Asia

A Concise History

Arthur Cotterell

WILEY

John Wiley & Sons (Asia) Pte. Ltd.

Other Wiley Editorial Offices

John Wiley & Sons, 111 River Street, Hoboken, NJ 07030, USA
John Wiley & Sons, The Atrium, Southern Gate, Chichester, West Sussex, P019
    8SQ, United Kingdom
John Wiley & Sons (Canada) Ltd., 5353 Dundas Street West, Suite 400, Toronto,
    Ontario, M9B 6HB, Canada
John Wiley & Sons Australia Ltd., 42 McDougall Street, Milton, Queensland 4064,
    Australia
Wiley-VCH, Boschstrasse 12, D-69469 Weinheim, Germany

Library of Congress Cataloging-in-Publication Data

ISBN 978-0470-82504-4 (Paperback)
ISBN 978-0470-82958-5 (e-PDF)
ISBN 978-0470-82957-8 (e-Mobi)
ISBN 978-0470-82959-2 (e-Pub)

Typeset in 10.5/13.5pt ITC Galliard by MPS Limited, a Macmillan Company
Printed in Singapore by Saik Wah Print Media Pte. Ltd.

Asia

A Concise History

For the
Class of 1968, V Arts,
St. Thomas' School, Kuching,
Sarawak

Contents

Contents

Contents

Preface

"Impossible. I've spent my entire life thinking about classical Greece." Thus George Forrest responded to a request for a 5,000-word article when telephoned one Friday evening in Oxford. Without hesitation, I told him to imagine that he was going to be shot by the junta next Tuesday and this was his last chance to leave behind a considered view. "I'll do it," he said to my relief as editor of the *Penguin Encyclopedia of Ancient Civilizations*. And I consider his contribution still unmatched as an introduction to the subject.

A not dissimilar feeling of impossibility assailed me when my publisher, Nick Wallwork, thought that a history of Asia was a good idea. Even though I have been allowed many more words, the subject is immense in terms of time as well as space. Only the conspicuous absence of any general treatment of a continent so important to the whole world persuaded me to undertake the task. Because Asia will have a great impact on the present century, we really do need to understand how events have shaped its peoples and polities.

Asia: A Concise History aims to provide this guide through a chronological survey of key areas: West Asia, South Asia, East Asia, Central Asia and Southeast Asia. While any book covering such an incredible range of human endeavour can never hope to be more than introductory, there is the possibility that the general reader will obtain a useful overview. At the very least, it is hoped that some bearings will be furnished for those who wish to explore the vast expanse of Asia's past.

What this book signals are the very different experiences of Asian peoples, not only among themselves, but in comparison with the peoples of other continents as well. Just to list a few of the individuals who have contributed to their history is enough to reveal Asia's significance in world affairs: Gilgamesh, Ashurbanipal, Zoroaster, Cyrus, the Buddha, Asoka, Jesus, St. Paul, Attila, Muhammad, Abd al-Malik, Confucius, Qin Shi Huangdi, Nagarjuna, Zhu Xi, Genghiz Khan, Yong Le, Hideyoshi, Shah Abbas, Akbar, Gandhi, Atatürk, Mao Zedong, Ho Chi Minh and Sukarno.

Preface

By tracing Asia's development from ancient times, and especially through the amazing diversity of the medieval era, the enduring traits of its various cultures can be discerned as they adapt to globalism. The catalyst for this far-reaching transformation was Western colonialism, whose recent retreat from Asia has produced an entirely new political landscape. Yet the most striking feature of the continent's history is the fact of its longevity, and not just the unusual length of Chinese civilisation, because Asian polities were the first to appear on Earth. What is new, however, is an awareness of how complex these earliest states were, thanks to the archaeological discoveries of the past 150 years.

In publishing this book I must acknowledge the invaluable contributions made by several people. First of all, my wife Yong Yap, through the translation of documents from Asian languages; second, an old friend Datuk Hj Harun Din, for advice on Islam; third, Graham Guest, another old friend whose extensive archive of pre-1900 illustrations, Imperial Images, has furnished material for the medieval and modern sections; and, last but not least, Ray Dunning, the creator of the maps and drawings spread throughout the book.

Perhaps the dedication needs a word of explanation. During the 1960s, I had the good fortune to teach in newly independent Sarawak, one of the states of Malaysia. Then I was struck by the communal harmony that existed among its more than forty distinct peoples, an undoubted legacy of the relaxed approach adopted by James Brooke, the first "white rajah". Only six of Sarawak's peoples were represented in the class mentioned in the dedication, but their different perspectives meant that our discussions were often a revelation. Besides making me aware of a wider range of possibilities, they planted an abiding interest in things Asian. I can only hope that this brief survey of Asia's past encourages a similar appreciation of its remarkable achievements.

Introduction

Asia invented civilisation. The earliest cities in the world appeared in Sumer, present-day Iraq, during the fourth millennium BC. Egypt was not far behind this urban revolution, but it was the Sumerians who shaped the consciousness of ancient West Asia. Their seminal thought is known to us from the library belonging the Assyrian kings. Translation of one royal text in 1872 caused a sensation because it comprised the Babylonian account of the Flood, a story believed to have been biblical in origin. When scholars discovered that this myth went all the way back to Atrahasis, the Sumerian Noah, they realised that here were some of the oldest ideas to survive anywhere on the planet.

In chapter 1, the Sumerian heritage is viewed through the empires of Babylon, Assyria and Persia, its successor states in ancient West Asia. Persian rule, however, was interrupted by Alexander the Great, whose conquests stretched as far as northwestern India. His generals could not hold on to these vast territories, so a revived Persia confronted the Romans in the Mediterranean. The seesawing struggle between Europe and Asia lasted well into the medieval period, with the Crusades and the Ottoman occupation of the Balkans. In ancient times, this intercontinental struggle had already acquired religious overtones. Because the multiplicity of deities derived from the Sumerian pantheon were largely replaced by the monotheism of Jewish belief through its powerful offshoot, Christianity. What the Christians retained in Jesus though, much to the later consternation of Muhammad, was the Sumerian notion of a dying-and-rising god.

Chapter 2 begins with the civilisation that arose in the Indus river valley about 2200 BC. Even though an inability to decipher the Indus script renders our understanding of this second-oldest Asian civilisation incomplete, archaeological remains point to a religious tradition that had a profound impact on Indian belief. Ritual ablution, yoga and worship of a mother goddess were passed on to the Aryans, who overran the Indus valley between 1750 and 1500 BC. Their chariot-led invasion made this war machine central to Aryan culture: its effectiveness is celebrated in the epic duels that are described in the *Mahabharata*, the second longest poem ever composed. Only the *La Galigo* cycle, belonging to the Bugis on the Indonesian island of Sulawesi, is more extensive in its account of the hero Sawerigading's exploits. Not so easily dealt with was Buddhism, the first pan-Asian faith. The Aryans had to come to terms with its singular concepts once the Buddha's message became popular. The patronage of the Mauryan emperors, as well as the Kushana kings, spread Buddhism into Central Asia by means of monastic foundations, whence monks carried the religion farther east to China, Korea and Japan.

The Kushanas were just one of the Central Asian peoples who controlled northern India during ancient times. Under the native Gupta dynasty a degree of stability returned before the arrival of the Huns. As did Attila in contemporary Europe, the Hunnish king Mihirkula took delight in the intimidation of settled populations. Before Gupta strength was worn down, however, the dynasty had rejected Buddhism in favour of Hinduism: henceforth the dominant religion in South Asia, despite Islam's penetration of the subcontinent during the seventh century AD.

The cradle of Asia's third-oldest civilisation in East Asia is the subject of chapter 3. There the Shang and Zhou monarchs witnessed the formation of China's uniquely continuous culture, which was to endure as an empire from 221 BC until 1911. Before imperial unification under Qin Shi Huangdi, the rival philosophies of Confucianism and Daoism had emerged, although the family-oriented system of Confucius would triumph under the emperors. Possibly the remoteness of China from other ancient centres of civilisation in South and West Asia explains its sense of being a world apart. Troublesome neighbours on the Central Asian steppe had led to the construction of the Great Wall, the boundary between the unsown land of the nomads and the intensive agriculture of the Chinese peasant farmers.

But the Great Wall was never enough to guarantee the safety of the Chinese empire once nomadic peoples were recruited as allies. In a parallel to the fate that befell the western provinces of the Roman empire, the whole of north China was conquered by Central Asian tribesmen in 316 AD. Yet the difference between the Germanic and Central Asian invasions could not have been more marked because, unlike Latin, Chinese survived intact and finally replaced the invaders' tongues as the official language. Only the Persian language achieved a similar longevity in its struggle with Arabic, although it was greatly transformed as a result.

The Central Asians, who took over north China, and indeed other parts of Asia as well as Europe, are discussed in chapter 4. How the Eurasian steppe acted as an intercontinental highway for charioteers and horsemen has come to be appreciated in recent years. Despite the usual direction of movement being from east to west, as nomadic herders headed towards lusher pastures kept green by Atlantic rain, China received the chariot from the Tocharians, a people originally living on the Russian steppe. Their trek eastwards remains an exception to the rule that migration was westwards, particularly after the Great Wall reduced opportunities for raids in East Asia. The scourge of the sown was how Central Asian nomads were viewed. Not until the Turks and the Mughals established dynasties, in West and South Asia respectively, would this perception begin to fade. Even so, Tamerlane was a terrible reminder that nothing could ever be taken for granted in Central Asia.

Chapter 5 introduces the medieval period in West Asia, an era defined by the rise of Islam, the second pan-Asian faith. Prophet Muhammad's mission was to have a far-reaching influence on the continent. Arab arms took his message to Central and South Asia, while Indian converts involved in trade carried the new religion to Malaya, Indonesia and the Philippines. A crucial decision was the replacement of Jerusalem as the Holy City with Mecca: it meant that the Arab custom of pilgrimage to the Ka'ba provided the means of unifying a community of believers spread right across Asia.

The Prophet's death brought about a poor compromise over the leadership of Islam, with the assassination of three of the four men who were appointed to succeed him, including his son-in-law Ali ibn Abi Talib. Only with the establishment of the Umayyad and Abbasid caliphates were the fratricidal tendencies of the Arabs tamed, although in 750 the former were slaughtered in a delayed revenge for Ali's murder. After the decline of the Abbasids, the Turkish Seljuks assumed the leadership of Islam, which was challenged by the Crusades between 1095 and 1229. Out of the mayhem of the Mongol onslaught, however, two major powers arose: Safavid Persia and the Ottoman empire. Today the splendid monuments that their leaders raised can be seen in Isfahan and Istanbul.

The coming of Islam to India is the starting point of chapter 6. Hindu and Buddhist kingdoms continued to flourish in southern India and Sri Lanka, but the medieval experience of South Asia was in the main foreign rule. From Central Asia came a series of Moslem invaders until in 1530 Zahir-ud-din Muhammad Babur founded the Mughal dynasty. The transformation of his semi-nomadic followers into the rulers of a great empire is one of the highlights of Asia's medieval era. That his most famous successor, Akbar, tried to accommodate Indian beliefs and customs is still evident in the Indo-Islamic architecture at Fatehpur Sikri, the city he built near Agra.

Foreign interference was not restricted to overland invaders because Europeans arrived by sea. The Portuguese and the Dutch were the first competitors for Asia's seaborne trade, but the contest for mastery pitted the French against the British. Arguably, it was their rivalry that turned the English East India Company into the dominant power, once Arthur Wellesley broke the Maratha confederacy in 1803. Well might a Mughal emperor still sit on a throne in Delhi, but real authority resided at Calcutta, the capital of British India.

Having recovered from the Central Asian occupation of north China, the Chinese empire enjoyed an impressive renaissance under the Tang and Song dynasties. In chapter 7 the splendour of their rule is reflected in the two main capitals they constructed: Chang'an and Kaifeng. The former Tang capital, with two million inhabitants, was then the largest and most populous city in the medieval world.

Such was the zenith reached by Chinese culture that its influence flowed strongly into Korea and Japan, shaping their own traditions in a lasting manner. Only feudalism prevented the Japanese from becoming as Confucian as the Koreans. Interminable civil wars ensured that no Japanese emperor ever acquired the authority of the Chinese throne. Despite the Mongol conquest of China between 1276 and 1368, the Chinese restored their empire under the Ming dynasty, strengthening the Great Wall and dispatching fleets under the eunuch admiral Zheng He into the southern oceans. Had the Chinese not turned away from the sea after 1433, Vasco da Gama would have found his tiny fleet sailing alongside a Chinese navy with vessels four times the size of his caravels. The emptiness of Asian waters gave the Portuguese, the Spaniards, the Dutch, the French and, finally, the English a false impression that they were the first explorers to sail there.

Central Asian arms were at their most irresistible during the medieval period. Not only did Genghiz Khan set the Mongols off on a series of conquests that made them masters of the largest empire ever to exist in

Asia, its subject peoples living as far apart as Russia, Persia, Korea, China, Cambodia and Java, but the Tibetans and the Manchus also carved out for themselves impressive states. Both the Tibetans and the Manchus harried China, but it was the semi-nomadic Manchus who founded in 1644 China's last imperial dynasty, the Qing.

In chapter 8 we note as well how Tamerlane's short-lived triumph could never be forgotten: his liking for severed heads resulted in 90,000 of them being cemented into 120 towers in 1401, after the capture of Baghdad. Despite his title, "the Sword of Islam", Tamerlane was by no means inclined to behead non-Moslems. In comparison with his Moslem enemies, Christians, Jews, Buddhists and Hindus escaped lightly. But on rare occasions, almost as though to appear even-handed, Tamerlane would unleash his fury against them too.

Chapter 9 is devoted to medieval Southeast Asia, whose various civilisations then came to the fore. First, Vietnam asserted its independence from China in 939, after a millennium of direct rule. Its rulers never shook off Chinese ways: Confucian learning endured long enough for Ho Chi Minh to despair in the 1900s at its continued use to recruit Vietnamese officials. South of Vietnam, Indian influence prevailed in Champa, Cambodia as well as the Indonesian archipelago, where Hindu-style kingdoms developed. Burma, modern Myanmar, received Buddhism from Sri Lanka, while the Philippines remained isolated from outside ideas before the advent of Islam and Christianity.

Christianity was brought to the Philippines by the Spaniards in the sixteenth century. At first they shared the spice trade with the Portuguese, but the Dutch decision to establish a permanent base on the island of Java gave them the upper hand in Indonesia, soon known as the Dutch East Indies. Another late intruder were the Thai, who left what is now the Chinese province of Yunnan during the fourteenth century.

Modern times commenced with Asian polities in full retreat. Western encroachment either overland or by sea reduced the majority to the status of colonies, protectorates or client states. Political realities were to alter dramatically after the Second World War, but the technological edge then enjoyed by the Europeans and the Americans gave them unprecedented dominance over Asian affairs.

Nowhere was this clearer in West Asia than in the collapse of the Ottoman empire, whose terminal decline is revealed in chapter 10 as the prelude to the formation of the countries into which the area is now divided. Opposition to Israel comprises one of the few policies these new states share, because their differences create an atmosphere of suspicion and uncertainty. Iraq and Iran are locked in bitter antagonism; Syria and Lebanon coexist in uneasy tension; Jordan and Saudi Arabia pursue their own separate courses, whereas the programme of modernisation sponsored by Atatürk has transformed Turkey into a potential member of the European Union.

For South Asia the key modern event was the Indian Mutiny of 1857. After the uprising, the deposition of the last Mughal emperor meant that the only way to escape from colonialism was independence, something that Gandhi did so much to achieve. Chapter 11 follows this strenuous effort, whose admirable emphasis on non-violence still failed to prevent bloodshed. But this was to be completely overshadowed by the communal disorder associated with the partition of the subcontinent in 1947, when 700,000 people lost their lives. Its bitter legacy was three wars fought between newly independent Pakistan and India, before the final one in 1971 permitted the emergence of Bangladesh as a sovereign state. Independent Sri Lanka also inherited communal problems that are still unresolved, despite the defeat of the Tamil Tigers.

Although theirs was not as extreme as the fate suffered by the Ottoman Turks, the Chinese were hard pressed by modern predators. The British demonstrated the Chinese empire's weakness during the notorious Opium War of 1840–42. Trafficking in opium resulted from the English East India Company's shortage of silver to pay for tea. Force of arms prevented the Chinese authorities from blocking this lethal import, a circumstance that encouraged others to meddle in China's internal affairs. Chapter 12 shows how the French, the Russians and the Japanese all pressed the tottering Qing dynasty for concessions before it was extinguished in 1911. The rise of Japan, the first Asian country to modernise its economy, altered the balance of power to such an extent that the imperial ambitions it ruthlessly pursued in Korea, China and, eventually, Southeast Asia fatally weakened colonialism everywhere.

The tribulations of modern Central Asia are treated in chapter 13. Rivalry with Britain in Afghanistan and Tibet was one reason for Russia's subjugation of its nomadic peoples, another was a desire to exploit the area's natural resources. At its worst under the Soviets, the Central Asian republics were converted into a vast cotton plantation that relied on cheap labour and the draining of the Aral Sea. Only now are its peoples becoming truly independent, notwithstanding a return of inter-tribal quarrels. Siberia and part of Manchuria remain under Russian control, while Afghanistan retains its capacity to frustrate foreign domination.

Chapter 14, the final chapter, brings this concise history of Asia to a close by reviewing the mixed fortunes of modern Southeast Asia. While the British conducted an orderly withdrawal from empire, after the historic decision to grant India early independence, the Dutch and the French endeavoured to retain their colonies in a totally changed world. For the Vietnamese, who led resistance to France on mainland Southeast Asia, the anti-colonial struggle proved devastating once the United States joined in. The Vietnam War is a salutary lesson of how misconceived were so many actions during the Cold War. Washington simply failed to grasp North Vietnam's essential aim: the reunification of the Vietnamese homeland.

For the Filipinos, the Pacific dimension of the Second World War made no difference to the agreed date of their independence, 4 July 1946. But the wanton destruction of Manila cast a shadow over this event, since the city suffered as much damage as Warsaw and Budapest during their liberation. As did Thailand and Myanmar, the Philippines learned that democracy offered no ready solution to public unrest, although so far it has avoided a military coup. Malaysia and Singapore, on the other hand, have managed the post-colonial period rather well, even though the Malaysian federation needed help to deter Sukarno's territorial ambitions during the 1960s. With the 1999 liberation of East Timor, another victim of the Republic of Indonesia's expansionism, the last European colony reasserted its sovereignty. Because of the abundant sandalwood forests, the Portuguese had established a trading post there in 1642.

List of Maps

All of the maps were drawn by Ray Dunning.

Photo Credits

Chapter 1

Pg 6   The ruins of the ziggurat, or stepped temple, at Ur.
        Source: Getty Images

Chapter 2

Pg 56   The Mahabodhi temple which marks the spot where the
        Buddha's enlightenment came to pass.
        Source: Getty Images
Pg 68   An entrance to one of the Buddhist cave sanctuaries at Ajanta
        in central India.
        Source: Corbis

Chapter 3

Pg 93   The Great Wall north of Beijing with its Ming dynasty stone
        facing.
        Source: Arthur Cotterell
Pg 96   The mound raised above the tomb of Qin Shi Huangdi at
        Mount Li.
        Source: Arthur Cotterell

Chapter 4

Pg 113 Rivers and streams from mountain ranges ensure the survival
        of nomads' herds.
        Source: Arthur Cotterell
Pg 117 The deserts of Central Asia meant that a variety of animals was
        needed.
        Source: Arthur Cotterell
Pg 123 Sunset on the Mongolian steppe.
        Source: Arthur Cotterell
Pg 128 The fortress at the western end of the Great Wall, whose
        rammed-earth construction is clearly visible.
        Source: Arthur Cotterell

Photo Credits

Photo Credits

Pg 331   The extravagant historical parade at Persepolis in October 1971.
Source: Getty Images

Pg 333   Ayatollah Ruhollah Khomeini returning home in 1979 after his exile in France.
Source: AFP

Pg 334   American missiles being fired in 2003 during the Second Gulf War.
Source: Getty Images

Pg 338   "Father Turk", Mustafa Kemal, in his garden in 1923 with his wife and a friend.
Source: AFP

Chapter 11

Pg 348   The Red Fort in Delhi, the last stronghold of the Mughals.
Source: Ray Dunning

Pg 349   From this audience chamber in the Red Fort, the Mughal emperor Bahadur Shah Zafar II could exercise no control over the mutinous sepoys.
Source: Ray Dunning

Pg 354   The Curzons' visit to Hyderabad in 1902.
Source: Corbis

Pg 356   The indomitable Gandhi as determined as ever in 1940 to end the British Raj.
Source: Getty Images

Chapter 12

Pg 374   Sun Yatsen in 1923.
Source: AFP

Pg 375   Guomindang troops skirmish in Shanghai with Japanese forces before the outbreak of the Second Sino-Japanese War.
Source: Getty Images

Pg 377   *USS Arizona* going down in flames at Pearl Harbor, 7 December 1941.
Source: Getty Images

Pg 379   On 1 October 1949 Mao Zedong proclaims the People's Republic in Beijing.
Source: Getty Images

Photo Credits

Chapter 13

Pg 390 Two views of Kashgar, a Moslem city that was pivotal in the Great Game (above).
Source: Ray Dunning

Pg 392 A towering minaret at Turfan, one of the Central Asian cities incorporated into the Chinese empire.
Source: Ray Dunning

Pg 395 High minarets such as this one at Bukhara have always fascinated visitors, including Genghiz Khan.
Source: Ray Dunning

Pg 402 Vladivostok, Russia's port on the Sea of Japan, was an early acquisition
Source: Getty Images

Pg 404 The Ark fortress at Bukhara, where in 1918 a 20-strong delegation of Russian Bolsheviks was executed.
Source: Ray Dunning

Chapter 14

Pg 412 A Land Dayak longhouse in Sarawak.
Source: Arthur Cotterell

Pg 416 Part of the Royal Palace at Phnom Penh.
Source: Ray Dunning

Pg 420 British soldiers surrendering at Singapore on 15 February 1942.
Source: Getty Images

Pg 422 A second atomic bomb exploding above Nagasaki, 9 August 1945.
Source: Getty Images

Pg 425 Singapore's Lee Kuan Yew with his Malaysian counterpart Tunku Abdul Rahman.
Source: AFP

Pg 427 President Sukarno rallies Indonesians against the return of the Dutch colonial authorities.
Source: AFP

Pg 428 Taman Ayun temple at Mengwi, a Hindu place of worship in Bali.
Source: PhotoLibrary

Pg 429   A typical Javanese village with its paddy fields.
          Source: Alamy
Pg 431   "Uncle Ho". The leader of Vietnamese resistance to the
          French and the Americans, Ho Chi Minh.
          Source: Corbis
Pg 433   Despite this display of technology in 1967, the United States
          was heading for defeat in Vietnam.
          Source: Getty Images
Pg 435   Mass opposition to President Marcos that led to his exile in
          1986.
          Source: Corbis

Special thanks to Imperial Images © and Ray Dunning for all the other
illustrations featured in this book.

Part 1

Ancient Asia

Chapter 1

Ancient West Asia

Exhausted, Ninhursag yearned for a beer.
The great gods languished where she sat weeping.
Like sheep they could only bleat their distress.
Thirsty they were, their lips rimed with hunger.
For seven whole days and seven whole nights
The torrent, the storm, the flood still raged on.
Then Atrahasis put down his great boat
And sacrificed oxen and many goats.
Smelling the fragrance of the offering
Like big flies, the gods kept buzzing about.

From the Sumerian story of the Flood

The First Civilisation: Sumer

Appreciation of Asia's antiquity is recent. Apart from China, whose uniquely continuous civilisation preserved a record of its own ancient origin, the rest of the Asian continent had to wait for modern archaeology to reveal the cultural achievements of the earliest city dwellers. Excavations over the past century and a half have uncovered lost civilisations in West Asia as well as India. Near Mosul in northern Iraq, exploration of a mound at the site of ancient Nineveh resulted in the recovery of the library belonging to the Assyrian kings, a treasure trove for understanding the world's first civilisation. Surviving texts provide a means of approaching the Sumerians, who founded their cities more than two thousand years before Nineveh fell in 612 BC to a combined attack of the Babylonians and the Iranian Medes. The destruction of this last Assyrian city ushered in the final era of ancient West Asian history, that of Persian power.

Because the royal library comprised a collection of Mesopotamian compositions going right back to Sumerian times, it is hardly surprising that their translation became a focus of keen interest. No one could have expected, however, the sensation caused in 1872 by the Babylonian story of the Flood, an event that appears first in *Atrahasis*, the name of the Noah-like hero of this oldest Sumerian epic. There is no mention of sinfulness as in the biblical account: instead, the gods inundated the Earth to stop the racket that people were making below the stairs. The sky god Enlil found sleep quite impossible, so plague, famine and flood were in turn employed to reduce the numbers then overcrowding the world. Warning of the final disaster was given to Atrahasis by Enki, the Sumerian water god.

Although in the 1920s discoveries of mounds in the Indus valley led to the excavation of two ruined cities at Mohenjo-daro in Sind and Harappa in western Punjab, and in the process redrew the world map of ancient civilisations, the finds had a less dramatic impact than the earlier Mesopotamian ones because of our inability to decipher the Indus script. Sumer and Babylon had long emerged in a civilised way of living at the time the inhabitants of the Indus valley built their remarkable cities. Only China was a late starter in Asia, the Indus civilisation having collapsed more than a century before its first historical dynasty, the Shang, arose about 1650 BC on the north China plain. In spite of the decipherment problem, the material remains of the Indus valley cities bear witness to an influence on the subcontinent's chief concern, namely religion. Defeated though they were by the Aryan invaders, the Indus valley people were not without their revenge because their beliefs came to have a profound effect on the outlook of the Aryans. Besides absorbing the Indus preoccupation with ritual ablution, they became

The arrival at the British Museum of an Assyrian bull statue that
was excavated at ancient Nimrud in 1847

fascinated by the possibilities of yoga, whose austerities were supposed
to empower the rishis, divinely inspired seers. That an Indus valley seal
shows a horned god in a yoga posture may explain the rise of Shiva,
"the divine rishi", to a senior position in the Hindu pantheon, displacing
warlike Indra. It had been Indra as Purandara, "the fort destroyer", who
gave the invading Aryans victory over the Indus valley settlements.

Nothing is known about the arrival of the Sumerians in southern
Iraq. As they believed that they had travelled in a westerly direction, the
discovery of the Indus civilisation has encouraged the idea of the Sumerians being earlier occupiers of northwestern India. But it is just as likely
that they moved into the Tigris–Euphrates river valleys from Iran, as did
other migrants attracted to their agricultural potential, although there
is also the possibility that the Sumerians always lived in Iraq. The name
by which they are called is Babylonian, which means the people who live
in Sumer, southern Babylonia. They named their own country Kengir,
"the civilised land": it stretched from the sea to the city of Nippur, one
hundred kilometres south of present-day Baghdad. A semi-arid climate
ensured that irrigation was essential from the start, artificial canals
eventually developing into an extensive network that required constant
supervision, dredging and repair. As a result of this management of

The ruins of the ziggurat, or stepped temple, at Ur

water resources, groups of villages came under the direction of larger settlements, the first cities ruled by princes or kings, who considered themselves to be representatives of the gods. The Sumerians seem only to have distinguished between city prince, ensi, and king, lugal, after 2650 BC, the approximate date for the establishment of the earliest known royal dynasty.

Fundamental to a Sumerian king's power was a large retinue of unfree retainers, in part recruited from captives whose lives the king had spared. This military tradition lingered into the medieval period: the Janissaries of the Ottoman sultan Mehmet II, who captured Constantinople in 1453, were all ex-Christian slaves. These lifelong soldiers even formed the sultan's personal bodyguard. Like the Janissaries, the Sumerian king owned his retainers body and soul: they ate with him in the palace and did his bidding in war as well as peace. In addition to this power base, rulers sought to broaden their support by making their authority available to the underprivileged in Sumerian society: they presided over a legal system designed to protect the least well-off from the rich and powerful.

Because cities expanded around temples, the nuclei of all significant foundations, the Sumerians looked to the resident deities for prosperity. In the southernmost cities, situated close to the marshlands, the city gods were connected with fishing and fowling; upriver divine influence was spread over fields and orchards, the date growers paying special attention to the prodigious powers of Inanna, goddess of fertility; in the grasslands, worship was given over to Dumuzi, the holy shepherd. Because she combined in her person several originally distinct goddesses, Inanna was the most important goddess in the Sumerian pantheon, a variant of her name being Ninanna, "mistress of heaven". Identified with the planet Venus as the morning and the evening star, Inanna was the bitter enemy of her sister goddess Ereshkigal, "the mistress of death", and once she had the temerity to visit the "land of no return" so as to assert her own authority there. At each of its seven portals, she was obliged to take off a garment or ornament, until at last she stood naked before Ereshkigal. After hanging on a stake for three days, the water god Enki sent two sexless beings to revive Inanna's corpse with the "food and water of life".

But after her escape from death, the goddess could not shake off a ghastly escort of demons who followed her as she wandered from city to city. They refused to depart unless a substitute was found. So Inanna returned home to Uruk, took offence in finding her husband Dumuzi at a feast, and let the demons carry him off to Ereshkigal's underworld. Thereafter Dumuzi's fate was spending half the year in the land of the living, the other half with the dead. Thus he became West Asia's original dying-and-rising god.

At Uruk there is compelling evidence that the king acted as an intermediary between the city and the city goddess through the New Year rite of a sacred marriage. The ruler impersonated Dumuzi, a high priestess Inanna. One text has the king of Uruk boast how he

> lay on the splendid bed of Inanna, strewn with pure plants . . .
> The day did not dawn, the night did not pass. For fifteen hours
> I lay with Inanna.

Capable of making endless love, the goddess was the awakening force that stirs desire in people and causes ripeness in vegetation. A ruler's enjoyment of "the sweetness of her holy loins" was regarded by the Sumerians as vitally important because this sacred coupling guaranteed a city's survival. It is tempting to see their joy during the festival as recognition that a new seasonal cycle was about to begin, marked by the return of Dumuzi from the underworld to Inanna's "ever youth-ful bed". In the *Song of Solomon* we find an unexpected parallel of such sensuousness, when "until the break of day, and the shadows fell away", the lover is exhorted to act "like a roe and a young hart on the mountains of Bether". This short love poem may well echo the rite of sacred marriage, even though an alternative view looks to Egypt for the source of inspiration. The authorship and the date of composition, not to say the inclusion of the *Song of Solomon* in the Bible, remain an unsolved mystery.

Uruk is also the setting of the Babylonian epic about Gilgamesh, a legendary Sumerian king whose original name was Bilgames. The city's earliest rulers fascinated later poets, much as the heroes of the Trojan War did the Greek epic poet Homer. They were the favourite subjects of court entertainment, their adventures being retold to ruler after ruler. Though it was the writing school of King Shulgi at Ur that set down for posterity the literary tradition of Sumer just before the close of the third millennium BC, the fullest surviving text of Gilgamesh's exploits comes from the Assyrian royal library at Nineveh. Translation of a small section of the epic was responsible for the furore in 1872, because it relates the visit made by Gilgamesh to his ancestor Utanap-ishtim, the one chosen to escape the Flood that "returned all mankind to clay". A later version of the Sumerian hero Atrahasis, this venerable sage was prepared to impart truth only to the man who dared to find him and was capable of doing so. The reason for Gilgamesh's visit to Utanapishtim was the grief that had overwhelmed him on the death of his companion Enkidu, something the distraught hero refused to accept as the inevitable end to life. Gilgamesh "wept over the corpse for seven days and seven nights, refusing to give it up for burial until a maggot fell from one of the nostrils".

Reaching Utanapishtim's subterranean house, Gilgamesh learns that his quest is hopeless, when Utanapishtim tells him he cannot resist sleep, let alone death. The only chance is a fantastic plant named "Never Grow Old" at the bottom of the sea. At great risk Gilgamesh fetches it from the deep and happily turns his steps to Uruk, but on his way home, while he dozes by a waterhole, a serpent smells the wonderful perfume of the leaves, and swallows the lot. Immediately the snake was able to slough its skin, and Gilgamesh realised that there was no way that he could avoid the underworld, "the house of dust".

Ereshkigal, "the mistress of death", and Inanna's
implacable enemy

Our knowledge of the Sumerians derives from their invention of writing, quite possibly the most consequential advance in all human history. This stroke of genius not only gave support to an expanding economy, through easing communication within crowded cities, but it also permitted the formation of reliable archives. Obviously the use of script, as a substitute for verbal agreements, was of immediate value in commercial transactions, the importance of which can be gauged from the protection afforded to trade routes by successive kings. Even more valuable for a record of the very first civilisation on the planet was the ability to set down in a permanent medium the ideas that informed its workings. Without the Sumerian script we would neither possess poetical works such as the *Gilgamesh* epic, nor appreciate

Life-size alabaster mask that once fitted
on a wooden statue of Inanna at Uruk

how deep was the Sumerian preoccupation with death. About 3000 BC, the Sumerians in Uruk hit upon the notion of creating hundreds of pictograms, plus signs for numbers and measures: these were pressed into clay tablets with a reed stylus to compose what is called the cuneiform system of writing.

The idea that it was possible to capture a language by means of writing travelled along the ancient trade routes. In Babylon the adoption of cuneiform for Akkadian, a Semitic tongue, meant that long after Sumerian became a dead language the educated remained familiar with it—just as Latin was prized in Europe until the Renaissance. The first Semites must have entered northern Babylonia not much later than the Sumerians, whom they eventually submerged through further waves of migration. Elam was the first state in Iran to follow Babylon's example and, given established trade links between Mesopotamia and India via the island of Bahrain, stimulus for the Indus script could well have derived from merchant enterprise as well. Those who suggest that the idea of writing spread beyond India to China are wrong, however. Finds at Banpo, a fortified village close to modern Xi'an, in Shaanxi province, indicate how about the same time that the Sumerians began writing on clay tablets, its inhabitants incised their pottery with the antecedents of Chinese characters. Although fully developed words are not in evidence until the Shang kings recorded queries to their exulted ancestors on oracle bones, the extreme antiquity of the Banpo signs argues against diffusion.

The unification of Sumer curtailed inter-city conflicts once disputes came to be settled by royal adjudication. This wider system of government formed the context of Uruinimgina's laws, which stand at the head of a long series including Hammurabi's famous code. King Uruinimgina of Lagash deplored his predecessors' confiscation of temple properties, which he returned. Driven from Lagash, he continued to rule as king at Girsu before being taken prisoner by the Semitic ruler of Akkad, where he died in 2340 BC. Even though the location of Akkad remains unknown, this ancient city was situated somewhere in northern Babylonia. For the Sumerians its rise as an imperial power spelt the beginning of the end of their independence. Yet Akkad's favourite instrument of power, wholesale massacre, could not ultimately ensure the survival of an empire that included Mesopotamia and Syria as well as eastern Asia Minor. Its nemesis

An early example of cuneiform, the writing system invented
by the Sumerians about 3000 BC

were the semi-nomadic Gutians, who descended from the mountains of Iran and terrorised Semites and Sumerians alike.

After the collapse of Akkad, there occurred a last flourishing of Sumerian culture, which was recorded by King Shulgi's scribes. His capital at Ur escaped the violent attentions of new raiders from Iran through the construction shortly before 2050 BC of "a wall in front of the mountains". But his successors were less fortunate when the Elamites, supported by their Iranian allies, launched a devastating attack on Sumer. A lament tells us how "water no longer flows in weed-free canals, the hoe does not tend fertile fields, no seed is planted in the ground, on the plain the oxherd's song goes unheard, and in the cattle pen there is never the sound of churning". The gods have gone, their temples defiled, and ancient ways "are changed forever". Not even the dogs of Ur remained in the ruined city.

The Great Empires: Babylon, Assyria and Persia

Archaeological recovery of Babylon's past followed in the wake of the discoveries in ancient Assyria. Despite being less spectacular than those of Nineveh, the excavation of northern Babylonia led to a realisation that here was another early Asian civilisation of great sophistication. How else could Babylon have once been renowned for its Hanging Gardens? Together with the city's walls, they were regarded as one of the seven wonders of the ancient world.

Babylon was founded shortly after the Elamite devastation of Sumer. During these troubled times its inhabitants had the benefit of a political stability absent elsewhere in Mesopotamia because, instead of a series of short-lived dynasties, the first royal house ruled Babylon for almost three centuries. The city was strongly fortified and its influence gradually spread far and wide. Instrumental in this growth of power was King Hammurabi, whose reign witnessed the acceptance of Babylon's suzerainty over all Mesopotamia. His inscriptions show that he styled himself as the ruler of Babylonia and Sumer; he was "King of the Four Quarters of the World". Although Babylon went on the defensive after Hammurabi's death in 1750 BC, the hegemony he secured for the city bestowed on it a lasting fame.

One of the steles on which King Hammurabi's law code was recorded

The mystique surrounding the city's name survives today, as does Hammurabi's law code, which was carved on forty-nine stone columns, 2.25 metres high. In the settlement of disputes between citizens, it reveals how the Semitic custom of "an eye for an eye and a tooth for a tooth" replaced the system of fines used by the Sumerians, who preferred to recompense physical injury with an appropriate payment, although murder and robbery were punished by death. Possibly Hammurabi considered this approach was inadequate for deterring crime in a newly acquired empire. The legacy of his harsh laws still informs attitudes in West Asia: turning the other cheek is not the usual response to a modern insult.

The eclipse of Babylon's first dynasty occurred in 1595 BC, when a raid by the Hittite king Mursilis I resulted in a sack of the city. Curiously, he withdrew to Asia Minor afterwards, and the Kassites took advantage of the power vacuum to seize control. They had begun to infiltrate northern Babylonia from Iran during the reigns of Hammurabi's successors, and Kassite kings were not seen as foreign intruders when their own long-lasting dynasty was in turn overthrown by the Elamites about 1152 BC. That the greatest king of the next Babylonian dynasty, Nebuchadrezzar I, was remembered for his chastisement of the Elamites only serves to underline the affection felt for the deposed Kassite kings. Nebuchadrezzar, the usual English spelling of Nabu-kudrri-usur, is based on a later Hebrew corruption of the name given to Nebuchadrezzar II in the Bible. Nebuchadrezzar was the fourth king of the new Isin dynasty, ruling in Babylon himself for twenty-two years.

In capturing the statue of Marduk, the patron deity of Babylon, the Elamites had utterly humiliated the Babylonians. A first attempt to return the cult statue to its rightful place in the great temple of Esagila was thwarted by an outbreak of plague in Nebuchadrezzar's army. Having received favourable omens for a second attack on Elam, Nebuchadrezzar gathered his chariotry together and advanced in sweltering heat one summer. We are told how gruelling the campaign was

> in the month of Dumuzu, when soldiers' axes burnt like fire in their hands, and the surface of the road scorched like flame. In the wells, there was no water, nothing was available to slake a terrible thirst. The strength of the horses gave out, and even the legs of the strongest warriors shook with fatigue.

But the almost disastrous advance caught the Elamites by surprise, and next to a river the dust raised by a great battle "blotted out the light of day". The right wing of Nebuchadrezzar's chariotry decided the outcome and in triumph the Babylonians bore Marduk home.

Whatever the military significance of the encounter, the chronicler says that "the great god Marduk has clearly relented his anger against his land and has returned to take care of it again". It may be that Nebuchadrezzar capitalised on the rare defeat of Elam by declaring Marduk to be not only the city god of Babylon but the supreme god of the Babylonian pantheon. In Marduk's temple the monarch participated in an annual ritual of renewal, a reaffirmation of his right to rule. To this ceremony the gods of the other major cities were brought as witnesses, until unsettled conditions towards the end of Nebuchadrezzar's reign caused a temporary interruption of the practice, because it was too risky for their cult statues to be carried to Babylon.

There were only minor skirmishes with Assyria, which occupied an area to the north of Babylon centred on the confluence of the Tigris river and one of its major tributaries. The rolling hills of Assyria sustained both herders and farmers thanks to a regular rainfall. Unlike Babylonia, dates could not be grown there but grapes were cultivated for fruit and wine-making purposes. At Nimrud, the biblical Calah, extensive wine cellars have been found along with lists of their contents. At some distance from the major Assyrian cities of Ashur and Nineveh, the city of Nimrud may have been the headquarters of the Assyrian army. One of its temples, dedicated to the war god Ninurta by Ashurnasirpal II, records this king's treatment of his enemies during the 870s BC. Not only did Ashurnasirpal "stand on their necks" and "with their blood dye the mountains red like wool", but more precisely he "cut off noses,

14

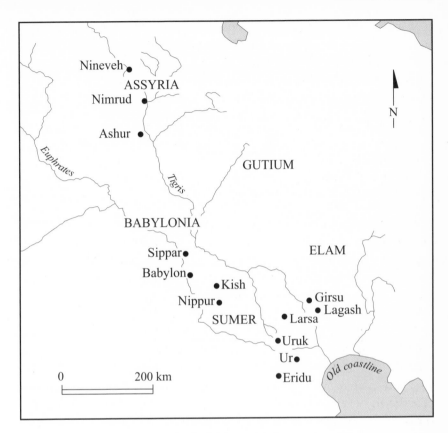

Ancient Mesopotamia

ears and extremities" of captives, "gouged out eyes", "burnt prisoners", "slashed the flesh of rebels" or "flayed" them alive. One disloyal ruler had his skin "draped over the wall of Nineveh". Massacre, pillage, wholesale resettlement—these were the favourite methods of Assyrian domination, whose sovereignty was "made supreme by the Ashur and Adad, the great gods". What allowed an Assyrian ruler to behave without apparent restraint was of course the power of his army.

At Nineveh, enjoyment of the grape is recorded in a wall relief from the palace of a later Assyrian king, Ashurbanipal. Though the monarch is shown reclining in Greek fashion on a couch, he does not drink in the company of men, as at a symposium. Only his wife, Queen Ashur-shurrat, shares the occasion with him. She sits on a throne in front of her husband, holding a wine cup to her lips while gazing upon her

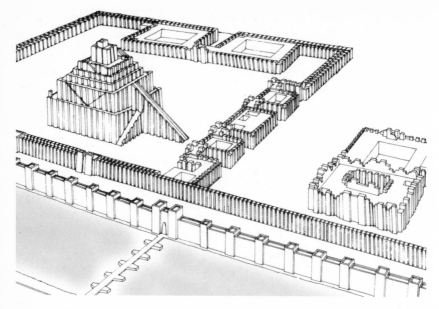

The ziggurat of Marduk opposite the Esagila temple at Babylon

lord and master. Servants busily wave fly whisks so that no insect may mar the royal couple's relaxation. But even here, in this restful garden scene, the bloody nature of Assyrian rule intrudes, as the severed head of King Te-umman of Elam is suspended from the branch of a nearby tree. Birds are gathered around to pick off the flesh and pluck out the eyes. Well might Ashurbanipal have imagined in his cups that Assyria was destined to dominate ancient West Asia for ever, but within fifteen years of his death in 627 BC, its empire ceased to exist. Undermined by the civil war in which his two sons struggled for supremacy, Assyria fell easy prey to the Medes and the Babylonians.

The slow growth of Assyrian power had much to do with its belligerent neighbour Mitanni, since for a long time it was a part of this northern kingdom. Mitannian strength derived from its chariotry, which was trained by Kukkuli, "the master horseman". That his famous training manual contains words closely related to Sanskrit, the language of the Aryan invaders of India, points to a connection between chariot warfare and successful takeovers of ancient lands. Similarities in chariot design in West Asia and India clearly suggests a western invasion of the subcontinent. Despite the chariot's invention on the steppe, ancient West Asia witnessed its first general use as a war

16

machine. Kukkuli's fame as a trainer for chariot horses was discovered through excavations at ancient Hattusha, present-day Boghazhöy in Turkey. There in the archive of the Hittite capital were not only clay tablets on which the original Mitannian version was written, but also translations of the manual into the Hittite and Akkadian languages, testifying to a very wide readership indeed.

Mitanni itself remains cloaked in obscurity, so that the number of Aryans living among the Hurrian-speaking Mitannians is still a matter of debate. Besides personal names and technical terms connected with horsemanship in Kukkuli's training manual, the main evidence for a sizable Aryan population are the gods who were invoked in treaties between Mitanni and other powers. One such deity is Varuna, the upholder of the moral order in India. Not until the Hittites crushed Mitanni in the fourteenth century BC, and two centuries later Hittite power itself disintegrated under the impact of the Sea Peoples, was there scope for the Assyrians to pursue imperial ambitions of their own.

The reasons behind the great migration of the so-called Sea Peoples are still not fully understood, but cities and palaces were razed to the ground in Greece, Asia Minor, Syria and Palestine. Assyria fought off those migrants who attempted to enter the Euphrates–Tigris valleys, while Ramesses III turned back most of the Sea Peoples in two hard-fought battles on the borders of Egypt. In 1182 BC the pharaoh overcame them on land as well as water. Successful resistance by the Assyrians seems to have inspired their own bid for universal dominion in ancient West Asia. The buildup of the Assyrian army was truly impressive: by the ninth century BC, some 60,000 were deployed against states in Syria and Palestine, a century later the regular forces had risen to 75,000, while under King Sennacherib, who ruled from 704 to 681 BC, the number jumped to an incredible 200,000.

It was Sennacherib who sacked Babylon after his son Ashur-nadin-shumi, the governor there, had been handed over to the Elamites by the rebellious Babylonians. A furious Sennacherib first defeated the Elamites and then captured the city of Babylon in 689 BC. Allowing his troops to sack it indiscriminately may have cost Sennacherib his own life a few years later, when he was assassinated by one or more of his surviving sons: for the destruction of Babylon was a sacrilegious act in the eyes of both Assyrians and Babylónians. The death of his favourite son at the hands of the Elamites had caused the Assyrian king to appoint Esarhaddon as the heir apparent. When the news of

King Ashurbanipal in his cups at Nineveh, with the severed head of the
Elamite king hanging on the far left

Sennacherib's murder reached Esarhaddon, he knew he would have
to fight for his accession. He said:

> My brothers went insane and did what is abhorrent to the gods.
> At Nineveh they hatched evil plots, resorted to arms, and striving
> for sovereignty they butted each other like billy goats.

Relying on the support of Assyrian nobles, who had already sworn
an oath of loyalty to the chosen successor, Esarhaddon marched
on Nineveh and put an end to the disturbances in the city, with the result
that the people there acknowledged his authority by "kissing his feet".

Esarhaddon's reign was a mixture of military triumph and civil
reconstruction. In Babylon, a major building programme sought to
heal the terrible wound inflicted by his father, especially through the
restoration of Marduk's temple. Abroad, Esarhaddon extended Assyrian
rule as far as Egypt, where he overran the Nile delta and advanced
upriver to seize Memphis. Because the Assyrians were unable to rule
Egypt themselves, they left this task to collaborators, who soon asserted
their independence. Later these petty rulers were replaced by one
pharaoh, Necho I, whose son Psamtik was to found the last effective
Egyptian dynasty before the arrival in 525 BC of the Persians, the
inheritors of Assyrian dominion. Continuous warfare was already putting
a severe strain on Assyria, bolstered though it was through the wholesale
resettlement of conquered peoples. It took surprisingly little to expose

Assyria's vulnerability to determined foes, the fall of Nineveh in 612 BC marking the end of its once mighty empire.

The Babylonians took advantage of the situation to gain control over the whole of Mesopotamia and Syria under King Nebuchadrezzar II, who was descended from the Chaldeans, a Semitic people living along the coast of the Persian Gulf. For some unknown reason, King Jehoiakim of Judah decided to throw off his allegiance to Babylon, with the result that in 597 BC Nebuchadrezzar besieged Jerusalem. The city was spared on its surrender through the payment of a heavy fine, but 10,000 Jews were taken as hostages to Babylon, where the prophet Daniel was already a resident.

In *The Book of Daniel* there are several stories about "the Babylonian Captivity". Along with three fellow exiles Daniel was trained to serve at court: the Babylonian names they answered to were Belteshazzar (Daniel), Shadrach (Hananiah), Meshach (Mishael) and Abednego (Azariah). Three episodes in particular stand out in the biblical narrative. The first was the refusal of Shadrach, Meshach and Abednego to bow down before "the golden image" that Nebuchadrezzar had set up.

Daniel in the lions' den, a Byzantine view of his miraculous escape

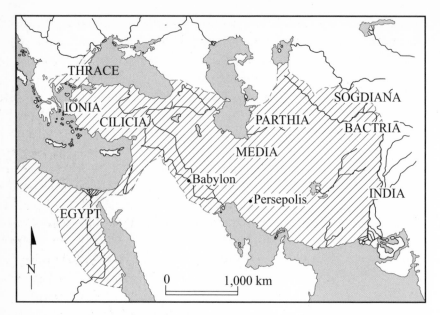

The Persian empire

When the king learnt of this insolence, he had them "cast into the midst of the fiery furnace" without ill effect. An angel, Nebuchadrezzar was convinced, had been sent by their god to save them. The second ordeal was suffered by Daniel under the new Persian administration for refusing to do homage to King Darius. When the new ruler discovered that Daniel's overnight stay in the lions' den had done him no harm, Darius admitted the power of the god that Daniel worshipped. A third episode, on this occasion not involving torture, is supposed to have predicted the Persian conquest of Babylon. During a feast hosted by Belshazzar, the grandson of Nebuchadrezzar, mysterious writing appeared on the wall, and only Daniel could read its message: "The days of the kingdom are numbered."

The Book of Daniel confuses Darius with Cyrus, the Persian king who occupied Babylon almost without a struggle in 539 BC. As the Babylonian empire was the most highly evolved state taken over by Cyrus, this founder of Persian power was anxious to conciliate its ruling class, to whom important posts were awarded on the basis of a willingness to serve the new regime. Their know-how was invaluable to the Persians and mediated between the conquerors and the most populous area of ancient West Asia. For the exiled Jews though, Cyrus was literally a godsend: the prophet Isaiah maintained that the rise of Persia was part of a divine plan to rebuild Jerusalem. A parallel Babylonian account of Cyrus' success relates how it was the work of Marduk, who "scanned and looked through every country, searching for a king who would grace his annual procession. Then he pronounced Cyrus to be the ruler of the world".

Cyrus and his successors opened up new perspectives to conquered peoples. They respected the religious beliefs and practices of their subjects, making generous donations to local sanctuaries. Instead of the customary mass deportation, the Persians allowed captives to return to their homelands if they wished. Rebellions were not unknown in Babylon or the rest of the Persian empire; but despite periodic usurpation crises, the violent repression of the Assyrians became a thing of the past. Yet trouble lay ahead for the Persians in the form of Macedonians. Having secured the eastern frontier through the annexation of northwestern India, Darius was stopped from doing the same in the west by the revolt of the Ionian Greeks in Asia Minor. His retaliation engendered a deep enmity between the Greeks and the Persians. During the great invasion of Greece in 480 BC, the Macedonians were obliged to side with the Persians because the enormous expeditionary force passed through their territory. One hundred and forty-six years later, however, Alexander the Great returned the compliment by invading the Persian empire at the head of his Macedonian troops.

Understanding the World: Religion and Myth

Ancient West Asians invented gods to understand the world. Convinced that creation could not be explained by itself, and needing to give it meaning, they envisaged supernatural beings who were responsible for creating the world and for ensuring that its processes continued satisfactorily. Totally anthropomorphic though they were in their approach to the gods, neither the Sumerians nor the Semites forgot the original function that each deity performed in the natural order. The great Sumerian goddess Inanna was still the power behind the rain that each spring brought forth pasture in the desert. It did not matter that Inanna's abundant sensuality also turned her into a love goddess, the protectress and colleague of prostitutes. In the *Gilgamesh* epic, she offers herself to the poem's hero and is enraged when he rejects her advances. The distracting effect of her charms is something Gilgamesh well knew: he had sent "the harlot Samhat" to tame the wild man Enkidu. "After he was sated with her delights," we are told, "Enkidu turned to face his herd, but the animals of the wild were already on the move." In the absence of a human family, he had grown up with them. Thus civilisation had claimed Enkidu, so fascinated was he with Samhat's account of the festivals held in Uruk, the attractiveness of the city's prostitutes and the fame of Gilgamesh, its ruler.

In Akkadian, the Semitic language in which the *Gilgamesh* epic has come down to us in its fullest form, Inanna is called Ishtar. Essentially the same goddess because of the Babylonian adoption of the Sumerian pantheon, Ishtar does later undergo a rather harsh transformation in Assyria. There she carried a bow and a quiver, her warlike aspect receiving emphasis with a curly beard. An Akkadian fragment, on badly damaged tablets, describes the wailing of Ishtar for Tammuz, whose annual death, resurrection and marriage suggests a fertility ritual connected with the agricultural cycle. Tammuz is the Akkadian equivalent of Dumuzi, the hapless husband of Inanna, whom she allowed demons to cart off to the Sumerian underworld. Worship of Tammuz as a dying-and-rising god spread to Palestine, where the prophet Ezekiel bitterly complained that even at "the door of the gate of the Lord's house . . . sat women weeping for Tammuz". Despite the *Song of Solomon*, it seems unlikely that Jewish kings ever consummated a sacred marriage in Mesopotamian fashion. Rather the celebration of the New Year in Jerusalem may have involved a nocturnal ritual during which the king was believed to have died and then returned to life in the morning. Psalms focus on such a theme, when the suppliant admits how

> the cords of death encompassed me,
> the torrents of perdition assailed me,
> the cords of Sheol entangled me,
> and the snares of death confronted me.

Whether some kind of humiliation was suffered by the ruler, followed by his joyful restoration, we have no idea. All that is clear is the anxiety of the prophets about the elaboration of cultic practices from the Exodus onwards. For them the worship of the golden calf in Sinai was a harbinger of the religious difficulties that faced the Jews once they

A Sumerian worshipper, dating from the third millennium BC

had settled in a land inhabited by peoples who subscribed to a multiplicity of West Asian gods.

Every Sumerian settlement gave worship to local deities, while the more important members of the pantheon held sway over the cities. The moon god Nanna resided at Ur, the sun god Utu at Larsa, the mother goddess Ninhursag at Kish, the water god Enki at Eridu, and the supreme deity Enlil commanded the sky at Uruk. References to the death of a god signal a view that blurred the line between immortals and mortals. And the Sumerians even deified their early kings. Such unregulated polytheism had not yet come under the influence of the Semites, who always maintained a strict separation of the human and the divine.

But where the Sumerians and the Semites were in complete agreement was on the question of fate. Both accepted that the destiny of everything in the world was determined by the gods, whose prime objective comprised a luxurious lifestyle for themselves. It might be said that the whole world had been programmed solely for their benefit. To continue with the computing analogy, the Sumerian account of creation contains an explanation of the glitches in the programme as well. After Enki fashioned from clay the first human servants, the gods gathered at a celebratory banquet, at which, overcome by strong beer, Enki and his wife Ninhursag became involved in a creation competition. Declaring that for each person she made it would be her decision whether "the fate is good or bad", Ninhursag's ineffectual creations set a challenge for Enki in finding them suitable employment. But his ingenuity "found them bread". The cripple became the servant of a king, the blind man his minstrel, the barren woman entered the royal harem and a sexless person joined the priesthood. What the myth explains are the destinies of individuals who do not take part in family life.

23

A fragment of the *Gilgamesh* epic

This means that the profession followed by the prostitute Samhat was divinely decreed, her acceptance of many "husbands" no more than an impersonation of Inanna herself. A tablet unearthed at Nippur underlines this link by recording a song that may have been performed during sacral prostitution. Though "sixty find relief on her nakedness, and the young men are wearied, the goddess is not wearied at all". Possibly a favourite in taverns as well as temples, the song's meaning cannot be missed. The Greek historian Herodotus, the chronicler of the Persian invasion of Europe, notes how every Babylonian woman had once in her life to sit in the temple and lay with a stranger, because it made her holy in Aphrodite's sight. Incorrect though this is, Herodotus was right in his association of the Greek love goddess with Sumerian Inanna and Babylonian Ishtar. A closer link would be the Canaanite goddess Astarte, whose cult was celebrated in Cyprus, the birthplace of Aphrodite. On that island, Herodotus relates, "a custom like that in

Babylon is followed". In Aphrodite, who was conceived at sea within sky god Ouranos' severed phallus, we have the export of Inanna–Ishtar–Astarte to Europe.

Only recently has it been realised how influential Sumerian ideas were not only in ancient West Asia but also ancient Greece. Oceanus and Tethys, the primeval couple of Greek mythology, could easily have come straight from the Babylonian epic *Enuma Elish*, which dates from the reign of Nebuchadrezzar I. This poem describes the war waged by Marduk against the primeval forces of chaos led by Tiamat, out of whose dismembered body he created the world after her defeat. Marduk is then crowned "king of the gods" by the divine assembly, and the epic ends with a recital of his fifty attributes. *Enuma Elish*, which takes its title from the poem's first words "When on high", continues,

> skies were not yet named nor earth below pronounced by name, sweet water Apsu, the first one, their begetter, and salt water Tiamat, who bore them all, had mixed together, but had not formed pastures, nor discovered reed-beds, when yet no gods were manifest, nor names pronounced, nor destines decreed, then the gods were born.

Like her namesake Tiamat, the Greek goddess Tethys dwelt on the edge of the world with her husband Oceanus, the encircling ocean. She had no established cult among the Greeks because no one knew anything else about her.

In Mesopotamia, on the other hand, Tiamat was the ocean, and in the Babylonian version of the creation, she was turned into a dreadful monster, the prototype of serpentine Satan. Her baleful character is at odds with the East Asian attitude towards dragons, which were always seen as benevolent deities and held in high regard. Throughout Chinese history the dragon was the rainbringer, the lord of waters—clouds, rivers, marshes, lakes and seas. On the western edge of the Asian continent alone, the dragon acquired an evil reputation whether it lurked in caves or in the sea, so that Leviathan, the "Coiled One", was a direct descendant of Tiamat.

The rise of Marduk to a supreme position in Babylon had three distinct consequences. First of all, Marduk was now a national deity, the guardian of Nebuchadrezzar I's restoration of Babylonian power. The return of his cult statue, after the successful campaign against the Elamites, implied that once more Marduk would defend the city.

But a second aspect of his enhanced worship, no matter how much it suited the king to place emphasis on Marduk's cult for propaganda purposes, was shaped by the cosmic role he played in the *Enuma Elish* epic. The city god of Babylon was well on the way to becoming a transcendent deity, no longer tied to a specific place. A final consequence of Marduk's elevation was paradoxically a growing closeness between the worshipper and the god. A personal religion had come into existence when devotees could say "Marduk is my god", a constant source of advice that anticipates the attitude expressed in the Old Testament. "Show me thy ways, O Lord", beseeches Psalm 25, "teach me thy paths. Lead me in thy truth, and teach me." Of course a worshipper of Marduk would never have gone on to express a profound sense of personal guilt. "A broken spirit, a broken and contrite heart" was not then "a suitable sacrifice" because the general concept of sin had yet to develop in ancient West Asia. Wrongdoing was still primarily a matter for city regulation.

Pollution and purity were always central ideas for the Jews, who had forfeited the paradisal garden of Eden through sin. Enticed by the serpent, Adam and his wife Eve ate of the forbidden fruit growing on "the tree of the knowledge of good and evil" and were driven from the garden for their disobedience. Though later associated with Satan, mention of the serpent in Eden may be intended to disparage Canaanite beliefs. Snake worship was part of the rain god Baal's cult, and the snake seems to have been a symbol of the mother goddess as well.

On Crete, an island that had once been ruled by West Asian kings, statuettes show goddesses or priestesses handling serpents. According to the Greeks, King Agenor of Tyre sent his five sons in search of their sister Europa, whom Zeus had abducted to Crete in the disguise of a bull. To this virile Greek deity she bore three sons, the most famous being King Minos of Knossos. He had the labyrinth built there for the Minotaur, a bull-headed man fed annually with seven girls and seven boys. Either a garbled account of the famous bull games or a misunderstanding of the nature of West Asian creatures with a bull's head on the body of a man, the killing of the Minotaur came to occupy an important place in Greek mythology. Rather than someone confused by its composite form, the bull-man was in Mesopotamia a reliable guardian against demons. That this was most likely his function on Crete goes some way to explaining Europa's abduction. It has indeed been plausibly argued that she was a Canaanite goddess of the night,

An impression made by a cylinder seal, showing the Sumerian sun god Utu rising behind mountains at the centre. Inanna stands on the left, Enki on the right, with the Euphrates and Tigris rivers pouring from him

as her name relates to the Semitic verb "to set": hence Europe, the continent where the sun sets.

In Eden the story of the Fall appears to be as much about divine omniscience as the discovery of sexuality. "Good and evil" means "everything", the knowledge reserved for a supreme deity. A variant in the *Book of Ezekiel* tells of a ruler who lived in a mountain paradise, but was cast down from this second Eden when he started to consider himself a divinity. Having "walked up and down in the midst of the stones of fire", the king became so enchanted by his own "beauty" that his "wisdom" was corrupted by the "brightness". A Sumerian account of paradise features Enki and Ninhursag; she is besides herself with fury when Enki impregnates her daughter, granddaughter and great-granddaughter, not least because the water god had sired them all himself. As a result of the last sexual encounter, Enki almost died when his semen overflowed the goddess' loins. In his exhausted state he ate the eight plants that Ninhursag had grown from the spilled semen, falling so ill that the gods expected his end. These forbidden plants seem to have sealed Enki's fate until a fox persuaded the underworld deities to intercede on his behalf with Ninhursag, who relented the curse of death she had laid on him. This myth differs in all its details from the Jewish narrative of the Fall, except for the eating of tabooed food.

27

An account of the restoration in 870 BC of Shamash's cult statue at Sippar.
Shamash was the Babylonian name for the sun god Utu

A reason for such a difference is the singular achievement of the Jews in perfecting a West Asian tendency towards monotheism: "The Lord our God, the Lord is One." While various arguments have been put forward to explain this development, the successive stages of Jewish consciousness are hard to discern. Was Abraham a monotheist? He lived in Ur, whose city god Nanna was credited with the fore-knowledge of destiny. Was the experience of Moses crucial? In Egypt he would have been aware of the pharaoh Akhenaten's efforts to give supremacy to Aten, the sun god. Or were the prophets, faced by the brute force of Assyria, the inventors of a divine plan for Israel?

Whatever the answer, we encounter a distinct mode of thought when the Jews consider the supernatural. "The gods of the peoples are idols, but God made the heavens": the psalmist means other West Asian deities were no more than a human invention. This conclusion is transparent in the apocryphal book *Daniel, Bel and the Snake*. To the Persian king Cyrus, Daniel demonstrates with the aid of ashes sprinkled on a temple floor that the footprints of those who came secretly to eat the food set out for the god Bel belonged to "the priests, with their wives and children". He also disposed of the sacred serpent by feeding it with cakes of boiled "pitch and fat and hair": these ingredients burst its belly asunder.

One West Asian inheritance the Jews did not reject outright was the Zoroastrian notion of a final judgement. In spite of Cyrus' policy of religious tolerance in his empire, the Persians themselves never faltered in their respect for the teachings of Zoroaster, whose prophecy was delivered at some date before 1000 BC. Then the Persians were still living on the Central Asian steppe, their movement southwards only beginning after their cousins, the Aryans, had conquered northwestern

A Zoroastrian funeral. A dog patiently waits next
to the priest at the centre

29

India. Calling themselves Iranians, rather than the Greek name Persians, they accepted Zoroaster's inspired utterances as the divine commands of Ahura Mazda, whose raiment was the sky.

All harm came from Ahriman, "the evil destructive spirit", in whose cosmic struggle with Ahura Mazda the world was caught up. Because no Persian god was ever thought to be omnipotent, Zoroaster believed that all creation had to assist Ahura Mazda's pursuit of ultimate victory. A series of saviours would be sent to guide the righteous, the last of whom has the power to raise the dead from the spot where life departed from them. Then the resurrected as well as the living were to be judged, after which the righteous would be saved and the sinners endure torments, before molten metal engulfed and purified the Earth.

For Jews, Christians and Moslems this final reckoning of accounts had immense appeal. Considering the undeveloped notion of an after-life among the Jews, whose Sheol was simply the place to which all the dead went, this Zoroastrian idea came as an absolute revelation. Derived from the Akkadian word for "desolation", Sheol was the equivalent of the Sumerian underworld: a place, according to the *Book of Job*, where the worm is addressed as father, mother and sister, for in corruption all "rest together in the dust". Not so attractive though were the funeral practices of the Persians, who according to Herodotus "never buried until the body had been torn by a bird or a dog". Bones that had been separated from the flesh were then placed in an ossuary. Even though the Old Testament never once states in so many words why the Jews had a duty to bury the dead, many passages make it obvious that a burial should happen with proper mourning rites: to this day, they bury their dead in the ground and eschew cremation. After Cyrus allowed the Jews to rebuild Jerusalem, however, the possibility of physical resurrection seemed no longer in doubt. "And many of those who sleep in the dust of the earth shall wake", the prophet Daniel could proclaim, "some to everlasting life, and some to shame and everlasting contempt".

Endgame: Greco-Roman Europe Versus Persian Asia

Aggressive though the Persians were in founding their empire, Cyrus chose to represent himself as a restorer of damaged or destroyed cit-ies and cults, beginning at Babylon with the improvement of Marduk's temple. A tablet recovered from its ruins relates how "Cyrus, king of the lands, loves Esagila".

Under his energetic successors, Cambyses and Darius I, Persian rule rapidly spread across all of ancient West Asia, except Arabia, and over Egypt as well as northwestern India. Darius in particular did not relax his efforts in extending the imperial frontiers. Long before the aid sent by the Athenians and the Eretrians to his rebellious Greek subjects in Asia Minor provoked him enough to dispatch in 490 BC an expeditionary force to Greece, Darius' ambitions in Europe were public knowledge. Persian ships had reconnoitred the Mediterranean coastline as far as Italy before Darius' crossing from Asia in 513 BC, so as to mount an offensive against the Scythians. When later in 480 BC Xerxes, Darius' son, marched the same way to invade Greece, he reviewed his army at a palace built in Thrace by his father. The Athenian victory at Marathon a decade earlier was no more than a pinprick to the Persians, although the determination of Darius to bring the Greeks to heel passed on to his son a family obligation that began a seesawing conflict between Europe and Asia that lasted into the medieval period.

The unexpected defeat of both Xerxes' army and navy were the greatest events ever for the ancient Greeks, who let the Athenians take the lead afterwards in forming a defensive maritime league against more Persian attacks. Rivalry between Athens and Sparta gave Persia a respite from a sustained counter-attack, but war against the old enemy

Xerxes enthroned at Persepolis. His invasion of Greece in 480 BC
inaugurated the conflict between Asia and Europe

31

Alexander the Great taken from a Roman mosaic. The Macedonian conqueror
was much admired by Julius Caesar

provided a ready battle cry for anyone who like Alexander the Great
wished to recruit the Greek city states in an overseas campaign. Once
this Macedonian king assumed the leadership of the forces being assembled in Greece for such a war, the days of the first Persian empire—the
so-called Achaemenid after Achaemenes the legendary forebear of
the royal house—were numbered.

This was because Alexander led the most efficient army then
deployed in the ancient world. At its core were superbly drilled Macedonian pikemen, whose five-metre-long weapon outreached other
thrusting spears. When in 334 BC Alexander crossed to Asia Minor
at the head of 32,000 infantrymen and 5,100 horsemen, he drove
his own spear into the soil and announced that he accepted Asia as
a gift from the gods. It was a prophetic claim, for his policy showed
how he intended that his Asian subjects were to be free and neither
part of a Macedonian empire nor slaves to the Greeks. On Alexander's part it was both belief and propaganda, and it touched many
Asian hearts.

Having visited Troy, the original West Asian enemy of the ancient
Greeks, the Macedonian king struck inland for the first of three battles

against the Persians. In this encounter he used only his Macedonian troops and some Greek horsemen. In the second and the third, his army consisted of Greeks, Balkan troops and Macedonians. Alexander was himself the spearpoint and the Macedonians the spearhead in battle, but the other soldiers were indispensable for the fulfilment of his grand plan. Once Persia was overthrown, he began to recruit West Asians as reinforcements. When he reached India in 326 BC his army had grown to 120,000 men, of whom Asian troops formed nearly half. But it was the Macedonians in Alexander's army who ultimately decided the limits of his conquests. They constituted the Macedonian assembly, the final arbiter of the king's wishes, and worn out by the effects of monsoon rain they felt they had been misled because the promised end of Asia was nowhere in sight. Alexander himself was baffled by India's size and, even though he wished to advance against Magadha in the Ganges valley, he recognised that this was now impossible and so he agreed to turn back.

Yet Alexander still achieved a conquest unmatched in ancient times, for he had overcome the Persians and added vast territories to their empire. His uniqueness was even more apparent in his ideal of a multi-ethnic kingdom, albeit organised on European lines, because Alexander made it plain that every person was to be judged in terms of worth, irrespective of parentage. He also insisted that he and eighty of his closest companions married the daughters of Persian noble families. Soldiers' Asian women and their children were made legitimate and educated at Alexander's expense, many of them settling in the seventy new cities he founded in Asia. Quite apart from the pressing need to augment his armed forces and find a way of bringing stability to his massive realm, Alexander firmly believed he had a divine mission to accomplish, which worried some of his Macedonian and Greek followers. As the Greek historian Plutarch put it:

> Alexander considered that he had come from the gods to be a governor and reconciler to the world. Using force of arms when he could not bring men together by reason, he employed everything to the same end, mixing lives, manners, marriages and customs, as it were, in a loving-cup.

Possibly the innovation that the Macedonians disliked most of all was the court ceremonial Alexander decided to adopt, because it included the Persian custom of prostration. Though he could have practised one form of ceremonial for the Macedonians and another for the Asians, his insistence on the new one shows the extent to which his mind was set on treating all his subjects alike.

Only Alexander's sudden death from fever in Babylon, at the age of thirty-three, cut short his great multi-ethnic experiment. When the dying conqueror was asked in 323 BC to whom he bequeathed his authority, he replied "to the strongest", correctly anticipating the struggle between his senior commanders. Their wars ensured the division of Alexander's conquests into separate kingdoms. Just one of these new powers, founded in ancient West Asia by Seleucus in 305 BC, stayed close to the ideal of a multi-ethnic society. At his eastern capital, Seleucia on Tigris, in present-day Iraq, a suburb was named Apanea after Seleucus' Asian wife, whom he had married at Alexander's behest. This marriage lasted, unlike others between senior Macedonians and Asian brides, and Apanea was the mother of Seleucus' eldest son and most able successor, Antiochus I.

Well before his death in 281 BC, Seleucus recognised the talents of his eldest son by appointing him co-regent, an unusual move that almost certainly ensured the dynasty's survival. Although Antiochus was sent to take charge of the eastern territories, it would be wrong to see anything formal in this division of responsibility: father and son were both monarchs with complete authority wherever they happened to be operating. The man on the spot needed to have the power of decision belonging to a ruler. From the start, Seleucus appreciated the problems involved in running a far-flung and diverse empire. This is the reason he styled himself as a latter-day Persian king, rather than a second Alexander, whose portrait rarely appears on his coins, unlike those minted by the great conqueror's other successors.

It was an approach enthusiastically endorsed by Antiochus who in 286 BC placed this Akkadian inscription in the temple of Ezida at Borsippa near Babylon. It begins:

> Antiochus, the great king, the mighty king, king of the world, king of Babylon, king of the lands, guardian of Esagila and Ezida, first son of Seleucus, the king, the Macedonian, am I. When I decided to rebuild Esagila and Ezida, the bricks I made with my own pure hands using the finest oil . . .

Antiochus I, whose Seleucid kingdom remained true to the
multi-ethnic vision of Alexander

Already Antiochus had introduced a new dating system for documents written in Greek and Akkadian. Its purpose was to signal political continuity by the bold assertion that Seleucid kings were no foreign intruders but legitimate rulers attuned to local deities and actively participating in their cult. The dynasty was, after all, half-Iranian.

That the Seleucid empire lasted so long had much to do with such pragmatism. Another factor in its longevity was the absence of strong enemies, once Seleucus settled his border dispute in northwestern India through negotiation with the Mauryan empire. Outlying territories such as Bactria might fall away, but not until the Parthians and the Romans both pressed hard was the Seleucid dynasty reduced to little more than Syria. Conflict with Rome stemmed from Antiochus III's revival of Selucid claims to Thrace in the 190s BC. Despite the Romans inflicting a heavy reverse on him at Magnesia in Asia Minor, Antiochus remained sufficiently strong to keep the semi-nomadic Parthians in check. They were indeed obliged to furnish mail-clad cavalry as well as mounted archers for the Seleucid army.

Later kings, however, were hampered by a usurpation crisis as well as the growth of Parthian power. The takeover of Iran by the Parthians and their invasion of Mesopotamia coincided with a Seleucid civil war, in which the Romans were only too pleased to meddle. Attempts to recover these important areas failed: by 126 BC the Seleucid kings had been driven west of the Euphrates, leaving them with a restricted economic base and no chance of mustering enough troops to fight back effectively. The extinction of the dynasty in 64 BC was therefore unavoidable.

Rome's annexation of Syria the same year brought the Romans and the Parthians face to face. Remarkable although the Iranian resurgence was under the Parthian kings, they were hardly the heirs of the Achaemenid Persians, because Parthia was never an all-powerful empire, but a loose union of virtually autonomous provinces. Nor were the Parthian kings as powerful as their Sasanian successors, despite the humiliating defeat inflicted on the Romans in 53 BC at Carrhae, where 10,000 legionaries were taken prisoner. Some were settled on Parthia's eastern frontier, beyond which they may have eventually faced Chinese soldiers near the Central Asian city of Turfan. A Chinese record tells of the surrender in 36 BC of a Hunnish chieftain, whose followers included a group of mercenaries suspiciously like ex-Roman legionaries from the description of their drill.

Parthian pressure on Rome's eastern provinces finally obliged its emperors to go on the offensive, with the result that on Trajan's death in AD 117 the Roman empire reached its widest extent. As holding on to the new conquests proved a less easy proposition, they were soon abandoned by an overstretched army. Mesopotamia was evacuated, the upper Euphrates valley forming the new frontier: it was still a dangerous one, especially after Parthia was taken over by the Sasanian monarchy in 226. Self-styled "Kings of Kings", Sasanian rulers held centre stage in the intercontinental struggle, first with the Romans and then with the Byzantines, the name by which their Greek-speaking successors in the eastern Mediterranean are known.

Although the Parthians and the Sasanians were Zoroastrian, the latter were more determined proselytisers of the faith, their conflict with Christian Europe taking on all the trappings of a crusade. The first Sasanian king, Ardashir, set the tone by seeking to recover all the territories that had been subject to Achaemenid Persia. But it was his son, Shapur I, who had cause to commission at Nash-i-Rustam, in southern Iran, gigantic rock carvings of his victories over the Romans. A submissive Philip is shown pleading for peace on his knees, while a second Roman emperor, Valerian, watches as a Sasanian prisoner

Persia triumphant. The famous celebration of Rome's defeat
at Nash-i-Rustam

of war. After his capture in 260, Valerian acted as Shapur's footstool whenever the Sasanian king mounted his horse.

Yet this dramatic advance did not lead to annexation, in part because Shapur's real interests lay elsewhere. He may also have been influenced by the radical teachings of Mani, a prophet who was born into an ascetic Christian community near present-day Basra in southern Iraq. Mani's advocacy of worldly withdrawal infuriated the Zoroastrian priesthood, and ended with the prophet's own violent death, but he enjoyed the protection of a sympathetic Shapur until 272. One of the sources of Mani's inspiration was Buddhism, which he encountered on a visit to India. In a very real sense Manichaeism, the belief named after Mani, was an attempt to incorporate in a single set of ideas the religious experience of ancient West and South Asia. After Shapur's death, the Zoroastrians reasserted their authority over the Sasanian court, the ayatollah-like priest Kartir persuading Bahram I to execute Mani and afterwards persecute Jews, Christians, Manichees and Buddhists.

The Sasanian king Khusrau II,
the determined opponent
of the Byzantines

During the ancient era the Sasanians were unique in systematically attempting to impose religious orthodoxy. As a less rigorous approach was also at work in the Mediterranean world, after Constantinople became the capital of a Christian empire, the Europe–Asia struggle was inevitably seen in religious terms. It was Emperor Constantine the Great who had converted the Roman empire into a Christian state. In 325 he even obliged bishops to settle their differences about the nature of Christ at the Council of Nicaea, present-day Iznik in Asia Minor. There the Creed was adopted at his behest. Constantine himself presided over the crucial debates, guiding discussion towards unanimous agreement. "Internal strife within the Church of God," he said, "is far more evil and dangerous than any kind of war or conflict."

The climax of the Europe–Asia contest happened during the reign of the Sasanian king Khusrau II. By 619 he had overrun Asia Minor, Syria, Palestine and Egypt. Not even the True Cross was spared as booty. For a moment it looked as though the West Asians had won: Constantinople was threatened by a Sasanian army stationed on the eastern shore of the Bosporus, and by the Avars on the western shore: Slavs and Bulgars poured into the Balkans, while the Lombards invaded Italy. But in the person of Heraclius the Byzantines found an emperor worthy of the worst military crisis that had ever arisen in the eastern Mediterranean. The loss of so much territory made meeting the army payroll almost impossible. Desperately short of money, Heraclius arranged for a massive loan from the Christian church and fought a series of gruelling campaigns against Khusrau. Almost a crusade, the conflict was accompanied by feverish religious enthusiasm and hatred on the Christian side, which spilled over into attacks on Zoroastrian fire temples in revenge for the desecration of Jerusalem.

It is one of the ironies of history that the bitter duel between Heraclius and Khusrau should have arisen from Byzantine political strife. In 590 the Sasanian ruler had been forced into exile by rebellious nobles, but he found in the Byzantine emperor Maurice someone who was prepared to restore him. In return for ceding most of Armenia to the Byzantines, Maurice sent an army that put Khasrau back on the throne. For hard-pressed Maurice peaceful relations with Sasanian Persia were priceless. He had inherited a badly depleted treasury as well as threatened frontiers. But his financial difficulties remained so burdensome that in 602 Maurice tried to save on rations by ordering soldiers in the Balkans to live off the land during winter. They not only mutinied but marched on Constantinople, where they slew the thrifty emperor and replaced him with one of their officers named Phocas.

Khusrau, vowing to avenge his benefactor Maurice, first supported a pretender alleged to by Maurice's son. After this young man died, Khusrau started to take possession of Byzantine lands in West Asia. An uprising against Phocas then brought a rebel fleet along with Heraclius to Constantinople in 610. We are told that:

> stark naked, Phocas was taken before Heraclius, who ordered that his right arm be removed from his shoulder, and his head impaled on a sword. Thus dismembered was Phocas paraded through the capital city, starting from the Forum of Constantine.

On the same day Flavius Heraclius was crowned, his claim to legitimacy being the overthrow of a usurper and the return of the empire to orderly government. Because Khusrau viewed this second coup as nothing more than continued Byzantine intrigue, which in a sense it was, he felt there was no reason to stop his military operations.

By 629, however, the exhausted Susanians were ready to sue for peace. A shaken dynasty relinquished all claims to recently conquered territory, and then endured a series of coups that fatally weakened its resolve to resist Arab invaders in 651. Even though the Byzantines met the Islamic onslaught with more success, they had to accept the loss of nearly all their West Asian possessions, for Islam's sudden expansion marked the beginning of the medieval period in West, Central and South Asia.

Chapter 2

Ancient South Asia

While the gods were drinking the elixir, a demon named Rahu got a mouthful as well. Warned by the Sun and Moon, mighty Vishnu cut off the demon's head before he could swallow the divine draught. It fell rolling on the ground and roared horribly. Ever since Rahu's immortal jaws have tried to devour the Sun and Moon.

The Mahabharata

Asia's Second Civilisation: The Indus Valley

In 1921 at Harappa, a small town in the Punjab, and in 1922 at Mohenjo-daro in Sind, evidence was discovered of cities nearly two thousand years older than any previously recognised in the subcontinent. Since then, more than a thousand settlements belonging to the so-called Indus civilisation have been identified, the most striking feature of which is their uniformity in town planning. Whether in the north or in the south, archaeologists have come to the conclusion that their finds indicate the ancient existence of a massive state, or federation of states: the geographical spread of the sites so far investigated marks the Indus civilisation out as the largest populated area of Asia's three cradles of urban life. The contrast with ancient Mesopotamia is staggering. Whereas the occupied land in the Tigris–Euphrates valleys was about 65,000 square kilometres, that in the Indus valley covered 1.2 million. Despite its present-day extent, China's Shang dynasty ruled an ancient kingdom less than one-third the size attributed to the Indus civilisation. Another fundamental difference was that, unlike the city-based society of Sumer, the Indus valley people lived largely in villages that the cities dominated. Populations of 40,000 for Harappa and 30,000 for Mohenjo-daro are of the same order of magnitude as Mesopotamian cities, but they were exceptionally big. Most Indus valley cities comprised small, isolated centres of authority dotted about the countryside. In Sumer and Babylonia, on the other hand, the settlements were often within sight of one another.

A final contrast with both ancient Mesopotamia and China is the shortness of the Indus civilisation. In its most developed form, Asia's second civilisation lasted slightly over half a millennium, from about 2400 to 1800 BC. At Mohenjo-daro the city only appears to come to life in 2350 BC, a date that may explain its lack of fortifications. Instead, the city stood on vast earthern platforms. Rising from a height of three metres in the south to six metres in the north, the "citadel" mound is built of mud and mud-brick, the latter being a critical component in dealing with flooding. Although the regular inundations of the Indus and its tributaries provided a rich soil on which to grow wheat and barley as well as fruit and vegetables, there was a constant need to maintain flood defences for riverside settlements. The discovery of burnt-bricks obviously allowed the reinforcement of mud platforms and walls, something very necessary at Mohenjo-daro, where the city was situated on the bank of the Indus. Now surviving in two sections, the "citadel" mound and the "lower city" one, this enormous artificial foundation represents an incredible investment of labour.

Because the few examples of the Indus script that have come down to us defy decipherment, we lack the insight that Sumerian and Akkadian texts so wonderfully offer in understanding events in ancient West Asia. The archaeology of the Indus civilisation is mute, except where the physical remains are in themselves able to suggest meaning. Of the excavated buildings at Mohenjo-daro three fall into this category: the great bath, the granary, and the pillared hall. The bath measures

The famous statuette of the priest at Mohenjo-daro

twelve by seven metres and is nearly three metres deep from the surrounding pavement. It is approached at either end by flights of steps, formerly furnished with timber treads set in bitumen. To ensure that the bath was watertight, the floor was constructed of sawn bricks set on edge in gypsum mortar; the sides were similarly mortared, and behind the facing bricks there was a layer of bitumen. Water was supplied from a nearby well, and the bath drained through an outlet in one corner. Around the bath were sets of changing rooms, while a stairway led to an upper storey. The function of this extraordinary building, situated on the highest point of the "citadel" mound, was almost certainly a religious one. It cries out ritual bathing as a prototype of the tanks associated with temples in later Indian history.

Use of the bath was perhaps restricted to a priesthood. And a portrait of a priest could be the famous stone figurine recovered from Mohenjo-daro, which shows a bearded man with an ornamental headband. His uncovered right shoulder would have been regarded as a sign of reverence during the lifetime of the Buddha. To the north of the great bath was a block with eight small bathrooms, which its excavator thought was the preserve of some kind of priesthood, although its users could as easily have been upper-class patrons, even their wives or daughters. The emphasis on washing at Mohenjo-daro must indicate religious rituals about which we remain in the dark. Less hard to interpret is the large granary to the west of the great bath. It once stood on twenty-seven blocks of brickwork criss-crossed by narrow ventilation

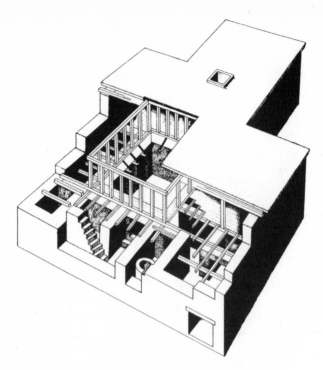

A typical Mohenjo-daro house

channels. The vanished superstructure was most likely made of wood, since the Indus valley forests had timber to spare, including the ebony that merchant vessels carried to the Persian Gulf and on to ports in southern Mesopotamia.

It seems that the granary was older than the great bath, a sure sign that the storage of grain underpinned the social order. The authorities would have paid employees, free or enslaved, in kind. The concentration of surplus foodstuffs in the granary at Mohenjo-daro, like the brick-built harbour at Lothol, farther south, indicates a tightly controlled system of production and distribution. A trading class doubtless existed in the Indus era, but the archaeological testimony points expressly to the dominance of the state. At Harappa, the northern counterpart of Mohenjo-daro, excavation has revealed a double granary, five rows of working platforms and two rows of warehouses. This facility, patently designed as a whole, suggests that government workers ground flour for the city's inhabitants.

The third large building of note at Mohenjo-daro is a pillared hall to the south of the bath and granary. Almost twenty-seven metres square, with an entrance in the middle of the north wall, the hall's roof was once held up by twenty rectangular pillars. Near this place of assembly are badly damaged ruins with a finely paved room and a walled courtyard, which may have been the private quarters of a high official. Reminiscent of later Indian audience chambers, the pillared hall in all probability served as a civic forum, where decisions were reached concerning the running of what was a major settlement. To it would have come the representatives of the "lower city", who dwelt to the east of the "citadel" mound on a less elevated mud platform.

The layout of the "lower city" is typical of Indus valley towns and cities. A carefully oriented grid of streets intersect blocks of buildings. Neither lanes nor smaller thoroughfares deviate from the pattern, in contrast to ancient Mesopotamian cities, whose maze of side streets remains a notable feature of many Moslem cities in West Asia today. What Mohenjo-daro also displays is a singular degree of uniformity in house design. Courtyards, walls, windows and ablution platforms all conform to a standard model, almost as if there were strict building regulations in force.

With the notable exception of Mohenjo-daro's bath, Indus valley cities and towns lack buildings with obvious religious purposes. But we should hesitate before concluding there was no organised belief, since the first cities built in the Ganges valley over a thousand years later exhibit no archaeological trace of religious architecture either. Here the first Buddhist monuments were all located outside city walls. One reason for this extramural development was a desire to place Buddhist monasteries near cemeteries, where the evident power of the monks and nuns in overcoming the malignant spirits lurking among the bones would impress the unconverted. Another reason was the need to avoid too close a contact with urban life. For Buddhists there always remained the problem of maintaining a spiritual authority based on separation and renunciation, while at the same time attracting popular interest and worldly support. Just as the Ganges valley cities possessed a powerful oral tradition that shaped their beliefs, Buddhist or otherwise, so an unwritten heritage must have informed Indus valley worship. All that we can do now is try and make sense of the apparent religious artefacts that are available. They consist of tiny statues and figures carved on seal-stones.

Conspicuous among them are repre-
sentations of a goddess, perhaps the Indus
equivalent of Inanna and Ishtar. Large
numbers of these terracotta figures have been
excavated at many sites. They show a standing
female adorned with a girdle, sometimes loin-
cloth and nearly always with a necklace and
a fan-shaped headdress. As no real artistry
went into their design, they may have been
used for domestic devotions because of the
low cost of manufacture. In the absence of an
Indus valley text to explain this goddess'
worship, we can only infer a fertility role. It
is tempting to suppose that she prefigures
the present head of the Hindu pantheon
Devi, whose triumph over the buffalo demon
Mahisa eclipsed the authority of both Shiva
and Vishnu, her chief male rivals.

The Indus mother goddess

Such a divine outcome would have been
unthinkable to other Indo-European peoples.
The ancient Greeks accommodated Hera, the
most powerful native goddess they encountered during their settlement of Aegean, by
marrying her to Zeus, their own supreme
deity. Hera's name could well relate to the
seasons and suggest the ripeness of women for marriage: a ritual bath she
took in a sacred spring each year was believed to restore her virginity. But
this did not stop her from nagging Zeus, nor prevent her from hounding
his illegitimate children, especially Heracles. Even in his cradle this hero
needed great strength to preserve himself, when he strangled two snakes
sent by Hera, creatures dear to her as an earth goddess.

A connection between the Indus valley fertility goddess and Devi
may not be that far-fetched. As the *Rig Veda*, the basic document of
the Aryan invaders, does not provide enough information on Shiva's
wife to tell if she bears any resemblance to his current partner Parvati,
whose name means "she who dwells in the mountains", it could well
mean that she was originally a pre-Aryan deity as well. Such a goddess
would be an appropriate mate for Shiva, a deity who prefers mountains
and the fringes of society. Reverence for Indus valley deities would have

outlasted the arrival of the Aryans, because the indigenous population, as the lowest class, the serfs, were not permitted by their conquerors to study the *Rig Veda*, the basis of the new pantheon. Yet it is "the divine yogi", Shiva himself, who suggests a tantalising link between the gods of the Indus valley people and those of the Aryans who subdued them. Indus seals show a horned figure in yoga posture: the legs are doubled up under the groin, and the soles of the feet pressed together. Again our inability to understand the inscriptions seems to leave us at a dead end, but in the later progress of Shiva, as in the case of Devi, we probably see the re-emergence of a much older stratum of belief that ultimately derives from the Indus civilisation.

Indus valley merchants traded raw materials as well as luxury goods. Docks existed at both Mohenjo-daro and Harappa, but the best-preserved harbour is at Lothol, which was discovered in 1954 some eighty kilometres south of modern Ahmadabad in Gujarat. The site comprises an enclosed area of 580 by 365 metres, which includes a spacious dock, once entered by a short canal from a now-dry river. The mud-brick perimeter wall and the platforms of mud and mud-brick were intended to deal with flooding, not intruders. Lothol's entrance, on the western side of the town, was simply an opening in the wall without any gate. The artificial dock, measuring 214 by thirty-six metres,

Indus seal showing a deity in a yoga posture

possessed burnt-bricks, gypsum mortar and bitumen to retain enough water for ships to enter and unload. A control mechanism ensured that the water level remained constant whatever the tide. Signs of flood damage, and frequent repairs, show that Lothol was an important trading port, its small rivercraft bringing up cargo from large vessels anchored in the river's estuary, twenty kilometres away.

The commodities that passed through Lothol were varied. Exports included timber, gold, semi-precious stones, even ivory, while we know that painted pottery was a favourite import. These pots were brought all the way from Mesopotamia, where a colony of Indus valley merchants once existed at Akkad. An inscription dated to about 2200 BC mentions a local man who apparently had a share in a trading ship from Meluhha, the name by which the Semites knew the Indus civilisation. After the fall of Akkad, the brief revival of Sumer saw the terminal for seaborne trade move downriver, where the Sumerian merchants at Ur gained the lion's share of Meluhhan commerce. Whether any Indus valley traders lived there is unknown, since Bahrain may have become a more convenient entrepôt. The island was then an independent trading state called Dilmin.

International commerce ceased during the second millennium BC. The reasons remain obscure. Changes in river courses may have been a factor, if some of them became prone to heavy flooding or, as seems likely among Indus' tributaries, they dried up and shifted elsewhere. At Mohenjo-daro we can trace a steady fall in the city's population, despite strenuous efforts to improve its flood defences. An even more general environmental alteration could underlie this decline, through overgrazing of the grass cover and the clearing of forests. By 1750 BC the Indus civilisation, the most egalitarian of all in ancient Asia, had collapsed with different results in Sind in the south, and in the Punjab in the

This tiny figure of a dancing girl was unearthed at Mohenjo-daro north. At Harappa some kind of settlement continued amid the ruins, reusing bricks from the city's older buildings, but a subsequent level of ash indicates a violent end. Unburied skeletons lying in the streets of Mohenjo-daro are just as suggestive. The culprits were the Aryans, who remembered burning cities and winning a great battle at Hariyupiya, increasingly identified with Harappa. That the *Rig Veda* refers exclusively to the Punjab as the initial home of the Aryan invaders may explain why in Sind vestiges of the Indus civilisation lingered on. This would make the apparent attack on Mohenjo-daro into no more than a raid. But with the advent of the Aryans, urban life disappeared in ancient South Asia for almost a millennium.

Epic India: The Aryan Invasion

Although they were to absorb certain Indus cultural traits such as ritual ablution, yoga and reverence for a mother goddess, the Aryans came as destroyers. The violence of their assault is celebrated in the *Rig Veda*, where through fear of the fire god Agni "the dark-skinned people fled, not giving battle, and left behind their possessions, for as Vaisvanara you did burn brightly and shine in destroyed cities". Between the Aryan invasion, somewhere between 1750 and 1500 BC, and the composition of the Vedic hymns, considerable time must have elapsed. A sign of this is that Dasyus, a word that previously meant the pre-Aryan inhabitants of northwestern India, had come to mean "slave". It was also used to denote demons with whom the gods were portrayed as fighting a never-ending war. The change of meaning must indicate an almost-forgotten movement of the Aryans from the Central Asian steppelands into the Indus valley.

Linguistic research now confirms that this was the route taken by the Aryan invasion of the subcontinent. The discovery of a close relationship among Greek, Latin, Sanskrit, German and the Celtic languages was made in 1786 by Sir William Jones, the founder of the Asiatic Society in Calcutta. A year earlier, another English East India Company employee had translated a portion of the *Mahabharata*, one of the longest poems in the world. This Sanskrit epic, to which we will shortly return, celebrates the extension of Aryan settlement from the valley of the Indus to that of the Ganges. As a result of Sir William Jones' work, systematic scholarship was able to demonstrate how the first speakers of

49

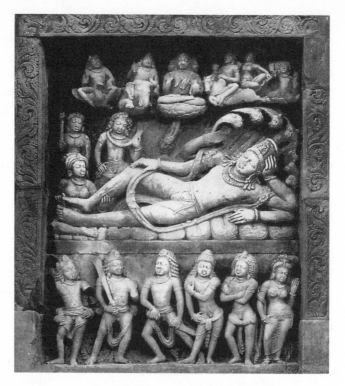

The preserver god Vishnu resting between incarnations on the
cosmic serpent Ananta

Indo-European languages—the forebears among others of the English,
the Persians and the Aryan invaders of northwestern India—once dwelt
somewhere on the steppe, which runs all the way from north China to
the Hungarian plain. At the moment, southern Russia is the favoured
spot for the dispersal of the Indo-Europeans, whose way of life was
dominated by stock breeding. Their horses gave them a mobility denied
to the settled agricultural peoples of West, South and East Asia: these
sturdy animals were harnessed to both wagons and chariots before the
invention of the snaffle-bit.

Without this crucial piece of equine equipment, the rider could not
communicate his intentions to his horse, although the absence of stirrups
still left the mounted archer or javelin thrower vulnerable in the event of
a collision. Even when the bronze snaffle-bit led to a shift from chariotry to
cavalry in the first millennium BC, the consequence was not the emergence

of the lancer, who had to await the combination of the stirrup and the built-up saddle, both Asian inventions. The use of stirrups renders mounting easier, increases control over the horse, and provides a steadier seat. When added to an effective saddle, it was to give the Franks with their wing spears and protective armour the shock of heavy cavalry, and laid the basis for knighthood in Europe. The Frankish charge was renowned and feared throughout medieval West Asia during the Crusades.

But it was the dust thrown up by Aryan chariots that announced the end of the Indus civilisation. Lacking an equivalent war machine, its people had to meet the Aryans on foot. The comprehensive victory that charioteers won in northwestern India conferred a prestige on this war machine that lasted for millennia. Long after chariots had ceased to be effective on the battlefield, Indian armies retained a chariotry. The vehicle's apotheosis, however, was to be the temple car, huge conveyances on which Hindu deities were paraded through city streets. Juggernaut is the word we have adopted in recognition of the sheer size of these great vehicles, some of which rolled along on six solid wheels whose diameters were twice the height of a man.

Where the exploits of Aryan chariot warriors receive epic teatment is in the *Mahabharata*. As we know that bards, the reciters of such heroic encounters, often accompanied their masters into battle as charioteers, their accounts of fast-moving chariot duels are full of detail. Set in the upper Ganges valley, the *Mahabharata* recounts a fratricidal struggle at Hastinapura, an ancient city now sited on the bank of a dry bed of the river near the town of Mawana. Many separate tales appear in the narrative, which reached its final stage of oral development in the fourth century AD. And because much didactic material was added along the way, the *Mahabharata* does not always feel like an epic poem. Yet it is still the quarrel between the Pandavas and the Kauravas over the succession to the throne in Hastinapura that propels the action right up to the final battle on the Kurukshetra plain.

The archery of Arjuna is praised in the *Mahabharata*. Just before the final battle, however, Arjuna falters in his resolve to fight and his charioteer, who is none other than an incarnation of the god Vishnu, explains why the Pandavan prince must not forget his duty as a warrior. Charioteer Krishna tells him that "the wise grieve neither for the dead nor the living" because "there never was a time I was not, nor you, and there never will be a time when we shall cease to be". Still unconvinced by Krishna's words about the spirit being "indestructible, immortal,

A magnificent Vishnu head discovered at Besnagar, an
early centre of Krishna worship

unchanging", Arjuna is told that he has no choice but to fight because
his path to enlightenment was through the way of action, not contemplation. "It is better," Krishna insists, "to do your duty badly than to do
that of another well." The reference to reincarnation, a concept central
to later Indian belief, suggests that the inclusion in the *Mahabharata* of
the *Bhagavadgita*, Krishna's extended sermon, came towards the end
of the epic's oral existence.

Spiritual guide though Krishna undoubtedly was to his wavering
companion, he acted as his experienced charioteer as well. How necessary
such an assistant was in combat can been observed in Arjuna's meeting with Kripa, when his undivided attention had to be focused on this
resolute opponent. Arjuna only gained the advantage by a swift dispatch
of arrows, when

> he pierced Kripa's four horses rapidly with four, smooth, gold-
> feathered arrows shot from his great bow. All the horses, hit with

the sharp shafts like flaming serpents, reared violently, so that his adversary lost his balance. When Arjuna saw how he had lost his footing, the slayer of enemy heroes refrained from striking him to preserve the other's dignity. When Kripa recovered his balance and fired ten heron-feathered arrows at Arjuna, the latter cut his bow in half with a single arrow and tore it from his hand. Next he blew off his opponent's corslet with sharp arrows that sought weak spots in the armour, but he did not hurt his body. Without body protection, Kripa looked like a snake that had shed its skin. Second and third bows were likewise knocked by Arjuna's arrows from Kripa's hand. Then the determined opponent seized a javelin and hurled it like a blazing thunderbolt, but again Arjuna broke the missile into pieces with his arrows. Still undaunted, Kripa stung Arjuna with ten sharp arrows from another of his bows, and in reply Arjuna loosed thirteen arrows with the splendour of fire; he smashed the yoke with one, finished off Kripa's horses with four, decapitated the charioteer with a sixth, struck the bamboo poles with three, the axles of the chariot with two, and split a battle-pennant with a twelfth arrow. Finally, Arjuna hit Kripa full in the chest with a thirteenth arrow like a thunderbolt. His bows broken, his chariot wrecked, his horses lying dead next to the charioteer, Kripa jumped to the ground and threw a well-studded club at Arjuna, whose arrows stopped it in flight.

The contest might have gone on had not Kripa's followers intervened. These foot soldiers showered Arjuna with arrows and carried off the wounded, but still unsubdued, chariot warrior. Of obscure identity, Kripa can nonetheless stand as the heroic fighter of epic India. Yet it was the politeness of Arjuna that not only let him fight a full archery duel through pausing until Kripa recovered his balance, but even more he did nothing to prevent his wounded opponent being carried away to safety. Honour having been satisfied, there was a chance that Kripa would live to fight another day.

The other great epic of the Aryan invaders is the *Ramayana,* a much shorter poem than the *Mahabharata* in spite of later additions. The original version is attributed to the sage Valmiki, who brought together bardic fragments and then, as Homer did in ancient Greece, reshaped them into poetry that set the standard for early Sanskrit literature. Study of both Indian epics demonstrates parallels with Homer, and especially between the *Iliad* and the *Ramayana,* which culminates with Rama's expedition to the island of Sri Lanka to recover his abducted wife Sita.

Both the Greek and Indian story-
tellers must have drawn upon a shared
mythological heritage that was recast to
suit the different experiences involved in
the occupation of Greece and the Ganges
river valley, in the middle part of which
the *Ramayana* is mainly set around the
city of Ayudhya. A real Mycenaean king
might well have led the Greek armada
to Troy, but Agamemnon's leadership
has been absorbed into a story of divine
rivalry, of gods as well as goddesses
settling their personal disputes by backing either the Trojans or the Greeks.
Yet even with Helen, the human cause
of the conflict, we are dealing with a
goddess rather than a wayward queen.
Hatched from an egg, this daughter
of mighty Zeus was probably a tree
goddess, whose cult encompassed
abduction as well as rescue.

South Indian bronze of Krishna,
the serpent-slayer

For the chief thing that the *Iliad*
and the *Ramayana* have in common is
the divinity of the abducted women,
Helen and Sita. At the end of a protracted
siege of the demon Ravana's stronghold on Sri Lanka, Sita is reunited
with Rama. Because he does not welcome her back as readily as Menelaus,
Helen's forgiving husband, Sita was swallowed by the earth as a testimony
of her innocence and purity. Inconsolable, Rama follows her by disap-
pearing in a river, water being the element of Vishnu, whose incarnation
Rama is. More so than Krishna in the *Mahabharata,* the divinity of Rama
can never really be forgotten. Time and again in the *Ramayana* we are
reminded of the reason for his incarnation, the defeat of the demonic host
commanded by Ravana, whose name means "the Screaming One". The
preserver god Vishnu was compelled to intervene in worldly affairs because
Ravana, through penance and devotion to the creator god Brahma, had
become immune to attack from either the gods or other demons.

So unusual is the idea that severe austerities could ever be a means of
obtaining immense power that we can only conclude that here is a prime

example of Indus valley influence. Having acquired the powers usually associated with the rishis, priestly seers capable of humbling even the gods, Ravana's inner strength encouraged him to challenge Rama, a foolhardy action in view of Vishnu's ability to descend periodically to the Earth and correct some great evil influence there. Just how strong was belief in the powers of the rishis is evident in the humiliation of Indra. When this sky god seduced the rishi Gautama's wife, the punishment meted out was nothing less than castration: the subsequent replacement of the divine testicles with those belonging to a ram merely served to underline the indignity Indra endured. No other Indo-European god ever suffered such a fate.

Undoubtedly Valmiki based the *Ramayana* on pre-existing oral materials, but he seems to have had an eye on a religious dimension from the start. The epic's story concerns above all the second incarnation of Vishnu, which resulted in the defeat of the earliest demonic attempt to gain universal power. Unlike Shiva, there was never anything sinister or dangerous in Vishnu's makeup that might have prevented him from becoming a saviour deity. He is credited with several incarnations, including one as the Buddha, "the magic deluder who corrupted the demons with many kinds of heresy, so they soon abandoned the teachings of the Vedas". While the anti-Buddhist tenor of this late myth remains transparent, there a distinct possibility that the emphasis placed by the Buddha on non-violence was so attractive to worshippers of Vishnu that they laid claim to "the magic deluder" to prove how it was their own god who had abolished animal sacrifice during this incarnation.

The Buddhist Revolution:
The Mauryan Empire

The location of Hastinapura and Ayudhya in the Ganges valley signals the eastern extension of Aryan authority. Neither the *Mahabharata* nor the *Ramayana* show any interest in the Punjab, the original place of Aryan settlement in ancient India. Not until the founding of the Gupta dynasty about AD 320 does Aryavarta, "the land of the Aryans", stretch "from the eastern to the western sea". This delay can only mean one thing: that the Aryans found the strong and distinct culture of Magadha, as the Ganges valley was then called, much harder to handle than that of the Indus valley. So accommodation rather than destruction was required, especially in matters of religion.

The Mahabodhi temple, which marks the spot where the
Buddha's enlightenment came to pass

An echo of Aryan frustration is apparent in a late addition to the
Mahabharata that refers to the godlessness and disorder of Magadhan
society. "This world is upside down: ignored are the temples of the gods,
and instead the Earth is marked by charnel houses. Even the lowest class
refuses to serve the brahmins." Only with the Sungas, the usurpers of
Mauryan power in 185 BC, would the brahmins be able to begin occupying the highest rank in society that they thought was rightfully theirs.
The Sungas were themselves brahmins. By the time the *Bhagavadgita*

was composed, a class system had become generally accepted but without the rigidity it was to acquire through the ideas of Manu. In the aftermath of foreign invasion, this lawgiver defined about AD 250 the varnas, the four classes into which ancient Indian society was properly divided. Manu also reduced the status of women, who like the lowest class and outcastes were henceforth ineligible to hear the recitation of the *Rig Veda*.

An early formulation of the varna is Krishna's description in the *Bhagavadgita*, when he informs Arjuna of the different characteristics of the priestly brahmins, the warlike ksatriyas, the hard-working vaisyas, and the lowly sudras. It is self-evident to Krishna that

> calm, self-control, austerities, purity, patience and uprightness, theoretical and practical knowledge, and religious faith, are the natural-born actions of brahmins. Heroism, majesty, firmness, skill, generosity and lordly behaviour are the natural-born actions of the ksatriyas. Farming, herding, and commerce are the natural-born actions of the vaisyas. Action that consists of service is likewise natural-born to the sudras.

This is caste status, inherited obligations that must be fulfilled without question. As a ksatriya, it was Arjuna's duty to slay enemy warriors, an action that amounted to nothing at all in the context of the endless cycle of death and rebirth, not to mention the immortality of the soul.

The special privileges claimed by the brahmins, such as exemption from taxes and charges for public services, were not readily conceded during the ancient India's second period of urban civilisation, which commenced in the Ganges valley about 500 BC. The brahmins had to compete with other cultic experts, whose beliefs derived from experiences quite alien to Aryan traditions. They indeed found in the Jains, the Buddhists and the Ajivikas such serious opponents that their own social advancement could only be guaranteed by adopting ideas from these indigenous beliefs. Two of them in particular were to have a lasting influence on Hinduism, the majority religion in modern India: rebirth and karmic retribution.

Impetus towards unification in northern India may have come from Alexander the Great's descent into the Indus valley in 326 BC, on the final stage of his conquest of the Persian empire. Even though he conquered the whole of the Indus valley, his Macedonian troops refused to advance against the Nanda state of Magadha. A few garrisons were left behind, but Alexander's early death put an end to his ambition of a worldwide empire, and by 317 BC the last Greek troops had quit the subcontinent, their commanders drawn westwards by news of the strife between his successors. The brief invasion made so slight an impression on ancient South Asia that it went unmentioned in any Indian record. Fanciful then is the suggestion that Candragupta, a young adventurer from the Magadhan clan of the Mauryas, was inspired to imitate the example of Alexander. Rather it would appear that, having extinguished the Nanda dynasty at Pataliputra, Candragupta took advantage of the political vacuum left by the Macedonian withdrawal to found the Mauryan empire in northern India. According to both Greek and Indian sources, Candragupta was of undistinguished birth, a son of the last Nanda king by a lowborn woman.

A Seleucid coin minted around 300 BC. It records the gift of Candragupta's war elephants

Candragupta saw off the remnants of Macedonian power in north-western India so effectively that Seleucus, the successor to Alexander's eastern provinces, ceded parts of present-day Afghanistan to gain a stable frontier. As a consequence of the agreement, Seleucus received 500 war elephants for use in West Asia. Seleucus also sent Megasthenes as an ambassador to Pataliputra, and while resident at Candragupta's court he compiled an account of the Mauryan empire. Megasthenes was amazed at the professionalism of the men who ran its standing army, which was organised under a committee of thirty, divided into subcommittees that controlled the infantry, the chariotry, the elephants, the navy and the supply train.

The emergence of Magadha as the major power in ancient South Asia, however, had as much to do with its civil servants as its soldiers. Candragupta was assisted by more than able generals, because he encountered in the brahmin Kautilya, an outstanding administrator. From the surviving writings of Kautilya, some of which were collected in the *Arthashatra*, it is clear that he understood how Mauryan authority depended on well-paid civil and military officials, whose salaries came from an efficient taxation system. The predictability of state revenue derived from agriculture was regarded as the basis of fiscal security, but

A carving of a stupa, a Magadhan "charnel house"
so disliked by brahmins

Kautilya also pointed out the need to keep an eye open for new sources
of tax such as trade, which increased greatly under Mauryan rule. His
linking of taxation, administration and military power was crucial in the
establishment of India's first empire.

At the same time that the political landscape was undergoing this
great change, another transformation thoroughly reshaped religion.
Two beliefs, Jainism and Buddhism, were then making startling headway. No less open to their influence than his subjects was Candragupta
himself. Disturbed by the ravages of a terrible famine, he abdicated
in 297 BC in favour of his son Bindusara, and travelled to southern
India, where he became a Jain recluse. A bas-relief today at Sravana
Begola, in Mysore state, records Candragupta's life, including his
final act of renunciation, the Jain rite of starving unto death. Perhaps

because he was such a new phenomenon in ancient Indian politics—the lowly usurper of power over an extensive area of land that previously was a patchwork of squabbling kingdoms—Candragupta could safely indulge his preference of Jainism, a more austere faith than Buddhism. Its ideas were located at the impersonal end of the spectrum of belief, far removed from any notion about the survival of the personality. Only through an act of sustained self-renunciation could the soul of a Jain make its escape from the sufferings of the world.

Both Jainism and Buddhism arose from a culture that was recognised as being non-Aryan, and as having funerary practices and an asceticism that offended the brahmins. Already these Aryan priests had condemned the construction of round sepulchral mounds in Magadha as the work of "the demonic people" because only a four-cornered shape was pleasing to the gods. Round sepulchral mounds of course were to become, as stupas, symbols of devotion wherever the Buddhist faith spread. But brahminical disdain for such monuments was a minor issue when compared with disagreements about the need for austerities, especially in the intensity with which Jain monks practised them.

Given the Indus civilisation's concern with yoga, it is possible to imagine a very ancient source for Indian asceticism. Even though we do not know whether the Indus seals that show yoga postures are actually pointers to such an indigenous tradition, it is certain in Jainism that we encounter asceticism in its oldest form. According to the Jain saviour Mahavira, a contemporary of the Buddha, four stages of meditation

A panel from Bharhut showing at the top; the Sacred Wheel of the Law: in the middle; the park in Benares where the Buddha first preached: and at the bottom; elephants acknowledging the truth of his mission

were necessary to remove the karmic burden that prevents liberation. In the first, the mind still moves from one object to another; in the second, it stops doing so and comes to a standstill; during the third and fourth stages, complete motionlessness of body and mind permits a satisfactory death to take place. How influential this yoga requirement of absolute self-control became in Indian belief is clear in a description, which occurs of all places, in the *Mahabharata*. "Having his mind firm", the yogi "is motionless like a stone. He should be without trembling like a pillar, and motionless like a mountain".

The Buddha entirely rejected this point of view. For him desire, or intention, was crucial. While Jain monks tried to suppress bodily as well as mental activity, Buddhist monks were guided by a psychological discipline founded on the banishment of both desire and fear. An undisturbed state of mind was the Buddhist goal, an entirely new solution to the problem of liberation. As the Buddha taught that the real problem did not lie in action, but with the driving force behind it, Jain commentators were delighted to ridicule the absence of anything physical in the Buddhist notion of karma. They noted with glee how a Buddhist who grills a child and eats it, but without knowing he does so, is supposedly free of blame, whereas that same Buddhist is blameworthy if he eats a gourd while thinking it is a baby. Fundamental to this difference in outlook was the Jain view of the soul being fettered by matter, so that the only method of gaining repose, as a free-floating soul at the top of the universe, was total disengagement from the physical world. A Jain monk wore a veil over the mouth in case he accidentally swallowed an insect, thereby adding to his karma.

As a dynasty the Mauryans were very eclectic in their religious beliefs: Candragupta favoured Jainism; in reaction, his son Bindusara clung to the determinism of the Ajivikas, a breakaway Jain sect that held that an individual had to live many, many times to secure release; while Candragupta's grandson Asoka was the world's first Buddhist ruler. About 270 BC Bindusara died and a succession dispute left Asoka on the throne. According to Buddhist tradition, it was the unprecedented bloodshed involved in a campaign in Kalinga, a part of Orissa state, that caused Asoka to lose confidence in Mauryan aggression. To pull himself together, he embraced Buddhism with a fervour that explains the spiritual revolution he inaugurated. For the rest of his life Asoka endeavoured to conquer through righteousness rather than warfare. In the process he turned Buddhism into a pan-Asian religion, two and a half centuries after the Buddha's death.

Although several kings were sympathetic towards the Buddha's teaching during his lifetime, there was no systematic attempt to adhere to the principles of living he preached. Not that this ever worried the Buddha, since he predicted that at a future date a great ruler would establish a Buddhist world order. This, Asoka came to believe, was none other than himself. As he said of the rock-cut edicts that he caused to appear in all his territories: "They are not everywhere yet, because of the extent of my dominions. But I shall have more prepared so that the people may know how to behave." Carved on tall stone pillars, sometimes on rock faces, the edicts of Asoka employed many languages including Aramaic as well as Greek. Inscriptions in these two languages, discovered by archaeologists in 1958 at Khandahar in

Prince Siddhartha, the future Buddha, in his chariot

southern Afghanistan, were intended to propagate Buddhism among the people Alexander had settled in cities there. Prakrit was the common language of ancient India north of the Deccan. Having split from Sanskrit well before the lifetimes of Mahavira and the Buddha, this Aryan tongue belonged to the masses. Sanskrit itself was now restricted to the brahmins, whose religious texts maintained the original language in an almost fossilised form.

Shortly before the Christian era the northern Buddhists turned to Sanskrit and Prakrit scriptures were translated into it, with new ones composed in that language. This change, most probably the result of brahmins entering the Buddhist order of monks, gives a clue to the subsequent falling away of Indian Buddhism under the Guptas. Brahminical delight in the elaboration of doctrine took the faith away from the directness of the Buddha's original message and, in what became known as Mahayana, developed a Buddhist pantheon. During the reign of Samudragupta, at the close of the fourth century AD, the Chinese pilgrim Fa Xian was not slow in observing how Buddhism was being steadily replaced by Hindu beliefs. Fa Xian provides the first datable reference to the practice of untouchability. He was bewildered that "if they enter a town or market, these outcasts sound a piece of wood to separate themselves". As a slightly later Indian source relates how many brahmins lost status because they unknowingly took food that had been polluted by contact with the leavings of a single outcast's meal, it is obvious that Manu's strict view of society had won the day. Although some Buddhist texts mention such a taboo, the Buddha had rejected the whole system of hereditary classes. A person's position, he always maintained, is determined not by birth but worth, by conduct and by character, rather than descent.

This democratic idea was not to be lost in Asia because Asoka had sent missionaries abroad. Cordial relations between Asoka and Devanampiya Tissa, the king of Sri Lanka, ensured that Buddhism transferred early to this island. One of the Mauryan ruler's sons even went there as a missionary. The form of Buddhism that flourished in Sri Lanka is called Hinayana, "the small ferryboat", as opposed to Mahayana, "the great ferryboat". Today it still eschews the deities and semi-divine figures that populate the Mahayana pantheon. Followers keep to its simpler creed in Myanmar, Thailand, Laos and Cambodia, whence it spread from Sri Lanka.

The Age of Invasion: From the Bactrians to the Huns

The disintegration of the Mauryan empire after Asoka's death has been blamed on his espousal of non-violence, but this Buddhist idea was not responsible for any military failure because Asoka never became a pacifist. All he hoped for was the minimum use of force by his successors. Had he been inclined to out-and-out pacificism there would have been no executions during his reign. Whatever the cause of Mauryan weakness, the dynasty ended in a palace coup when, in 185 BC, Pusyamitra killed the last Mauryan ruler and declared himself the first Sunga king.

Vulnerability in northwestern India led to an immediate clash with intruding Greeks from Bactria. A factor that indirectly brought about the series of invasions, which were to trouble India for centuries, was the unification of ancient China by Qin Shi Huangdi, its first emperor, in 221 BC. The consolidation and the expansion of the Chinese empire, most dramatically demonstrated in the construction of the Great Wall, put pressure on the nomadic peoples living on the Central Asian steppe. Two of them, the Da Yuezhi and the Hunnish Xiongnu, to use their Chinese names, waged a fierce war for control of the pasture lands to the north of the Great Wall. When the Da Yuezhi were soundly defeated, they migrated about 165 BC westwards to the borders of Bactria. Pushed along by the Da Yuezhi, the Sakas were driven to invade India as well as Persia. Before this intrusion in the first century BC, there were also Greek kingdoms in northwestern Indian, founded by Bactrian kings who supplemented their forces with locally raised troops.

The Bactrian king Euthydemus I as a young and old man

An unknown Kushana king
discovered at Mathura

According to the Greek geographer Strabo, a near contemporary of events in Bactria and India, the people whom Alexander settled in Bactria did so well because the Oxus river valley was fertile. "It is large and all-productive except for olive oil," he tells us. "Because of the excellence of the land, the Greeks who rebelled against Seleucid rule grew so powerful that they conquered both Ariana and India as well." By these places Strabo means southern Afghanistan and the Indus valley that, he adds, was overrun "all the way to the coast". Bactrian conquests in the subcontinent were to cover eventually an area "larger than that captured by the Macedonians".

He credits two kings with this expansion: Demetrius, son of Euthydemus, and Menander, the subject of praise in Buddhist literature. Though worsted in battle with Antiochus III, the last of the Seleucids to attempt holding on to Alexander's Central Asian provinces, Euthydemus I was by 200 BC king of an independent Bactria. His successor, Demetrius, thrust into India soon after Pusyamitra's overthrow of the Mauryans. One of his armies concentrated on the Indus valley, while a second under the command of his son-in-law Menander took control of the upper Ganges.

A tradition that Menander built a stupa in Pataliputra seems to refer to a second invasion of Magadha when he was himself the Bactrian king. Then the Sungas were forced to move their capital to Vidisa, on the northern edge of the Deccan. A column standing in a field near the present-day town boasts an inscription carved at the behest of a Greek envoy from King Antialcidas, who ruled in the Indus valley about 100 BC. The column was raised in honour of Krishna, whose emerging cult fascinated the Bactrians. Hardly surprising then is the Buddhist column raised by Menander in the Ganges valley, because memorial pillars were in vogue. It mentions "the Great Saviour, Just and Invincible Menander", who was "King of Kings". These grandiose titles did not stop him from becoming a lay Buddhist and, after entrusting the throne to his son, Menander entered a monastery, where he attained enlightenment.

Bactrian power was shattered by the arrival in India of the Sakas, whom the Greeks knew around the shores of the Black Sea as the Scythians. These nomads had already seized Bactria, only to be driven out by the Da Yuezhi, who conquered the whole area up to the Hindu Kush. As they were not pastoral nomads even in their original homeland, the fertile Oxus valley proved an irresist-

The great Buddhist philosopher Nagarjuna

ible place of settlement for the Da Yuezhi: there they were content to be farmers and traders until one of their clans, the Kushanas, followed the Bactrians and the Sakas along the route to northwestern India. Little is agreed about Kushana history before the accession of King Kanishka in AD 78. Like Asoka before him, Kanishka was remembered as a great patron of Buddhism. It was through his Central Asian territories that the Mahayana version of the faith was introduced to ancient China. How great Kanishka's kingdom was in ancient India is still a matter of dispute, although he seems to have held sway over the Indus valley and that of the Ganges as far as Pataliputra. His control of large areas to the north allowed him to profit from the diversion of the Silk Road from China through the Khyber Pass and down the Indus valley, whence merchandise went by sea to the head of the Persian Gulf.

Kanishka may have suffered a defeat at the hands of the Chinese general Ban Chao, who was ordered to punish a Kushana king for having the temerity to demand the hand of a princess in marriage. Ban Chao's western advance was probably a response to intimidation of China's Central Asian allies. From his headquarters in Kuchu, an oasis city in the Turfan depression, Ban Chao marched in 90 against the Kushanas, defeated them somewhere in Bactria, and then advanced all the way to the shores of the Caspian Sea, the closest a Chinese army has ever got to Europe. The intervention did not have a lasting effect on the Kushanas, who in India were well on their way to becoming naturalised. Almost as eclectic as the Mauryans, they showed an interest in all the subcontinent's beliefs, while on their coins they reveal an even wider spiritual outlook because European as well as West Asian deities are often represented alongside South Asian ones. It was at Kanishka's command, however, that a gathering known as the Fourth Buddhist Council met to discuss doctrinal differences. Attending were representatives of no fewer than eighteen Buddhist sects.

In spite of the discovery at Mathura of a Kushana inscription praising a bodhisattva, the depth of Kanishka's personal belief cannot be gauged. At this stage, Mahayana Buddhism was not established in any secure manner. Already possessing distinct features of its own, like the bodhisattvas, "beings whose essence is enlightenment", the movement had to await Nagarjuna for a full exposition of its philosophy. It was through his efforts that figures such as Amitabha, the Buddha of the Western Paradise, the future Buddha Maitreya and Avalokitesvara, the epitome of compassion, were launched on their trajectories as demigods. Avalokitesvara's ability to change his shape into male, female or animal forms accounts for his amazing transformation as Guanyin, the Chinese goddess of mercy. Fa Xian saw all of them paraded through city streets on elaborately decorated ceremonial carriages, accompanied by crowds of singers, musicians and monks. Like Hindu temple cars, these vehicles rose to a height of five storeys, overtopping all but the chief buildings and city gateways.

At this period, relations between Buddhism and Hinduism were peaceful, but Mahayana and Hinayana scholastic debate had descended to a level of abuse that would have appalled the Buddha. As Nagarjuna put it, "the Good Law is in great danger". With remorseless logic he exposed the weaknesses of all contending Buddhist schools of thought and, when challenged to provide an explanation of his own, Nagarjuna said he was unable to do so because none could ever exist. In the swirl of sense impressions no mind could expect to comprehend the world. Because nothing has an inherent existence, Nagarjuna argued, there is no possibility of formulating any satisfactory account of phenomena. Everything is unreal because it is based on relations the nature of which we can neither understand nor explain. Appreciation of the empty quality of all things, this alone Nagarjuna claimed, leads to the intuitive wisdom that discloses ultimate truth. It was this deeper understanding that the Buddha had meant to communicate to his followers. Opponents accused

Nagarjuna of having destroyed the whole of Buddhism with his teaching of emptiness, but he replied that they misunderstood sunyata, "emptiness". The Buddha had acknowledged two kinds of truth: everyday experience of objects and, below this apparent reality, the unreality of everything that is supposed to exist. Only when Buddhists awoke to this deeper truth would they find release from the dream-like experience of daily life and approach Buddhahood.

With such a quest as the fundamental purpose of Mahayana Buddhism, the focus of endeavour among monks and lay devotees alike, there was no reason to apply a brake on the development of its pantheon. The various Buddhas and bodhisattvas were merely pointing the way. By postponing release from the travails of the world, a bodhisattva was indeed the supreme example of compassion in that he or she was prepared to become the saviour of all, whatever their worth or their claim to attention. So much so that Mahayana apologists were able to distinguish between a bodhisattva's unselfishness and the selfishness of a Hinayana monk, who sought personal enlightenment in the seclusion of a cloister.

The Kushana empire reached the height of its influence under Kanishka. His two sons, Vasishka and Huvishka, had less success in maintaining the throne's authority. But during his long reign of thirty-four

An entrance to one of the Buddhist cave sanctuaries at Ajanta in central India

years, this did not stop Huvishka from taking a great interest in religion. He actively supported the Hindu revival, which under the powerful Gupta dynasty was about to marginalise Buddhism in northern India. The last of Kanishka's family, his grandson Vasudeva, was completely Hinduised. His name is one of those belonging to Krishna, and his coinage does not display any of the divinities drawn from different pantheons that had appeared on earlier Kushana coins. It was during the twilight of Kushana rule, nevertheless, that the most remarkable Buddhist monument of all in ancient India was taking shape. Independent rulers on the Deccan oversaw the construction of twenty-nine caves, carved into the inner rim of a horseshoe-shaped valley formed by a bend of the Waghora river. Their interiors at Ajanta, some seventy kilometres north of modern Aurangabad, are adorned with statues and paintings depicting events in the lives of the Buddha: his final mission that ended with him entering nirvana, or "enlightened extinction", and his previous lives as bird, animal and man.

At Ellora, a cave complex closer to Aurangabad, there is situated a Hindu equivalent to Ajanta. Its outstanding feature is a rock-cut temple dating from 783. Into the mountainside two parallel gorges were driven and, from the monolithic block left between them, a full-size temple was carved and dedicated to Shiva. Ellora remains a startling witness to the victory of Hinduism over Buddhism in the subcontinent. Farther south Hindu kingdoms were also raising temples and carving into the living rock stories of Shiva's exploits. On the seashore at Mamallapuram, south of present-day Chennai, the Pallava king Mahendravarman I commissioned rock-cut sculpture to celebrate the descent of the Ganges. Through the tangled mass of Shiva's hair the onrush of water in this mighty river, as it first poured down from heaven, was safely guided to earth, where it washed away the ashes of generations of the dead. King Mahendravarman was in 610 converted from Jainism to the worship of Shiva by the ascetic Apparsvamin. Today Mamallapuram consists of a petrified collection of animals carved from boulders, temples hewn from larger rocks, and of course the famous carving of the descent. The cultural influence of the Pallavas, and their successors the Cholas, was to be felt in the medieval era as far away as Cambodia, Vietnam and Indonesia.

A degree of stability returned to northern India with the establishment of the Gupta dynasty, which lasted from 320 to roughly 550. Its second king, Samudragupta, undertook a whole series of campaigns, eliminating small kingdoms that had emerged during the rundown of Kushana rule and he extended his dominion into the upper reaches

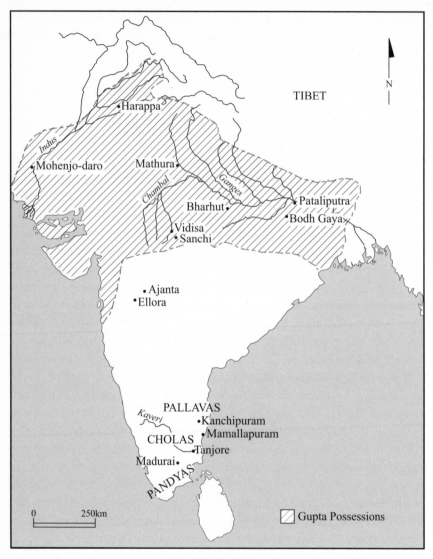

The Gupta empire

of the Indus, and some distance beyond, a feat of Indian arms unequalled since the reign of Asoka. The Guptas seem deliberately to have imitated the Mauryans, with one notable exception: they were staunch supporters of the Hindu gods. To demonstrate his control of "all between the oceans" Samudragupta staged an Aryan horse sacrifice.

The rite was a perfect way for Samudragupta to demonstrate the extent of his authority, since it descended from a practice in remote times when a chieftain asserted his ownership of herds and the grounds on which they grazed. When such an early ruler wished to announce himself as a paramount chief, he would do so by letting loose his best stallion. This splendid animal was allowed to wander wherever it liked, followed by a guard of young warriors, ready to defeat anyone who might attempt to capture the horse. The Gupta king's horse sacrifice included such a year-long roam as well as rituals designed to purify both the horse and the ruler.

Before setting the horse free, the prospective victim was washed in a pool while a dog was killed and thrown in the water. Then the Gupta warriors accompanying the stallion made sure that there was no contact with mares, or further immersion in rivers or streams, during the year it wandered the world. Towards the end of the year a huge pyre was erected, and Samudragupta underwent several observances in readiness for the sacrifice, which lasted three days. On the second day, when the actual slaughter took place, the king drove in a war chariot drawn by the sacrificial stallion and the other horses. The victim was anointed by Samudragupta's three foremost wives, and its tail decorated with pearls. At the sacrifice of the horse, a sheep and a goat were also killed. The stallion was then smothered to death, presumably to avoid damaging its body, whereupon the king's first wife, his queen, symbolically coupled with the sacrificed horse under covers, while the royal court gave her encouragement with obscene remarks. Afterwards, the victim was dismembered and burned on the pyre.

Satisfied as Samudragupta was with this rite in 376, his realm did not quite measure up to his claims. On the Deccan he was obliged to rely on compliant kings, whose good behaviour had to be enforced by military pressure. And his claim that the Sri Lankan ruler became his vassal is unfounded, because the purpose of the mission dispatched from the island to Pataliputra was not a token of submission. The rich gifts sent to Samudragupta were intended to persuade him to look with sympathy on a request to build a monastery and a resthouse for Sinhalese pilgrims at Bodh Gaya, the place where the Buddha attained enlightenment.

Shortly after Samudragupta's death, Gupta power was shaken by another Saka invasion. To stave off certain disaster, his son Ramagupta offered to present the Saka king with own wife in exchange for a truce. But Candragupta, his younger brother, went to the Saka camp disguised as a woman and slew the enemy ruler instead. Later Candragupta killed Ramagupta as well, before succeeding to the throne. On an iron pillar, now standing in the Quwwat-ul-Islam mosque, south of Delhi,

As Durga, the goddess Devi slays the buffalo demon Mahisa. From Ellora

is recorded Candragupta's "defeat of a confederacy of hostile chiefs . . . and the reconquest of the seven mouths of the Indus".

The boast proved to be hollow, for a more ferocious foe was already headed in the direction of the subcontinent. Arriving in the fifth century, the Huns devastated Gupta lands in much the same way that Attila's followers fought their way across the Roman empire. In Europe, the Huns first occupied the Hungarian plain, the westernmost extension of the great Central Asian steppe; there they grazed their horses until the comparative smallness of the pasturelands forced them to relinquish their tradition of murderous raids on settled communities in favour of regular supplies and recruitment to their army. Operating a protection racket on a grand scale, the Huns were happy to be bought off whenever the price was right. But the system of exploitation fell apart after Attila's death in 445. His quarrelsome sons destroyed the unity that was necessary to maintain such a productive balance of oppression and reward.

Something very similar happened in northern India, where for nearly a century the Huns wore down Gupta strength. The Hunnish king Mihirkula was a second Attila, uncouth in manner and an absolute terror when opposed. Greatly he enjoyed watching the slaughter of Buddhist monks and the sacking of their monasteries. Mihirkula died in 542, by which date the disunited Huns posed much less of a threat, although the tide of the Hunnish invasion did not recede until the end of the century. Then the Huns were under sustained attack from the Sasanian Persians and the Turks, who had settled in Bactria. Later northern India was to experience the Turks at close quarters in yet another series of Central Asian invasions of the subcontinent, after the arrival of Arab arms in the lower Indus valley.

Chapter 3

Ancient East Asia

> The capital of Shang was a city of cosmic order,
> The very pivot of the four quarters.
> Glorious was its fame,
> Purifying its divine power,
> Manifested in longevity and peace,
> And the sure protection of descendents.
>
> *A description of Anyang*

The Cradle of the East: The Shang Dynasty

Before the foundation of Anyang, the Shang dynasty had moved its capital several times. The first requirement of a Chinese state was a permanent capital, but these not infrequent moves were a necessity until the perfect location, one that most pleased the Shang kings' divine ancestors, was discovered.

The pivotal importance of the ruler as the Son of Heaven formed the basis of Chinese thinking about politics ever since Shang times, the earliest period in which written records were kept. Right down to the abolition of the empire in 1911, the occupant of the dragon throne was regarded as the custodian of social order. Never seen however as a divinity, kings and emperors were considered to possess a heavenly mandate to rule, a concept that ultimately derived from the ritual practices of the Shang dynasty. From oracular inscriptions it can be deduced that the ruler alone possessed the authority to ask for the ancestral blessings, or counter the ancestral curses, which affected society. It was Shang Di, the high god of Heaven and the ultimate Shang ancestor, who conferred benefits upon his descendents in the way of many sons, good harvests and victories on the battlefield. Through divination the advice of the Shang king's immediate ancestors could be sought as to the actions most pleasing to the supreme deity.

Ruling by divine right then, the Shang monarch was known as "the One Man", whose charismatic authority was enhanced by an annual cycle of religious ceremonies at which he presided. His predecessor was believed to have ascended heavenwards as a "god-king" to serve in Shang Di's court. After the overthrow in 1027 BC of the last Shang ruler, the notorious Di Xin, the change of dynasty was explained by this ruler's unsuitability as a divine servant. "God on high," we are told, "hated the laxity of Shang rule and, turning his gaze to the west, chose the land of Zhou as his dwelling-place." Despite needing to be on our guard against a tendency among Chinese authors to account for dynastic change in terms of virtue sweeping aside corruption, the replacement of the Shang by the Zhou was seen as a process of renewal and, throughout the subsequent history of China, this idea provided a means of explaining the change of ruling families.

But the Shang system of succession was complicated and more than half the kings were the son of an elder brother. It was perhaps a misfortune for the dynasty that this convention of lateral succession finally gave way to primogeniture, since it ensured that Di Xin came to the throne. Except for the tyranny of this ruler's reign, the Shang king was an awesome figure since his priestly power was connected with shamanism. Heaven was where all the wisdom of human affairs lay and only the king, through the mediation of his divine ancestors, could access this invaluable information. A fifth-century BC document gives the reason for this, when it states that

> in ancient times, men and spirits did not intermingle. Then there were certain persons who were so articulate, single-minded, and humble that their understanding enabled them to make sense of what was above and below. Thus they could explain what was distant and profound. These possessors of such powers . . . supervised the positions of the spirits at ceremonies, sacrificed to them, and otherwise handled religious matters. As a consequence, the spheres of the sacred and the profane were kept distinct. The spirits sent down blessings on the people, and accepted from them their offerings. There were no natural calamities.

All was thrown into disorder when every household tried to usurp the role of these spiritual specialists, the shamans. The people lost their reverence for the spirits, who became too familiar with the world so that disasters were commonplace. To rectify matters the gods returned everything to its proper place, thereby "cutting the communication between Heaven and Earth".

This myth neatly explains the original meaning of wang or "king". Its character consists of three horizontal strokes, representing Heaven at the top, humanity in the middle, and Earth at the bottom; they are joined together by "the One Man", a vertical stroke at the centre of the character, since he was now the sole channel of communication between all three. Thus Shang kings were expected to keep in constant touch with their biological forbears. By the end of the dynasty there were few days in the year when this priest-king was not occupied with a sacrifice to them.

To consult the ancestral spirits divination took the form of observing cracks on scorched animal bones and tortoise shells. At first Shang kings used oracle bones that had been expertly prepared. They were sawn, cut, scraped, polished and drilled to induce more cracking. Tortoise shells were a later addition. It was as a result of divination that King Pan Geng decided to move the capital to Anyang. In the

Signs incised on pots such as this one from prehistoric Banpo anticipate fully developed Chinese characters

76

Inscribed Shang oracle bone dating from the
eleventh century BC

Book of History, a collection of documents edited during the fourth century BC, are recorded the difficulties faced by Pan Geng when he wished to move the capital. Speaking firstly to his most senior courtiers, he countered their resistance in these words:

> Our king Zu Yi came and fixed on this location for his capital. He did so from a deep concern for our people, because he would not have them all die where they could not help one another to preserve their lives. I have consulted the tortoise shell and obtained the reply: "This is no place to live." When former kings had any important business they paid reverent attention to the commands of Heaven. In a case like this they were not slow to act: they did not linger in the same city. If we do not follow the examples of old, we shall be refusing to acknowledge that Heaven is making an end to our dynasty. How small is our respect for the ways of former kings! As a felled tree puts forth new shoots, so Heaven will decree us renewed strength in a new city. The great inheritance of the past will be continued and peace will fill the four quarters of our realm.

Separately Pang Geng charged his nobles with stirring up trouble among "the multitudes" through alarming and shallow speeches, a grievous crime he pointed out, considering how their own ancestors shared in the sacrifices offered to former kings. Unless they treated the ruler with proper respect, there would be inevitable punishments and afflictions laid on Shang by an outraged Heaven.

To ram home his point, Pang Geng then addressed "the multitudes", who were "charged to take no liberties in the royal courtyard and obey the royal commands". He told the people about the reason for the removal, stressing the calamity that the founder ancestor of the dynasty would surely inflict on the existing capital, and let it be understood that nothing would affect his "unchangeable purpose". Having achieved his aim by direct speech, Pan Geng transferred everyone across the Yellow river to Anyang, where he instructed his officers "to care for the lives of the people so that the new city would be a lasting settlement".

One of the elaborate bronze vessels used by Shang
kings for ancestor worship

The episode is interesting for a number of reasons. Implicit is the threat of the priest-king to invoke the aid of the royal ancestors to punish dissidents, yet the sheer strength of Pan Geng's conviction of impending disaster without a change of residence cannot be denied: he genuinely believed that only his "great concern" stood between the Shang people and their ruin. For had not Heaven itself given the crucial sign by way of cracks in the tortoise shell? How could he afford to ignore a warning that his own divination had revealed? "When great disasters come down from Heaven," he commented, "the former rulers did not fondly remain in one place. What they did was with a view to the people's welfare, and so each moved their capital to another place."

This duty to "the multitudes" is the other aspect of this episode that deserves notice. In it is the germ of the idea of reciprocity between ruler and ruled, which would become so influential in the philosophy of Confucius. Eventually this notion would be expressed in the saying: "Heaven sees what the people see; Heaven hears what the people hear." By the fourth century BC Mencius, Confucius' greatest follower, could argue that whenever a ruler lost the goodwill of his subjects and resorted to oppression, the tian ming, "the mandate of Heaven", was withdrawn and rebellion justified. This democratic theory, a kind of safety value in the Chinese constitution, derived from Mencius' view that the ultimate sovereignty lay with the people. Heaven granted a throne but succession depended on the people's acceptance of a new ruler. Uniquely Chinese was the idea of cooperation required from "the multitudes". Though we should not overlook how such a humanist idea emerged from a religious context, Shang beliefs were more this-worldly and people-centred than any other ancient Asian outlook.

The location of Shang capital had been changed several times before Pan Geng moved it to Anyang about 1300 BC. There the traditional rammed-earth method of construction was employed to raise the ceremonial buildings. According to the *Book of History*, "The multitudes set their plumb-lines, lashed together the boards to hold the earth, and raised the Temple of the Ancestors on the cosmic pattern." In this new building, "the king used the tortoise shell to consult the ancestral spirits, after which the court and the common people agreed about a course of action. It is called the Great Accord." What we have described here is the patrimonial nature of Chinese rule, royal or imperial. The authority of the Shang king over his people was no more than an extension of his patriarchal control over his own family, an idea later developed by

Ritual axe discovered at Anyang, the last Shang capital

Confucius into a political justification for the state. Because Confucius envisaged the state as a collection of families under the care of a leading family, the virtue of obedience was the chief characteristic that defined the relationship between a ruler and his subjects. When asked about government, he replied: "Let the prince be a prince, the minister a minister, the father a father, and the son a son."

While he regarded correct familial relations as the cornerstone of society, Confucius also possessed a profound sense of personal responsibility for the welfare of mankind. After his philosophy became dominant under the Former Han emperors in the first century BC, the Chinese empire's administrators came to see themselves as protectors of the people, inheritors of Pang Geng's fatherly concern for their prosperity.

Underpinning the layout of the ancient Chinese capital, with its ceremonial centre for royal ancestor worship, was a conscious attempt to mirror the cosmic order itself. As "the pivot of the four quarters", it was designed to facilitate the role of the king in fulfilling his responsibilities to Heaven for what happened on Earth. The organising feature of every capital city was the ruler's ancestral temple, whose position was determined by geomancers, ancient experts in feng shui. They sought a site that was set among landforms generating auspicious, or at least benign, influences, but such locations were sometimes unavailable, so that often geomancers were required to concern themselves with defence against evil influences seeping into the residences of the living and the dead. The good fortune of

Marble carvings of an owl and a tiger found in royal tombs at Anyang

a dynasty could only be assured if all the sites chosen, and not least that of royal tombs, were properly adapted to local cosmic currents. By the reshaping of hills, the removal of boulders and the excavation of ground considered to be unlucky, geomancers could help redeem otherwise inauspicious locations, while just by planting trees and shrubs they were able to assist in restoring a necessary balance of the yin–yang element.

Attuning to the rhythm of nature was a vital consideration for the ancient Chinese, who explained its perfection in the yin–yang theory: it envisaged two interacting forces, not in conflict but existing together in a balance that if disturbed would bring swift disaster. This perception of natural forces could have arisen nowhere else than in the loess plains of north China, where a sudden downpour might dramatically alter the landscape.

Because the ancient Chinese believed that the divine and human realms were connected through kinship, the current ruler's sacrifices always formed a key link between them. As the *Book of Rites* puts it, "Rites banish disorder just as dikes prevent floods." In the ancestral temple there were ritual specialists who assisted in the conduct of ceremonies, but the central position of "the One Man" meant that no priesthood ever developed in the earliest stage of Asia's third civilisation. This singular feature of Chinese society was to be challenged in the medieval era by Buddhism, China's greatest import before modern times. Its late arrival probably explains the failure of this Indian faith to dislodge

Confucianism. While the struggle was accompanied by scenes of mass fervour, the strength of the rational, sceptical mould of Confucian philosophy ultimately prevailed. A tradition that took for granted strong central authority, embodied in the ruler as the Son of Heaven, and the duty to ancestors in the perpetuation of family lineage, was too firmly rooted for Buddhist evangelists to alter permanently either the social or the spiritual landscape. Once ancestor worship had spread beyond the confines of the highest social rank, and become a concern of every Chinese family, there was no possibility of placing the attainment of individual salvation before an expression of gratitude to one's forbears.

Not only did the Shang dynasty possess no priesthood, unlike those that arose in the civilisations of ancient West and South Asia, but even more its culture was communicated from generation to generation by a unique method of writing. The Chinese script evolved from pictograms engraved on bone and wood. Because they were always associated with the knowledge held by the ancestral spirits—a question was first inscribed on an oracle bone and then the answer added after interpretation of the cracks produced by scorching—Chinese characters were always thought to have an intrinsic value. Respect for the power of the written word was evident in Confucian temples through the provision of special ovens for the ritual disposal of unwanted paper with writing on it. One myth even recounts the spiritual impact of writing. When the legendary Yellow Emperor's chief minister devised the original Chinese characters, all the spirits cried out in agony because the innermost secrets of the world could thereafter be recorded. Instead of using clay as a durable writing material, small tablets of sliced and scrapped bamboo were strung together with string. They functioned as paged books before paper was invented in the first century AD. Even after paper came into general use, the continued popularity of bamboo is explained by this wood being as plentiful in China as palm leaves were in South Asia.

Classical China: The Zhou Dynasty

The fall of the Shang, China's first historical dynasty, was blamed on the waywardness of Di Xin, whose infatuation with his favourite consort Dan Ji brought about a reign of terror. She encouraged him to take delight in hurting others. When Di Xin's uncle Pi Kan decided that the state of affairs was grave enough to risk death in reproving the monarch, a furious Di Xin exclaimed, "I hear the heart of a sage has seven holes," and had Pi Kan cut open to see whether he was one.

Hardly surprising then was the ancient Chinese view that the Shang dynasty was overthrown through a justified rebellion, when the Zhou toppled a worthless tyrant and re-established good government. But the reasons for the dynastic change were far more complicated. Late Shang kings appear to have squandered resources on campaigns along their eastern and southern frontiers, where allied peoples had come to resent Shang rule. A consequent neglect of the western approaches to their kingdom may account for the rise of the Zhou people, who shortly before Di Xin's deposition were still half nomadic and half agricultural. The contest between the Shang and the Zhou was by no means the pushover that the *Book of History* suggests, for the issue was for some time in doubt. Only the statesmanship of Duke Tan, who acted as regent for the young Zhou king, seems to have finally secured the new dynasty.

This minister was credited with great wisdom by Chinese historians. Looking back on these early years from the confusion at the end of Zhou rule, many scholars, Confucius among them, regarded this period as a lost ideal. For Tan had shown proper respect for the fallen royal house by investing a Shang prince with a fief so that the ancestral sacrifices might be continued, while his treatment of Shang officials was a sign of the value he attached to peace. When they were given posts under the new dynasty, Tan told them how Zhou's superseding of the Shang dynasty was the will of Shang Di, a telling explanation of the changeover because this supreme deity was none other than the ultimate ancestor of the Shang people.

Although the Zhou possessed divine ancestors of their own, Tan's acknowledgement of Shang Di as "the mighty god on high" was his greatest contribution to Chinese civilisation. Possibly motivated as much by apprehension over Zhou's prospects of becoming a successful dynasty as a genuine sense of awe at the elaborate rituals involved in the worship of Shang Di at Anyang, where Tan had once lived for some years, the endorsement he gave to Shang religion conferred upon ancient China a sense of continuity that would inform its system of government until the beginning of the twentieth century. It crystallised the theory of the heavenly mandate to rule, difficult though Tan admitted this entitlement was to retain. "Heaven is hard to rely on," he said, for its favour "is not constant". The corollary of such realism was the need for the Zhou king and the Zhou people, as well as others who were living in the kingdom,

A wine container used in Zhou ancestor worship

jointly to seek Heaven's approval. "To begin well is common," Tan warned the Shang officials, "but to end well is rare indeed." So complete was Tan's explanation of the ancient Chinese state that Confucius could claim with some truth that he was a "transmitter" rather than a "creator" of ideas about government. "I believe in things of old," he told his disciples, "and I love them."

As a child, Confucius often set out the sacrificial vessels and, as an adult, he acquired a reputation of being expert in matters of ritual. This delight in the ceremonies of ancestor worship led him to formulate a code of conduct that placed the individual firmly within the family. For Confucius proper behaviour was embodied in the concept of rites, which is usually rendered as etiquette or ritual, but really means propriety. The Chinese character tells us what he had in mind, for the strokes represent a vessel containing precious objects as a sacrifice to the ancestral spirits. Confucius saw, therefore, the rite of ancestor worship as the focus of a moral code in which proper social relations were defined: the loyalty of a minister to a ruler was the same as that owed to a father by a son.

Confucius said that, in accordance with traditional rites, affection and respect should be expressed during the lifetime of one's parents through obedience and after their death by an appropriate burial and offerings of food. Filial piety meant the continuation of deference to parents into full adulthood; it was never simply the natural gratitude of children. Also involved in this fundamental relationship was the duty of thanking one's ancestors by providing a better life to one's descendents, an attitude still fundamental to the Chinese outlook today.

Management of familial relations was thus the foundation of a good society and the only context for a good life. What ancient China needed, Confucius argued, was compassionate rulers who would instruct their people by their own example in following traditional usage. Pointing out that a written law code represented a dangerous break with custom, he astutely predicted that the code of punishments inscribed on a tripod by the ruler of Qin state would be learned and honoured by the people above all else. Never again would those in authority be able to call upon tradition to declare their judgements correct. Not for a moment was Confucius suggesting that arbitrary decisions were ever justified. As he remarked:

> If you lead people by regulation and regulate them by punishments, they will seek to evade the law and have no sense of shame. If you lead them by virtue and regulate them through rites, they will correct themselves.

A sense of shame was indispensable: without it, the individual had no chance of self-reform. Here the combination of virtue and rites underlines Confucius' emphasis on the courtesy expected from an educated person, because good manners were always a sign of moral character.

So deeply did Confucianism instil an appreciation of the enormous role played by nurture, by education as a preparation for civilised living, that subsequent Chinese speculation can be said to have been an interpretation of this principle. Referring to the Daoists, the indigenous opponents of this philosophical position, Confucius said: "They dislike me because I want to reform society, but if we are not to live with our fellow men, with whom can we live? We cannot live with animals. If society was as it ought to be, I should not be seeking to change it." It is a point constantly made down the ages by Confucian scholars whose outlook rested on a sense of responsibility for the welfare of mankind. This stress on service was the chief reason for the adoption of Confucianism as the imperial ideology. For Confucius persuaded China that a would-be leader of men could not rely on inherited status as a qualification, but

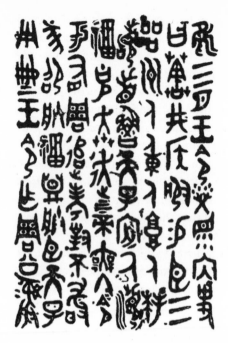

An inscription on a bronze vessel dedicated
to the Duke of Zhou

only on these qualities deriving from personal integrity that commanded respect, whether in a ruler or a teacher.

Right down to his death in 479 BC, Confucius' zeal for reform was driven by the obvious breakdown of feudalism. Even though the Zhou was the longest-lasting dynasty in Chinese history, royal authority ebbed away after the court moved to Loyang in 771 BC. Well might a Zhou king present lacquered bows and arrows as a token of the empowerment of leading nobles, who were supposed to be restoring order on his behalf, but the political reality was that these great men were virtually independent in all but name. They actually fought each other to acquire greater territory and prestige. In the eighth century BC some 200 feudal states existed: by 500 BC less than 20 of them could boast their existence. The climax of the struggle occurred in the aptly named Warring States period, which ended with the triumph of Qin in 221 BC. Then just seven contenders tried to advance their positions through incessant warfare.

To its competitors, the rise of Qin seemed phenomenal. Its hard-bitten rulers cut their way to absolute power so decisively that they were compared to silkworms devouring a mulberry leaf. Situated in the old homeland of the Zhou people, around present-day Xi'an, Qin turned itself into China's first key economic area, a place where the supply of tax-grain was so superior to that of other places, that the ruler who controlled it could control the whole country. Having been given the equivalent of the western march by Zhou, when the dynasty shifted its capital downriver to Loyang, Qin leaders were able to maintain the fighting skills of their people, through almost continuous warfare against barbarian invaders, and build up their own economic strength through large-scale irrigation schemes. There was a feeling that Qin was hardly Chinese at all.

But semi-barbarian origins alone cannot explain the reluctance of the Qin court to embrace feudal etiquette. Frontier conditions required a robust outlook and inclined it to adopt with enthusiasm a new spirit of government, a quest for efficiency without regard to traditional moral-ity, that already permeated several states. This harsh philosophy, known as Legalism, was brought to Qin in 356 BC by Shang Yang, who was given permission to introduce a new legal code that strengthened the state's military power by weakening the influence of the nobility, breaking up powerful clans, and freeing the peasantry from bondage. In place of customary ties he substituted collective responsibility as a method of securing order.

So Shang Yang ordered the people to be organised in groups of five and ten households, mutually to control one another's conduct. Those who did not denounce the guilty were cut in half; those who denounced the guilty received the same reward as those who had decapitated an enemy. Everyone had to assist in the fundamental occupations of agricul-ture and weaving, and only those who produced a large quantity of grain were exempted from labour on public works. Merchants were enslaved along with the destitute and the lazy. Shang Yang's singlemindedness made him unpopular and he did not long survive his master's death. Yet his fall was not followed by the abolition of the reforms, for Qin rulers were very well aware of the advantages of centralised authority, a disciplined bureaucracy and a strong army. They also appreciated Shang Yang's dictum: "Better to face the enemy than to fall into the hands of the police." It allowed the rulers of Qin to behave in an increasingly authoritarian fashion, right down to the unrestricted power enjoyed by Qin Shi Huangdi, China's first emperor.

But Qin's dedication to Legalism came at a heavy price. As the philosopher Aristotle wisely remarked of Sparta's miserable failure in

The grave of Confucius at Qufu, where his followers mourned for three years

Greek politics after the defeat of Athens in 404 BC, an exclusively military outlook was no preparation for peace and, in the last resort, was itself a cause of defeat. The Spartans "do not appreciate leisure and never engage in any kind of pursuit higher than war . . . Those like the Spartans who specialise in one and ignore the other in their education turn men into machines." In a similar manner, the shortcomings of a military hierarchy were to undermine the Qin empire, once the strong hand of its founder was removed. Qin Shi Huangdi's younger son found himself in 209 BC beset by subjects driven to outright rebellion through the overbearing behaviour of Qin officials.

Though the patent disdain for commerce in Shang Yang's reform programme may seem strange, the lowly position of merchants in ancient China was a result of princely supervision of industry from earliest times. At Anyang there were separate areas of settlement for chariot makers, metalworkers, potters and weavers. It was, however, the Warring States period that witnessed the emergence of China's four famous classes. In order of precedence, they were the gentry, the peasant farmers, the artisans and the merchants. Out of the conflict between feudal states, and within them, rose the gentry, whose growing surplus of younger sons, educated but without rank, took advantage of whatever opportunities presented themselves. These were usually employment with a state or noble family, and from their ranks Confucius drew some of his most able disciples.

Yet the later supremacy of Confucius' ideas did not mean that there were no philosophical challengers during the Zhou dynasty. An older contemporary of Confucius, Lao Zi, the founder of Daoism, was the keeper of the royal archives at Loyang. Access there to more ancient records than anything available to Confucius may have persuaded him of the falseness of traditions glorifying the feudal past. Unlike Confucius, Lao Zi was convinced that the causes of disorder in ancient China lay not in the weakness of Zhou institutions but in feudalism itself being an unsatisfactory method of achieving order. Benevolence and righteousness were too often a mask for ambition. The book associated with Lao Zi's name, *The Way of Virtue*, set political rivalry in a cosmic perspective:

> Who would prefer the jingle of jade pendants,
> Once he has heard stone growing in a cliff?

Man's rootedness in the natural world, an inner strength that made all men wiser than they knew, was the Daoist means of salvation. The artificial demands of a feudal society had so disturbed the innate abilities of the people that instead of following the natural way of living, they were circumscribed through codes of honour and duty. Daoist quietism was practised by a number of Lao Zi's followers, one of whom, Zhuang

Han commentary on *The Spring and Autumn Annals,*
a work once believed to have been written by Confucius

Zi, even rejected the premiership of a major state in their early third century BC. As he succinctly commented: "A thief steals a purse and is hanged, while another steals a state and becomes a prince."

Such an attitude was of course anathema to Confucian thinkers, who regarded public service as a moral obligation. The problem for the Daoists was that China had no popular institutions similar to those that appeared in Greece: there was nothing for them to use in the furtherance of a practical democratic philosophy. Withdrawal from service in government, or becoming a hermit, could never be more than political protest. The only revolutionary glimmer to survive at all was in Daoist religion, a transformation brought about largely by the need for solace among the peasantry when crisis overtook the early empire in the third century AD. Chang Daoling, the first heavenly teacher of the Daoist church, even established for a time a small, semi-independent state. His organisation of the peasants in a quasi-religious, quasi-military movement was the first of many such ventures. It is reported that Chang Daoling dramatically acquired immortality when in 156 he disappeared except for his clothes. That, like Lao Zi himself, he had no tomb indicates more than an indifference to ancestor worship. It shows that Daoism was always concerned with the pursuit of the elixir of life.

Imperial Unification: The Qin and Former Han Emperors

From 237 BC onwards, the ruler of Qin, Zheng, had the advice of a second Shang Yang in his councillor Li Si. As determined a Legalist as his predecessor, Li Si guided Qin in 221 BC to its complete defeat of rival states. As the last Zhou king had already been dethroned, there was nothing to prevent Zheng declaring himself Qin Shi Huangdi, the First Sovereign Qin Emperor. The reference to divinity in this new title was more than a political device. As early as 219 BC, the same year that work started on his own incredible mausoleum at Mount Li, the first imperial envoys were sent up mountains to establish relations with the Immortals who were believed to dwell on their summits. For Zheng's objective was a supply of the elixir of life. Two assassination attempts had not only served to increase his dread of dying, but they had encouraged his aloofness from all but a small circle of advisers and, indirectly, abetted those intrigues so disastrous to the Qin dynasty on his sudden death in 210 BC.

Although the Qin dynasty was brief, it represents a turning point in East Asian history, because the bureaucratic form of government developed under the Qin emperors became the model for future Chinese political organisation. The significance of the change that Qin Shi Huangdi began, and Liu Bang, the founder of the following Han dynasty, completed, cannot be overstated: despite periods of disunity, the unified empire gave China two millennia of internal stability and external influence.

In his drive for uniformity Qin Shi Huangdi relied on military force alone. Feudal holdings were abolished and noble families compelled to take up residence in Xianyang, now the capital of all China; the peasants were given greater rights over their land but became liable for taxation; weapons were also brought to the capital, where they were melted and cast into twelve colossal statues; the empire was divided into administrative districts, garrisons planted strategically, and a body of inspectors established to audit accounts as well as check on the administration of justice; there was standardisation of weights and measures, currency, written script and axle wheels; a national road network was built and canals improved for the supply of the army and, as a counter to the Xiongnu, the Huns who later invaded the Roman empire, the Ordos desert region was annexed and defended by the construction of the Great Wall, which ran for more than a thousand kilometres from modern Gansu province in the west to the Liaodong peninsular in the east.

Qin Shi Huangdi was anxious to halt any drift of the Chinese people to the north in case the farmers of the northern outposts might abandon agriculture and take up stock rearing, thus strengthening the nomad economy on the Central Asian steppe. The Great Wall was intended to keep his subjects in as well as his enemies out. To encourage a southward population movement imperial armies had by 210 BC extended Qin Shi Huangdi's authority as far south as present-day Hong Kong. While the southern peoples were by no means assimilated or firmly controlled, they were irrevocably tied to the empire.

When the Chinese empire was consolidated under the Han dynasty, the people of what is now north Vietnam were also incorporated into the imperial defences, remaining under Chinese control for a millennium. The Vietnamese became independent only when China itself fragmented for half a century following the fall of the Tang dynasty in 906 AD. Even then, Ngo Quyen, the first Vietnamese ruler, looked northwards for the model of his new kingdom; a sinicised aristocrat, he recognised no

An assassination attempt on the life of Qin Shi Huangdi

alternative. Before its complete subjugation in 111 BC southern China was called Nan Yueh, from which the name Vietnam derives.

When, in 213 BC, Qin Shi Huangdi discovered that his edicts drew criticism from Confucian scholars, he accepted the advice of Li Si and burned all the books except those on medicine, forestry, agriculture and divination. Li Si's exemption of works on divination was calculated, given his master's interest in the spirit world, but he must have known that the deeply rooted belief in its efficacy would make suppression very difficult. "The disloyal," Li Si asserted, "can no longer use the past to discredit the present." Radical though this attempt was to make knowledge an imperial monopoly, the proscription of books under Qin rulers was not new: Shang Yang had destroyed the *Book of History*. When, in 206 BC, a rebel army burned the Qin capital of Xiangyang, the conflagration engulfed the imperial library and destroyed the sole surviving copies of many books. The loss caused a definite break in conciousness, for when, under the patronage of the Former Han emperors, ancient texts were painfully reconstructed from memory and badly tattered copies hidden in 213 BC at great risk, the feudal age seemed remote. The book burning gave later Chinese scholars a lasting hatred of the Qin dynasty, although this did not entirely prevent censorship under later imperial houses. What effectively ended any official attempt at regulation was the Chinese invention of printing, which made both censorship and copyright impossible to enforce.

Renewed criticism in 212 BC drove Qin Shi Huangdi to conduct a purge of scholars in Xiangyang, some 460 being condemned to death.

The Great Wall north of Beijing with its Ming dynasty stone facing

For daring to oppose this repression, Prince Fu Su was exiled from the imperial capital. Nothing could now stem Qin Shi Huangdi's rising tide of anger at "alchemists who had wasted millions without obtaining any elixir and scholars who said the throne lacked virtue". Perhaps such frustration was inevitable: there had never been anyone like him before, the undisputed ruler of a China still isolated from the other centres of ancient civilisation.

Given his utter obsession with immortality, the elaborate funeral arrangements that Qin Shi Huangdi commissioned at Mount Li were intended to prepare an abode suitable for a future Immortal, none other than himself. A description of his burial chamber relates how in it were placed

> models of palaces, towers and official buildings, as well as fine utensils, precious stones and rarities . . . All the empire's waterways, including the Yellow and the Yangzi rivers, were reproduced and made to flow mechanically. Above, the heavenly constellations were depicted, while below lay a representation of the Earth.

And to the amazement of archaeologists since excavations began in 1974, the emperor's tomb is guarded by several thousand life-size ter-racotta warriors and horses, standing ready for action in subterranean chambers. Columns of foot soldiers are modelled wearing iron-mail coats, even the heads of the rivets being shown. Most significant of all, though, is the vanguard of crossbowmen whose weapons would have turned the shields of contemporary Macedonian or Roman soldiers into colanders.

When this Chinese invention eventually reached Europe during the medieval period, the crossbow caused consternation because of its effectiveness against armour. It claimed many knightly and even royal victims, including the English king Richard I in 1199. Unlike in the West, there was never any superiority belonging to any section of society, because the balance of military power was never one-sided in China. That the crossbow was such a great leveller explains the feasibility of Mencius' doctrine about justified rebellion against tyrannical government.

The inherent weakness of Qin rule only became obvious after Qin Shi Huangdi's early death in 210 BC. Having on a tour of inspection a dream of a sea god interpreted as an evil spirit keeping him from con-tact with the Immortals, the emperor roamed the seashore of Shandong province until he dispatched what was most likely a stranded whale with a repeater crossbow. Shortly afterwards he sickened and died, but Li Si and Zhao Gao suppressed the news and brought the imperial litter

Bronze dragons unearthed at Xi'an, the site of ancient Chang'an. For Qin Shi Huangdi the dragon was an imperial guardian

back to Xiangyang, behind a cartload of mouldering fish to disguise the stench of the emperor's corpse in high summer. Such was the terror inspired by the imperial title, there was neither an onlooker to question the arrangements for the homeward journey, nor on arrival in the imperial capital an official to oppose the forged will they used to place Qin Shi Huangdi's worthless younger son, Hu Hai, on the throne.

Li Si's motive in plotting against the heir apparent Fu Su appears to have been personal anxiety, a flaw in his character skilfully played upon by the chief eunuch Zhao Gao. Neither of the conspirators gained from their actions. Zhao Gao engineered Li Si's execution in 208 BC, and in the ensuing year forced Ershi Huangdi, the Second Sovereign Qin Emperor, as Hu Hai was titled, to take his own life, but the usurpation then attempted by the scheming eunuch was effectively opposed by the Qin bureaucracy. Afterwards Zhao Gao strove to maintain his position as best he could. He advised Qin Shi Huangdi's nephew to be content with a lesser title than emperor, because Qin was once again one state among several. "Now these states have reasserted their independence and our territory has shrunk accordingly," Zhao Gao said, "it would be improper to retain an empty dignity."

Having with the connivance of Li Si eliminated in Prince Fu Su the only member of the imperial family capable of holding on to power, Zhao Gao left Qin defenceless against rebellion. The continuous use of conscript labour had strained the allegiance of the peasantry, especially when it was enforced by means of cruel punishments. As a result of the progressive expansion of state demand for workers, there was a drop in agricultural output, with all the miseries that a shortage of food entails. It was indeed the dislocation of the rural economy that formed the background for the popular risings against the Qin dynasty. The impoverished peasants who in 209 BC staged the first large-scale uprising in China's history were unconsciously responding to the unique circumstance of a unified empire: they were marking out the limits of future power for a centralised government.

In early 206 BC Qin Shi Huangdi's hapless nephew was the prisoner of Liu Bang, the first of the rebel leaders to reach Xiangyang. The arrival of the main force shortly after the Qin surrender brought death to the entire imperial clan in a general massacre. The violence was unprecedented. Liu Bang had treated the inhabitants of Xiangyang with restraint, forbidding his men from plundering its riches or taking captives. The devastation of Xiangyang, and the subsequent division of

The mound raised above the tomb of Qin Shi Huangdi at Mount Li

China between the rebel leaders, was beyond Liu Bang's prevention, but three years later he was ready to make a bid for the dragon throne. By carefully husbanding his strength, Liu Bang triumphed over all his rivals, becoming in 202 BC the Han emperor Gaozu, or "High Ancestor".

Then it could not be foreseen that China under the Former Han dynasty would become a society divided by literacy, a prerequisite of success in the examination system for public office that Liu Bang's successors developed to recruit men of talent to manage the empire. Barely literate himself, Liu Bang had a peasant dislike of the excessive ceremony attached to learning. When some scholars came to him in costume, he snatched one of their elaborate hats and urinated in it. But he was moderate in disposition, a signal virtue in that very violent age, and it made his accession popular: people felt that he would govern in their interests, unlike the absolute rulers of Qin. Liu Bang neither aped aristocratic manners nor slackened his compassion for the peasantry, and his habit of squatting down, coupled with an earthy vocabulary, unsettled polite courtiers. He knew the value of learned advisers, however, and to bring order to his new palace at Chang'an, which means "Forever Safe", across

Part of the terracotta army, with individually sculpted faces for each soldier

the Wei river from the ruins of Xiangyang, he commissioned from one of them a court ceremonial for his boisterous followers. His only instruction was "Make it easy."

Despite the brief unification imposed by Qin Shi Huangdi, China remained a collection of recently independent states with vigorous regional cultures. But Confucian standards and rituals together with inherited Qin administrative practice brought some cultural unity. By turning to scholars untarnished by the harsh policies of Legalism, Liu Bang paved the way for the ultimate Confucianisation of a bureaucratic empire. The transformation was a slow one because the first Han emperor settled for a compromise after the oppression of Qin. He allowed the restoration of certain feudal houses and granted fiefs to his own close relatives, but these diminished holdings were intertwined with districts controlled by imperial officials. In 154 BC a rebellion among the vassal states was used to alter the laws of inheritance: afterwards inherited land had to be divided between all sons in a family, a requirement that hastened the breakdown of the largest units.

The accession in 180 BC of Wen Di, Liu Bang's grandson, accelerated the development of the imperial civil service. A profound modesty, almost a sense of unworthiness, persuaded this emperor to summon to Chang'an "wise and bright men who will speak frankly and reprimand me, that I may repair my shortcomings". Unlike other ancient Asian rulers, no Chinese emperor ever considered the state to be his private property after the totalitarianism of Qin. The repressiveness of this short-lived dynasty taught the Chinese to distrust despots, with the result that Former Han emperors were frequently reminded that they were the inheritors of an empire founded by Liu Bang, the first ruler to call for "men of wisdom" and "men of virtue" to help in its administration. Even though Wen Di expanded this practice, it was the urgent need of Wu Di for reliable civil servants to oversee his policies of state intervention that finally established the imperial bureaucracy. Its total strength, from ministers to minor officials, in 5 BC was 135,000, a figure thought to be slightly higher than under Wu Di, the first emperor set examinations for would-be civil servants.

Terracotta horse from Mount Li. The Former Han emperor
Wu Di sought larger mounts from Central Asia to send
armoured cavalry against the Xiongnu

An ideal official, a graduate from the imperial university in Chang'an, was said to be distinguished by abundant talents, respect for the family, loyalty to the emperor, moral rectitude and deep learning. Education had begun its enduring role as arbiter of power and prestige outside the imperial house itself. The blocking of all venues of social advancement to merchants always meant that a poor scholar without an official position would prefer farming as a means of livelihood, lest he spoil any future opportunity of a civil service career.

During Wu Di's long reign, which lasted from 141 to 87 BC, both external and internal difficulties troubled the ancient Chinese empire. Raids by the Hunnish Xiongnu drove this forceful emperor into a long, expensive and, ultimately, unsuccessful war on the steppe, although for the first time it took Chinese armies to Central Asia. Action was also impelled in the economic sphere over mounting problems in the production and distribution of basic commodities, the worsening condition of the peasantry, the growing wealth of merchants, and inflation caused by the private minting of coin. Currency reform was followed by a

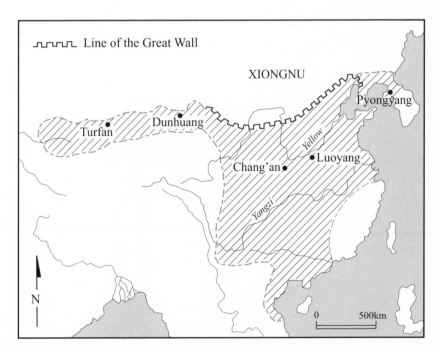

The Han empire

clampdown on merchants, who were forbidden to own land, and the imposition of a state monopoly over the iron and salt industries. And to counter speculation in foodstuffs, Wu Di established public granaries and ordered provincial officials to buy when prices were low and sell in times of shortage.

The end of Wu Di's reign was blighted by a witchcraft scare between 92 and 90 BC in Chang'an. Fear of black magic, and the hysterical response it evoked at court, led to the execution or enforced suicide of senior officials and members of the imperial family, while in the streets large numbers of people were killed in the fighting that broke out. The sixty-six-year-old emperor, now hopelessly ill and impressionable, was at the mercy of those who reported deeds of magicians and witches. He seems to have been quite unaware that the turmoil was a consequence of rivalry between the families of his six consorts. By starting the practice of entrusting power to relations of his favourite women, Wu Di had sown the seeds of the dynasty's downfall. Court intrigue undermined his successors and brought the high official Wang Mang to power in AD 9. For two decades Wang Mang's family had been influential before he usurped the dragon throne.

Imperial Crisis: The Failure of the Later Han

The earliest documented event in Korean history involves China. After an unsuccessful rising against the first Han emperor Gaozu, the defeated rebels sought refuge beyond the imperial frontier and one of them Wiman, took control of Choson, a Korean state in the north of the peninsula. Wiman, or Wei Man in Chinese, astutely showed favour to Korean courtiers, thereby making it plain that he had no intention of putting Choson under the control of China. Language alone was enough to make Wiman cautious. The settlers of the Korean peninsula seem to have come originally from present-day Siberia, and they spoke a polysyllabic and highly inflected language, in striking contrast to the monosyllabic and uninflected Chinese tongue. Despite the obvious differences between Chinese and Korean, the Chinese script was adopted because it represented then the sole means of writing in East Asia. Its mastery also allowed access to the Chinese classics, the contemporary standard for civilised living. But this cultural exchange did not mean that the Koreans lacked the determination to defend their own independence, hard pressed though they were during Wu Di's war against the Xiongnu, because an alliance between these nomads and the Koreans was feared most of all. Only through the occupation of Choson could this threat be averted, but Chinese arms were less powerful under the Later Han emperors, so the new Korean state of Koguryo recaptured most of the lost territory. But this reassertion of Korean independence had no adverse effect on China's cultural influence because large numbers of Chinese settlers stayed on. They were to have an impact on Japan as well as Korea because the peninsula became the main conduit through which Chinese traditions reached the Japanese islands.

While the Xiongnu had troubled Wang Mang during his usurpation between 9 and 25, and were indeed a factor in his bloody overthrow, the Later Han emperors found a degree of relief by playing one group of nomads off against another. Now based at Loyang, near the site of the second Zhou capital, they were fortunate in the disunity that prevented the steppe tribesmen from combining against the Chinese empire, which once again extended its authority to Central Asia. But these territorial gains were taken over by the Xiongnu in the 150s, the same decade as pressure was steadily applied to the northeastern defences by the Xianbei. These nomads of Turkic descent seem to have freed themselves from Xiongnu subjection towards the end of the first century. "After 168," a Chinese chronicler sadly notes, "no year passed without a serious nomad incursion."

Frontier problems in the north were mirrored in the south. In the 40s a major rebellion occurred in northern Vietnam. Its leaders were two aristocratic sisters, Trung Trac and Trung Nhi. Recognised as queen by the Vietnamese nobles, Trung Trac became the focus of resistance to the tax-collector mentality that lay at the heart of Chinese imperial government. General Ma Yuan was sent to crush the uprising with an army of 20,000 men and a fleet of 2,000 ships. An initial reverse caused Ma Yuan to pause and reflect on the unsuitable nature of the climate for a strenuous campaign. Tropical humidity sapped the strength of his men and undermined their morale. "When we were encamped," the general remembered, "and the rebels not yet subdued, rain fell, vapours rose, and the heat was unbearable. I even saw a sparrowhawk overcome by it: the bird fell into a lake and was drowned." Yet the noble supporters of Trung Trac had also begun to lose heart and, in the hope of keeping their forces in the field, she gave battle and the Vietnamese were

Terracotta sleeve dancer

heavily defeated. The heads of Trung Trac and her sister Nhi were sent to Loyang in late 42. That the rebellion faltered at the first reverse is an indication of how greatly things had changed during the century and a half of Chinese overlordship: the Vietnamese no longer possessed the certainty of earlier times. An element of disaffection with Trung Trac's leadership was the growing influence of the patriarchal values introduced by the Chinese. The Vietnamese nobility abandoned Trung Trac because she was a woman.

An outspoken but loyal supporter of the first Later Han emperor Guangwu Di, Ma Yuan believed that economic progress and political stability in the Vietnamese commanderies depended on direct rule. "Wherever he passed," we learn, "Ma Yuan promptly set up prefectures and districts to govern walled towns and their environs, and dug ditches to irrigate the fields to sustain the people living in those places." Garrisons protected the imperial officials, who were responsible for implementing the regulations by which the general bound the

Vietnamese people to the empire. Although the legacy of Ma Yuan was full Chinese administration, the Vietnamese language survived and within a generation the local magnate proudly spoke it alongside the official Chinese tongue.

The second Later Han emperor Ming Di had cause for concern about a problem closer to home, his half-brother Liu Ying. A letter that the emperor sent to him in 65, addressed Liu Ying as one "who recites the subtle words of Daoism and respectfully performs the gentle sacrifices of the Buddha". It is the earliest reference to the Indian faith in China. This characteristic mixture of the two beliefs derived as much from the circumstances of Buddhism's arrival in China as from the purposes to which its doctrines were put. Eclecticism was forced upon the ancient Chinese by a shortage of scriptures, the small number of converts who could read them in the original Indian languages, and competition between the different Buddhist sects.

That Liu Ying was fascinated by both Daoism and Buddhism, and surrounded himself with magicians as well as monks, suggests that his goal was not the dragon throne, as spies maliciously reported to Loyang, but immortality. When in 70 he was denounced for sorcery, Ming Di received a strong official recommendation that his half-brother should be executed for treason. The emperor ignored the advice, exiling Liu Ying instead to south China, where he soon committed suicide. Study of Buddhist texts never constituted a criminal offence, and during the increasing political troubles that beset China after the fall of the

Birds such as these were often placed in Later Han tombs

103

Later Han burial pillar with a crouching guardian on top

Later Han dynasty many scholars were drawn to them. That they encountered in the first Chinese translations a ready use of Daoist expressions caused Buddhism to be regarded as a sect of the indigenous belief. Daoists may well have served to spread certain Buddhist ideas, thus playing a role analogous to that of Jewish communities that helped to extend Christianity's influence in the Roman empire.

The restored imperial house, the Later Han, was less firmly based than the Former Han. As Ma Yuan commented on Guangwu Di's accession: "In the present times, it is not only the emperor who selects his subject. The subjects select their emperor too." Because Guangwu Di had beaten eleven other rivals to power, he owed much to the great families that had supported him. As had the Ma clan, they became entrenched in the imperial bureaucracy to such an extent that some emperors turned to the palace eunuchs for assistance. So powerful were the Liang during the 150s that, in desperation, Emperor Huan Di got the eunuchs to organise the physical destruction of this powerful clan. Its overthrow represented of course a victory for the eunuchs as much as the throne and their influence grew accordingly in Loyang. By the succession of the twelfth Later Han emperor Ling Di, in 168, the imperial government was virtually in eunuch hands. But nomad incursions and peasant rebellions obliged this weak ruler to raise extra military formations, one of whose newly appointed commanders was Cao Cao, the father of the first ruler of the Wei dynasty, an imperial house that was destined to replace the Later Han in 220. The killing of one of the commanders by the eunuchs, a few months after Ling Di's death in 189, finally drew the army into politics. The immediate response of the murdered general's troops was to storm the palace and slaughter every eunuch in sight. "Some men without beards," we are told, "were mistaken as eunuchs and also killed."

Xiwangmu, "the Queen Mother of the West", whom
Daoists believed could grant immortality

The ultimate beneficiary of the coup was Cao Cao, who assumed authority in all but name. The situation was almost a repeat of the Warring States period, with the Son of Heaven fulfilling a ceremonial role once again at Luoyang. The fiction of the Later Han continued as long as it was politically expedient. But when Cao Cao's son Cao Pi deposed the puppet emperor and founded the Wei dynasty, his military rivals set up ruling houses of their own: Shu in the southwest at Chengdu and Wu in the south at Nanjing. With the foundation of these kingdoms, the edifice of empire began to crumble.

The struggle between these so-called "Three Kingdoms" was finally ended in 280 by the Western Jin dynasty, which had toppled the Wei house fifteen years earlier. The first Western Jin emperor, Sima Yan, was another general in the mould of Cao Cao, though he outdid him by achieving the reunification of the empire. His brief triumph was facilitated by the extra strength he derived from nomad and semi-nomadic peoples who were permitted to settle within the Great Wall. This policy of barbarian settlement was to have the same dire consequences for China that it had for the western provinces of the Roman empire. For the Western Jin dynasty lasted only till 316, the year in which most of the northern provinces of the Chinese empire passed into the hands of people from the steppe and the remnants of Sima Yan's line fled southwards to Nanjing, where they founded the Eastern Jin dynasty.

This first Central Asian takeover of north China will form part of the next chapter's narrative. Two salient features of this period of division, which lasted from 316 until 588, were the survival of Chinese culture and the rise of Buddhism. In the 490s, the Tuoba Wei emperor,

Xiao Wen Di, prohibited at court both Turkish speech and clothes. His courtiers were expected to adopt Chinese ways. Such an astonishing instance of the absorptive power of China explains the enduring strength of its empire. The impact of German settlement on Rome was entirely different, since a definite cultural break took place with the retreat of Latin learning behind monastery walls.

The second great event was Buddhism, which spread throughout the whole of China. There was indeed a revolution in Chinese belief, with the appearance of large-scale, organised religious movements. Daoist and Buddhist inspired, they provided new visions that transcended ties of kinship, locality and social hierarchy. In the confusion of the times, their ideas met emotional needs that were left unsatisfied through the collapse of the traditional Confucian state. Even though a foreign faith, Buddhism had an immense influence on the Chinese people, who were absorbed into a pan-Asian outlook for the first time. In competition with this new belief, Daoism also transformed itself into an institutionalised church, with temples, monasteries and gardens for contemplation. There were, however, differences of approach between the Central Asian-occupied northern provinces and the southern provinces still under Chinese control. In the north, state sponsorship of Buddhism was associated with more rigorous regulation of monks, to the extent that a Tuoba Wei emperor appointed a chief monk. Whereas southern monks had gained the privilege of not bowing to an emperor, on the grounds that they already lived beyond the world, this northern chief monk took the opposite position, by suggesting that the Tuoba Wei emperor was an incarnation of the Buddha, so all monks should bow to him. It was quite usual for steppe peoples to regard their rulers as being divinely inspired.

Chapter 4

Ancient Central Asia

Last year the wolves of the north were let loose upon us from the far-off crags of the Caucasus, and quickly swept through entire provinces. Countless monasteries were captured, innumerable streams ran red with human blood. Herds of captives were dragged away. Arabia, Syria, Palestine and Egypt were all seized by fear.

The Hun attack of AD 395

The Steppe: An Intercontinental Highway

News reports in 1994 claimed that the discovery of mummies belonging to a non-Asian people in northwestern China had stood "history on its head". That they were already housed in a museum at Urumchi, in Xingjiang province, hardly registered at all. Because the excited accounts of these tall, blonde Europeans stemmed from the fact of their incredible preservation: they were not wizened and eviscerated like the swathed occupants of Egyptian tombs, but dressed in their everyday clothes. So well preserved were the bodies, and others

THE
EURASIAN
STEPPE

Ural Mountains

•Moscow

Danube

Rome•

Constantinople

Oxus

•Rey

Damascus•
Jerusalem•

Euphrates

Tigris

•Baghdad

•
Isfahan

subsequently removed from the graveyards around Urumchi, it was clear that they reveal ancient Western settlement of the Tarim basin.

Who were these people? And how did they arrive there between 2000 and 1700 BC? Speculation about them was finally settled in favour of the Tocharians, Indo-European speakers like the Aryans and the Persians, and indeed most of the present-day inhabitants of Europe. Tocharian documents were known in the late nineteenth century, but it was not until 1947 that a large number became available for study. Then

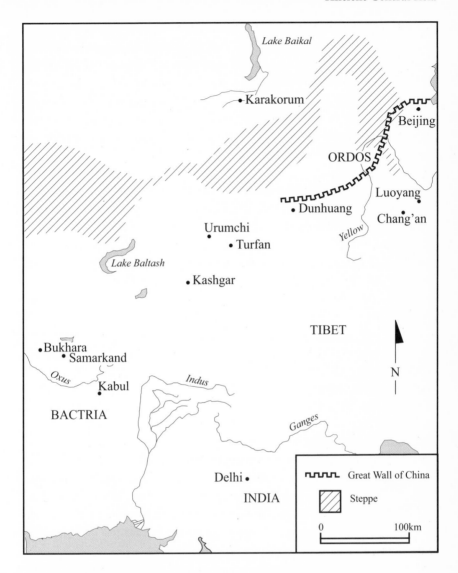

it was realised that the Tocharian language had a close affinity with the speech of the ancient Celts, Greeks and Italians. The surviving texts are largely concerned with Buddhism, although a few commercial documents have come down to us. Yet it was the discovery of the Sanskrit word tokharika, meaning "a woman from Kucha", in a bilingual text, that confirmed the Tocharian people's identity.

Having determined the people to whom the remarkable mummies belonged, attention then turned to their original homeland. Where did they come from and, just as important, how did they manage to travel so far eastwards? An amazing array of possible homelands has been proposed, but all that can be established with any degree of certainty is that at some point in the distant past the Tocharians dwelt on the steppe-lands of southern Russia, a location that goes a long way to answering the second half of the question about the Tocharian mode of transport. The Tocharians had trekked along the grasslands of the steppe, an intercontinental highway extending from the Hungarian plain to the Great Wall of China.

A reason for initial hesitation over the direction the Tocharians took, from west to east, is that the western end of the Eurasian steppe boasts lusher grasslands than elsewhere. Its grassy plains at the mouth of the River Danube, and along the northern shore of the Black Sea, continue all the way to the Ural mountains, the dividing line between Europe and Asia. Despite a temperature range that is marked by hot summers and cold winters, rain-bearing clouds from the Atlantic ensure that adequate pasturage exists throughout the year along the whole length of steppe here.

But in Central Asia conditions change dramatically. The steppe is higher, colder and drier than its European counterpart. Sparse grass does grow, even where rainfall is low, but the rivers running off snow-capped mountains really guarantee the herders' survival. Their steady flow of water also supports oasis dwellers, whose skills in irrigation have always added to the food supply. The severity of the environment explains the normal east-west pattern of nomad migration, as it does the periodic southward movements into both India and China. Once Qin Shi Huangdi turned China's northern defences into the Great Wall, shortly before his death in 210 BC, the scope for moving south in ancient East Asia was so curtailed that nomad peoples in competition for limited grassing land were obliged to defeat their rivals or move west.

Essential to the understanding of Central Asia is the steppe, whose potential for long-distance travel was first exploited by the Tocharians. That they could make their way so far east depended on the domestication of the horse. Though most people assume riding and horses are inseparable, the horse was not the first animal to be ridden regularly. The ass was adopted as a mount but because of its small size, it could only occasionally be ridden. The same held true for the horse, until breeding produced a larger and more robust specimen. Even then, the absence of the horseshoe meant that mounted warriors were at a disadvantage when

Second millennium BC chariot seal from Syria

compared with charioteers. Asses have harder hooves than horses, whose original habitat was the semi-desert or steppe. The horse's hoof grows continuously, but the extra weight of a rider will soon wear it down, especially if the ground is dry and hard. The problem proved insuperable in ancient times whenever horsemen wore armour.

Domestication of the horse on the Russian steppe was therefore not initially for the purpose of riding. Besides providing a source of meat, the horse was required to pull wagons, carts and chariots by accepting bone and metal devices in its mouth and straps on its head and body. Horseshoes, stirrups, saddles and the snaffle-bit having yet to be developed, it is easy to understand why the earliest domesticated horses were used in teams rather than as mounts. Cavalry did not become a feature of Asian armies until the first millennium BC, and even then charioteers still had a role to play on the battlefield. Shooting arrows while riding and steering a galloping horse remained far harder than firing a bow from a speeding chariot. Only the nomadic riders of the steppe ever fully mastered this difficult art.

So the Tocharians went eastwards as waggoners and charioteers. Their journey was aided by the horse's digestive system, which allows it to survive on large quantities of low-protein fodder. When grass falls into short supply, a horse can eat brush or scrub vegetation as well. And a horse is quite capable of digging its food from beneath snow. The special adaptation to its mouth that is necessary to graze on marginal land proved invaluable when it came to harnessing. There is a gap between the grinding teeth and the incisors at the front of the jaw in which a bit

111

can be readily fitted. The Greek historian Herodotus provides a description of ancient nomadic chariot teams. Speaking of the Sigynnae, most likely a Scythian tribe who lived to the north of the Danube, he tells us that they used "little, snub-nosed, shaggy horses, with hair about four inches long all over their bodies. These horses cannot carry a man, but are very fast in harness, with a result that driving is here the rule."

The Tocharian trek from southern Russia was arduous, but they had the advantage of wheeled transport, an invention that had been perfected in ancient West Asia. The impact of chariot warfare, something the later Aryan invaders of northwestern India exploited to the full, would have been startling for the other nomads whom the Tocharians encountered on their journey east. Chariot warfare, however, relied on three things: the spoked wheel, the domesticated horse and the composite bow. In West Asia, as well as along the western steppe, the deliberate sacrifice of protection for the lightness so necessary to ensure a chariot's speed was the result of poor harnessing. On a long-necked animal such as a horse, neck straps were inefficient because they impaired its breathing by pressing on the trachea whenever it was forced to pull hard. Despite the variations tried with this kind of harness, there remained a degree of suffocation. Outside ancient China the problem was only solved by reducing the weight of the vehicle itself. The Chinese invention of the

An Assyrian groom. Horses were first domesticated on the steppe

Rivers and streams from mountain ranges ensure the survival of
the nomads' herds

breast-strap harness alone permitted a horse to throw its entire weight
against a load because the harness pulled on the shoulders, leaving the
throat unaffected. Other Chinese advances in chariot design allowed this
war machine to reach perfection in ancient East Asia, once it had been
borrowed from the Tocharians.

A second aspect of chariot warfare was the composite bow. Typically
it consisted of a wooden core, with a layer of sinew applied to the back and
a layer of horn to the face, the whole bow being covered with a protective
bark sheath. The chariot only became militarily significant when it was first
combined with this weapon, which had long been a luxury item reserved
for rulers and their closest friends. Hunting in chariots would have been
the activity that inspired someone to consider what might happen on the
battlefield, if several chariots carrying archers fought together.

Tocharian charioteers armed with composite bows would have
been such formidable opponents that they could have settled anywhere
they liked in ancient Central Asia, although their main place of settlement remains a mystery. From the Urumchi mummies we are aware

113

that some of the Tocharians made their home in the Turfan basin, south of the steppe itself and close to the borders of ancient China. It seems likely that other Tocharians remained on the steppe in the vicinity of Lake Balkash, an area renowned for its horses. In 115 BC the Han emperor Wu Di sent an ambassador to negotiate with the horse-breeding peoples there. For stud purposes Wu Di wanted their large horses, because they could be used to carry heavily armed men against the troublesome Xiongnu, who rode the smaller Mongolian pony. As a result, one of the chieftains living near Lake Balkhash, in modern Kazakhstan, asked for the hand of a Chinese princess and sent a thousand horses as a bethrothal present.

The western origin of the chariot may not have been forgotten when Wu Di looked to Central Asia for answers to Chinese military shortcomings along the northern frontier. Though we have no way of knowing, it could be that the emperor's western horses were simply a repeat of the earlier assistance received by the Shang dynasty, when it acquired the chariot. Oracular inscriptions from the reign of Wu Ding, the twenty-eighth Shang king, indeed reveal the alacrity with which this foreign import was adopted for warfare as well as hunting. One inscription tells of the king pursuing "a rhinoceros" when his chariot

A Scythian archer stringing a composite bow

A Zoroastrian text from northwestern China that reveals
how ideas travelled along the steppe

collided with another and "the king's chariot overturned". On the battlefield, oracular inscriptions show an interest in military formations, as we learn of chariots being accompanied by hundreds of foot soldiers.

Whether Shang kings had direct contact with Tocharian leaders is unknown. But a recently made suggestion that Westerners penetrated the Shang court as magicians and fortune tellers points to a way by which chariot expertise may have arrived in ancient China. Chariot makers could have been enticed to take up residence in Anyang, or they may have been brought there as prisoners of war. Tiny carvings of men with a non-Asiatic appearance have been recovered from the site of the palace at Anyang. Their conical headgear is similar to that worn by certain steppe peoples, and on the top of one of these figures' heads is the Chinese character for magician. Should this indicate a Tocharian presence, then it is quite possible that the manufacture, and indeed the maintenance of the Shang chariotry, was under Tocharian supervision. So like the West Asian chariot are the vehicles unearthed at Anyang, and especially in the construction of wheels, that there can be no question about this war machine arriving in China via the steppe.

115

Nomads: The Scourge of the Sown

When riders discovered, with the aid of a bronze bit, how to control their horses, the nomads possessed the means of raiding settled communities. Relations between the steppe and the sown, between the mobile peoples of the Eurasian grasslands and the farmers living to the south have always been problematic. Oases were always regarded by nomads as legitimate targets, but a new mobility, astride fast-moving horses, allowed them to treat adjacent areas of Europe and Asia as gigantic oases as well. The ferocity of their sudden assaults was feared throughout ancient and medieval times, the nomad threat to China not being finally removed until the 1760s, when the Qing emperor Qian Long completed the conquest of the Mongols. The Chinese had never been free of invasion from the northern steppelands, the Great Wall being massive testimony to this problem. But Qian Long's commanders devised a successful strategy against the nomads when they used the agricultural resources of China to keep the Qing army permanently in the field, and then settled Chinese farmers to sustain garrisons on conquered lands.

Mounted warfare became general in the seventh century BC, although on the steppe it may have begun in the preceding century. Essential for the success of ancient cavalry was the use of the composite bow, a weapon suited to open country such as the steppe. Shooting an arrow and hitting a target from the back of a galloping horse, however, were skills that a rider could attain only through long hours of practice. They also required a horse completely obedient to the rider's voice and body commands, since in shooting an arrow the hands of the rider were occupied with the bow.

As the Romans painfully learned from the Parthians at the battle of Carrhae in 53 BC, a mounted archer could fire in all directions, since he was able to twist his upper body, face the rear, and even shoot an arrow at a pursuer. It was a tactic specially designed to encourage the enemy to break ranks. The Greek historian Plutarch relates how the Parthians

> wheeled their horses round and made off. Immediately the Roman cavalry followed and even the infantry managed to keep up. Hope had filled them with eagerness and joy; they imagined that they were victorious and were engaged in a pursuit until, after they had gone a long way forward, they realised the trick

that had been played upon them. Now those who appeared to be running away wheeled about again and at the same time were joined by fresh horsemen in even greater numbers. The Romans halted, expecting the enemy would come to close quarters with them, since there were so few of them. However, the Parthians merely stationed their armoured cavalry in front of the Romans and with the rest of their cavalry, in loose order, rode all round them, tearing up the ground with their horses hooves, and raising great clouds of dust so that the Romans could scarcely see or speak. Huddled together in a narrow space and getting into each other's way, they were shot down with arrows.

This account of the impetuous charge led by Publius, the son of the Roman general Marcus Licinius Crassus, was typical of the whole battle. Drawing upon their heritage as ex-nomads, the Parthians refused to take the unnecessary risk of engaging the Roman legions in hand-to-hand combat. They had no need to do so because the main body of Roman soldiers was so densely packed together that it was impossible for the Parthians to miss. The arrival of camel trains loaded with extra arrows

The deserts of Central Asia meant that a variety
of animals was needed

sealed Crassus' fate: his severed head was taken in triumph to Ctesiphon, the Parthian capital.

The decisive military feature of mounted warriors was of course their mobility. Raiding parties of horsemen could reach their destination quickly, take the occupants by surprise, and ride off before a relief force arrived. The exposure of the northern Chinese state of Zhao to this hit-and-run problem led its prince, Wu Ling, to a radical solution. So difficult did the Zhao army find repelling these fast-moving intruders that Wu Ling not only formed a large corps of cavalry, but even more trousers were borrowed from the nomads to make riding easier. Trousers were then looked upon by the ancient Chinese as a garment only suited to barbarians.

The famous debate of 307 BC in Wu Ling's court about the adoption of mounted archery was concerned, however, with more than the defence of Zhao's northern frontier. The arguments for and against such a change should be seen in the overall weakness of this small state. For Wu Ling was conscious of a general lack of military strength, whether facing nomads or Chinese competitors. He knew that nothing short of a thoroughgoing military revolution would be enough to preserve Zhao. There was no room for half measures. So he said:

> The way of rulers is to be mindful of the virtue of their ancestors while they are on the throne; the rule for ministers is to devise ways to enhance rulers' powers. Thus it is that a virtuous ruler, even when totally inactive, can guide his people and conduct his affairs with success; when active he can achieve such fame that it may exceed the past, to say nothing of the present . . . Now I intend to extend the inheritance I have received from my forebears and make provinces out of nomad lands; but though I spend my entire life in this enterprise, my eyes will never see its completion. I propose to adopt the horseman's clothes of the Hu nomads and teach my people their mounted archery. Just think how the world will laugh. But though all China laughs, I shall acquire the lands of the neighbouring nomads.

When a distinguished minister expressed grave reservations about this policy, Wu Ling frankly told him of the vulnerability of Zhao. "We have river frontiers but command not a single boat upon them. We have land frontiers without a single mounted archer to defend them. Therefore

Saka nomads, one of the tributary peoples shown at
Persepolis, the Persian capital

I have collected boats and boatmen to guard the first, and deployed mounted archers in suitable attire to guard the second." Abashed, the minister apologised for appreciating neither the gravity of the situation nor the ruler's strategy for dealing with it. Instead he had had "the temerity to mouth platitudes". A delighted Wu Ling immediately presented him with a set of horseman's clothes.

Afterwards the balance of forces in the Zhao army tilted towards cavalry as chariots were abandoned completely and the size of the infantry reduced. And Wu Ling stood firm against all objections: he was sure that the terrain over which his forces had to operate was best suited to mobile archers. As he pointed out:

> My ancestor built a wall where our lands touch on those of the
> nomads and named it the Gate of No Horizon. Today armoured
> foot soldiers cannot safely go beyond this wall. As benevolence,
> righteousness and ritual will not civilise the nomads, we must go
> and subdue them by force of arms.

So it was that Wu Ling "dressed in barbarian garments, led his horsemen against the Hu nomads, leaving the Gate of No Horizon".

The stunning success of this first campaign opened up to Zhao the possibility of acquiring vast new territories. It also demonstrated the military value of mounted archers. Derision greeted Wu Ling's innovation throughout ancient China but, in other northern states facing regular nomad incursion, the advantages offered by the cavalry were not missed by their rulers. They could see how greater mobility was a means to dominate the steppe and the marginal tracts of land adjoining it. Through Wu Ling's ability to reform the Zhao army, mounted archers became the specialised troops of China's northern frontier, and especially for the forays beyond the defences which were eventually incorporated into the Great Wall.

Less successful in dealing with the nomad threat was the Greco-Bactrian kingdom in ancient Central Asia, which was overrun by the Sakas, the name given to the Scythians in ancient Central Asia. Both the Scythians and their cousins, the Sarmatians, were Indo-European speakers. For twenty-eight years, after the fall of Nineveh in 612 BC, the Scythians had plundered large areas of ancient West Asia. "In their arrogance," we are told, "they destroyed everything. They not only assigned and extracted tribute from one and all but in addition, by riding all around, each group plundered whatever they could." Thus Herodotus introduces the Scythians, a people that this Greek author knew from first-hand experience in the Black Sea. They were later decisively defeated by the Persians and driven back to the steppe.

When it suited them, the Scythians cooperated with the Persians. Their languages were still close enough for them to understand each other without translators. That the Persians themselves were renowned as archers is a sign that they had also descended from the steppelands. A related people may have been the Kimmerians, who were pushed into Asia Minor by the Scythians. The Kimmerians, writes Herodotus, had once lived in the Crimea, to which they gave their name, but they were expelled by the newly arrived Scythians. The latter were not satisfied merely to drive the Kimmerians out of the Crimea, but continued to chase them all the way through the Caucasus to Asia Minor, where the Kimmerians roamed, a desperate horde of men, women and children. Somehow the Scythians took the wrong turn and found themselves in Mesopotamia.

That the twenty-eight-year Scythian intrusion was not a migration, but a prolonged raid, is quite clear from an episode Herodotus recounts. Because they had left their families behind on the steppe, in the husbands' absence the Scythian women turned to their slaves as lovers, and the sons from these irregular unions formed an army that tried but failed to bar the elderly Scythians' return. Regarded as no more than one of Herodotus' stories, an interesting anecdote rather than an

Another Central Asian people who served the
Persians, the Sogdians

actual event, details of the Scythian pursuit of Kimmerians and then the
brief Scythian supremacy still remain valuable as an illustration of what a
large-scale nomad raid was like.

Now we can be less certain that Herodotus got it wrong, because
newly discovered Assyrian sources mention the assistance given by King
Ashurbanipal to hard-pressed Gyges, the king of Lydia. They mention
that Lydia, an ancient power in western Asia Minor, was under assault
from none other than the Kimmerians. According to one Assyrian text,
Gyges learned of Ashurbanipal in a dream sent by Ashur, the divine
begetter of the Assyrian king. Gyges was advised to

> Lay hold of Ashurbanipal's princely feet!
> Revere his sovereignty and implore his rule.
> With tribute-bearing prayers, invoke his name
> And conquer your enemies. On the same day
> Gyges sent a rider to ask for the great king's aid.

The short poem ends satisfactorily from both the Lydian and Assyrian
viewpoints because the gods Ashur and Marduk as well as the goddess
Ishtar lent Gyges their assistance on the battlefield. "In handcuffs, iron
manacles, shackles and iron fetters," captured Kimmerians were sent to
Nineveh along with "rich gifts". But another Assyrian record says that later
on the defeated Kimmerians recovered sufficiently to rise up, slay Gyges,

and then lay Lydia waste. The reason given for this unexpected reverse was that the Lydian king had foolishly forsaken the Assyrian gods.

Although we possess no equivalent detail about the nomad attack on Bactria in the second century BC, the Saka invasion was a preliminary to the occupation of northwestern India. And we cannot be certain whether the Saka followed the battle rituals of the Scythians. Once a Scythian archer had overcome an opponent, either on horseback or on foot, he sprang off his mount, scalped his victim and drank some of his blood. For scalps, rather than severed heads, were the Scythian means of demonstrating prowess. Possibly sped on their way by the arrival in Bactria of the Da Yuezhi, the Sakas moved south and became the first nomads to invade India.

The impetus behind the Da Yuezhi's western migration was the Xiongnu, Hunnish nomads who lived to the north of the Great Wall. Their sudden rise to power was the result of a strict code of discipline introduced by Maotun, who assumed the leadership of all the Xiongnu tribes in 209 BC. With unswerving loyalty his personal followers carried out his every command, including the execution of his rival half-brother, his stepmother and those chieftains who refused to support him. Just how ruthless Maotun was can be gauged from his method of training his men, who were expected to shoot anything he struck himself with a special whistling arrow. Having in this manner disposed of a favourite horse and a favourite wife, Maotun knew they were trained to perfection. Obediently, his bodyguard had fired arrows at both these targets.

Maotun's establishment of a steppe empire coincided with the re-establishment of a unified China under Liu Bang, who founded the Han dynasty in 202 BC. So great was Xiongnu pressure two years later that Liu Bang personally campaigned against Maotun. With an army of 300,000 men the Chinese emperor felt confident enough of the outcome but, at present-day Datong, he was cut off from the main body of his forces for a week. Liu Bang would have been taken prisoner if Maotun had pressed the issue to a conclusion. He seems to have decided that there was more to gain from an advantageous peace treaty, which involved the receipt of Chinese gifts of silk, alcohol and food several times a year. He also received the hand of a princess, an event that invalidates an alternative explanation of Maotun's decision. According to this version, his wife persuaded him to reach a settlement when Liu Bang threatened to send a bevy of beautiful consorts to Maotun, knowing that they would cause the Xiongnu leader to lose interest in her. It is quite

Sunset on the Mongolian steppe

possible that Maotun needed to have peaceful relations with the Chinese empire: he was still not the undisputed nomad leader on the steppe until the Da Yuezhi were driven westwards to Bactria.

Afterwards, Xiongnu authority on the steppelands beyond the Great Wall remained secure for more than two centuries, making these nomads a constant worry for China. Even when they were disunited, Chinese emperors still had to be on their guard against sudden attacks. The seventh Han ruler, Wu Di, endeavoured to secure the northern frontier by force of arms, a forward policy that advanced Chinese influence into the Tarim basin. But the larger horses that Wu Di obtained from this part of ancient Central Asia did not bring the victories he needed. The new cavalry helped to increase Chinese mobility, but the steppelands were still a dangerous place to serve, in 102 BC some 20,000 of its soldiers falling in a single engagement.

In 99 BC, Li Ling, one of Wu Di's best field commanders, was obliged to surrender to the Xiongnu after an engagement that could have led to a revolution in tactics. Li Ling was stationed near Dunhuang with the duty of defending the line of extended Great Wall. Hearing of an advance against the Xiongnu, he received permission to mount a separate advance, although there was no cavalry immediately available to support him. Up till now the Chinese had attacked the nomads on horseback, but Li Ling thought the crossbow would offer sufficient protection against the composite bow.

Emperor Wu Di seems to have appreciated Li Ling's need for protection and ordered a cavalry commander to meet him half-way on his return. Because this man held the rank of a general, while Li Ling was a mere chief commandant, he protested that such coop-eration would make him into a subordinate. Through this unseemly dispute Li Ling's force had to fight 30,000 Xiongnu horsemen on its own. When Li Ling positioned his crossbowmen behind a wall of shields and spears, the effect of their fire was devastating and several thousand Xiongnu fell before the rest fled. Had Li Ling then chosen to withdraw to the line of the Great Wall, he would probably have saved his tiny force. A pursuit of the shaken Xiongnu left it dangerously exposed to a counter-attack, which came with the arrival of more nomad archers. With crossbow bolts running low, Li Ling ordered his men to find their way back to China as best they could. Only 400 men reached the safety of the Great Wall, and Li Ling himself was taken prisoner. As the Xiongnu had been informed by a Chinese traitor that there was no hope of cavalry coming to support Li Ling, they had screwed up their courage to attack again.

When the news of the Xiongnu victory arrived at the imperial court in Chang'an, Wu Di hoped that Li Ling had died with his troops, as was customary Chinese practice. The emperor was therefore besides himself with fury on hearing of Li Ling's capture, although Wu Di eventually appreciated how he was to blame himself for not insisting that a cavalry column went to his aid. The emperor sent for the chief commandant, but he refused to return to China, so his family was destroyed. The encounter on the steppe is one of the few documented cases of direct competition between the crossbow and the composite bow. Had the Romans access to this Chinese invention at Carrhae, the legionaries could have easily kept the Parthians at bay. As it was, they had nothing to outrange Parthian arrows. Not only would crossbows have unhorsed the Parthians, but even more their bolts would have ripped through armour and shields belonging to Rome's less mobile

Kushana warriors

enemies. As ancient charioteers and cavalrymen had long known in China, speed was no longer enough to keep them safe from the attentions of crossbowmen.

Because no emperor could afford a prolonged war lest the burden on the ordinary people caused a rebellion like the one that overthrew the Qin dynasty, Chinese foreign policy was always dictated by the need to contain nomad pressure, never by an ambition for conquests in ancient Central Asia itself. By 91 BC, Wu Di had to admit that there was no sense in further campaigning. A return to gift giving was inevitable and trade resumed with the nomads in markets sited outside the gates in the Great Wall. Imperial China was also fortunate that the successors of Maotun were unable to maintain unity that he had established. Tribal animosity did not entirely remove the nomad threat, although during the Later Han period it brought almost a century of comparative peace. Not until well after the extinction of the Han dynasty would the Central Asian nomads threaten China through their involvement in its own internal disputes. By the start of the fourth century, they found themselves in a position to conquer the whole of north China, obliging the Jin imperial house to seek refuge as far south as the lower Yangzi river valley.

The Spread of Buddhism: The First Pan-Asian Faith

On his deathbed, the Buddha advised his disciples to rely on monastic discipline, so that his message would be safely passed from generation to generation of monks and nuns. The contrast with the messianism of the early Christians could not have been more striking: instead of charismatic preachers spreading far and wide as Jesus' disciples and converts such as St. Paul were to do, the closest followers of the Buddha formed a monastic order. They did not share the urgency of St. Paul, who assured his listeners that they would not die before Jesus returned. This is clear in his first letter to the Thessalonians, the earliest book of the New Testament. St. Paul seems to have written it because the death of Christians in that community had cast serious doubt on the timing of Jesus' second coming. His answer was an absolute belief in physical resurrection: "the dead in Christ will rise first", St. Paul boldly asserted. Because such a West Asian concern with escape from the grave was irrelevant in ancient India, where the endless round of rebirth was the key religious issue, Buddhists living there devoted themselves to contemplation.

A Tuoba Wei column dated to 536. It celebrates the Buddha's mission

Their new faith was not indifferent to the sufferings of the lay community, else it would never have evolved and developed so dramatically over the millennium following the Buddha's death in 479 BC, but Buddhism remained on the fringes of Indian society before the conversion of Emperor Asoka. His enthusiasm for its teachings, and the conscious effort that he made to bring them to general notice in his territories and beyond their borders, set Buddhism on an international path. A council that Asoka convened at Pataliputra, the Mauryan capital, actually discussed the best method of propagating the faith. A rock edict, carved in the 240s BC, mentions an Asokan target of increasing the number of monks and nuns by 150 per cent.

Even though the tremendous support that Asoka gave to Buddhism greatly increased its prestige and wealth, Buddhist influence outside the subcontinent only became significant during the reign of King Kanishka, in large measure because this Kushana ruler controlled much of Central Asia as well as northern India. The advent of monasteries in ancient Central Asia persuaded later Buddhist commentators that Kanishka was nothing less than a second Asoka who devoted himself to making his realm faithful to the Buddha's teachings. The religious eclecticism of the Kushanas argues otherwise, although the Chinese pilgrim Xuan Zhang saw in the 630s AD the ruins of a gigantic stupa raised by Kanishka at present-day Peshawar. It had been more than one hundred metres in height. In 1908 the stupa's excavation revealed a relic box placed there by the Kushana king. Xuan Zhang also found that large numbers of Buddhist monasteries had fallen into disrepair, victims of resurgent Hinduism. He reckoned there were several thousand active institutions still in existence, but in many areas of India there were none at all. Not surprisingly the premier centres of Buddhist learning survived the longest in the Ganges valley, the original focus of Buddhism. They were not finally destroyed until the Moslems overran the region in the medieval era.

When the Buddhist faith spread into Central Asia, it encountered many different peoples living there under Kushana rule, which lasted into the 240s. There were the descendents of Greek settlers planted by Alexander the Great in Bactria, the native Bactrians, the Sogdians dwelling to their north, the Parthians and the Sakas. We know that the earlier

An early Tuoba Wei stele with a bodhisattva at the centre

The fortress at the western end of the Great Wall, whose rammed-earth
construction is clearly visible

Greek kingdoms in northwestern India were attracted to Buddhism—
Menander being a prime example of royal patronage—but it was the
ease of movement within Kushana territories that really allowed the faith
to travel northwards, and then eastwards to China, Korea and Japan. And
of course the generous endowments made by Kaniska himself allowed
Buddhist communities to form for the first time in ancient Central Asia.
Because it was a monastery-based faith, state sponsorship was always
required for Buddhism to flourish.

Where the faith was welcomed by rulers in China, Tibet and
Korea, the Buddhist community became closely associated with affairs
of state, and monks even assumed important administrative and political
responsibilities. The zenith of Buddhist influence in China happened in
the early medieval period, so that before the great persecution of 845 a
total reshaping of religious outlook seemed likely. That year the Tang
emperor Wu Zong shut down 44,600 retreats, shrines, temples and
monasteries housing 260,500 registered monks and nuns. The Japanese
monk Enin, who was studying in China then, tells us that "numerous
monks and nuns were sent away with their heads wrapped up", while

the "bronze and iron statues of the Buddha are smashed, weighed, and handed over to the Salt and Iron Bureau".

Mild in comparison with the actions of later military dictators in Korea and Japan, Wu Zong's assault on the Buddhist establishment represented, nonetheless, a severe blow for the Indian faith. Even though the struggle for spiritual supremacy had been fiercely contested, the strength of the rational mould of the Confucian outlook prevailed, with the result that Buddhism thereafter came under the regulation of the imperial civil service. Private ordination ceased: officials had to give their consent to anyone who wished to join a monastery.

How this religious crisis occurred is really the subject of this section, for the good reason that the Central Asian takeover of northern China in 316 opened the way for Buddhism's eastern movement. As early as the first century there were Buddhists in China, but it was the uncertainty of barbarian rule that turned Buddhism into a succour for the subject Chinese, while at the same time gaining the patronage of their Central Asian overlords. During the long years of division, reflective Chinese speculated on what had befallen the empire, and on the precarious lives they led. They turned to Daoist texts, finding in them an alternative view of existence to the apparently outmoded duties of Confucianism. Another source of inspiration was Buddhism, once its ideas were accessible and intelligible. The infiltration of the new faith among the educated elite was indeed the work of scholars involved in the Daoist

A painted brick from a tomb on the edge of the Gobi desert

129

The great Buddha at Bingling Si in Gansu province, striking testimony
to the Indian faith's arrival in north China

revival, who believed that they found a reflection of their own concerns
in Mahayana Buddhism.

But the task of translation proved very difficult. Initially, a foreign
monk, knowing no or very little Chinese, recited the text, which was
translated by an interpreter, and then commented upon by Chinese
monks. Devout laymen might have a hand in shaping the final version
too. This cumbersome method continued until just before the Central
Asian conquest of north China. It was ended by Dharmaraksa, a man
born of a Da Yuezhi family resident in Dunhuang. As he had spoken
Chinese from birth, Dharmaraksa was able to translate nearly one hundred Buddhist texts himself. He gave to China what was to become its
favourite sutra, the *Lotus of the Good Law,* which promised salvation to
all who sought enlightenment as had the Buddha. Continued problems
with translation seem to have produced Buddhist teachings that encouraged the Chinese to evolve their own versions of the faith: in the plural,
because the sayings attributed to the Buddha left plenty of scope for

different interpretations, even without the competing Buddhist schools of thought that had already appeared in India.

Four Chinese schools of Buddhism emerged, bearing no Indian imprint at all. The first was the Tiantai, which was espoused by the educated and the well-to-do. It resolved the apparent differences between texts by suggesting that they ceased to exist when the devotee realised the unity of all phenomena. This typically Chinese synthesis of Buddhist doctrines meant that all men could achieve enlightenment because they shared the nature of the Buddha. The sect's name derived from Mount Tiantai, in modern Zejiang province, where about 550 a gifted young monk named Chih-I settled. It was said that he had realised the truth about the transitoriness of existence when he saw a library destroyed by soldiers. The experience confirmed the central teaching of the great Indian philosopher Nagarjuna: that nothing possesses an inherent quality.

Guanyin, the Chinese goddess of mercy. The Sui dynasty sculpture follows the style established by the Tuoba Wei

A second Chinese sect that appealed to the intellect was known as the Hua-yen, founded by Fa Zang fifty years after Chih-I. It would appear that Fa Zang's ancestors were Sogdian, but he was born in Chang'an and grew up as a Chinese. Despite the presence of so many Sogdians in north China, where they had become part of the gentry, there is no firm evidence that they were responsible for the introduction of Buddhism. As polyglots, the Sogdians could well have helped in the transmission of Budhist texts, but Chinese tradition always looks upon Dharmaraksa as the first great translator.

Fa Zang's basic tenet, like that taught by Chih-I, was emptiness. Where he differed from Tiantai, however, was in claiming that the universe represented a harmony, its forms being no more than different waves on the same body of water. Chih-I seems to have conceived

131

them as manifestations of a supreme mind, whose objective was the fulfilment of the Buddha's mission. Less abstruse, and therefore more popular, was the Pure Land School, which flourished at first in south China. About 380 its founder, Hui Yuan, gathered a community of monks about him, whose worship was devoted to Amitabha Buddha, in whose paradise of the Pure Land they sought to be reborn. Here this Buddha, who virtually replaced the historical Buddha himself, was believed to have the bodhisattva Avalokitesvara as his chief minister: Avalokitesvara was called "the lord of compassionate glances". That this saviour of monks, householders and animals would also become Guanyin, the goddess of mercy, was yet another Chinese change to the Mahayana pantheon.

Hui Yuan persuaded the Chinese emperors, who clung on to power in Nanjing, that monks should be excused going through the outward signs of obeisance. Already living beyond this earthly world, a monk ought not to bow. No such concession was ever granted by the Central Asian rulers of north China. It was even suggested, in 574, that the Buddhist monasteries be closed down there so that the whole area became one harmonious temple, with the ruler presiding over his believing subjects as an incarnation of the Buddha.

Although the fourth distinctive Chinese school of Buddhism started in the south, it soon extended to the north, and abroad to Korea as well as Japan. In China it was called Chan, in Korea Son and in Japan Zen. An admixture of Buddhist and Daoist elements, Chan advanced the idea of a shattering insight arising from contemplation of ordinary things. Its founder, the enigmatic Indian monk Bodhidharma, is said to have spent years looking at a wall. Having arrived from India by boat, Bodhidharma had an audience in Nanjing with Xiao Yan, the Liang dynasty emperor, who was a fervent Buddhist. When Xiao Yan asked what merit he had acquired by good works, Bodhidharma replied, "No merit at all!" Amazed, he then asked his visitor about the first principle of Buddhism. "There isn't one," was the reply, "because where all is emptiness, nothing can be called holy." After this splendid encounter, Bodhidharma travelled northwards and sat in contemplation before a wall that he particularly liked at the Eternal Peace Monastery in Luoyang, the Tuoba Wei capital.

The Tuoba Wei dynasty was the ultimate beneficiary of the Xiongnu conquest of north China. By 452, this Xianbei house, part Turkish and part Mongolian in descent, had disposed of its rivals and ruled a territory

Part of the vast Buddhist cave complex at Dunhuang, near the western end of the Great Wall

that stretched from Dunhuang in the west to Korea in the east. Apart from a brief interval in the 430s, when its third ruler adopted Daoism and sought to suppress Buddhism, the Tuoba Wei dynasty was closely identified with the Buddhist faith. The first step in the state absorption of the Buddhist order took place with the appointment of a chief monk. Already highly sinicised, the Tuoba Wei house saw itself as the true successor of those who sat upon the dragon throne from Qin Shi Huangdi onwards. For this reason Xiao Wen Di decided to rebuild Luoyang as his imperial capital, where the heavy concentration of Chinese people living in the vicinity meant that nomad customs could not easily take root there. To underline his intentions, he even prohibited Turkish speech and dress in his court.

Such an incredible transformation is a witness to the enduring strength of China's culture. As the Son of Heaven, Xiao Wen Di could rule like a Chinese emperor but he was still close enough to nomad beliefs to be regarded as a Buddha himself. At the cave complex of Yungang, near the former Tuoba Wei capital situated at modern Datong, the process of identification began when it was discovered that a huge carving of the Buddha possessed spots on the face and feet corresponding exactly to black moles on the emperor's body. So revered were the 51,000 sculptures in the fifty-three caves at Yungang that, when the Tuoba Wei court moved to Luoyang, its inhabitants insisted upon another cave complex being carved nearby. It was to become the famous Longmen grottoes with an incredible total of more than 90,000 carved figures.

So impressed was Bodhidharma at the level of state patronage for Buddhism in Luoyang that, on his arrival in 526, he commented: "In my hundred and fifty years of existence, I have been everywhere and travelled in many countries, but a temple of beauty like the Eternal Peace Monastery cannot be found anywhere in the lands of the Buddha." The monastery's 250-metre-high pagoda could be regarded as the height of devotion, or extravagance. It was adorned with gold ornaments and gold bells, something unpaid Tuoba Wei soldiers noticed when they met there, before rioting in the city. Unrest continued right down to the abandonment of Luoyang in 534. As the last Tuoba Wei rulers were no more than the playthings of military commanders, the Central Asian experiment in Chinese-style administration foundered and tribal rivalries reappeared. One emperor even prayed to the Buddha not to be reborn as a ruler, just before he was strangled. Then the great pagoda at the Eternal Peace Monastery caught fire during a snowstorm, reducing the pride of the Buddhist order in Luoyang to ashes.

The first Sui emperor, who reunited China in 588 and built a new capital at Chang'an, inherited northern enthusiasm for Buddhism as well as the less rigorously controlled version of the faith in south China. Inclined as he was to Buddhist beliefs himself, Emperor Wen Di recognised that he had to revive the imperial civil service on Confucian lines if there was to be any possibility of restoring order in the Chinese empire. Thus he set the scene for the dramatic confrontation of 845, which resulted from intense competition between Daoism and Buddhism for imperial patronage. In the ensuing débâcle Confucian officials were able to return China to its traditional approach to religion, a moderation summed up in Confucius' most famous remark: "I stand in awe of the spirits but keep them at a distance."

The Great Raid: Attila the Hun

Although the attack by the Huns on the Roman empire was not the first Central Asian invasion of Europe during ancient times, its ferocity is remembered today in the use of the word Hun for a merciless foe. Before the arrival of Huns in the middle of the fifth century, the Romans had already met on the battlefield another Central Asian people, the Sarmatians. They tried to cross the River Danube on several occasions until peace was agreed in 175. Under its terms, the Sarmatians had to furnish the Roman army with 8,000 cavalrymen, most of whom went to Britain as part of the garrison along the Hadrian's Wall. Their settlement within the Roman empire did not stop others from attacking elsewhere, because the Sarmatians boasted several quarrelsome tribes. Their language was close to Scythian. According to a story preserved by Herodotus, the Sarmatians were descended from Scythian men and roving Amazons, which may account for their womenfolk joining the fray whenever it was necessary. In alliance with the Romans, the Sarmatians proved to be valuable allies and helped to secure a major victory in 332 over the Goths. As a reward, another 300,000 Sarmatians were settled in the Balkans.

Rome's policy of settlement was dictated by the increasing pressure on its northern frontier. Aggressive German peoples were a problem well before Attila burst onto the scene. Whenever they demanded to be

Emperor Valens was defeated at Hadrianopolis, present-day Edirne

135

settled within the Roman empire, or they had already broken through its defences, there was a stark choice to be made. Either let them settle and assist with defence or fight them in a war of extermination, a strategy now largely beyond the strength of the Roman army.

The whole Roman approach was left in tatters after the battle of Hadrianopolis, present-day Edirne, where in 378 the eastern emperor Valens fell along with most of his army. This comprehensive defeat at the hands of the Visigoths seemed to contemporaries as "the end of the world". Yet an even worse invasion occurred in 406, when the Vandals and other starving German peoples crossed the frozen Rhine at present-day Mainz. The invaders devastated France and Spain, whence the Vandals crossed to north Africa. Within half a century the Vandals had taken control of almost the entire coastline. No less demoralising was the Visigoth sack of Rome itself in 410. Even though the Visigoths moved off to Spain afterwards, the days of Roman power in the western Mediterranean were clearly coming to an end.

Into this confused situation King Attila led his Huns, who were related to the Xiongnu, if indeed not one of their constituent tribes. No one in the Roman empire had ever heard of the Huns until the 370s, a generation before the birth of Attila. Then reports reached Roman forces stationed on the Danube of the sudden appearance of a savage people moving westwards along the steppelands. The Goths failed to block the Hunnish advance onto the Hungarian plain, and by the 430s the Romans were regularly buying King Rua off. After Rua's death, his nephew Attila became the king of the Huns and in 441 he

The western Roman emperor
Valentinian III

Honoria, Valentinian's
disaffected sister

crossed the Danube, routed the Roman forces sent against him and put the Balkan provinces to the sword. A further period of peace was bought by a large annual payment in gold, but six years later he once again ravaged Roman lands.

It would seem that Attila was losing interest in the eastern provinces well before Honoria, the sister of the western Roman emperor Valentinian III, gave him a pretext for moving westwards. Annoyed at her enforced engagement to an aristocrat of Valentinian's choice, Honoria secretly sent a eunuch slave with a message to Attila, asking him to save her from an unsought marriage. Accompanying the request was a ring bearing the seal of the headstrong princess. The Hunnish king told the slave to inform Honoria that the wedding would never take place. Instead, she was to become the next wife of Attila himself. In spite of her genuine disdain for the middle-aged husband Valentinian wished upon her, Honoria was motivated as much by dynastic ambition as anything else: she wished to be the wife and mother of emperors.

When news of Honoria's dealings with the Hunnish king reached his ears, Valentinian was so annoyed that he rebuffed Attila's envoys in late 450. They disingenuously proposed that Valentinian should agree to sharing power with Honoria, something the emperor could never accept. For more than a century the Roman empire had been ruled simultaneously by emperors in the eastern and western Mediterranean. Weak though his position was, Valentinian saw no reason to share power in the west with his difficult sister, especially as her future husband would be none other than Attila.

How ill prepared Valentinian was to resist Attila became obvious when the Huns invaded Italy. It was Pope Leo I who negotiated with Attila and obtained his withdrawal. Regrettably, no eyewitness report survives of the meeting between Attila and Leo, although legend says how faced with the sternness of the ecclesiastical gaze and the magnificence of gold-embroidered pontifical robes, the Hunnish king fell silent. No less impressive perhaps were the gifts presented to Attila, and in a famine-stricken Italy the Huns would have found a prolonged stay out of the question anyway. Reports of successes by eastern Roman troops across the Danube may have given Attila cause to withdraw as well. He could not afford to campaign in the west without a firm guarantee of security along the Danube. As in earlier raids, the Huns returned with their wagons piled high with plunder to the Hungarian plain, now their permanent steppe base.

Paradoxically, it was to be Roman troops stationed in the western provinces who eventually inflicted a significant defeat on Attila in 451, at the battle of the Catalaunian Plains, some distance from modern Orleans. A combined force of Romans and Goths under the command of Flavius Aetius had already strengthened the city's defences with ditches and earthern ramparts. Seeing these formidable works, Attila turned his army away and the Goths and Romans followed close behind. Near the modern city of Troyes the two sides began fighting in the early afternoon. It was an engagement fought at close quarters, "fierce, convulsed, dreadful, unrelenting", we are informed, "like none ever recorded in times past". The battle only died down at nightfall. Next morning the heavy losses suffered by all combatants were visible "in the shattered corpses of the slain spread right across the battlefield". Attila was unmoved by the sight and challenged Flavius Aetius to return to the fray, but neither he nor his Gothic allies had the stomach for more fighting. They withdrew and, shortly afterwards, so did Attila.

Ancient commentators blame Flavius Aetius for not launching another assault, but he may have been unsure of the final result. Losses were heavy and the Huns utterly determined to fight to the finish. Attila was supposed to have raised a huge pile of saddles and told his men that he would throw himself onto this funeral pyre rather than "be taken alive by his enemies". Not that the Roman general got any thanks for blunting Attila's assault. An ever anxious Valentinian had come to believe that Flavius Aetius was aiming at imperial power and, in 454, he slew him in the audience chamber with the assistance of a eunuch. The murder

St. Nicasius's martyrdom at Reims. The Huns quit the city when the
bishop's severed head went on speaking

cost Valentinian his own life the next year, when two of the general's
former barbarian bodyguard took their revenge.

The Vandal king Gaiseric exploited the confused situation by
mounting a seaborne attack on Rome, carrying back to north Africa
huge amounts of loot, plus the widow and daughters of Valentinian.
Overlooked by the Roman emperor when he murdered Flavius Aetius was
the invaluable experience of this commander. Having been successively
held hostage by the Goths and the Huns, whose languages he learned,
he could negotiate the complicated world of shifting alliances that typified the final years of Roman authority in the western Mediterranean.

Attila would never have been so foolish as Valentinian. The Hunnish
king had a deserved reputation for violence but this character trait was
reserved for his enemies, not his own men. Once he secured his own
position, Attila ruled the Huns with a degree of restraint in comparison
with his nearest equivalent, the Mongol leader Genghiz Khan. The
removal of Flavius Aetius and Valentinian meant that there was no
longer any chance of Roman power surviving in the western part of
Europe, already swamped by the Germanic settlers. The last emperor,
whose name Romulus Augustulus ironically recalled Rome's legendary
founder as well as its very first emperor, was dethroned in 476, and
afterwards the Ostrogoths turned Italy into their kingdom.

By then Attila was dead. His end came not on the battlefield but
in his bedroom: a haemorrhage of blood from the nose choked him

on his wedding night. Which number wife the beautiful Ildico was we simply do not know. When she was discovered in the morning weeping hysterically over her dead husband's lifeless body, Attila's enemies put the inglorious end of the great war leader down to binge drinking. "Thus did drunkenness destroy him," a delighted Gothic historian noted in 453. With Attila's death, the Hunnish empire fell apart and the Huns broke into small hordes, never recovering the unity that had made them such a menace. At Attila's funeral his followers seem to have realised how the zenith of Central Asian power in Europe had passed, when they cut their hair and slashed their cheeks "so that the greatest of all warriors should be mourned not with the tears of wailing women, but with the blood of own men".

With the sharp decline of Hunnish power, their place was taken by a whole series of nomads travelling westwards along the steppe. The first to arrive were the Avars, who sent an embassy to Constantinople in 557. The Byzantines thought they were much like the Huns, although their use of stirrups revolutionised cavalry in Europe. The eastern Roman army adopted them at once, since they permitted a rider to swing a sword and handle a spear without danger of being unhorsed. In a repeat of the great raid that Attila had mounted on Europe, the Avars based themselves on the Hungarian plain. Their most adventurous move was a combined attack with the Sasanian Persians on Constantinople in the summer of 626. Both the Sasanians and the Avars were repulsed.

Part 2

Medieval Asia

Chapter 5

Medieval West Asia

Awake Umayyads! Your sleep has lasted
Far too long. Your caliphate is ruined!
How are the faithful to know God's caliph
When he stays among tambourines and lutes?

A rebuke of al-Mahdi, the third Abbasid ruler

Islam: The Second Pan-Asian Faith

rophet Muhammad brought the development of religion in West Asia to a close. He was the voice of Allah, whose emergence from the welter of ancient deities had first been championed in Israel. But unlike Moses, who received the Ten Commandments when he led the chosen people there from Egypt, Muhammad enjoyed a more sustained period of divine contact; and the directness of his message in the Qur'an may have owed something to his early upbringing in a desert encampment, ringed at night by nothing but the stars. Whatever shaped his uncompromising monotheism, the Prophet at once explained to his Arab followers the way of life most pleasing to the deity. Fully aware of the lateness of his prophecy, Muhammad told them that their "appointed time compared with that of those who had gone before is as from the afternoon prayer to the setting of the sun".

The Arabs were nomads who inhabited the Arabian peninsula and its northern extension, the Syrian desert. In border areas, however, the distinction between Arab and non-Arab was blurred, because some Arabs combined agriculture with pastoralism and others settled in towns as traders. The Arab tribes were notoriously conflict ridden through competition for scarce resources, their differences erupting in tribal warfare and bloody revenge. Arabs are first mentioned in an account of the battle of Qarqar, fought in 853 BC between the Assyrians and a confederation of Syrian and Palestinian states. According to Assyrian scribes, the latter fielded an army comprising 3,930 chariots, 1,900 horsemen, 42,700 foot solders and 1,000 camels under the command of Gindibu the Arab. Of interest here are the camels, whose domestication permitted the Arabs to master desert lands. Similarly to the horses used by the Central Asian nomads, camels were the means by which the Arab tribes could emerge from any part of the desert in sudden raids on settled neighbours. It was this predilection for raiding that persuaded Muhammad and his successors to encourage Arab expansion: to keep the peace in Arabia, the feuding tribes were directed not to attack each other but someone else instead.

But it was neither a nomadic nor an agricultural community that produced the Prophet. Muhammad was a trader in animal skins. His birthplace, Mecca, had commercial links with Africa as well as Syria and Iraq. Long before the advent of Islam, Ethiopia had established a presence in Arabia through military expeditions and trade. During much of the sixth century, southern Arabia was actually occupied by Ethiopians, who also sent traders to live in cities, such as Mecca, that were not under their direct control. That Muhammad's wet nurse Baraka, better known as Umm Ayman, was an Ethiopian reveals how far Africans had integrated with Arab society.

Before his call as the Prophet, Muhammad had been a caravan leader for fifteen years, a role that may well have taken him to Ethiopia. His sympathy for this country can be judged from the dispatch of some of his followers as missionaries: he must have believed that his message would receive a welcome there. This perception undoubtedly derived from his own knowledge of the Ethiopian Bible, which had been translated from the Greek. We know that Ethiopians read it aloud in Mecca,

Pre-Moslem religious decoration in southern Arabia

where Muhammad used to stop and listen. Without such a public recital of the Old and New Testaments, Meccans would not have understood references to biblical figures in the Qur'an. In particular, those who embraced Muhammad's message realised why it denied the divinity, the crucifixion and the resurrection of Christ. The Qur'an does not accept anything that constitutes mainstream Christianity.

A famous discussion between the third Abbasid caliph al-Mahdi and the Nestorian bishop Timothy the Great in 781 exposes very different perceptions of Jesus. When the caliph asked about veneration of the cross, Timothy explained how the death of the Son of God had redeemed mankind. The caliph then asked whether this meant that God could die, and after listening to Timothy's careful distinction between Christ's divinity and humanity, he replied that "they did not kill him, nor did they crucify him, but he made a likeness for them". Christians, such as Timothy, who lived under Moslem rule encountered monotheists of an entirely different kind to themselves. Their own controversies about the nature of the Trinity and Christ's incarnation totally clashed with the Moslem emphasis on God's unity. There was no room for theological compromise in Islam for the good reason that the Arabs would have no truck with dying-and-rising deities.

Arguably, the composition of the New Testament in Greek was a decisive factor in preventing Christianity from becoming a pan-Asian

ع وَاِرَ عَلَيْهِ ۞ اِنَا الْبَشِيّ رَبَانِ فِي الْقَزَ يُضِلُّ بِهِ الَّذِينَ كَفَرُوا وَالْجُلُوسُ عَاماً
وَنَسَاً عَاماً ۞ خُطَبَ عَلَيْهِ السَّلَامُ وَمَا ... أَنَّ الزَّمَانَ قَدِ اسْتَدَارَ كَهَيْئَةٍ

A fourteenth-century miniature of Muhammad preaching

religion like Buddhism and Islam. Jesus spoke Aramaic along with his disciples, although it seems likely that St. Paul preached and wrote mostly in the Greek language. Many Christians in Syria and Iraq did not use Greek for sacred texts, but their churches were swamped by the triumphant wave of Islam. Their monks eventually spread Christianity as far as China, where the second Tang emperor, Tai Zong, received them with courtesy. These missionaries had some effect in the larger Chinese cities, but it was on the Central Asian steppe that they met with greater success. Yet the use of Greek for religious purposes in the Mediterranean area would ensure that the main thrust of Christianity was westwards, a movement accelerated by St. Jerome's Latin version of the Bible. Accomplishing this enormous task of translation, he set the scene for the development of medieval Europe's two forms of the faith: the Greek-based Orthodox church and the Latin-based Catholic church.

There can be no question that the adoption of Greek placed the Gospels within a tradition of philosophical speculation that inevitably generated theological argument. Parallel with early Christian disputes was the conflict between rival Buddhist schools of thought in ancient India. While these differences were to an extent composed through Nagarjuna's penetrating analysis of phenomena, a cause of their intensity

146

may well have been the language used for discussion. The translation of Buddhist texts into Sanskrit, an Indo-European cousin of ancient Greek, served to facilitate debate: classical Sanskrit provided as ready a means for argument as Greek did in contemporary Christian controversy.

During the late medieval and early modern periods Christianity spread to other continents, but in Asia it only made significant progress in the Philippines as a result of Spanish colonialism. Even there it was challenged by Moslems living in the southern part of the archipelago. By the time of the arrival of the Portuguese and the Spaniards in the sixteenth century, Christianity was viewed by most Asians as a European religion.

For the Byzantines, Arabia was never more than "the breeding ground of heresies". Its Christians were beyond the pale: the Arians, who emphasised the humanity of Jesus and rejected his divinity; the Monophysites, who accepted Christ's divinity, but one group of whom held that before the crucifixion Judas Iscariot was substituted for Jesus; and the Nestorians, who laid stress on the humanity of Christ more than his divinity. At Najran, south of Mecca, the Nestorians ran a church with a large Arab congregation. A caravan city, Najran would have often been visited by Muhammad when he as a merchant. And we know that he heard a sermon delivered by the Nestorian bishop of Najran, when this cleric preached astride a camel at a trade fair. In due course Muhammad was seen by the Byzantines as a heretic, his prophecy no more than another deviation from biblical truth.

About 610 Muhammad started to receive the revelation of the Qur'an. Afterwards he called upon the Arab people to acknowledge the glory of Allah and pray to him. Muhammad's first convert was his wife, followed by his close relatives. What galvanised his listeners was his utter certainty that those who failed to recognise Allah as the one true god would be consigned to hell. At first the reception of his message was mixed in Mecca and, after persecution, Muhammad took up residence in Medina. Trouble had begun for the Prophet when he disparaged local deities. This was considered offensive by most Meccans, who thought that Muhammad was actually suffering from a mental illness. They tried to obtain medical treatment for him, but his absolute espousal of monotheism meant that there was no choice but removal elsewhere. At Medina, where he lived from 622 onwards, the large community of Jews resident there was initially sympathetic. But just as Christians could never comprehend how the Jews persisted in their refusal to accept Jesus as the Messiah, so Muhammad was in the end baffled by a Jewish unwillingness to regard him as the Prophet. The rejection caused Muhammad to accuse the Jews of falisfying revelation and secure their expulsion from the city. Many of them were killed or sold as slaves.

While Muhammad's religion was being elaborated, he continued to receive revelations, and by his death in 632 the entire content of the Qur'an had been revealed. The duties of the faithful were already established—washing, prayer, almsgiving, fasting and pilgrimage—and the subordinate role of women accepted. The Qur'an speaks of believers having up to four wives as well as the entitlement to divorce them. Except for the inferior status of women and slaves, there were to be no inequalities among Moslems other than those of religious merit. The prohibition of alcohol, an Arabic word in origin, once seemed no more than nomad disdain for the corruption of city life.

But tending vines was very much part of Arab culture because the Nabatean Arabs had long made wine. So where did Muhammad's stern injunction come from? The answer is by no means straightforward, although there are several possibilities. One is the influence of ascetic practices among Christian communities situated on the outskirts of the Syrian desert, where wine was forbidden as well as all animal products because "food was Satan's great weapon and drink his sharpened sword". Another source describes a group of monks who wandered between Syria and Persia. They were called "the shepherds as they had no houses, ate neither bread nor meat, and drank no wine", their extreme diet consisting of uncooked vegetables and seeds, soaked in olive oil. Apart from attempting to liberate the spirit through such physical punishment, these Syrian ascetics were putting a safe distance between themselves and pagan cults, in which wine was offered alongside meat in sacrifice. They saw it as impure and corrupted by evil spirits.

Another possible reason for the prohibition may have been the role that wine came to play in the central Christian ritual of the Communion. The Jews were ambivalent about wine. Moses was told to make "a burnt offering" and one of "wine, as a sweet savour for the Lord". Though regarded as a heavenly blessing, indeed a specific sign of divine approval, wine was understood by the Jews often to be the cause of wickedness. Despite John the Baptist taking neither wine nor any other fermented drink, Jesus' attitude was quite different. He used traditional Jewish imagery of wine to depict the newness of his own message, and during the wedding at Cana he demonstrated his miraculous power by turning water into wine. Even more, wine seems to have become a spiritual drink

The Ka'ba, the sacred stone that Muhammad purged of idols.
A twelfth-century Turkish tile

at the Last Supper, when it assumed a commemorative role. After he had taken a sip, Jesus said: "This cup is the new testament in my blood: this do ye, as oft as ye drink it, in remembrance of me." All this must have been deeply offensive to Prophet Muhammad, for whom Allah was far removed from earthly things. And it would seem earlier that St. Paul shared some of Muhammad's worry about the apparent closeness of the Last Supper to pagan feasts. There was a danger that Christians might get sidetracked into old ways of worship again. Though the Qur'an stresses the importance for health of avoiding alcohol, what Muhammad probably sought to achieve through this prohibition was a complete separation of Islam from Christianity and the beliefs of the Jews.

Having recaptured Mecca, Muhammad purged the Ka'ba of idols, confirming the sacred stone as the chief object of pilgrimage. Originally Moslems had prayed in the direction of Jerusalem but, after the violent break with the Jews, the direction was altered to Mecca. Believed to have been set up by Abraham and his son Ishmael, the black stone of the Ka'ba could be a survival of ancient veneration of rocks among the Arabs. A similar reverence was accorded to the Mount in Jerusalem, the site of the old Jewish Temple: it was held to be where Abraham's sacrifice had occurred, the place from which Muhammad ascended

A page of the Qur'an in nakshi script. Early Moslems believed that Arabic was spoken by Ishmael, Syriac by Abraham and Hebrew by Isaac

heavenwards, and the setting for the Last Judgement. As far as Muhammad was concerned, the presence of the Ka'ba in Mecca justified Islam's claim to be the "religion of Abraham". Whereas Isaac, the son whom Sarah bore Abraham in their extreme old age, was destined to become the founder of the Jewish nation, Abraham's existing son Ishmael, whose mother was an Egyptian concubine named Hagar, in turn founded the Arab tribes. Belief in Abraham as the common ancestor of the Jews and Arabs naturally made the refusal of the former to accept Muhammad's message much harder to bear. They seemed to be unnecessarily stubborn in refusing to accept a Gentile prophet.

The death of Muhammad at the age of sixty brought Islam to a standstill. He simply could not be replaced: even more, another divinely inspired prophet would have nothing to add to the Qur'an, his definitive revelation. What should Moslems do? Ali ibn Abi Talib, Muhammad's son-in-law, was a possibility for leadership, although he was perhaps too young to be generally accepted. Anyway, Ali was more concerned with making the arrangements for the Prophet's funeral than the politics of the mosque. So Abu Bakr became khalifat Allah, "the deputy of God". Even though a compromise choice as caliph, the usual rendering in English of this title, Abu Bakr was able to hold the volatile Arabs together because he had considerable assets. He was related to

Muhammad, whose revelation he had early endorsed; he possessed a vast knowledge of the Arab tribes as well as the reasons for their endless squabbles; he was diplomatic in his dealings with chieftains but, like Muhammad, he never forgot the essentials of Islam and, above all else, he was an old man, which meant that there was scope in the near future for the ambitious to succeed him. Of the four caliphs who were appointed after Muhammad's death, Abu Bakr alone escaped the dagger of an assassin. Umar ibn al-Khattab, Uthman ibn Affran and Ali himself were all struck down before the Umayyad clan in newly conquered Syria founded a dynasty that lasted for almost a century. Even though in 750 the Umayyads were overthrown in a bloodbath by those who favoured the restoration of the Prophet's family to power—in a kind of delayed reaction to Ali's murder—Umayyad caliphs effectively established Islam and made Arabic the key language in medieval West Asia. Only in Persia did the conquered tongue, greatly altered in script, grammar and vocabulary, survive as a written language. There it was destined to be the vehicle of the great literary achievements of the medieval era.

The Umayyad and Abbasid Caliphates

As Muhammad intended, his successors exported Islam from Arabia by force of arms. These military expeditions were never nomadic migrations, because families only followed the bedouin after a conquest was complete. But victories over the Byzantines and the Sasanians seemed to confirm the power of Allah, encouraging yet more Arab conquests. Once the concept of holy war took root, there was no reason for dialogue with non-Moslem states. The world was divided into two starkly different zones, the Dar al-Islam, the "House of Islam", and the Dar al-Harb, the "House of War", with the result that peace was not seen to be interrupted by war but rather continuous warfare against infidels came to a halt whenever outright victory or a truce occurred.

The Arab onslaught could not have been launched at a better moment for the attackers. Perhaps as much as one-third of the West Asian population outside Arabia had been carried off by plague, even before the bitter struggle between the Sasanian Persians and the Byzantines added widespread destruction. Yet the unexpected Arab advance in the last decade of Emperor Heraclius' reign so shattered Byzantine confidence that some of his subjects thought that it indicated the loss of divine approval

The Dome of the Rock, Jerusalem

for the Christian empire. Sophronius, the patriarch of Jerusalem, said the Moslems would not have triumphed had the Christians remained truly devout. Instead, they had "injured the gift-giving Christ and impelled his wrath against us". It fell to the lot of this senior churchman to surrender his city to the second caliph Umar ibn al-Khattab in 638.

The Arab general who conducted the siege offered either conversion to Islam or capitulation and the payment of a fine for the safety of the inhabitants; otherwise, he informed Sophronius, they faced death. The patriarch knew that Damascus and Aleppo had already come to terms, their Christian places of worship being spared any damage or confiscation. At Aleppo indeed there would be no change at all: so few Moslems took up residence in the city that a monumental mosque was unnecessary. A violent assault could only mean the destruction of the Holy Places, so Sophronius offered to surrender Jerusalem to the caliph, without realising how much the Moslems esteemed the city themselves. Umar received news of Sophronius' offer while in Syria and responded at once, arriving post-haste on a camel. The two men met on the Mount of Olives. Taken aback by Umar's shabby appearance, Sophronius lent the caliph a cloak until his dirty camel-hair garment could be washed. A Moslem version of the story, however, puts an entirely different slant on the historic encounter. It relates how Umar changed his dirty riding clothes and rode into the city, where the Arabs refused to acknowledge him as the true caliph until he changed back into them.

Whatever the truth, the caliph and the patriarch were impressed with each other. The 79-year-old Christian recognised Umar's humility and, as a monk who followed a regime of daily prayer, Sophronius appreciated the Moslem leader's need to pray. He even provided a mat for this purpose. In return, the caliph gave Sophronius a document that exempted the steps of the church on which he prayed from congregational Moslem worship. He told the patriarch that his use of the church itself would have led to its inevitable seizure by Moslems because the caliph had worshipped inside. All Umar did before leaving Jerusalem was build a small shrine on the Temple Mount. The agreement Sophronius reached with Umar extended toleration to Christians and Jews, allowing the followers of both faiths to freely worship in the city. This peaceful era lasted until 969, when control passed to the Fatimids of Egypt. Their less tolerant Shi'a outlook led to the destruction of synagogues and churches, a policy continued by later rulers and a cause of the Crusades, which culminated in the capture of Jerusalem in 1099.

Under the Umayyad caliphs, Arab power grew apace. To cut down inter-tribal feuds, blood money was paid to pre-empt retaliation and tribes were dispatched in different directions. Not everyone was pleased with distant campaigns, although it did not stop Arab forces reaching as far west as Spain and as far east as India. The naval expedition to India of 644, the year that witnessed Umar's assassination, was not followed up until 711 when another force of 12,000 men reached the Indus delta. Rapid progress ensued, as it did in Central Asia where, in 751, a Chinese army met defeat at Talas river. But unappreciated at the time was that this

Umayyad milestone in the sufic script, the earliest one used for Arabic. It says Damascus is 120 kilometres away

153

victory marked the limit of Arab ambitions there. The Umayyads had usurped the caliphate in the confusion following the assassination of Ali, Muhammad's son-in-law. Their power base was Syria, where they had a local following well before the arrival of Islam. As they understood the desire of other prominent Arab families to secure their own positions, the first Umayyad caliphs had come to terms with those who controlled the provinces, thereby gaining the support of influential leaders without conflict. Such a decentralised form of government actually suited the Arab temperament. Only in Iraq were there any difficulties, but fortunately for the caliph's court at Damascus this populous province could never agree on unified action.

Bronze falcon made in Persia about 796

The accession of Abd al-Malik in 685 brought an effective ruler to power. Not only did he reform the administration but he also introduced a standard coinage that bore no images at all. Moslem disdain for imagery spilled over to the Byzantine empire in the form of iconoclasm, or "image breaking". Emperor Leo III ordered the removal of an image of Christ from over the entrance to the imperial palace at Constantinople, an action that in 730 provoked condemnation from the pope. The figure's replacement by a cross was considered to be blasphemous. Although the roots of iconoclasm go back to the Ten Commandments, which forbid the making and worshipping of "graven images", the amazing military success of the Moslems encouraged some Byzantines to think that their own failure might be connected with divine disapproval of icons. Islam was always iconoclastic, and its movement eastwards involved the destruction of many images. Probably the best known was the dynamiting of the Buddhas at Bamiyan in Afghanistan. This dramatic example of Taliban iconoclasm was condemned as artistic vandalism, the world's press overlooking the fact that the colossal statues had lost their faces long before the explosion in 2001.

Abd al-Malik's construction of the Dome of the Rock, one of the world's architectural masterpieces, drew upon Byzantine building techniques and craftsmanship, but it was an unequivocal statement of Islam's establishment as a great religion. Besides celebrating this event, Abd al-Malik had a political motive too. A rival "caliph" briefly seized Mecca, so the Dome of the Rock offered an alternative centre for pilgrimage. The strain of constant warfare, and especially the struggle against the Byzantines in Asia Minor, had thrown up this opponent. For half a century after the death of Abd al-Malik in 705, the Umayyads held on to the caliphate despite renewed outbursts of tribal conflict. Opposition to the rule of Damascus was never anti-Moslem, since rebellions were driven by the ambitions of Arab leaders and the discontent of their followers. But their agitation was enough to bring down the Umayyads, who were killed with the sole exception of Abd al-Rahman. Fleeing westwards, he seized power in southern Spain where he ruled for more than thirty years. Abd al-Rahman showed that he had learned from the violent overthrow, because he had the assassins sent after him killed and their severed heads returned to Damascus.

Because the revenues of Iraq, the home province of the Abbasids, were critical to the new government, the second caliph al-Mansur shifted the capital in the 760s to Baghdad, which soon became the largest city in the world outside China. Within little more than a century the Arabs had transformed themselves from desert dwellers into the owners of a metropolis. Though the Abbasid family claimed descent from the Prophet, some of their most prominent supporters were of Arab origin but spoke Persian, having intermarried with local people.

Coins showing two Abbasid caliphs: al-Muqtadir drinking on the left and al-Radi strumming a lute on the right

Dancing girls pouring wine

Certainly the Abbasid caliphate was not exclusively run by Arabs, as had been the case under the Umayyads. If anything, al-Mansur and his successors emphasized the equality of all Moslems regardless of their ancestry. Notice was being given that the Moslem empire was no longer solely for the benefit of the Arabs. Welcome though this attitude was for the different peoples who lived within its borders, the Abbasids found in the end that it was not enough to prevent either territorial fragmentation or sectarian conflict.

The most famous Abbasid caliph, Harun al-Rashid, whose accession in 786 followed his older brother's murder, made every effort to strengthen the power of the court, but the regime remained militarily weak. Even though he managed to assert his authority over provincial interests, Harun al-Rashid was the last ruler to exercise undisputed dominion in the Moslem world. Reliance on Turkish soldiers recruited from the Central Asian steppelands left his successors so dangerously exposed to rebellion that even Baghdad endured a year-long siege in 812, from which the dynasty never really recovered. Although the caliphate was still regarded as an ideal, the political tide flowed towards provincial autonomy and the independence of rulers outside northern Iraq, the sole area under direct Abbasid control.

In parallel with this breakup of the Moslem empire, a sharp fissure opened within Islam itself. The two opposing sects were the Sunni and the Shi'a. Whereas the former believed that the caliphate was a legitimate institution, and the Abbasids were entitled to exercise religious as well as secular leadership, the latter held that only the heirs of the fourth appointed caliph, Ali ibn Abi Talib, could be accepted as the true successors of Muhammad. Today Osama bin Laden is a Sunni Moslem who regrets the abolition of the caliphate. The followers of the Iranian ayatollahs, on the other hand, are Shi'a. It is tempting to see the modern antagonism between Iraq and Iran as a continuation of this old sectarian divide.

The Coming of the Seljuks

Despite Abbasid Baghdad witnessing a cultural flowering in poetry, medicine and philosophy, the city was largely irrelevant to Moslem affairs at the close of the tenth century. While the Byzantines recovered lost territory in Asia Minor and Syria, turning Aleppo into a valuable buffer state, the Abbasids clung to power as best they could. The forces that they sent against the Byzantines at Aleppo were no match for the Christian army, which numbered 30,000 horsemen and 40,000 foot soldiers. The Byzantine offensives might have recovered more land had not a new people arrived in the form of the Oghuz Turks, a nomadic people

A Seljuk ruler

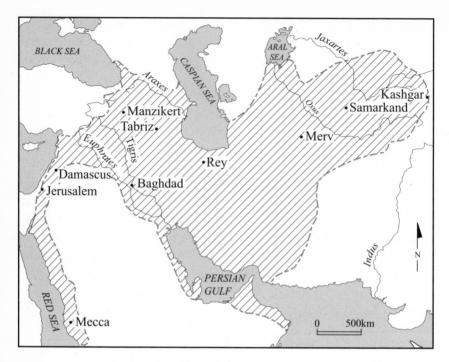

The Seljuk empire

along with their animals and their tents, propelled by poverty and pressure from enemies on the Central Asian steppe. More than the Arabs perhaps, and much more than the Persians, the Turks sank their identity in Islam, inaugurating a Sunni revival that eventually took them into Europe, where they lay siege to Vienna in 1529 and 1683. The Seljuk family did not lead the Turkish movement westwards from the Aral Sea, but their own conversion to Islam ensured that, once recognised as leaders, the Oghuz became Moslems.

The Abbasid caliphs had begun to use Turkish slave-soldiers in the ninth century. A verse relates the supposed value of such retainers:

> One obedient slave is better
> Than three hundred sons;
> For the latter desire their father's death,
> The former his master's glory.

This revival of a practice going back to Sumerian times failed to mend the military fortunes of the Abbasids, because the slave-soldiers soon became semi-independent forces with an agenda of their own. Before the migration of the Oghuz, most Turks would have largely encountered Islam as targets of slave raids. In India there were even Moslem "slave-rulers", the Delhi sultanate being a prime example. There the Ghaznavid Turks would overcome relatively immobile Indian armies and install a fellow slave as sultan in the twelfth century.

Effective in the establishment of the Seljuk empire was the battle of Manzikert in 1071. Fought on a plain ideally suited for a cavalry engagement, to the north of Lake Van, the Seljuk victory broke the Byzantine border defences and opened Asia Minor to Moslem settlement. Alp Arslan, the second Seljuk leader, had done what earlier rulers failed to do for centuries. That Alp Arslan also took the Byzantine emperor Romanus IV Diogenes prisoner, and then released him, only tended to make the battle more memorable. One account tells us how the Seljuk victor had Romanus led around the Moslem camp with a rope round his neck, so that he might be sold as a slave to the highest bidder. When he learned that the emperor had been traded for a dog, Alp Arslan said: "That is just, because the dog is better than he is! Give him the dog and set him free." Considering the dislike of so many Moslems for this particular animal, it was a prophetic remark. For on his return

Seljuk soldiers

to Constantinople, Romanus was indeed treated as less than a dog: he was blinded.

Loyal though they were to Alp Arslan, the Oghuz Turks remained fiercely independent like other nomads, finding the discipline of an Islamic sultanate irksome. As a result, the core of Alp Arslan's army consisted of slave-troops, Turkish in origin but from non-Oghuz tribes. This force of some 15,000 men was supplemented by Oghuz warriors whenever it required support on the battlefield. But as the first Moslem family of prominence among the Turks, the Seljuks began the process in the western part of Asia whereby the Turkish people came to give up their nomadic ways. An early sign of this change was the replacement of the title khan with sultan. To assist in running an administration, the Seljuks turned to Persian bureaucrats, expert in such matters since Abbasid times.

A wonderful example of Seljuk wood carving

Another reason for their involvement was the location of the Seljuk capital at Rey, a few kilometres from modern Tehran.

Although the encouragement of Oghuz attacks outside Iraq and Iran might be seen as no more than a continuation of nomad raiding, Alp Arslan regarded Seljuk expansion as holy war, a Sunni onslaught on Christians and Shi'a Moslems alike. The battle of Manzikert was essentially a sideshow for Alp Arslan, an engagement that happened when he heard of the Byzantine emperor's presence in Asia Minor while he was wresting Syria from Fatimid control. His chief targets were Syria and Palestine, from which he intended to roll back Shi'a influence to Cairo. The extent of the Manzikert victory probably surprised Alp Arslan. What he did not realise was that disaffected relatives of the previous Byzantine emperor had spread the rumour that Romanus faced defeat at the very moment he was winning. Soldiers fled, leaving the emperor and those fighting around him to be easily captured by the sultan.

Within twenty years of Alp Arslan's death in 1072, the Seljuk empire disintegrated. But conflict between its successor states had no effect on the migration of Turkish people from Central Asia, more than one million of them settling in Asia Minor where they formed not the largest ethnic group but the only one spread throughout that region.

The Crusades

Halfway through a tour of France in 1095, Pope Urban II presided over a council at Clermont that issued this decree:

> Whoever for devotion alone, not to gain honour or money, goes to Jerusalem to liberate the Church of God can substitute this journey for all penance.

The call to arms roused Europe to a concerted effort against Islam. Armed pilgrimage to Jerusalem predated the Clermont decree, as a group of German knights had sported crosses thirty years earlier, but Urban's desire to "restrain the savagery of the Saracens" converted individual initiative into a recognised way of salvation for European warriors. The pope's emphasis on Moslem atrocity was of course intended to stop any criticism of what was blatant warmongering. No less than the Byzantine justification of wars as a defence of Christendom, the papal blessing that Urban conferred upon Crusaders made them soldiers of Christ. As a holy war, the Jerusalem expedition was made special by the indulgences that were awarded to those who took the cross. Though they are sometimes equated with the Islamic struggle against infidels, the Crusades arose from a specific cause, the barring of Christians from access to the Holy Places in Jerusalem. "The House of War", on the other hand, was for Moslems a continuous activity. Just as they had to fight an internal battle for personal purity, so they also had to defeat those who refused to acknowledge Allah.

Having just sponsored a war against Moslems in Spain, Urban transformed a Byzantine request for military aid into a campaign of religious revivalism, personally preaching a crusade that raised between 50,000 and 70,000 men. When the Crusaders reached Syria in late 1097, they could not have come at a more opportune moment. They found a politically frag-

Pope Urban II preaching the First Crusade

mented land, where local rulers could reach no agreement at all. Yet it was only through treachery that they were able to take Antioch. An Armenian by the name of Firouz assisted the Crusaders in entering the city one night, after a frustrating eighteen-month siege. Once the fury of the sack had abated, the Crusaders had to decide on their next move. They were encouraged, however, by the discovery in Antioch of the Holy Lance: it had pierced Christ's side during the crucifixion. Despite the existence of another lance at Constantinople with a longer established claim of authenticity, they accepted the find as the genuine article, perhaps in the hope that it showed how the Crusade was truly blessed.

The defence of Jerusalem was the responsibility of the Fatimid governor, who expelled all its Christian residents, drove off the flocks and herds from the pastures outside the walls and filled up the wells there too. Once again the Crusaders could not take the fortifications by assault, and learning of the approach of an army from Egypt, they fell back on penance. To the mockery of Jerusalem's defenders, the entire army walked barefoot round the city and then listened to three sermons on the Mount of Olives. Inspired by this, the Crusaders made another attempt to take the city by storm, which succeeded. The ensuing massacre of Moslems and Jews, who had stayed behind when the Christians left, deeply shocked Moslem opinion, but Western observers described it approvingly in apocalyptic terms. The subsequent defeat of the Fatimid relief force at Ascalon seemed to confirm their view, because a single charge by Frankish knights was enough to secure victory.

Yet because following "in the footsteps of Christ", as the First Crusade was described, had ended in such violence, churchmen still felt obliged to explain the event in theological terms. "In our time", reflected Guibert, the Benedictine abbot of Nogent, "God has instituted holy warfare so that the knightly order and the errant mob," rather than engaging in mutual slaughter, "might find a new way of deserving salvation." Within two centuries, this idea was used to justify any action taken against Islam when Humbert de Romans, the Dominican Master General, boldly declared that the followers of Muhammad deserved only destruction for the reason they would never convert. Killing Moslems or being killed by them won for the crusader the ultimate prize, eternal life. "The aim of Christianity," Humbert added with absolute conviction, "is not to populate the world but to populate heaven."

The discovery of the Holy Lance at Antioch

Following the First Crusade's capture of Jerusalem in 1099, four Christian states were set up in Syria and Palestine. They were known as the Outremer, "the land beyond the sea", an admission of their distance from Catholic Europe. Holding this bridgehead became a major preoccupation in Rome, particularly when Saladin's tremendous victory in 1187 at Hattin, close to Lake Galilee, was followed by the recapture of Jerusalem and the reconquest of almost all the Christian holdings. Possibly because Salah al-Din ibn Ayyab was a

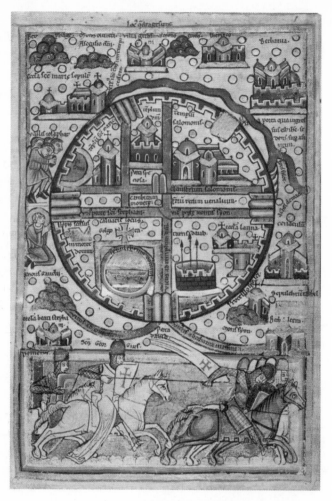

A European map celebrating the capture of Jerusalem in 1099.
Frankish knights see off Moslem cavalry at the bottom

Kurd, he was largely overlooked by Moslem historians, who also resented his accommodation of the Third Crusade. But in Europe Saladin gained legendary status as a non-Christian paladin of chivalry.

The response to Saladin's great victory in Europe was immediate, the kings of Germany, France and England taking the cross. A special tax, called the Saladin Tithe, was instituted in France and England to help finance the Third Crusade, the work of its predecessor in 1145–49 having been undone at Hattin. Only the army that Frederick Barbarossa, king of Germany and the Holy Roman emperor, led overland failed to arrive in strength, because Barbarossa was drowned in 1190 trying to cross a river in Asia Minor.

The English and French monarchs did not embark until this date, and on the way Richard Lionheart took the opportunity to conquer Cyprus, which remained in Catholic hands until 1571. Although Acre fell to the Crusaders, this port-city to the north of modern Haifa was merely a staging post for the assault on Jerusalem. Having repulsed Saladin's attempt to drive them back into the sea, King Richard twice marched within a few kilometres of the Holy City only to withdraw each time, arguing he had insufficient troops to take or hold it. Because Richard could not strike at Saladin's power base in Egypt, the military stalemate led to negotiations through which the Crusaders were left in control of the coastline and Christian pilgrims allowed access to Jerusalem.

By failing in its main objective, the Third Crusade determined the pattern of later support for Christian kings in Moslem West Asia. Seaborne aid was all they received down to their eclipse in 1291. The Fourth Crusade of 1198–1204 actually turned into a Venetian-inspired attack on Constantinople, while the Fifth Crusade of 1213–29 had only the appearance of a triumph. Holy Roman Emperor Frederick II merely negotiated a compromise with the Egyptian sultan that gave Christians control of their Holy Places except for the Temple Mount, which remained under Islamic religious authority. For Christians it was an extraordinary spectacle to have a crusading emperor arrive amid fanfares, and then, hardly unsheathing his sword, to have him reach an agreement with the Moslems by diplomacy. What they misunderstood was Frederick's main objective: securing access to Jerusalem for pilgrims, rather than winning glory on the battlefield. It was something he had to achieve to safeguard his own position in a bitter struggle with Pope Gregory IX, who held that the emperor was subordinate to the papacy.

With the treaty agreed, an excommunicated Frederick could now style himself as Defender of the Church and King of Jerusalem, but the local Christians were not at all satisfied. So unpopular was he with them that when at Acre Frederick embarked for home he was pelted with offal. His negotiated arrangement lasted until 1244, when Jerusalem was seized by Turkish freebooters in the pay of Egypt. The city remained under Moslem rule until 1917. The rollback of Christian power had less to do with Moslem heroics than European exhaustion: the Outremer was simply too far beyond the sea.

Safavid Persia

A whole series of invasions engulfed Persia between the Arab defeat of the Sasanians in 651 and the splendour of the Safavid dynasty in the seventeenth century. One thing that the Arab, Turkish and Mongol conquerors could not erase, however, was the Persian language. While many languages were replaced by Arabic or Turkish, Persian survived in much the same way that English was transformed after the Norman Conquest. Instrumental in this development was Ferdowsi, whose great poem the *Shahnameh*, "Book of Kings", was composed in the late tenth century. Essentially the national epic, it celebrates the deeds of Rustam, a Persian equivalent of the Greek hero Heracles. Rustam's adventures not only recall the famous labours of Heracles, but they also indicate

Sufis dancing

a common Indo-European heritage. By avoiding Arabic words and eulogising pre-Islamic kings, Ferdowsi deliberately laid emphasis upon the traditional values of Persia, besides giving the Persian language a new lease of life.

That the Persians were not Semites probably helps to explain their resistance to Arab culture. The Turks and the Mongols presented less of a cultural challenge: the Seljuks and the Ilkhanate, founded in the late 1250s by Hulegu, a younger brother of Mongke Khan, both relied on Persian officials to run their administrations. Yet the reassertion of Persian influence over these conquerors remains an extraordinary event on a par with the Chinese absorption of the Turks and the Manchus. Even more remarkable is the fact that this period saw an upsurge of creativity, producing in Rumi one of Persia's greatest writers. Jalal al-Din Molavi Rumi was born in Balkh in 1207, but his family moved to Asia Minor on the approach of the Mongols. There he encountered Sufism, whose mysticism informs all his poetry. It celebrates the unity of the human spirit with the deity. An overwhelming desire for reunion with Allah, a personal relationship upon which no other human being can intrude, runs through his unconventional verse; and its directness still unsettles modern Persians, when he writes:

> All fear of God, all self-denial, I deny; bring wine, nothing but wine.
> For I repent my worship, a hypocrisy that reeks of self-display.

Acknowledging his subordination to his older brother Mongke Khan, Hulegu called his dynasty Ilkhan, meaning "lesser khan". He had been sent westwards to deal with peoples who still dared to oppose the Mongols. After the accession of Kubilai Khan, relations between the Ilkhanate and the Mongol homeland remained close, but there was never any question of the Great Khan actually nominating a new Ilkhan. The Mongol empire had broken into separate powers, with Kubilai Khan gaining the lion's share. Even though Nestorian Christians were influential in the Ilkhanate, as indeed they were in Mongolia, it was Islam that was finally adopted as the state religion. The first Ilkhan rulers did not abandon their nomad ways, preferring to live outside city walls in tents, with the rich pastures of Azerbaijan their favourite location.

The Mongols living in Persia owed their conversion to Islam to Ghazan Ilkhan. Shortly after 1295, he ordered that Buddhists, if they were unwilling to convert, should leave the country and that their temples be destroyed. Christians and Jews were able to worship freely,

Isfahan, "half the world", according to medieval Persians

although they became second-class citizens, as was the standard practice in Moslem states. The Mongols showed a marked interest in Sufism, Islam in its mystical form, partly because Moslem mystics were the missionaries who penetrated Central Asia, having organised themselves into orders, each with a leading Sufi and its own rituals. Often they incorporated indigenous religious ideas, which made Sufis suspect in the eyes of urban clerics, now the guardians of orthodoxy in Moslem schools and colleges. Leading Sufis such as Shayk Safi al-Din Ardabili, founder of the Safavid order and ancestor of the Safavid dynasty, were treated with respect and favour by the Ilkhans. Shayk Safi sought to purify Islam so that the faithful might have a spiritual experience akin to that granted to Muhammad himself. It involved the banishment of all worldly concerns when approaching the divine.

Ghazan's conversion led to a fundamental change in Mongol attitudes. The Ilkhans began to rebuild neglected cities, restore the irrigation schemes on which agriculture relied and construct at Tabriz a permanent capital of their own. This eventual accommodation with traditional Persia was cut short by Tamerlane, a ferocious warrior from Central Asia, whose people were of Mongol stock but had become Turkish in speech and had adopted Islam. In a repeat of Hulegu's conquest of

West Asia, Tamerlane spread terror wherever he went. Most of all, he liked to raise pillars of human heads: 70,000 were set in 120 pillars outside Isfahan alone. In the aftermath of this wonton destruction, various dynasts struggled to maintain themselves until the Safavids became the ruling dynasty of Persia during the sixteenth century.

How the Safavid order of Sufis came to reunify Persia under a strong monarchy is still unclear. And why the Safavid kings then turned against the Sufis, despite their own Sufi heritage, remains yet another puzzle, especially as the ultimate beneficiary of this persecution were Shi'a clerics, the forerunners of the present-day ayatollahs.

But there is no question that the Safavid period has defined how the world views medieval Persia. Always recalled is Shah Abbas the Great's splendid building programme at Isfahan: it famously transformed that city into "half the world". So impressed was the French traveller Jean Chardin by

> the great number of magnificent palaces, the agreeable and pleasant houses, the spacious caravanserais, the really fine bazaars, the water channels and the streets lined with tall plane trees

that he could overlook the confusion of the back streets and lanes that had escaped reconstruction. Such was his attention to detail that Chardin employed two clerics to provide information about the mosques that he was unable to enter himself. Chardin was greatly impressed by the exploits of Shah Abbas' new model army, which was well supplied with firearms. Two years after their defeat in 1514 at the hands of the Ottomans at Chaldiran, north of Tabriz, the Safavids manufactured 2,000 muskets with the aid of Ottoman deserters, and they produced 40 copies of an Ottoman cannon recovered from a river bed. They also used their diplomatic contacts to obtain up-to-date weapons from abroad. By 1598, the year that Shah Abbas designated Isfahan as the capital, Persian musketeers were the equal of any opponent they might meet in battle. But Safavid armies were never as large as Ottoman ones, because at most Shah Abbas could field only 40,000 regulars.

Less favourable was Chardin's view of those who followed Shah Abbas. He considered that they had frittered away Persia's new military strength through "luxury, sensual indulgence and indolence on one side and study and literature on the other". They had "allowed themselves to become effeminate—but nothing has contributed more than the spirit of jealousy and the arbitrary exercise of power". It seemed to

The great mosque at Isfahan

the Frenchman utterly reprehensible that Shah Abbas had contributed to the decline himself by letting his sons grow up in the harem, where "envy rather than courage was the chief motivation". As a result of this laxity, Safavid rule had lost real leadership, becoming much more interested in parades than training for war.

Notwithstanding Chardin's own reservations in the late sixteenth century, many Europeans were already drawn to Persia's magnificence. Not everyone came as peaceful traders, however: the Portuguese had seized the island of Hormuz at the mouth of the Persian Gulf in 1515, before the high point of the Safavids' power, which coincided with Shah Abbas' reign from 1587 to 1629. Shah Abbas centralised power, established secure borders, introduced new institutions, facilitated trade and, above all else, sponsored art and architecture. Inevitably his achievement is compared with that of the Ottoman sultan Suleyman the Magnificent, whose European campaigns were a continuation of the Crusades. The latter added large territories to the Ottoman empire before his death in 1566, but at a cost because the revenue they generated barely covered the expense of their occupation. Shah Abbas was less concerned with conquest, although a robust foreign policy initially set the tone for the Safavid dynasty. It collapsed through widespread rebellion in

1722, when division among the ruling family was exacerbated by clerical interference with the administration.

The Ottoman Empire

Although the ignominious Fourth Crusade dispossessed the Byzantine emperor of Constantinople and parcelled out Greece among Frankish nobles, the setback for the Greeks was temporary. In 1261, Emperor Michael VIII Palaeologus recovered the capital and then concentrated on driving away these intruders. But it proved to be a mistaken policy, because neglect of Asia Minor gave the Ottomans scope for territorial gain. Tradition credits Osman son of Ertughrul with the foundation of the Ottoman empire. News of his victories over the Byzantines attracted large numbers of Turkish fighters and, in 1326, Osman was strong enough to capture the city of Bursa, the first Ottoman capital.

Osman gave his name to the Ottoman, or Osmanli, dynasty. But it was under his son Orhan that the city of Bursa began to acquire a settled aspect. Its great mosque, the Ulu Cami, was not constructed until 1396–99: the costs were defrayed by spoils from the defeat at Nicopolis of

Suleyman the Magnificent's mosque at Istanbul

a crusading army lead by King Sigismund of Hungary. It was the grandest mosque erected in Asia Minor during the two centuries before the Turkish capture of Constantinople. Sultan Bayezid I actually lifted his siege of that city to march in 1396 to the relief of the Danubian fortress of Nicopolis. The impulsiveness of the Frankish knights determined the outcome of the battle, once their futile charge at the start of the action left Sigismund's men-at-arms exposed to a counter-attack by the far stronger body of Ottoman cavalry. The Christian losses were heavy, although Sigismund himself escaped. Other Western leaders were less fortunate and the ransoms of those who survived provided the funds for building Ulu Cami.

A costly failure though the attempt to expel the Turkish garrison from Nicopolis was, this advance into Romania had the effect of drawing the sultan's attention away from beleaguered Constantinople, already surrounded by Ottoman holdings on both sides of the Bosphorus. Shortly after 1361 the Ottoman capital had been moved from Bursa to Edirne, over 200 kilometres west of Constantinople. Bursa was still revered as the first seat of the Ottoman government, the burial place of Osman and the first five sultans, but the shift into Europe marked the direction of future Turkish ambitions. Extending control beyond Budapest was as important to the Ottomans as their advance in West Asia to the Persian Gulf,

Sultan Orhan's tomb at Bursa

Sultan Mehmet II, the conqueror of Constantinople

and in North Africa along the Mediterranean coast. Twice Vienna was besieged. But the second siege of 1683 represented a severe reverse for the Ottomans. Afterwards the Holy League, a coalition of anti-Ottoman powers, inflicted defeats on land and sea with the result that in 1699 the Treaty of Carlowitz awarded Hungary to the Austrians and Athens and the Peloponnese to Venice.

At the start of the eighteenth century, three Moslem empires straddled West and South Asia: those belonging to the Ottomans, the Safavids and the Mughals. They were land based, with only the Ottomans developing any real naval capability. But all of them faced the same problem: how to transform themselves into stable organisations no longer dependent on semi-nomadic followers. The Ottomans did this by adopting the style of Islamic sultans who ruled over an agrarian empire. The Safavids turned to Shi'a clerics for support. The Mughals found dealing with the Indian subcontinent ultimately impossible, since their client rulers called in Europeans to settle differences on the battlefield. Unlike the Ottomans and the Safavids, the Mughals never relied on slave-soldiers, preferring to raise extra troops from their restive vassals.

The Ottoman Turks secured their lasting foothold in Europe with the capture of Constantinople. Its conqueror in 1453, Mehmet II,

The Byzantine church of Saint Sergius and Saint Bacchus in Istanbul. Begun in 527, it was the prototype of Haghia Sophia and Ottoman mosques

claimed to be the heir and possessor of the Roman empire. There was consternation in Europe, but Christian rulers were unable to expel the Ottomans. Assistance from an Hungarian engineer called Urban provided at long last the Ottomans with a method of breaching Constantinople's massive defences. In the summer of 1452 this man had offered his services to Emperor Constantine XI Palaeologus Dragases, but the Byzantine ruler could not pay him the salary he thought to be his due, nor could he provide him with the raw materials he required to make powerful artillery. Urban therefore went to the Ottoman sultan, who was delighted at the prospect of a gun that was capable of firing balls heavy enough to shatter masonry.

Even though the monster that Urban made for Mehmet could only be fired seven times a day, its impact was devastating and weakened whole sections of Constantinople's landward defences, and in early 1453 the Ottomans broke into the city. Realising that nothing could be saved, Constantine discarded his imperial insignia and died fighting in the breach. His body was never identified, despite a stuffed head supposedly belonging to him being sent round the leading courts of the Islamic world by the triumphant sultan.

Mehmet's success in 1453 derived as much from his peaceful succession as Urban's technology. Two years before, by means of a written will his father had managed to prevent the violent quarrels that accompanied each sultan's elevation. Thus the Fatih, "the Conqueror", was free to take the initiative against Constantinople without having to face a succession crisis, fuelled by the thwarted ambitions of rival claimants. According to Turkish tradition, Osman alone was peacefully succeeded by his son Orhan, after his brother Ali Pasha had voluntarily renounced his claim and retired to a life of contemplation. Although Orhan never had a brother, the story is correct in that he became sultan with none of the bloodletting that characterised the start of subsequent reigns. Civil wars were an inevitable result of the Ottoman acceptance as ruler of almost any legitimate heir of the sultan, irrespective of precedence. In spite of the will that had named him as the next ruler,

Haghia Sophia, the former Church of the Divine Wisdom. The Ottomans added the minarets when it became a mosque

175

A Janissary band, whose playing made "Turkish music"
fashionable in Europe

Mehmet took no chances and executed his infant half-brother as soon as
he entered the palace.

The Ottoman empire was first and foremost a Moslem polity, a fact
emphasised in the 1540s, when Suleyman announced that he was the
caliph, the successor of Muhammad and the four caliphs appointed after
the prophet's death. Yet this bold attempt to assume the leadership of
Islam could not disguise the presence of a large non-Moslem population
that, in most of the European provinces, actually comprised the majority.

Yet even in West Asia, the Moslem population was far from homogeneous. Kurdish tribesmen had little in common with Arab bedouin roaming the deserts of Syria and Arabia. And there were also Christian and Jewish communities to be taken into account. Although Islamic courts acted as the primary ones of the empire, Ottoman officials were prepared to let different peoples settle their affairs at the local level as far as possible. Punishment for unresolved non-capital offences consisted usually of the lash or fines, or a combination of both.

Those who wished to join the ruling class, whether or not they were Turkish by descent, had to practise the Moslem religion, loyally serve the caliph, and integrate with Ottoman society. The Janissaries, the Yeni Ceri or "New Troops", were the most obvious example of non-Moslem recruitment. Agents went periodically through the provinces, conscripting the brightest Christian youths for military service, while Christian captives formed the other source of recruits. Employment in the palace itself was the apex of the system, and the children of existing high officials tended to make this their preserve. Promotion through the ranks of the army, including the Janissary corps of foot soldiers, was an alternative way of mounting the social ladder. But Ottoman forces suffered a series of defeats that began at Vienna in 1683 and ended with Napoleon Bonaparte's invasion of Egypt in 1798. Not only did the Ottomans have to cede territories to the Russians, but the separation of the Crimean khanate from the empire meant the loss of valuable manpower at a time when the Janissaries ceased to be such an effective fighting unit. The Crimea, long a dependency of the Ottomans, had been made independent in a peace treaty, but this was no more than a cover for Russian interference. In 1783 Catherine the Great annexed the region by simply announcing that the khan and his people were Russian subjects.

Chapter 6

Medieval South Asia

Ever since the reign of Akbar, it has been ordained that the names of the inmates of the harem should not be mentioned in public, but that they should be designated by some epithet derived from the place where they were first noticed by the monarch with the eye of affection.

Shah Jahan on the Mughal seraglio

The Arrival of Islam

In 711, the year the Arabs invaded Spain, an expeditionary force of 6,000 cavalry and 6,000 infantry marched through southern Persia to the Indus delta, while supplies and siege equipment were sent by sea. The target was Daybul, a port on the site of modern Karachi. The specific cause of the attack was piracy, because an Arab ship carrying precious gifts from the ruler of the Maldives to the Umayyad caliph had been intercepted by marauders from Daybul. There were Moslem women on board as well. The Hindu king of Sind, who had recently annexed Daybul, disclaimed any responsibility for the pirate assault, so the Arabs decided on direct action.

After the walls of Daybul were demolished by huge catapults, a large number of the people living there were shipped off as slaves. Though conversion does not seem to have been an Arab priority, many Indians became Moslems as a result of Daybul's capture, especially those with a low-caste status, who were hardly integrated with Hindu society at all. In Sind, and elsewhere in the subcontinent, Moslem invaders were to find that Islam's marked egalitarian outlook would prove attractive to people whom fellow Hindus regarded as their social inferiors. Buddhists also seem to have been prepared to convert, possibly because in Sind they were largely merchants whose capital was then at stake. This positive response did not stop the Arabs, however, from accepting to a degree the social divisions propagated by the Indian lawgiver Manu. Despite Muhammad's insistence on equality, Islam was able to accommodate segregation in India for the reason that the Prophet's point of view was narrowly interpreted to mean only the relation of a believer with Allah, rather than between men. During the decline of the Mughal empire in the eighteenth century, Islam's claim to universal brotherhood faltered to such an extent that Moslems in India even began to devise subgroups of their own, based on ethnic origin and occupation. Muhammad's teachings had conspicuously failed to have any decisive impact on the caste-ridden structure of Indian society.

From the start, pragmatism shaped the approach of the Arab conquerors. Once it was realised that they intended no damage to either Hindu or Buddhist temples, cities upriver from Daybul were prepared to submit. Given the size of the indigenous population, the small number of incoming Arabs had little choice but tolerate local beliefs. The invasion was therefore never regarded as a holy war but rather a move that was deemed necessary to safeguard trade. Already Arab merchants were settled in other parts of India and Sri Lanka, their trading activities greatly enriching Arabia, Iraq and Syria. At the southern Iraqi port of Basra, the harbour was actually called "Hind and Sind". Later European powers were to be driven by a similar concern for the protection of commerce to assert themselves in the subcontinent.

Many Arabs left at the end of Umayyad rule and, though the subsequent Abbasid caliphate dispatched expeditions as far as Kashmir, it fell to Turkish tribes from Afghanistan to firmly establish Islam in the subcontinent. These semi-nomads came as raiders but stayed on as rulers. Their conquest

Carved marble panel. Ghaznavid, ninth century

took place in several stages, starting with the Turkish Ghaznavids. They brought to northwestern India an amalgamation of Islamic and Turkic cultures but within a strong Iranian framework. Under Seljuk rule the influence of a Persian-staffed bureaucracy was so pervasive in West Asia that the use of the Arabic language ceased to be universal. Even more in medieval South Asia, Persian became the every-day Moslem language, thereby restricting Arabic to a scholarly role.

What the Ghaznavids also imported was iconoclasm, destroying in 1026 the famous Hindu temple at Somnath, long a place of pilgrimage in Gujarat. Their leader, Mahmud ibn Sebruktigin, was heaped with praise for this act of destruction, in large measure because his stern approach was underpinned by a view of society that left no room for any dissent. According to Mahmud's admirers, the ideal state required an absolute ruler whose powerful army kept the population trembling at his feet. To be expected then was the wholesale confiscation of treasures belonging to Hindu temples to defray the costs of administration. After Mahmud's death, the Ghaznavids suffered severe reverses in Central Asia, so they were obliged to concentrate their energies on fighting Hindu kings instead. This did not stop the Ghaznavid capital at Lahore from developing into a significant centre of Islamic learning as well as Sufism.

Here the first comprehensive study of Moslem mysticism was written in the Persian language. It described a Sufi as one who is "purified by love, absorbed in the Beloved, and has abandoned all else".

An even more recently converted tribe of Turkish extraction, the Ghurids, then descended from Afghanistan and ended Ghaznavid rule in 1186. Afterwards the Ghurids advanced to the south and the east before setting up at Delhi, the so-called "Slave Sultanate". Victories over the armies belonging to Hindu kings were gained through mounted archers and foot soldiers armed with crossbows. When their leader died as a result of a polo accident, his son-in-law Iltutmish was installed as the first "slave sultan" in 1210. Iltutmish secured his position through patronage and the recruitment of people fleeing the Mongol onslaught in Central Asia. Though it was known for certain that the sultan had been sold as a child into military service, a genealogy was soon produced to show how he was descended from legendary Persian rulers. With Iltutmish's elevation, Islamic authority was now established in the centre of the subcontinent, where it would remain until the British deposed the last Mughal emperor after the Indian Mutiny in 1857.

A fine Ghurid bronze made in Central Asia

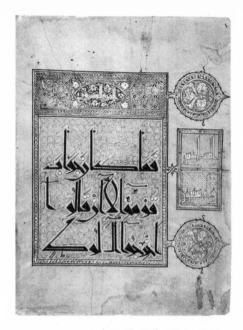

The script favoured by both the Ghaznavids and the Ghurids

Ghurid sultans were not iconoclastic like their Ghaznavid pred-ecessors. They imitated Indian types of coinage showing Hindu deities such as Shiva and Vishnu's wife Laksmi, the goddess of good fortune. Iltutmish was still concerned, however, that his followers should appre-ciate how his rule fitted into the overall pattern of the Islamic world. A coin he issued described himself as "the Helper of the Leader of the Faithful", a ruler loyal to the tradition of the Abbasid caliphate. One reason for this bold assertion was the restricted authority that Iltutmish possessed, hemmed in as he was by powerful courtiers and critical Sufis. The latter now increasingly intervened in politics whenever they were unimpressed by the sultanate's expression of piety.

The era of the Delhi slave sultans could have been cut short in 1221, when Genghiz Khan was only dissuaded from a full-scale invasion of India by the appearance of a unicorn: it told a member of his bodyguard that the khan should return at once to Mongolia. Yelu Chucai, his secretary-astrologer, informed Genghiz Khan how the green-coloured creature was a symbol of peace and its warning against further bloodshed should be heeded. Some argue that this Qidan adviser merely played on the khan's superstitious nature. Others accept the genu-ineness of Yelu Chucai's interpretation of the event, because he sacrificed on the spot where the unicorn had appeared. Genghiz Khan himself was never entirely at the mercy of oracles or signs, so the thrust into north-western India may have been no more than a probing raid. Whatever the motives involved, the Mongols abandoned a plan to return home by fighting their way through northern India and across Tibet.

During the fourteenth century Islam spread across much of the subcontinent. Two Delhi sultans in particular were responsible for this happening: Khalaji and Tughluq. The former declared himself sultan in 1296. Called Sikander Sani, "the Second Alexander", Ala al-Din Khalaji stopped the Mongol raids and reduced to vassal status the Hindu rulers of Rajasthan, Andra and Karnataka. But this rapid extension of authority did little more than add states to Delhi's existing tributary network, the

The Qutb Minar in Delhi, built by the Ghurids about 1199

One of the temples at Khajuraho, where Ibn Battuta
found Moslems studying yoga

usual method of Moslem control. Most of the defeated kings were left in
place, after their treasuries had been emptied. Much more determined was
Tughluq, the son of a slave-soldier in Khalaji's service: whereas Khalaji
had been content with loot, Tughluq sought to extend sovereignty.

After Khalaji's son was killed by his favourite slave, a convert from
a low-caste Hindu family, order was restored by an able soldier named
Ghazi Malik, the son of a Turkish slave and a Hindu mother. Urged
by the Moslem nobles in Delhi to ascend the throne, under the title of

Ghiyath al-Din Tughluq Shah, he founded a new dynasty, the Tughluqids. An early death in 1325 led to the accession of his son Muhammad ibn Tughluq, who moved the court to Daulatabad on the Deccan to expand his empire southwards. With the aid of Sufis, he tried to persuade the Deccani Indians to convert to Islam because he wished to combine in his own person religous with secular authority. Frustration over their reluctance to embrace the Moslem faith may have forced him to return to Delhi, although the strain on the sultanate was obvious well before Muhammad's death in 1351.

The second shift of the capital resulted in many Moslems being left behind on the Deccan, where they were to set up autonomous states. Even in Delhi the policies of the Tughluqids became the subject of heated debate, especially the effort made by Muhammad to enlarge the Moslem community through mass conversion. Critics held that the sole guarantee of continued Turkish dominance in India was ethnic exclusiveness. To stifle this criticism, grants of extra land were awarded to the aristocracy and exemption was given from paying certain taxes. Thus the Tughluqid sultanate secured a longer lease of life, but it had to pay a heavy price for its aristocratic support. When Tamerlane's army descended on Delhi in 1398, it lacked sufficient authority to marshal an adequate defence, even though it took another fifteen years to come to an end, with the death of the last Tughluqid sultan in 1412.

The Morrocan traveller Ibn Battuta suggests one reason for a return to repressive measures directed against Hinduism. On a visit to Khajuraho, a centre of Hindu as well as Jain worship not far from present-day Jansi on the Deccan, he discovered Moslems studying yoga. He tells us how

> near temples, which contain idols that have been mutilated by the Moslems, live a number of yogis whose matted locks have grown as long as their bodies. And on account of extreme asceticism they are all yellow in colour. Many Moslems attend these men in order to take lessons from them.

Such a blatant interest in Indian beliefs could not but worry the Delhi sultanate, concerned as it was for the purity of Islam as well as its own prospects of survival.

Idn Battuta has left us a portrait of Muhammad ibn Tughluq, whom he knew from his time as a judge in Delhi. Ibn Battuta writes that

> of all men he was addicted to the making of gifts and the shedding of blood. His gate is never without some poor man enriched or

some living man executed, and there are well-known stories of his generosity and courage and of his cruelty and violence towards criminals. For all that, he is of all men the most humble and the readiest to show fairness and to acknowledge the right. The ceremonies of religion are strictly complied with at his court, and he is severe in the matter of attendance at prayer and in punishing those who neglect it.

Only the generosity of Muhammad saved Ibn Battuta from his creditors. "Three sacks of money" were required to repay what he had borrowed from merchants to cover his travelling expenses, a gift purchased for the sultan, and the cost of his stay in Delhi. Even though he received a good salary as a judge, Ibn Battuta found that it was insufficient for his needs.

The Hindu and Buddhist Kingdoms

Two new Hindu powers arose to oppose the further expansion of Islam in the subcontinent. Both replaced states previously ravaged by Moslem arms, an experience that strengthened a will to defend Hinduism. They were situated in Karnataka and Orissa, where their rulers sought to strengthen this faith by raising great temples dedicated to patron deities. Most successful in resisting Islam was the southern kingdom of Vijayanagara, literally "the City of Victory", founded at the behest of a devotee of Shiva, the awesome god of destruction. "Out of fear of Shiva," a medieval text runs, "the wind blows, out of fear the sun shines, out of fear fire and the king of heaven rush to their work." But as Nataraja, "king of the dancers", Shiva appears as a less frightful deity. Elegant bronze statues from southern India reveal his role as a cosmic saviour. Shiva is shown encircled by a ring of flames, the vital processes of universal creation, and with one leg raised he stands upon a tiny figure crouching on a lotus. This dwarfish demon represents human ignorance, the delusions that must be overcome through wisdom to escape from the bondage of the world. In one of his four hands Shiva holds a drum, the sign of speech, the source of revelation and tradition; his second hand offers blessing and sustenance; in the palm of his third hand a tongue of fire is a reminder of destruction; and the fourth hand points downward to the uplifted foot, already saved from the power of delusion. His pose here signifies the refuge available to Shiva's devotees through asceticism.

South Indian bronze of Shiva Nataraja, "king of the dancers"

Although the kings of Vijayanagara never overlooked this aspect of the great Hindu god, their main concern was the assistance that Shiva could provide them in dealing with the Bahami sultanate, a Moslem state on the Deccan that threatened to overrun the whole of southern India. Vijayanagara was at the zenith of power and splendour in the first half of the sixteenth century, when the impressive temples and elephant stables still standing today at the village of Hampi were erected.

According to tradition, the first Vijayanagara king Harihara and his brother Bukka were encouraged to look upon Shiva as a supernatural ally by the renowned teacher and ascetic Vidyaranya. The brothers were lapsed Moslems, having converted on their recruitment to Tughluq's forces. Vidyaranya is said to have persuaded them to rescue Shiva and the other Hindu gods languishing under Moslem rule. Quite likely the kingdom was called Vidyanagara for a time in honour of the sage before it became known as Vijayanagara. Notwithstanding the piety of the Vijayanagara kings, which was demonstrated in the fine temples that they raised within the walls of their capital, they were still willing to employ Moslem mercenaries and allow them to train their Hindu troops in new techniques of warfare. One of them went so far as to construct mosques for the benefit of the Moslem fighters garrisoned there. When around 1520 the Portuguese traveller, Domingo Paes, visited Vijayanagara he was amazed to observe this religious tolerance. He goes on to describe the city

> as large as Rome and very beautiful to the sight. There are many canals that bring water right into Vijayanagara, and in places there are lakes. The palace of the king, which is larger than the castle at Lisbon, is close to a palm grove and other richly bearing fruit trees. Below the Moorish quarter there is river . . . and along its bank fruit trees growing so closely together that they look like a thick forest.

Work on Hindu temples continued after the fall of the city in 1565, following a defeat inflicted on the Vijayanagara army at Talikota by combined forces of the Moslem rulers of Bijapur, Ahmadnagar and Golkanda. It has been suggested that the elephant stables at Vijayanagara were a mosque, Hindu craftsmen adapting their temple-building traditions to the needs of Islam. Some support for this idea comes from the mosque built later at Bijapur, because the stables' seven circular vaults could well be the prototypes of this mosque's unusual array of domes.

Temple band from Vijayanagara

The Kailasanatha temple at Kanchipuram, the Pallava capital

Long before the defeat at Talikota, Vijayanagara had become the last bastion of Hinduism in India. The Tamil dynasties of the Pallavas, Pandyas and Cholas had already passed away, but not before Indian concepts were transmitted to Southeast Asia. The first important southern dynasty was that of the Pallavas, whose kings converted from Buddhism to the worship of Shiva in the seventh century. So deeply rooted was Buddhism in southern India that the speed of the Hindu revival was quite unexpected. The great Chinese pilgrim Xuan Zhang had studied Buddhist scriptures there shortly before the Pallava conversion. Afterwards Pallava temple construction standardised the architectural approach of Tamil kings and also influenced those built in Cambodia as well as Indonesia. It looks as though the Kailasanatha temple, built about 700 in the Pallava capital of Kancipuram, acted as the model for Angkor. From the Pallavas the medieval Cambodians and Indonesians got the idea that sparks of the infinite, nothing less than a divine essence, were incarnate in their kings.

About 900, the Chola king Aditya conquered the Pallava kingdom to the north and, shortly afterwards, his son took Madurai, the capital of the Pandyas to the south, and then went on to invade Sri Lanka. This island virtually passed under Chola control, as did the eastern coastline of India all the way to Bengal. About 1025 a devastating Chola raid was launched against the Burmese kingdom of Pegu and not long afterwards another struck Srivijaya, a Hindu-inspired state on the island of Sumatra. These seaborne expeditions are testimony of a formidable navy that turned the Bay of Bengal into a Chola lake, until overstretch allowed the resurgent Pandyas to eclipse the Cholas in the twelfth century. The present-day temple city of Madurai remains dominated by the four gigantic gate-towers belonging to a complex dedicated to Shiva. This is a comparatively recent construction though, the original Pandya temple with fourteen towers having been razed to the ground by the Moslem invasion of 1310. Madurai had been seized and brought for a time under the control of the Khalaji Sultanate after the intervention of Delhi forces at the request of one of two warring Pandyan princes. It was a prime example of an older Hindu centre of authority in the subcontinent being obliterated by Moslem horsemen, which left behind a vacuum that was soon filled by the able fighters who established Vijayanagara.

Madurai's replacement temple was still incomplete three centuries later. One myth seeks to locate this earlier temple's foundation in the caste system, when it claims that Indra came to the site after his defeat of Vritra. This great deed in the perpetual struggle between the gods and the demons overthrew the tyranny of Vritra, a drought-serpent that had swallowed the cosmic waters and lay in coils on the mountains. By splitting open the serpent's belly with a thunderbolt, Indra ended a crippling drought, much to the delight of the gods until they discovered that Vritra was a brahmin. A distressed Indra apparently recovered his composure beside "a pond of golden water lilies", the tank of the Madurai temple. Chola championing of Shiva worship was actively continued by the Pandyas, one of whose kings rid the city of Madurai of Jains by impaling the heads of 8,000 ascetics outside that god's temple. Tamil tradition recounts the desecration of Vishnu temples too, but the main Pandya targets were usually Jain and Buddhist shrines.

In Sri Lanka the religious differences between Hindu southern India and Sinhalese Buddhism inflamed Chola aggression. During the last Chola invasion of 993, the ancient capital of Anuradhapura was subjected to systematic destruction by the invaders. The Cholas moved the

The standing Buddha at the Gal Vihara rock temple, Polonnaruva

capital to Polonnaruva, some 100 kilometres to the southeast, but from the ruins it would seem that this new settlement acted primarily as a ceremonial centre. King Vijayabuhu, who united Sri Lanka in resistance to the Cholas in the 1060s, was crowned in Anuradhapura but made Polonnaruva his own capital when he restored the Sinhalese monarchy. The Polonnaruva kings were at first allies, and then enemies, of the Pandyas, who repeated the Chola invasion of Sri Lanka.

After the collapse of the Polonnaruva kingdom, Sri Lanka suffered further invasion. In 1247 a Buddhist ruler ousted from the Malayan peninsula overran the northern part of the island, until he was in turn ejected by the Pandyas. Once again it became a dependency of the

Pandyan empire. But the Moslem capture of Madurai destroyed the Pandyas, their capital briefly becoming a Moslem sultanate. During this upheaval an independent Tamil kingdom arose in northern Sri Lanka at Jaffna, whence cinnamon was exported by a large merchant fleet. By the arrival of the Portuguese in 1505, the Sinhalese kingdom of Kotte, centred near modern Colombo, had united nearly all of Sri Lanka. But the construction of a Portuguese fort there meant the end of independence for the Kotte kings, the last of whom, the Catholic convert Dharmapala, was forcibly moved to this stronghold. When he died in 1597, its Portuguese governor claimed that Dharmapala had bequeathed his kingdom to the Portuguese crown.

The Mughal Empire

Tamerlane's sack of Delhi ended the first Moslem era in northern India that began in the 1200s with the slave sultans. It was followed by Afghan and Mughal rule until the early eighteenth century, when the Mughal emperor Aurangzeb subdued nearly all of the subcontinent. His conquests were to be undermined by the Marathas, a confederacy of warring clans inspired by Hindu warrior traditions in western India. Ironically, the Marathas themselves succumbed first to the rule of the English East India Company through the victories of Arthur Wellesley at Assaye and Argaum in 1803, half a century before the last Mughal emperor was dethroned.

After his Indian campaign, Tamerlane added war elephants to his army and defeated the Ottomans at Ankara in 1402. Europe feared that Tamerlane's pursuit of glory would lead to an immediate invasion, as word spread of the assembling of a fleet in Black Sea ports, but instead the insatiable Central Asian conqueror turned east and died on the Chinese frontier. Tamerlane's blood had hardly turned cold when the internecine conflict he predicted broke out. From this constant jostling for position among the Turkish tribes there emerged the Mughal empire, founded by Zahir-ud-din Muhammad Babur between 1526 and 1530. He had invaded northen India and overthrown the Lodhis, the only Afghan dynasty to rule from Delhi. Under Babur's successors the Mughal empire brought Moslem civilisation to its climax in India. In his journal, Babur sadly wrote that this country has

> few charms. Its people have no good looks or manners, no character or genius . . . no nobility or chivalry. In arts and crafts

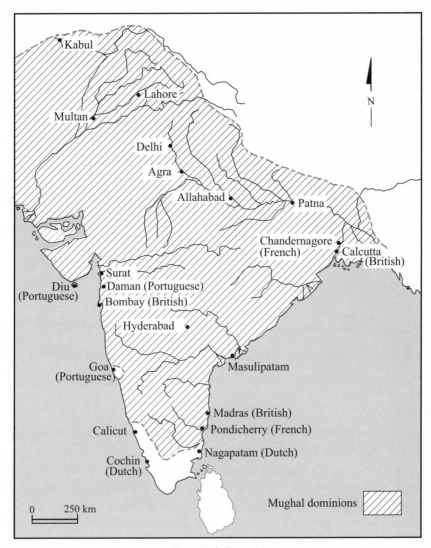

Kabul

Lahore

Multan

Delhi

Agra

Allahabad

Patna

Chandernagore
(French)

Calcutta
(British)

Surat
Diu
(Portuguese)
Daman (Portuguese)
Bombay (British)

Hyderabad

Goa
(Portuguese)

Masulipatam

Madras (British)
Calicut
Pondicherry (French)

Cochin
(Dutch)
Nagapatam (Dutch)

N

0   250 km

Mughal dominions

The Mughal empire

there is no regularity . . . There are no good horses, no good dogs, no grapes . . . or first-rate fruits, no ice or cold water, no good bread or cooked food in the bazaars, no baths, no schools, no candles, no torches or candlesticks . . . Except large rivers . . . there is no running water either in their gardens or residences, which possess no elegance in design.

India's saving grace were "masses of gold and silver" and the "innumerable and endless workmen of every kind" who were organised

Indo-Islamic decoration at Fatehpur Sikri, Akbar's new city
30 kilometres from Agra

by "a fixed caste so that the work of the father is always followed by the son". For Babur good government meant well-fortified cities, full granaries and a treasury overflowing with tribute. All the Mughal emperors subscribed to the same view, even pugnacious Aurangzeb, who dreamed of an India full of prosperous Moslems, rather than abject Hindu poverty. But on his deathbed he admitted an inability to reduce the hordes of beggars.

For the Mughal emperors were confronted in India by a dilemma for which there was no readily available Islamic solution. The Moslem faith remained a minority religion in every part of the subcontinent, and the nature of Hinduism made it unlikely that this situation would ever change. So Jalal ud-din Muhammad Akbar, Babur's grandson and the third Mughal emperor, realised that he would have to set the interests of state above those of Islam in legitimising his rule. Previous Moslem dynasties governed their unconverted subjects by means of naked force: they had gained neither their affection nor active support. So Akbar married the daughter of a Rajput ruler, whose father like other leading Rajputs were indifferent towards Akbar's religious beliefs. It did not worry his Hindu father-in-law that Akbar sponsored debates among spokesmen of different religions, nor that he restricted the power of Moslem clerics, many of whom the emperor thought were corrupt. Even more radical was Akbar's abolition of the tax traditionally levied on non-Moslem subjects.

Akbar's brilliant courtier, Abu al-Fadl, encouraged the emperor in his own reinterpretation of Islam. A prophetic halo was now believed to adorn the emperor's head. Abu al-Fadl himself took a conciliatory attitude towards Hinduism, which manifested itself in the Indo-Islamic style of architecture at Fatehpur Sikri, Akbar's newly built capital near Agra. There the emperor demonstrated his own piety by sweeping the floor of the mosque and occasionally leading prayers, actions that failed to impress Jahangir, Akbar's son by the Rajput princess. This prince even had Abu al-Fadl assassinated in 1602, three years before Akbar died.

Yet the aura surrounding Akbar was akin to divinity. He was credited with remarkable powers of healing besides the ability to control the waters in both rivers and clouds, so much so that European visitors reported how the emperor was "learned in all kinds of sorcery". As a result, Mughal historians have tended to overlook Akbar's faults, especially a determination to have his way in all matters, plus ownership

Some of the monumental buildings at Fatehpur Sikri

195

of a harem 5,000 strong. In addition, he had more than 300 wives through marriages he contracted when making political alliances. Yet it has to be recognised that these marriages to non-Moslem princesses, though pursued for political ends, had a considerable influence on his own attitude to Indian society as a whole. Such marriage alliances also gave an altogether different complexion to his efforts at territorial expansion, so that Akbar ceased to be regarded by Hindus as a foreign adventurer like other Moslem dynasts before him.

Akbar's religious tolerance was later condemned as an attempt to establish a new, composite faith that would embrace elements from all Indian beliefs. Akbar had stopped the slaughter of cows, attended court with a Hindu ritual mark on his forehead, worshipped the sun in Parsee fashion and heard Catholic masses. Such a width of belief seems quite

The Mughal emperor Jahangir looking at a portrait
of his father, the great Akbar

exceptional today, but at this time there existed a considerable overlap of religious points of view, with the notable exception of Christianity.

In Hinduism, the bhakti movement encouraged the notion that through simple devotion a worshipper could, at the end of his or her life, achieve union of some kind with the deity. Even though this approach can be traced as far back as Arjuna's humble adoration of Krishna, bhakti first became a major force in southern India during the early medieval period. There, Tamil devotees of Shiva had declared how this god resided in the hearts of all those who fixed their minds on him in loving devotion. Others looked to Vishnu, and especially at Srirangam, a temple town with six encircling walls. Once each month from the inner enclosure, the enormous temple chariot is still pulled round its streets. At noon, when about three-quarters of the procession is completed, the two pulling ropes are put down and the curtains drawn in front of the cult statue, those who cannot take part in pulling the temple chariot, for reasons of health or age, come and touch the ropes lying on the ground, which transforms the occasion into a communal event very unlike brahmin-controlled rituals. It is a reminder that here Vishnu's worship involves a personal relationship between the deity and the devotee, whatever their caste.

A similar impulse appears to have persuaded the Sufi saint Hasan Teli of the futility of established Moslem rites. Living in the Punjab, this contemporary of Akbar rejected pilgrimage as well as communal prayer. Hasan Teli maintained that they were unnecessary when a believer truly worshipped the Ka'ba one hundred times a day from the bottom of the heart. Thus the rejection of externals was applied to Hindu as well as Moslem practices, since in both they were seen as a hindrance to the personal experience of true belief. Neither Hindu image worship nor the daily cycle of Moslem prayer satisfied a deeper spiritual need.

An obvious product of religious convergence was the new creed of Sikhism. According to the first Sikh guru Nanak, who died three years before Akbar came to the throne in 1556, there was every reason to combine the best elements of Hinduism and Islam. Nanak was a strict monotheist and a determined opponent of caste, preaching the equality of all mankind and declaring that everyone could obtain liberation of the spirit through devotion and contemplation. In an ultimate sense his deity remains unknowable, formless and eternal, but Nanak insisted that observation of the divine presence in everything offers the means of salvation to those who are prepared to open their eyes. Often though Sikhism is associated with beards, turbans and valour, its essential core

Shah Jahan, creator of the Peacock Throne and
the Taj Mahal

remains the patient meditation upon "the One God". Nanak ensured
the survival of this belief by gathering a band of followers near Lahore
and before his death nominating a second guru. The word Sikh means
"disciple", one who has left behind the trammels of traditional worship.
Possibly because Sikhism was established at this rare moment of religious
equipoise in India, it was never felt necessary to proselytise.

But this great transformation had no influence on Akbar's son
and the next Mughal emperor Salim Jahangir. Despite his hatred for
Abu al-Fadl, Jahangir ignored religion altogether, allowing three of his
nephews to become Christians. There was even a splendid procession
through the streets of Agra on the day of their baptism. Jahangir himself
was described by François Bernier, a French physician, as someone who
"died, as he had lived, destitute of all belief ". A fondness for pork and
wine was always at its strongest during the fasting month of Ramadan.

The suggestion that Khurram Shah Jahan, his son and successor,
demolished Christian churches and forbade marriages with non-Moslems

in reaction to this laxity cannot be discounted, but this thrustful prince was at odds with his father before Jahangir died in 1627. Shah Jahan always wanted his own way, as had Jahangir, who had rebelled against Akbar. Quarrels within the imperial family were to trouble the Mughal empire throughout its existence, Shah Jahan's imprisonment at the end of his life was perhaps the most famous example of the conflict between fathers and sons.

Although Shah Jahan was a capable commander who maintained the aggressive military pressure of his predecessors along the empire's borders, his reign is remembered for the luxury that crippled the imperial treasury and led to his deposition. The Venetian adventurer Niccolao Manucci has left this description of his court:

> The throne on which Shah Jahan was seated stood in front of, and near to the women's quarters, so that as soon he came out of the

Shah Jahan's tribute to Mumtaz-Mahal, the famous Taj Mahal

door he reached it. The throne looks like a table, adorned with all sorts of precious stones and flowers in enamel and gold. Around the throne, at a distance of one pace, are railings of gold . . . within which no one may enter except the ruler's sons.

One of Shah Jahan's extravagances was this Peacock Throne, a jewel encrusted seat whose finest ruby "worth a million rupees" was a present from the Safavid ruler Shah Abbas. Millions were spent on the decoration, which took its name from two peacocks with "outspread wings that were studied with jewels of every description".

The ornamented throne was but part of the emperor's determination to put his stamp on Mughal India, or rather on its art and architecture. Substantial alterations were made to existing buildings at Agra and Lahore for the benefit of the imperial family; an entirely new capital named Shahjahanabad was laid out at Dehli, despite there being

The Taj Mahal viewed from the Agra Fortress, where Shah Jahan spent his final years as a prisoner

no reason to quit Agra other than Shah Jahan's desire to emulate his grandfather Akbar; in Kashmir the Shalimar Gardens already boasted an unprecedented array of trees, flowers and waterways; and, on the death of his favourite wife Mumtaz-Mahal, construction began on her mausoleum, the Taj Mahal. Fussing over the latter, Shah Jahan would visit the site and try to gauge the quality of the work. When he asked a stonemason, who was cutting with great care a piece of marble, exactly what he was doing, the workman replied to the emperor's satisfaction: "I am building the Taj Mahal, old man, and if I keep answering idle questions I shall never be able to finish the most beautiful monument on earth."

Mumtaz-Mahal, "Most Exquisite of the Palace", died in childbirth at the age of thirty-eight in 1631, four years after Shah Jahan ascended the throne. She had given him fourteen children, including his deposer Aurangzeb. Serious illness provided the opportunity that this seventh child seized to become emperor in 1658. Once Shah Jahan took to his bed, a power struggle between his sons plunged the Mughal empire into a bloody civil war during which Aurangzeb overcame his opponents in turn and then compelled Shah Jahan to surrender, after the water supply was cut off to the fort at Agra where the ailing emperor was staying: afterwards Shah Jahan was imprisoned there until his death in 1666. The various titles of the usurper were largely disregarded by Aurangzeb's subjects, who simply called him Alamgir, "Seizer of the Universe". It probably explains his absence from Shah Jahan's funeral, when his father was quietly buried alongside his beloved wife in the Taj Mahal.

To ease his conscience, Aurangzeb patronised Islamic learning and imposed a strict version of the faith at court. Ornament was proscribed as well as music and poetry: the emperor seems to have spent most of his time off the battlefield copying the Qu'ran, something he achieved twice. An attempt to subdue southern India and enforce conversion backfired so badly that by Aurangzeb's death, in 1707, the Mughal empire was a shadow of its former self. One of the largest Asian powers in medieval times, its population still exceeded 100 millions but the grip that its rulers had previously kept on a network of client states was now less firm. After yet another succession crisis caused by the rivalry of Aurangzeb's sons, the eldest was finally acknowledged as Emperor Bahadur Shah. Rebellions were soon to accelerate Mughal decline, the first of which was started by the Sikhs, who sought to avenge the deaths of Govind Singh's two youngest sons. He was the tenth Sikh guru. Unable to obtain redress from Bahadur Shah, whom Govind Singh had supported in his struggle for the throne, the Sikhs overran the Punjab and defeated in a pitched battle the forces sent against them. Mughal reinforcements pushed the Sikh rebels from the plains, but they had no chance of ending in the hills a guerrilla war that was sustained by wide popular support. Fighting was still going on in 1712, when Bahadur Shah died at the age of seventy.

Another war of succession left his weakest son Jahandar Shah without any authority at all. Unable to do anything, the new Mughal emperor drank heavily with his favourite concubine Lal Kunwar. Their indulgence meant that unpaid soldiers refused to march against the inevitable rebellion. In desperation, the palace was stripped of its finery as precious cups, jewels, even wall decorations were put on sale. Anarchy ensued. The elevation of yet another puppet emperor ruler in 1719 did nothing for Mughal morale, and outlying provinces and subject rulers asserted their independence. So vulnerable did the Mughals become that in 1739–40 a Persian army captured Delhi, looted the city, slaughtered its inhabitants and carried off the Peacock Throne. Despite their loss of power, the prestige of the Mughal emperors lived on in the imitation of their ways at other Indian courts, since palaces and gardens in the Mughal style appeared in Hindu as well as Moslem states. And in 1857 the last Mughal emperor was still thought important enough to legitimise the Indian Mutiny.

European Rivalry

Trade was the motive power behind European penetration of medieval South Asia. The first to arrive were the Portuguese in 1498, when Vasco da Gama sailed to Calicut in southwestern India via the cape of Good Hope. There, anti-Moslem sentiment among the Portuguese got the better of common sense and they worshipped at a Hindu temple a goddess said to be the Virgin Mary, in part because no sign of Islam was in evidence. The religious fanaticism of the Portuguese, whose own sense of identity had been largely shaped in a struggle against Islam, introduced a new dimension to international commerce when they transferred to Asian waters the warfare of the Mediterranean. Arab and Chinese records speak of the hazards of the sea, of storms and shipwrecks, but they are silent about physical force other than brushes with pirates. What the Portuguese brought with them was the notion of exclusive rights to maritime trade, something quite alien to Asian commerce.

Vasco da Gama, the first European admiral to reach India by sea in 1498

For Portuguese belligerence received the support of successive popes as a continuation of the Crusades. In 1502, King Manuel of Portugal told the ruler of Calicut that all Moslems should be expelled from his kingdom, as they were the enemies of Christ. Then it seemed a not unreasonable demand because the Portuguese met little naval opposition in the Indian Ocean. The Chinese empire had turned its back on the sea, while Egypt, Persia and Vijayanagara were without navies. And this stroke of good luck was continued with the foundation of the Mughal empire, a land-based power uninterested in the sea. Emperor Akbar responded with puzzlement when he stood on a beach and first saw waves.

In desperation at the Portuguese seizure of the spice trade, the most profitable of all commercial ventures in Europe, Venice requested that the Mamluk sultan of Egypt should ensure that the routes through the Red Sea were kept open. In no position to do so himself, the sultan asked the pope to intervene on pain of Egyptian harassment of Christians and the destruction of sacred sites in Jerusalem. Not until the Ottomans had conquered Egypt and extended their power to the Persian Gulf in the 1540s would the Portuguese become stretched at sea. By then there was a chain of fortresses to sustain the authority of the Estado da India, "the State of India", the name by which the Portuguese knew their Asian empire. Its headquarters was Goa, a Moslem stronghold that fell in 1510 to the second viceroy Alfonso de Albuquerque. Even though he was thwarted in an attack on Aden three years later, Albuquerque secured control over much of the spice trade by fortifying Hormuz, an island at the entrance to the Persian Gulf, establishing an enclave at Diu in Gujarat, and finally capturing Malacca with a fleet of seventeen ships.

In India, however, the Portuguese were most concerned about Aurangzeb, even though his drive southwards threatened trade but not the existence of Goa itself, because no Mughal emperor could afford to provoke the Portuguese into blocking pilgrim ships sailing to Arabia. More serious for the Estado da India was the advent of the Dutch, whose quarrel with Spain encompassed Portugal for the reason that from 1580 until 1640 the two countries were temporarily united under the Habsburgs.

The Dutch blockaded Goa for eight years, and even harassed ships sailing from Lisbon. Merchants' losses mounted and commercial traffic hitherto centred on Goa migrated to other Indian ports, mostly outside Portuguese control. The situation was made worse by the loss of Hormuz, although the Estado da India held on to Muscat. But Portuguese naval patrols from Muscat found it impossible to control shipping in the Strait of Hormuz after 1622. The Dutch did not easily wrest control of the spice trade from the Portuguese, who fought hard to defend their stake in Asian commerce. Despite having a foundry in Goa, Portuguese guns were inferior to Dutch cannons. At Trincomalee, the Portuguese fort dominating its fine harbour was taken in 1639 after a bombardment made a wide breach in the walls. Unable to resist Dutch firepower, the Portuguese grip on Sri Lanka was steadily loosened: by 1652 the Dutch ruled a considerable territory and had gained control of the trade in cinnamon.

Quite unexpected by the Dutch was the extent of intermarriage between the Portuguese and the Sinhalese. They discovered that men of mixed descent had fought alongside the Portuguese in large numbers and were partly responsible for the prolonged resistance to Dutch arms. Perturbed though they were by the power of the Catholic priesthood, their Calvinist outlook was most offended by Buddhism, the island's traditional religion. The Dutch harried Portuguese priests, with the result that many of them left, but they stopped short of attacking Buddhist beliefs. Johan Maetsuyker, the governor-general, made the best of the situation by following the Portuguese practice of integration. He encouraged Dutch settlers to marry Asian women, arguing that their children would be better acclimatised than those born of European parents. But Maetsuyker's colonial experiment foundered because those who served in the garrison were German, Scandinavian, French and English mercenaries, rather than Dutch men. Additionally there was the aloofness of senior Dutch officials, whose superior attitude would culminate in apartheid. In Java, where the Dutch were to establish a permanent presence, there were soon severe penalties for Dutch settlers who married Malay girls.

Although they had European and Indian competitors, the Dutch met no determined opposition in India, where a trading post was established as early as 1606. From there cloth went eastwards to the Indonesian archipelago, China and Japan, and westwards to Europe and the West Indies. Southeast Asian markets accounted for an overwhelming proportion of the total trade in Indian textiles, because the Dutch used cloth as a medium of exchange for spices. Dutch business in Gujarat, an established textile centre, rested almost entirely on spices. The principal

A street in Goa, from 1510 onwards the headquarters of the Portugese in Asia

ones sold there in the port of Surat, and farther inland at Agra, where the Dutch had an outlet close to the Mughal court, were cloves, nutmeg and mace. The willingness of the Moslem aristocracy to pay inflated prices for cheaply procured Indonesian spices baffled Dutch merchants, who considered lowering prices to widen the market until they realised there was a danger of other traders buying them for re-export to Europe.

To the English East India Company, the conduct of the Dutch looked similar to the earlier Portuguese attempt to monopolise Asian commerce. Three wars were fought in European waters before it was accepted in 1674 that neither the English nor the Dutch could decisively prevail. They simply had to tolerate each other on the high seas.

First the Portuguese, then the Dutch, had developed the idea of a fortified settlement as a haven for shipping. Whereas the Portuguese forts concentrated on taxing seaborne traffic, those of the Dutch were used to dominate local trade, in particular the production and distribution of spices. In the case of the English, the commitment to fortified settlements was slow to evolve and had much to do with the decline of Mughal power. Situated in close proximity to the area disputed by the Mughals and the Marathas, Bombay could not be left without adequate defences. This settlement had been ceded by Portugal in 1661 as part of Charles II's marriage settlement. Yet the king's Portuguese queen, Catherine of Braganza, brought more than the island of Bombay with her to England, as her taste for tea set a fashion that would transform the English East India Company into the world's greatest trader.

The problems experienced by English merchants were complicated by the Mughal–Maratha conflict. Hardly surprising then was the view of Bombay governor Charles Boone, who said in 1718 that the threat of violence was essential: "no naval force no trade, if no fear no friendship". It was endorsed later by Robert Clive, the architect of France's defeat in India, where the English East India Company owed its triumph to the ripple effect of Anglo-French rivalry in Europe.

From Pondicherry, the administrative centre of France's trading posts in India, François Dupleix was only too pleased to intrigue with Indian rulers to undermine Madras, the nearby English settlement. The Muhgal ruler of Karnataka, Anwar-ud-din, urged both the French and the British to keep peace, sending in 1746 his son Muhfuz Khan with a 10,000-strong army to enforce his prohibition on fighting. On the bank of the Adyar river Muhfuz Khan encountered a French force comprising 230 Europeans and 700 Indians en route for Madras. When he tried to stop it, the French commander ordered his men to open fire: the decision was a turning point in colonial history because it demonstrated how successive volleys from a small but disciplined force could disperse a Mughal army.

All the European powers in Asia, from the Portuguese onwards, had attempted to compensate for their numerical weakness by recruiting local troops, but the French were the first to systematically train these recruits to fight in a European manner. After 1751 they supplied them with not only muskets but European officers as well. The lead was followed by the English East India Company, which in the process laid the foundation of the British Indian Army. Here was an inexhaustible reservoir of military manpower. As Field Marshal Slim commented after the Second World War, victory over the Imperial Japanese Army in Burma had been achieved by "an army that was largely Asian".

Having taken Madras, the French tried to capture Fort St. David as well. Situated closer to Pondicherry, the stronghold was defended by barely 300 men, but among them was Dupleix's nemesis, the twenty-one-year-old Robert Clive, who had escaped Madras and been granted an ensign's commission on his arrival. To aid the beleaguered fortress Anwar-ud-din sent 2,500 men, who were sufficient to oblige the French to retire to Pondicherry. Dupleix realised that he had to come to terms with the Mughals and, with the plunder taken at Madras, he was able

Bombay became English in 1661 as a result of Charles II's marriage
to Catherine of Braganza

to bribe Anwar-ud-din to abandon the English. He even allowed the Mughal flag to be hoisted over Madras for one week.

Peace in Europe officially ended hostilities in India but not Dupleix's intrigues. So successful were they in southern India that the English East India Company sanctioned action against France's Indian allies. Although Clives's intervention on the battlefield decisively checked French influence and caused the recall of Dupleix to Paris, the military expenditure cut deeply into company profits, as it was not yet realised how the China trade could sustain its activities in India. Tea had still to become the commodity in highest demand: it would increase one hundredfold in value from £8,000 in 1701 to £848,000 in 1774, almost all of which was consumed in Britain and its American colonies.

Soon Clive was called upon to deal with another crisis in Bengal, where the Mughal governor Siraj-ud-daula believed that the work being undertaken by the English on fortifications at Calcutta and by the French on theirs at Chandernagore was aimed against him. Not waiting to discover that these settlements were getting ready for another Anglo-French conflict, Siraj-ud-daula captured Calcutta, where in 1756 the notorious "Black Hole" permanently blackened his reputation. Within a year Clive had restored the situation and for good measure expelled the

The British stronghold at Madras

Robert Clive with the Great Mughal, shortly after the battle of Plassey

French from Chandernagore. Less fighting probably occurred during his defeat of Siraj-ud-daula at Plassey than in any other eighteenth-century battle, for the issue was determined by an attack late in the day on the Bengali camp. Much time had been taken up by an exchange of artillery fire and, believing after a downpour that the English would undertake no further action that afternoon, Siraj-ud-daula's soldiers began moving back to camp. Seeing the chance to advance, Clive led his troops forward at the double and, fearing for his life, Siraj-ud-daula disappeared on a fast camel. Once again a small Anglo-Indian army had routed a larger Indian opponent, in all probability 30,000 strong.

The fall of Siraj-ud-daula made the English East India Company dominant in Bengal. In southern India the French were also discomfited at the battle of Wandiwash, where the English commander Eyre Coote achieved a second Plassey. Better discipline ended France's ambitions of empire in India, for, without relief from the sea, Pondicherry surren-dered in 1761. Clive retired to England a rich man, an achievement that encouraged others to try their fortune in India. The British government was never happy with the enrichment of English East India Company officials but so valuable was its trade to the national economy that their trials in London tended to end in acquittal.

Arthur Wellesley about to be unhorsed at Assaye in 1803

The British Triumph

Clive's successors in arms gradually expanded the power of Calcutta, now the permanent headquarters of the English East India Company in the subcontinent. If anything, the loss of the North American colonies redirected British imperial interests eastwards, where Lord Cornwallis found some compensation for his ignominious surrender at York-town. By shrewdly arranging for £500,000 to be paid each year to the Exchequer in London and maintaining an upright image in the United Kingdom, this governor-general got away with outright imperialism in India. It was the appointment in 1797 of Richard Wellesley, however, that really expanded the company's role beyond trade, despite his wars having to be financed by the sale of opium in China. India ought to be "ruled from a palace, not a counting house," he said, "with the ideas of a prince, not those of a retail trader in muslins and indigo".

Richard Wellesley was more than fortunate in having on hand his younger brother Arthur, who was commanding the 33rd Foot. Yet the international situation could not have then been worse for the British. They were at war with France as well as Holland and Spain; their last remaining ally, Austria, had just been defeated by the rising French general Bonaparte, and compelled to sign a separate peace treaty; while mutinies at the Nore and Spithead seemed to indicate that morale in the Royal Navy was breaking down. Undaunted by the threat of French intervention in Indian affairs, the new governor-general set about improving Calcutta and striking down those who defied its instructions. First of all, he conquered Mysore in southern India, long a thorn in the company's side. Then he sent Arthur Wellesley to deal with the Marathas. Though the French threat from Egypt was now less serious, Richard Wellesley was not alone in thinking that Napoleon might still try to invade India, either overland or by ship from the Red Sea. To Napoleon the subcontinent was always more than a British possession: in him it inspired a vision of conquest crowned by Asian wealth and splendour.

One reason for tackling the Marathas was that they were no longer seen with such alarm as they had been during the First Anglo-Maratha War of 1775–76. Richard Wellesley considered that the time had arrived for bringing their confederacy under Calcutta's control. In this aim he was inadvertently assisted by the British government, which directed him to expel the remaining French from India. As most of these soldiers of fortune were in Maratha employ, the directive gave the governor-general

A Calcutta street, with masts of trading ships indicating the city's purpose

211

scope to go to Baji Rao's aid. This nominal head of the Maratha confederacy had been ousted from Poona and his appeal to Calcutta delighted Richard Wellesley because Baji Rao was prepared not only to cede territory but also accept vassal status.

Marching from Madras, an expeditionary force under the command of Arthur Wellesley reached Poona without difficulty and reinstated Baji Rao. Besides improved logistics, its passage was smoothed by the absence of looting, an unheard-of occurrence in India whether the army on the march was friend or foe. Arthur Wellesley's Anglo-Indian army was more receptive to such an order than ever his British forces were during the Peninsular War. Near present-day Jafrabad, he caught up with the Marathas at the village of Assaye and gave battle with a much smaller army. The hard-fought victory here, and another at Argaum, established Britain as the major power in India. Arguably the Marathas might have fared better if they had relied upon their traditional hit-and-run cavalry tactics. By copying European infantry formations, they pitted themselves against English East India Company sepoys as well as British regulars.

A footnote to this triumph was the Vellore mutiny. That Richard Wellesley's displacement of so many Indian princes would cause trouble was not foreseen, in spite of change coming so quickly to such a large area of the subcontinent that it was bound to spread unease among the sepoys, who were jealous of their own beliefs and customs. When these soldiers were ordered to don a European-style uniform and shave off their beards, a mutiny broke out at Vellore in southern India. Most hated was the shako, a cylindrical hat with a peak and a leather cockade, because it was rumoured that dressing sepoys like British troops was the first step to making them become Christians. At Vellore in 1806 the sepoys suddenly attacked European soldiers stationed there, killing and wounding nearly 300 men. A few survivors held out in a bastion above the main gateway until a relief force arrived.

Afterwards it was considered that the Vellore mutiny was purely a military matter, but the incident had serious implications for British power: Indian officers as well as other ranks had responded to a prophecy that its end was at hand. When a Moslem sepoy warned that there was a plot to murder the Europeans in the garrison, his story was referred to a committee of officers, most of whom were sympathetic to the conspiracy. They reported that his allegation had no foundation, and the sepoy was jailed as a troublemaker. The most worrying aspect of the disturbance was the first mention of religion as a grievance, a factor that would reappear in the Indian Mutiny.

Medieval East Asia

Because filial piety and social duties prevent him from seeking solitude in the mountains, a virtuous person refreshes his spirit by taking imaginary journeys through a landscape painting in which the artist has combined the beauty, grandeur and silence of the natural world.

The Song artist Guo Xi

Tang and Song China

The sinicisation of the Central Asian rulers in north China left the way open for reunification. As did the Qin dynasty that first united the country as a single empire, the Sui began its reconquest in the northern provinces, only to fall itself within a few decades. And, once again, a subsequent imperial house built on the foundations it laid. Under the Tang emperors China experienced a cultural renaissance that reached its climax during the Song dynasty.

Notwithstanding his forbidding manner, the first Sui emperor Wen Di understood how military domination of the southern provinces would not alone restore unity: traditional beliefs must be revived, so imperial patronage was extended to both Daoism and Confucianism. By 595 examinations for civil service candidates were open to all again, except merchants; but examination questions were based exclusively on the Confucian curriculum, despite Wen Di's personal sympathy for Buddhism, because Confucianism provided the only available body of political theory and ritual precedents for running the state. Confucian learning was once again the passport to office and wealth, although the chief intellectual interest remained Buddhism, whose rapid development in China attracted monks from Korea and Japan.

Emperor Wen Di's awareness of the urgent need for unity was not shared by his son and successor, Yang Di, who was believed to have hastened his father's death in 604. His preoccupation with massive public works and successive foreign campaigns alienated the Chinese people, whose exhaustion was revealed in a series of peasant rebellions that began in 611. A shaken Yang Di ordered the empire back to peacetime pursuits, but his edict rang hollow in provinces already in rebel hands. In 617 Li Yuan, one of the most powerful Sui generals, captured the capital at the prompting of his able second son Li Shimin. "Follow the desire of the people, raise a righteous army," he advised, "and convert calamity into glory." Even though the assassination of Yang Di a year later gave the rebellious general scope to consolidate his position at Chang'an, the exceptional service rendered by Li Shimin in the struggle to secure the Tang dynasty provoked an immediate crisis. Rivalry with the heir apparent turned into a bloody feud that left Li Shimin's elder and younger brothers dead and his father dethroned.

The support of his own troops in the coup of 626 made the second Tang emperor, Tai Zong, or "Great Founder", very sensitive to dangers from the army, and led him to shift power from military to civil officials. He increased the number and frequency of civil service examinations and instituted a scholarship system to encourage learning, with the result that during his reign the imperial administration was taken over by professional bureaucrats recruited on the basis of personal talent and education. The rise of such men committed to a central government altered the position of the emperor. No longer was he just the chief aristocrat, whose pedigree might even be suspect, because with no aristocracy to challenge his authority and with a loyal bureaucracy, the imperial family became set apart from the people in quite a new way. That is why Tai Zong's chief minister Wei Zheng was so outspoken in

Sui bodhisattva. Though the first Sui emperor was a devout Buddhist, he also patronised Daoism and Confucianism

his dealings with the emperor. He realised that, without a revival of the traditional joint ruler–minister approach in decision making, there was a real danger of despotism.

The fame of Wei Zheng as an upright adviser was not unconnected with the relief that Confucian officials felt at a return to a fully bureaucratic system of government. Because Tai Zong was a very self-conscious ruler, a weapon that Wei Zheng was adept at using against his unwise policies was the judgement of posterity. In China it was customary from the Han empire onwards for specially appointed scholars to write an account of their times. As each document was composed, it was deposited in an iron-bound chest, which was to remain locked until the dynasty ceased to rule. Then the chest would be opened and the documents edited into "a veritable record". When Tai Zong asked about the possibility of examining the documents before they were deposited, he was respectfully fobbed off. Pressed again, one of the scholars said: "My duty of office is to uphold the brush, so how could I not record bad points? That is the reason they are never made available." Still worried about how the deaths of his brothers were being treated, the emperor seems to have asked Wei Zheng to intervene, and there is some evidence that sections of the dynastic history dealing with this distressing episode were rewritten.

The closeness of the emperor and his chief minister did not mean that their relationship was unstrained. Frustrated by Wei Zheng's refusal in 640 to endorse the expansion of Chinese influence in Central Asia, Tai Zong in a towering rage cried out, "I am going to have to kill that old country bumpkin!" Wei Zheng's daring independence rested on an unshakeable conviction that unnecessary foreign wars had ruined the Sui dynasty. Five years later, conflict with Korea turned into a disaster when a great blizzard caught the imperial army on its march home.

Remembering the prudent advice he had
always received, Tai Zong sadly said: "If
Wei Zheng were still alive, he would not
have allowed Us to do this."

But it was the openmindedness of
Tai Zong that inaugurated a unique
cultural flowering, an era of significant
artistic and intellectual advance. Quite
typical of the emperor's attitude was the
audience he gave to a Christian missionary. An inscription set up in the capital
at Chang'an records how a Nestorian
monk was welcomed by Tai Zong, who
listened carefully to what he had to say
and then opined:

Prostrating Tang official

> The Way has more than one name. There is more than one Sage.
> O Lopen, a man of great virtue, has brought images and books
> from afar to present them at the imperial capital. After examining
> his teachings, We find them profound and pacific, stressing what
> is good and important. This religion benefits all men. Let it be
> preached freely in Our empire.

The inclusive habit of mind in evidence here, coupled with Confucian
scepticism, tended to keep religion and a priesthood as minor elements
in Chinese society, so that religious persecution barely figures in the historical record. The severe, though short, repression of 845 can be seen
therefore as an attempt to prevent Buddhism from securing a strangle-
hold over China's economy. Its method was confiscation of property and
the compulsory laicisation of supernumerary monks and nuns.

Another pilgrim to whom Tai Zong granted a personal interview
was Xuan Zhang, on his return from India with Buddhist texts. Although
the emperor inclined to Daoism, he supported Confucianism for the
sake of the civil service, besides welcoming Buddhism and other foreign
faiths. The emperor intended to give Xuan Zhang only a few minutes'
audience, but he was so interested in the monk's account of the lands
through which he had passed that Tai Zong asked him to become his
adviser on Central Asian affairs. Reluctantly the emperor agreed that
Xuan Zhang could embark on his programme of translation in exchange
for a written account of his distant travels. At the end of his life Tai Zong

216

seems to turned to Xuan Zhang as a spiritual adviser, because the monk was with him when he died in 649.

Intrigue at court resulted in the ninth son of Tai Zong succeeding him as the emperor Gao Zong. Weak and prone to illness, Gao Zong was overshadowed by his empress, Wu Zhao. About this attractive and talented woman we can be sure of very little because, as the antithesis of the Confucian ideal, her involvement in public affairs received no sympathetic record at all. Yet Wu Zhao virtually ran China before her husband's death, and afterwards she pushed aside two of her sons before,

The pilgrim Xuan Zhang persuaded Emperor Gao Zong
to erect this pagoda at Chang'an as a library for Buddhist scriptures

in 690, becoming the only woman to don the yellow robe. Allowing for Confucian commentators' hatred of her usurpation, it is clear that Empress Wu was exceptionally gifted. A streak of cruelty created terror, but she was always careful to balance those who served her violent ends with talented administrators. Perhaps her most enduring claim to fame was introducing poetry in examinations for higher civil service qualifications. The subsequent poetical outpouring was block-printed in an anthology comprising 48,000 poems by no less than 2,200 authors.

Empress Wu's indulgence of favourites was her undoing, and especially the notorious Zhang brothers who gained her affection in 697, the year of her seventy-second birthday. Their close relations shamelessly profited from the special relationship to enrich themselves, one openly accepted bribes for arranging official appointments.

Xuan Zhang's tomb at a monastery on the Silk Road.
This Buddhist pilgrim greatly impressed Tai Zong,
the second Tang emperor

Women under the Tang emperors enjoyed a freedom unmatched in the later Chinese empire

Having taken gold and personal papers from a graduate who had not yet received a post, this man demanded that an immediate appointment be made. When the official responsible admitted to misplacing the graduate's papers and asked who he was, he was told it was Xie something-or-other, and fearing for his own position, he appointed more than sixty graduates with that name.

In 705 Empress Wu was deposed and she died of despair the next year. The two sons she had pushed from the dragon throne briefly reigned until her grandson, Xuan Zong, was unexpectedly elevated through another palace plot. The longest-reigning Tang emperor, Xuan Zong, restored the Chinese empire to its former greatness and is remembered as one of China's most famous rulers. Yet he still precipitated a disaster that nearly destroyed the empire.

At first Xuan Zong had no favourites, but later the influence of the emperor's favourite concubine Yang Yuhuan prepared the ground for the disastrous rebellion of An Lushan, a Turkish general in command of the imperial forces on the northeastern frontier. Exploiting the growing idleness of the emperor, this ambitious soldier made a bid for supreme power. Possibly it was the rich cultural life of the capital that most served to highlight the devastation caused by the ten-year conflict, for in recognition of its splendour Xuan Zong was styled Ming Huang, "the Brilliant Ruler". Every Chinese knows how the ageing emperor indulged Yang Yuhuan and, at her urging, bestowed undeserved honours upon An Lushan. And how driven from Chang'an in 656 by the rebels, his personal bodyguard insisted on Yang Yuhuan's execution, backing this demand with a threatened mutiny.

The Tang fightback was slow and humiliating for Su Zong, Xuan Zong's successor, who needed the aid of Uighur Turkish cavalry to restore the situation. But Uighur aid was insufficient to save Chang'an from the Tibetans, whose medieval empire seriously threatened China. It was fortunate for the Chinese that Tibet was soon wrecked by internal troubles, as a dispute between its king and the great Buddhist monasteries left the latter dominant in Tibetan society.

The Tang empire, though now much reduced, enjoyed another century of peace before popular revolts arose, those telltale signs of impending dynastic change. The eunuchs became a power once again, a legacy of Empress Wu's attempt to circumvent uncooperative branches of the imperial bureaucracy; military commanders were harder to handle, making taxes difficult to collect; and, beyond the northern frontier, danger was already arising on the Central Asian steppe. When the last Tang emperor was dethroned in 907, the empire split into nearly a dozen states, a fragmentation doubtless connected with the recent invention of gunpowder.

One event stands out during the late Tang era: the curbing of Buddhism. The Daoist-inclined emperor Wu Zong shut down 44,600 retreats, shrines, temples and monasteries. Despite the persecution ending on Wu Zong's death in 846, Buddhism in China never again rivalled the Confucian state. A motive of Wu Zong's was a desire to obtain the elixir of life, a will-o'-the-wisp peculiarly attractive to Chinese emperors. He had been told that the Buddhists were blocking his chance of attaining immortality, since the Immortals were reluctant to appear on the artificial mountain that Wu Zong had raised in the palace gardens.

The half-century of disunity that separates the Tang and Song dynasties was ended by another northern general, who was elevated to the throne of the northernmost state by his mutinous troops. But Zhao Kuangyin, who took the title of Tai Zu as the first Song emperor, was determined that his own would be the last military coup, and he persuaded his senior officers to retire early. Then the administration was overhauled so that the army no longer controlled territory, the entire conduct of affairs being placed under civil officials. The other petty states into which China had split viewed these changes with interest, and two of them submitted straight away. The majority surrendered after brief campaigns, while the last held out only till 979. When one ruler begged for continued independence, Tai Zu asked, "What wrong have your people committed to be excluded from the Empire?"

As it was, 979 was not a good year for the Song empire, however. A defeat at Gaolinghe, near modern Beijing, left the semi-nomadic Qidans in occupation of a large area inside the Great Wall. The Qidans called their state Liao, a sinicised name, and absorbed Chinese culture. As admiration was not the same as incorporation, this cession remained outside of the empire for centuries until through it came the Mongols to conquer all China. Apart from the Liao kingdom, the northern frontier was also threatened by the partially sinicised Tibetan state of Xi Xia. In 1044 an annual gift of silver and silk was agreed as the price of peace. In striking contrast to the Han and Tang empires, Song foreign policy was never expansionist but aimed at the containment of Central Asian peoples. Foreign invasion remained a threat and was the cause of the dynasty's final overthrow, but the subjection of military officials to civilian control reflects the pacific tenor of this third great period of Chinese civilisation.

The Song empire after the fall of Kaifeng to the Jin in 1127

The cemetery of the Xi Xia kings at Yinchuan. Its tombs
were robbed by Genghiz Khan

Although the Song capital of Kaifeng on the lower Yellow river was
somewhat smaller in its walled area than Tang Chang'an, it was again the
largest city in the entire world. Consumer demand was so great that there
was a general relaxation of state regulation on trade. New firms sprang
up and soon made Kaifeng the richest city in China, its commercial tax
yielding five times that of Hangzhou, the nearest rival. Before the Song
dynasty the traditional Chinese city had only a limited commercial role,
because it was essentially a political creation, the headquarters of the local
administration. All this changed with the shift of the empire's centre of
gravity southwards, and even more after fugitive Song emperors were
obliged to reside in Hangzhou, a long-established centre of trade.

Just how critical the business community had become for government revenue in what was now a money economy can be judged
from a comparison of Tang and Song figures. In the eighth century less
than 4 per cent of tax was paid in money, but in the eleventh century
the amount exceeded 50 per cent. In Hangzhou the imperial bureaucracy had no choice other than accept the emergence of banks, credit
and shareholders. The controversial reforms of Wang Anshi, who won

the confidence of Emperor Shen Zong in 1070, tried to make sense of this monetary revolution: their failure stemmed from the fact that they most affected the propertied classes, from whose ranks officials were mainly recruited. Practical measures, such as the technical subjects introduced into the civil service examinations, were attacked as dangerous lapses from traditional values, but Confucian rhetoric could not disguise the self-interest of the large landowners whose surplus wealth was available for buying out struggling peasant farmers. The austerity of Wang Anshi's own life was not enough to persuade others that radical change was necessary. In the end, the maintenance of large armies along the northern frontier overburdened the empire's finances and, in 1127, led to the fall of Kaifeng.

One Song prince refused to accept the dynasty's submission to the Jin, a nomadic people who had already overwhelmed the Qidan state of Liao, and he rallied populous south China against the northern invaders at Hangzhou. Marco Polo called this city "the most splendid in the world, in point of grandeur and beauty, as well as abundant delights, which might lead an inhabitant to imagine himself in paradise". Spared by a timely surrender to the Mongols, Hangzhou deeply impressed the Venetian traveller with its waterways and 12,000 bridges

One of Kaifeng's gateways, the Song capital until 1127

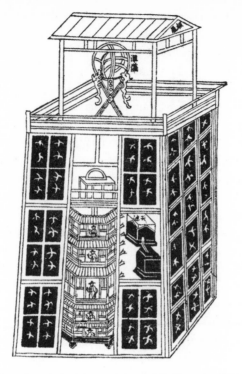

An astronomical tower set up at Kaifeng in 1088.
It was the original mechanical observatory

that spanned them. His native city would not boast the famous Rialto for another three centuries.

But totally misunderstood by Marco Polo were Hangzhou's inhabitants, whom he considered to be "naturally pacific". He was unaware of the thirty years of war that were necessary before the last member of the Song imperial house perished in 1279. And Marco Polo was also wrong to translate Kinsai as "the celestial city". He did not realise that it was a corruption of "temporary residence", the only title the Song emperors could bring themselves to confer on Hangzhou. Yet it was here that Confucianism reached its classic form in the writings of Zhu Xi, whose *Family Rituals* perfectly summed up Confucius' idea that virtue comprised self-control and ritualised behaviour. "The most serious instance of filial impiety," Zhu Xi insisted, "is depriving a family of posterity." But his reluctance to accept an official appointment in what he considered to be a corrupt administration made Zhu Xi enemies during his lifetime.

His funeral in 1200 was dubbed "a gathering of scoundrels mourning the teacher of rebellious falsehood", but within a generation Zhu Xi was accorded sacrifices in Confucian temples.

Confucian Korea

Chinese interest in the northern part of the Korean peninsula centred upon the fear that its rulers might ally themselves with Central Asian peoples living on the steppe, beyond the Great Wall. To counter this threat, both the Sui and the Tang dynasties sent armies to contain the Koreans, who were then divided into several warring states.

Most is known about Silla at the extreme south of the peninsula. It was a typically aristocratic state with a weak monarchy. Warfare must account for this arrangement, because grants of land and prisoners of war after successful campaigns served to strengthen the position of the nobles. An independent peasantry, subject as in China to taxation, labour duties and military service, comprised the largest section of society, but constant warfare had reduced its numbers and lowered its status.

Villages formed the basis of the kingdom, each under the authority of a headman. Higher officials lived in towns or cities, but the adoption of Confucianism never gave to a Korean ruler the authority of a Chinese emperor because the imported bureaucratic titles defined hereditary privileges, rather than described official functions. The so-called "bone-rank" hierarchy of Silla clearly reflects the structure of an aristocratic society. The top rank, "true-bone", was reserved for the royal house of Kim and close relatives: the aristocracy held several lower ranks called "hard to get"; below these ranks, at least in theory, there existed three further gradations among the ordinary people. Without membership of an appropriate upper rank, it was impossible to occupy any of the seventeen levels of official appointments.

The strong aristocratic tradition of Silla hindered the southern advance of Buddhism as well. Whereas the new faith was readily accepted elsewhere, Buddhist monks met with concerted resistance in Silla until Pophung came to the throne in 514. He overruled the nobles and in 534 ordered the construction of the first Buddhist monastery at Kyongju, the Silla capital. The self-sacrifice of a devout courtier named Ich'adon finally gave Pophung the upper hand by accepting execution as the price to be paid for advocating the introduction of the faith. According to the *Lives of Eminent Korean Monks,* Ich'adon predicted two miracles that would prove "the virtue of the Buddha". He said that after decapitation, his head would fly up to a mountain top, and his blood would shoot up like milk 100 metres in the air. Legend says that these events were accompanied by an earthquake and a darkened sky, which caused the overawed nobles to embrace the new religion.

It was during this period that many Korean monks visited China in search of instruction at Buddhist monasteries. One of them by the name of Wonhyo was sidetracked on his way there. One night he took shelter in what he thought was a cave, and drank from a cup he found there. At daybreak he was horrified to discover his bed was a tomb and his cup a skull. First nausea, then enlightenment overwhelmed him. As did Nagarjuna, the profound Indian exponent of Buddhism, Wonhyo suddenly appreciated that nothing was as it seemed to be, a realisation that saved him the bother of going on to China.

Wonhyo's son, on the other hand, rejected Buddhism in favour of Confucianism, whose increased influence in Silla brought about the introduction of examinations for official posts. After 788 candidates were graded according to their proficiency in reading the Chinese classics. But because admission to higher study was still restricted to the aristocracy, this innovation failed to undermine the Korean preference for hereditary privilege. It is an irony that the bone-rank monopoly brought about the downfall of the Silla nobility. By blocking all avenues of political advancement, it forced other families to look elsewhere for opportunities. Trade thus developed with China and Japan: in Shandong province there were permanent settlements with Korean magistrates and temples, while on the island of Tsushima the Japanese employed extra Korean interpreters. Foreign trade had been carried on previously by official missions, but these gave way to private enterprise, with the result that wealth and, ultimately, power shifted away from the capital at Kyongju toward commercial centres in outlying places. One of these was Kaesong, to the north of modern Seoul, the home of the grandfather of Wang Kon, the founder of the Koryo dynasty.

The loosening of ties between the provinces and the capital allowed local leaders to collect forces together and fortify their residences. Known as "castle lords", they controlled much of the countryside and made it impossible to collect taxes from the peasants. The reduction of revenue provoked a determined effort by the government, which merely resulted in a series of revolts, as the peasantry found itself squeezed between an extravagant court and the exactions of the castle lords. The initial uprisings were not contained by Silla troops, and insurgent bands combined into large forces capable of holding wide territories, once leaders arose to direct their energies. In 927, one of them was strong enough to sack Kyongju, execute the Silla king and carry off the royal treasury.

The ultimate victor was Wang Kon, whose familiarity with international commerce, and his proven abilities as a general, seemed to offer Korea the best chance of lasting unity. But not until the accession of the fourth Koryo king Kwangjong, in 949, would stability return to the peninsula. This ruler struck at the manpower held by military commanders through the freeing of those enslaved because of poverty or war; appointed officials unconnected with powerful families, and even scholars from China who had no power base in the country; and regularised the system of grants of land to officials as stipends so that these properties reverted to the state when they died. As soon as the bone-rankers dared to show their displeasure at his reforms, Kwangjong slew them without hesitation.

After this determined king's death, a new aristocratic order slowly formed under the ministry of Ch'oe Sung-no, a scholar who believed in a powerful central administration but not a powerful monarch. Ch'oe Sung-no told King Songjong that he could not afford to ignore the contribution made by the nobles to Korean society. Though the Koryo dynasty did manage to stop the age-old tendency of Korea to fragment into antagonistic regions, it was unable to impose a full Chinese-style administration upon a united country. Powerful families recovered the ground they had lost under Kwangjong, and they were quick to acquire slaves to the extent that a quarter of the peninsula's population was soon tied to this status, a situation without parallel in medieval East Asia.

In 1136 a challenge emerged from an unexpected quarter, when a rebellion headed by the Buddhist monk Myoch'ong had to be crushed. Having gained ascendancy at court by means of his skill in divination, Myoch'ong tried to move the capital away from Kaesong so that he could seize the reins of power for himself. Arguing that the dynasty would be reinvigorated by a change of location, the king was almost convinced that the removal of the court was necessary until the Confucianist minister Kim Pu-sik moved against Myoch'ong's conspiracy.

Buddhism was soon to be put firmly in its place by the military dictator Ch'oe Ch'ung-hon, who in 1196 took direct control of the palace guard and stationed his own units near Kaesong. During the next sixteen years he deposed two kings, set four others on the throne, dismissed civil officials, and expelled Buddhist monks from the capital. A chronicle relates how Ch'oe Ch'ung-hon decided all matters of life and death, all decisions previously made by the government. "The king stood above his subjects holding only an empty authority," we are told. "Alas, he was nothing but a puppet." By crushing armed monks with military force Ch'oe Ch'ung-hon removed one of the complicating factors in Korean politics. The Buddhist clergy had acquired considerable influence through illegitimate princes becoming monks and then maintaining a close relationship with the court.

After the Mongols took over control of Korea, and squandered its resources on abortive seaborne assaults on Japan, the peninsula sank into abject poverty. National renewal had to await the establishment of the Yi, Korea's last dynasty, which would rule from 1392 until 1910, when Japan annexed Korea to its empire. The dynastic change was welcomed in China because of the strong Confucian commitment of Yi Song-gye, the first Yi ruler, who had been enthroned like Wang Kon by his rebellious supporters.

In 1394 Yi Song-gye moved his court to a new capital at Hansong, the site of modern Seoul, a name in the Silla dialect meaning "chief city". Its city walls were built in six months by 200,000 conscript labourers.

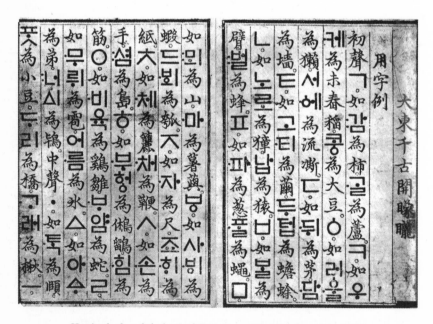

Han'gul, the alphabetical Korean script introduced in 1446

228

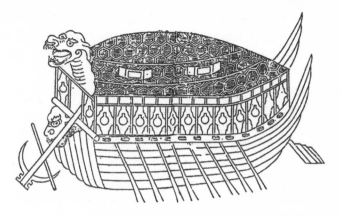

One of Yi Sun-sin's revolutionary "turtle boats"
with its iron plates

During the next four years Yi Song-gye lived in a splendid palace until illness and conflict over the succession led to his retirement to a Buddhist monastery. The bitter squabble among his sons would have boded ill for the dynasty had it not been for the restraint exercised by Confucian ministers. The Yi dynasty survived and, during King Sejong's reign from 1418 to 1450, Korea experienced its most brilliant cultural era. Sejong established the Hall of Worthies, assigned outstanding scholars to it and had them study ancient statutes and institutions of China. One result of their work was a six-volume codification of Korean law. But Sejong's greatest cultural contribution was the official adoption of han'gul, the twenty-eight letter script used ever since for the Korean language. Employed initially for the translation of Chinese texts, it soon provided a means for Koreans to write in their own tongue.

King Sejong's death was unfortunately followed by factionalism at court, a weakness in government that could have cost Korea dearly a century later. Then the Japanese warlord Toyotomi Hideyoshi ordered Seoul to join in an attack on China, or suffer conquest itself. Unwilling to oblige, Korea suffered for five years as Japanese forces tried to subdue the peninsula. Chinese forces were sent to reinforce Korean resistance, but Toyotomi Hideyoshi's plans were defeated not on land, but at sea. In the Korean admiral Yi Sun-sin, Japan encountered a naval genius who added iron plates to his ships, along lines previously developed by the Chinese, and sank one Japanese fleet after another. "Annihilation was complete within a matter of hours," reported Yi Sun-sin with satisfaction.

"Many of the Japanese leaders present either drowned themselves by jumping overboard in full armour, or killed themselves with their own swords." By 1598 the last of the Japanese invaders had quit Korea. Though mortally wounded by a stray bullet, Yi Sun-sin ordered his condition to be kept a secret until the final naval engagement at Noryang sent every Japanese vessel to the bottom.

Yet the effect of Japanese intervention was dreadful. Systematic destruction of towns and villages by the invaders, coupled with the denial of succour by the defenders, left the peninsula in an exhausted condition that was difficult to alleviate. Recovery was made the more difficult by another onslaught from the north, the Manchu attack of 1627. The balance of power on mainland East Asia had been irrevocably changed by the Manchu leader Nurhachi's defeat of the Chinese garrison in what is today Liaodong province. Afterwards it "was easy for the Manchus to subdue Korea," a Chinese chronicle laments, "and end its faithfulness to the Son of Heaven." Unknown at the time was how a later Manchu conquest of China would make the Yi kings subordinate once again to the Son of Heaven, albeit not a Chinese one: it forms part of the next chapter.

Feudal Japan

Although Japan lay beyond the perimeter of the Chinese empire, its rulers were regarded by Chinese emperors as subordinate princes. Recognising the distance that Japanese ambassadors had to travel to the Tang capital at Chang'an, it was decided in 631 that an annual visit was unnecessary. This did not imply any special favour because Chinese officials had already reprimanded them for presenting a communication that began: "The Son of Heaven in the land where the sun rises addresses the Son of Heaven in the where the sun sets."

What was always appreciated in Chang'an was the full extent of Japanese borrowing from China. In 604 Shotoku had published a state constitution whose precepts introduced Chinese ideas about the supremacy of a ruler within a centralised state, administered by salaried officials. To overcome the intense strife between contending Japanese clans, he endeavoured to unify the country on the model of the Sui dynasty and the Silla kingdom, then attempting a unification of Korea. The Confucian emphasis of Shotoku's constitution is apparent in the first of its seventeen articles. It reads:

Harmony is to be valued and quarrels avoided. All men are inclined to partisanship and few are truly discerning. Hence there are some who disobey their lords and fathers or who maintain feuds with neighbours. But when those above are harmonious and those below are conciliatory and there is concord in the discussion of all matters, the disposition of affairs comes about naturally. Then what is there that cannot be accomplished?

Prince Shotoku was regent for his aunt, the empress Suiko, who had been enthroned in 592 after a ferocious struggle between two rival groups of aristocrats. Her husband, the Japanese emperor, had died in this conflict, so it was with some relief that she entrusted government to Shotoku, whose name can be translated as "royal moral authority".

Shotoku transformed Japan into a land of Buddhist belief and Chinese learning. With that peculiarly Japanese talent for absorption and imitation, Shotoku made foreign precepts his own. But his support of the native Shinto religion also seems to have been genuine, possibly for the reason that worship was already entwined with the imperial family, which traced its divine descent from the sun goddess Amaterasu. Her supposed gifts of a bronze mirror and a sword remain in the present-day imperial regalia.

The constitution that Shotoku formulated gave to the throne an opportunity to copy the organisation of the Chinese empire in Japan. Referred to as the Great Change, an edict of 646 ordered that Japan be divided into districts and provinces as in China. Change would have been far reaching had not the nobles occupied most of the senior posts in the provinces, where they were able to preserve their power bases. Rebellions indicated the unease of many great clans but in 710 the imperial house was still able to lay out a capital at Nara, the first permanent foundation in Japan. As it was believed by the Japanese that a dwelling place was polluted by death, the court had previously moved to a new site whenever an emperor died. But Nara was no second Chang'an, because its street plan had to make allowance for existing Buddhist and Shinto buildings. These monasteries and shrines, and forty-eight new Buddhist temples built there, were to form the nucleus of Nara after the removal of the court to Kyoto. At Nara the imperial government was supposed to be a replica of China, but the situation was quite different because Japanese officials sent to the provinces were often kinsmen of local magnates. And the imperial university failed to open up the bureaucracy to talent for, as in Korea, it served rather as a finishing school for the sons of aristocrats.

Nonetheless, the impact of Chinese culture on Japan was profound through the adoption of the Chinese script. Unsuited though its characters were for a polysyllabic language such as Japanese, scholars in Japan persevered and greatly excelled in calligraphy. Inspired by the Tang example, they produced in 760 the first national anthology, the *Collection of Myriad Leaves*, containing more than 4,000 poems.

On the site of modern Kyoto, Emperor Kammu built in 794 a city called Heian-kyo, "Everlasting Peace", after the name of Chang'an. By denying the Nara monasteries the right to relocate to the new capital, the emperor hoped to check the growing influence of Buddhism. He was destined to be disappointed as Buddhist warrior monks, a typical Japanese innovation, soon engaged in full-scale wars. To protect their growing assets, enhanced by tax exemptions and land grants, the great monasteries fielded their own soldiers in an increasingly unstable Japan. That they copied the samurai, literally "those who serve", was in itself an indicator of resurgent

Tobatsu Bishamon trampling demons. He was originally an Indian deity who overcame evil

feudalism. Samurai were the armed retainers of the provincial aristocracy, not the throne, and were recognisable by their box-like armour of metal and leather, extravagantly horned helmets and razor-sharp swords slung from a belt. Their conduct, with its emphasis on loyalty, was codified as bushido, "the way of the warrior".

Amazingly, the feudal recovery had no impact upon the imperial dynasty. Between the ninth and the nineteenth centuries there was no need to end the line because hardly an emperor can be said to have ruled. Those who ran Japan—in turn the Fujiwara, Taira, Minamoto,

Hojo, Ashikaga and Tokugawa families—simply ignored the throne. For in Japan, unlike in China, the absence of a bureaucracy to hold the power of a military aristocracy in check meant that surplus sons tended to join its ranks, rather than strive for any imperial revival. All pretence at central government ceased as the country moved back to the loosely federated feudal holdings that had prevailed before Shotoku's constitution.

It remains a paradox that wars between monasteries devoted to the worship of the gentle Buddha should mark the advent of military domination in Japan. Since the move of the capital there had been bitter rivalry between the old foundations of Nara and the new ones built on Mount Hiei, outside Kyoto. In 989 the enormous monastery complex of Enryakuji sent warrior monks from this mountain to attack one of the Nara monasteries. In 1036, after a dispute over the election of an abbot, Enryakuji even turned on its twin foundation of Miidera, and burned that monastery to the ground. It was the most belligerent Buddhist foundation and often sent 6,000 warrior monks into the streets of Kyoto, carrying celestial artillery in the

An episode from one of Japan's civil wars. This event happened in 1440

233

The gatehouse of the Nanzenji temple in Kyoto, Japan's second imperial capital

form of portable shrines. Fearful of giving the deities in question any offence, the capital's inhabitants would anxiously await the decision of the court on the monks' latest demand. These actions brought about the displacement of the Fujiwara by the Taira, and then, the Minamoto. Taira power was finally broken in 1185 at Dunnoura, a sea battle in the waters separating the islands of Kyushu and Honshu. By directing archers' fire at the oarsmen in the Taira boats, the Minamoto admiral disabled them and caused a mass samurai suicide. His Taira counterpart donned two suits of armour to weigh him down, before joining his men over the side. American sailors were to be amazed at chilling repetitions of such voluntary drownings during the Second World War.

In 1192 the emperor made Minamoto Yoritomo the shogun—best translated as "generalissimo"—in recognition of his military supremacy. As this was the first such appointment to be made permanent, Minamoto Yoritomo employed his new authority in an entirely different way to either the Fujiwara or the Taira families. He ruled as a military dictator from Kamakura, a coastal city near modern Tokyo. No one was left in any doubt about Minamoto Yoritomo's intentions, after he ruthlessly eliminated the Taira family and its supporters. Then he confiscated all their lands. Every part of a now feudal Japan was expected to obey the shogun's will, or suffer immediate attack. When the Minamoto family went into decline from 1219 onwards, Hojo regents dominated Kamakura through puppet shoguns, just as previously the Fujiwara and Taira had kept emperors on the throne in Kyoto.

It was a misfortune for the Hojo family that it was called upon to defend Japan against Mongol attack. Under the energetic leadership of Hojo Tokimune, the samurai were readied for battle and defences prepared on the islands of Kyushu and Honshu. The offshore island of Tsushima fell in 1274 to an overwhelming expeditionary force, but once the Mongols landed on Kyushu the odds were less unfavourable for the Japanese, although the Mongols still had some surprises ready. The first was tactics. Whereas the Japanese warrior always sought to be the first into battle and the greatest collector of severed heads, the Mongol soldier willingly sank his individuality and behaved as a member of a combat unit. No matter how bravely mounted samurai charged, they could not break up the Mongol formation. A second shock was the invaders' weapons. Besides powerful crossbows and catapults, they had missiles that exploded in the air. A Japanese chronicle reports:

> When the fighting began, mighty iron balls were flung towards our men. Some were simply rolled along the ground, but they still sounded like thunder and looked like bolts of lightning. Over 3,000 balls were used at a time, so that horses were terrified and men wounded with iron fragments. Many died of burns.

The determination of the samurai surprised the Mongol generals, who were also aware that reinforcements would soon approach from Honshu. When the Korean sea captains advised that the invasion fleet should sail so as to avoid being dashed on the rocks by an imminent storm, the generals evacuated the coast, although they still lost some of their vessels on the way back to Korea.

Between 1274 and 1281 Kubilai Khan was too busy sorting out his conquests in China to worry about Japan. Hojo Tokimune knew that he had time to prepare for a full-scale invasion. His main decision was to build a long wall to deny the Mongols the landing place they had used at Hataka, the best anchorage on the island of Kyushu. This could not repel the invaders alone, and arguably Tokimune might have launched ships instead, but the five years spent building the wall certainly stiffened the Japanese will to resist.

The Japanese warlord Oda Nobunaga

When the invasion fleet was sighted in the summer of 1281, there was confidence among the defenders, until it was realised that the ships were only an advance squadron of a combined armada from Korea and China, carrying 140,000 men. As the assault was about to start, a typhoon suddenly struck the entire Mongol fleet. The kamikaze, or "divine wind", was believed to have been sent by Amaterasu at the behest of the emperor. All that the crippled ships could do was flee the supernatural blast. The invasion threat was over, yet the changed circumstances on mainland East Asia were not understood in Japan, where large forces were kept together for several years. The burden of defence was heavy, especially because the invaders left no spoils. This was dangerous for the Hojo family when in 1331 Emperor Go-Daigo exploited its declining authority to reassert the power of the throne. Not even the sack of Kamakura and the suicide of the last Hojo regent were enough, however, for the realisation of Go-Daigo's imperial dream. Already, his ally Ashikaga Takauji was moving with quiet determination towards the establishment of the next shogunate.

When Go-Daigo tried to block this move, Ashikaga Takauji took Kyoto and installed another emperor. The shift in political power from the imperial palace to the shogun's tent was paralleled by a transformation in religious belief. With the advent of a thoroughgoing feudal society and the loss of court patronage, Buddhist monks were obliged to consider the spiritual needs of the lesser aristocracy and the ordinary people. One sect that borrowed heavily from China was Jodo, "the Pure Land", whose concentration upon Amitabha Buddha's compassionate concern for individual salvation threatened the primacy of the monasteries through its downgrading of traditional worship. The second Jodo leader Shinran seemed to justify their concern. Having abandoned all constraints, this monk left the cloister, married and started a family. Shinran never ceased to defy the ecclesiastical authorities and carry his gospel of personal hope direct to both warriors and peasants. After his death in 1262, the True Sect, as Shinran's followers were now called, became a quasi-political organisation capable of holding its own in an increasingly violent Japan. Yet the most enduring sect was Zen. It was introduced in 1191 by the equally poor Eisai, who had studied Chan Buddhism in China. Eisai brought tea back with him as well, a beverage long regarded by the Chinese as an aid to meditation.

It was the inability of the Ashikaga family to hold on to power that opened the way for the rise of warlords such as Oda Nobunaga and Toyotomi Hideyoshi. In 1568 Oda Nobunaga seized Kyoto on the pretext of restoring the Ashikaga shogun and returning stolen property to the emperor. The destitution of the throne had already surprised the Jesuit missionary Francis Xavier, who was required to pay a fee for an audience. In a show of munificence Oda Nobunaga built a new palace for the shogun, and also one for the emperor, whom he treated with respect. Toyotomi Hideyoshi, his successor as chief warlord, continued this policy of subsidy for the imperial house, despite a marked indifference to the views of the throne. The last Ashikaga shogun was less prepared to be ignored and fled Kyoto, hoping to raise support in the provinces. He had no success and when he died in 1597 the title lapsed. There was no shogun till 1603, the year Tokugawa Ieyasu assumed the role.

Oda Nobunaga's task in reunifying Japan was immense. Ranged against his army were the considerable forces of the provincial nobility, now equipped with imported Portuguese firearms, while the capital itself was threatened by the warrior monks of Enryakuji. Oda Nobunaga forbade the great monastery access to Kyoto, and licensed Jesuits to

preach openly instead. These measures were soon followed up with a
surprise attack to forestall an alliance
between militant Buddhists and
dissident aristocrats. The notorious
assault of 1571 on Enryakuji was a
grim warning to the warlord's opponents. Every building was burned and
every person found there was slain.
Jesuit Luis Frois described the event
in a letter to Europe as an act of divine
providence. Catholic priests were
ready to play on Oda Nobunaga's
enmity towards Buddhism, but their
involvement in Japanese affairs was
counterproductive. Once it became
apparent that their teachings were in
conflict with "the way of the warrior",
the end of missionary endeavour
was in sight. In 1612 an edict of

Toyotomi Hideyoshi had no
sympathy for Christianity and
deplored everything foreign

Tokugawa Ieyasu prevented samurai from professing the Christian faith,
and two years later the Jesuits were expelled. Compliant Dutch traders
had conveniently arrived to replace the zealous Portuguese.

Before Tokugawa Ieyasu became shogun, Toyotomi Hideyoshi had
already shown a profound dislike for Christianity. This humble samurai
had avenged Oda Nobunaga's assassination, reduced all Japan to obedience and diverted the restless energies of the nobility in an invasion of
Korea, as a prelude to the conquest of China. His rage in 1596, when
Chinese enoys offered him recognition as king of Japan in return for
peace in Korea, reportedly caused "vapour to rise from his head". Because
he wished to ensure that no other ex-peasant should repeat his own
singular self-promotion, Toyotomi Hideyoshi disarmed the population
except the samurai, whose stipends were guaranteed by a rearrangement
of landholdings. For all his efforts, the samurai in later centuries were to
become increasingly anachronistic, once there was virtually no scope for
fighting. Military skills gave place to ceremony and display.

But China remained the moral point of reference for Japan during
all but the last years of the Tokugawa shogunate, because Japanese

scholars made the study of Chinese synonymous with that of Confucius. In particular, Yamaga Soko, who died in 1685, drew attention to the ideal picture of ancient Zhou feudalism as described in the original teachings of Confucius, since it provided a model for the application of Confucian morality in the paramilitary world of feudal Japan.

The Ming Revival

For most of East Asia the thirteenth century had meant the end of a world—a world that acknowledged the regional power of the Chinese empire. As we will see in the next chapter, Mongol arms not only conquered China, but incorporated it into the largest continuous land empire in the history of mankind, controlling territory stretching from the Pacific to the Mediterranean. But shortly after the accession of Kubilai as the "khan of khans", the Mongol empire split into separate states, one of which was China itself. Unrest there under the Mongols became so acute in 1368 that Togontemur Khan fled Beijing for a nomadic existence on the Central Asia steppe. Unlike the Turks who had stayed on after the fall of the sinicised Tuoba Wei dynasty and contributed to the remarkable achievements of the Tang dynasty, the Mongols disappeared altogether.

That Kubilai khan's city at Beijing survived the Mongol overthrow intact had much to do with the discipline of the Ming soldiers on their unopposed entry to the great double-walled city. Their good behaviour accorded with the view of Zhu Yuanzhang, the first Ming emperor, who recognised that China needed a period of recuperation. "We should not pluck the feathers of a young bird," he said, "nor should we shake a newly planted tree." An agricultural metaphor because like Liu Bang, the founder of the ancient Han dynasty, Zhu Yuanzhang was a man of the people, an ex-beggar and bandit. Both came to power through a combination of outstanding leadership and peasant cunning, and they were equally prepared to use the administrative skills of scholars to consolidate their authority, although in the relationships they had with officials there were marked differences.

Anxious to disassociate himself from the totalitarian excesses of Qin rule, Liu Bang deliberately adopted the role of a Confucian prince, the benevolence of whose actions would elicit virtue from a people still steeped in feudalism. The situation in 1368 was quite different. As the leader of a national uprising against foreign invaders, Zhu Yuangzhang's personal power was more absolute than any previous Chinese ruler. When ministers and generals were charged with sedition, he had no hesitation in ordering mass executions. Well may his dynasty have been called Ming, or "Bright", but the shadows of despotism were gathering around the dragon throne, so that once again the eunuchs would become a dangerous court faction. In the third Ming emperor, Yong Le, whose title means "Perpetual Happiness", this despotic tendency clearly manifested itself. While Yong Le would have loved his subjects to have regarded him as

The third Ming emperor, Yong Le

Monumental sculptures lining the road leading
to the Ming imperial tombs near Beijing

an ideal Confucian ruler, who listened to his advisers, he always kept his officials on a short leash. A mixture of ruthless brutality, moral idealism and sheer hard work made this emperor the perfect absolutist ruler.

Even before he deposed his nephew in 1402, Yong Le had foiled a Mongol counter-attack, when he marched beyond the Great Wall and caught the nomads before a full concentration could take place. Possibly his awareness of continued danger from Central Asia was one reason for Yong Le's decision to make Beijing his capital. Stable foreign relations were a major concern for Yong Lee, who dispatched a great fleet under the command of the grand eunuch Zheng He to restore Chinese suzerainty in the southern oceans. Between 1405 and 1433 there were seven major seaborne expeditions that caused the authority of the Son of Heaven to be acknowledged by rulers as far away as India and Africa, even Egypt sending an ambassador to China. In 1415 the sultan of Malindi sent an embassy with exotic gifts, among them a giraffe for the imperial park. At the palace gateway, Yong Le personally received the animal, together with a "celestial horse" and a "celestial stag". The giraffe was looked upon as "a symbol of perfect virtue, perfect government and perfect harmony in the Empire and the Universe". To mark the emperor's appreciation the ambassadors were conducted all the way home to Africa on the fifth voyage of 1417–19.

The Ming seaborne expeditions had nothing in common with those of the Portuguese, the first Europeans to sail in Asian waters. Instead of spreading terror, slaving and planting fortresses, the Chinese engaged in diplomatic missions, exchanging gifts with distant rulers from whom they were content to accept merely formal recognition of the Son of Heaven. No greater contrast could be drawn between the peaceful trading of Zheng He in Calicut in southeastern India and the atrocities practised there in 1502 by Vasco da Gama, who bombarded the city and slew several hundred fishermen who were caught up in the action. There was never a Chinese equivalent of the Portuguese custom of entering an Indian port with corpses hanging from the yards.

The giraffe from Malindi

Court ladies playing cards

To deal with the depredations of Japanese pirates a network of fortifications had to be built along the coastline. When these defensive measures were discovered to be inadequate against fast-sailing squadrons, Yong Le sent to the Ashikaga shogun a delegation carrying the regalia of a subordinate ally: a crown, robes of state and a seal of solid gold that was too heavy to be lifted with one hand. The acceptance of these presents in 1405 meant that the pirate bases were no longer safe in Japanese waters and the attacks on China declined in number. For Japanese chroniclers, however, the episode was fraught with indignity, because it seemed to be an unnecessary admission of Chinese suzerainty.

On the death of Yong Le in 1425, the programme of ocean voyages was suspended and, despite the seventh expedition of 1431–33, the era of maritime diplomacy came to an end. Not all the reasons are apparent for this reversal of policy, which left a power vacuum in the Indian Ocean into which the Portuguese unwittingly sailed. A combination of circumstances seems to have been responsible. The scholar officials, strongly against the voyages from the start, were even more opposed to the prestige that Zheng He and the eunuchs derived from their success. They were also becoming less profitable as trading ventures and the cost of mounting them pressed hard on the imperial exchequer. A final reason for a turning away from the sea was the northern location of the capital, because the laying out of a new city at Beijing made the Great Wall of prime importance.

Impressive though the Ming dynasty's rebuilding of the Great Wall undoubtedly was, for the first time China fell behind other countries in technology and science, experiencing a rude shock when in the 1590s imperial troops exchanged fire in Korea with Japanese forces sent there by Toyotomi Hideyoshi. The invaders were armed with better guns based on the Portuguese matchlock. Although the Manchu conquerors

Part of the emperor's private quarters in
the Forbidden City, Beijing

An inner doorway at the Forbidden City, Beijing. The last Ming
emperor, Si Zong, hanged himself in the distant pagoda when
Li Zicheng took the city in 1644

of China never possessed superior weapons, they were assisted by a complicated civil war that followed the usurpation of the dragon throne by
Li Zicheng, whose rebel army captured Beijing in the previous year.
It is not impossible that Li Zicheng, a man of the people like the first
Ming emperor, could have established another Chinese dynasty, but he
did not take into account the feelings of Wu Sangui, the commander of
the forces in the northwest. When Wu Sangui learned that Li Zicheng
had added his own favourite concubine to the imperial harem, the
angry soldier reached an agreement with the Manchus and opened in
the Great Wall the "First Gate to all Under Heaven" at Shanhaiguan.
In the ensuing battle, which occurred in a fierce storm, the decisive
moment came when 20,000 iron-plated Manchu horses galloped into the
rebel host. Unnerved by the unexpected attack, the rebels broke ranks
and fled, following their leader's example. While Wu Sangui pursued
Li Zicheng, we will see in the next chapter how another Central Asian
people occupied Beijing and installed their king as the first Qing
emperor.

Chapter 8

Medieval Central Asia

For the strength of Eternal Heaven, the Universal Sovereign of the Empire of the Great Mongols. This is his order.

The seal of Guyug, the third Mongol khan

The Turks and the Qidans

Between the tenth and the fourteenth centuries most Turks converted to Islam and some tribes moved westwards to found powerful dynasties such as the Seljuk and the Ottoman. Another movement took a southward direction to India, where Zahir-ud-din Muhammad Babur founded the Mughal empire. Babur's initial intention was to dominate medieval Central Asia, but too many other Turkish leaders had the same idea. His ancestry seems to have been Turko-Mongol: for he claimed direct descent from Tamerlane on his father's side, and Genghiz Khan on his mother's. Both the Turks and Mongols had a great deal in common as nomad warriors who lorded it over semi-nomadic and agricultural peoples.

The remote position of Mongolia prevented Islam from making inroads there, while the Moslem population of China remained largely connected with international trade. Sino-Turkish families usually tended to be Buddhist, a legacy of the Tuoba Wei emperors' patronage of this religion before the reunification of the Chinese empire under the Sui dynasty. Its first emperor, the redoubtable Wen Di, was so in awe of his strong-willed Turkish wife that he is remembered as the most hen-pecked of all Chinese rulers. When the empress noticed how attracted Wen Di was to the charms of a young girl, she secretly had her killed. Finding out what had happened, the emperor rode off alone into a remote mountain valley and had to be brought back by his closest courtiers, who admonished him for putting his own life at risk. "I may be honoured as the Son of Heaven," Wen Di replied, "but I haven't any freedom at all".

The determined empress was actually part Xiongnu and part Uighur, her sinicised family having lived a long time in north China. Known as the Uighurs, the name of the chief tribe bordering the Great Wall, these Turks established about 850 at Qocho, a city near Turfan, an empire that lasted until almost 1250. According to Chinese sources, the Uighurs adopted Manichaeism under their third ruler, Mou-yo. In 762 he had encountered this Iranian faith in Luoyang while his horsemen were there assisting the Tang dynasty against An Lushan's rebellion. He became a convert and shortly after imposed the new belief on the Uighurs. A Chinese envoy to Qocho noted in 982 how

> in this country it neither rains nor snows, and the heat is extreme. Every year, when summer is at its hottest, the inhabitants move underground . . . There is a river which flows from a mountain defile in such a way that its waters pass around the capital, irrigate its fields and gardens, and move its mills . . . The nobility eat horse-flesh, while the rest of the population eat mutton, ducks and geese . . . There are some fifty Buddhist monasteries and a Man-ichaean temple . . . No one is destitute because those who cannot provide for themselves are cared for by public welfare. Many people reach an advanced age.

Qocho is now an archaeological site, but under the Turks the oasis city functioned as a staging post on the Silk Road, its half-millennium of existence being not untypical of medieval Central Asia cities. It depended upon international trade and was wary of nomadic neighbours.

The Qidan successors of the Turks ruled much of Central Asia during the twelfth century, one of the least understood periods of its history. The Qara Qidai empire seems to have been a military domination of an area stretching from the Aral Sea to the Altai mountain range, with its southern border adjoining Tibet. The subject population was mostly Moslem. The Qidans who had moved westwards to dominate Central Asia briefly were propelled by the collapse of the Liao state in northeastern China. Those

A gilded Qidan crown with a Daoist divinity at the top

Qidans who stayed behind in 1114 and accepted Jin rule included the ancestors of Yelu Chucai, a future adviser of the Mongol khans. The semi-nomadic Qidans had occupied an area of land on both sides of the Great Wall from the 970s onwards. The Jin would never have overcome the Qidans were it not for an alliance they made with the Song dynasty. Chinese cooperation with the Jin was incredibly short-sighted, as the defeat of Liao removed a buffer state from the Song frontier and exposed the capital at Kaifeng to a direct Jin attack, which occurred in 1127. Afterwards the Song imperial house was obliged to settle south of the Yangzi river at Hangzhou.

After the Jin conquest of Liao, the fugitive Qidans who travelled westwards and established the Qara Qidai empire did not embrace Islam. They tolerated the various religions of their subjects—Moslem, Jewish, Nestorian Christian, Manichaean and Buddhist—but remained wedded to tribal beliefs that involved animal sacrifices. Before a campaign it was customary to dedicate a grey ox and a white horse to the celestial realm, the Earth and their ancestors. Possibly the reasons for Islam failing to convert the Qidans as it did other peoples of nomad origin in the middle part of Central Asia were the relatively short period of Qara Qidai rule as well as the religious complexity of their empire. But Qidan resistance may well have been reinforced by Chinese attitudes, since the Liao kingdom was thoroughly sinicised before its disappearance.

Best known is Yelu Dashi, the founder of the the Qara Qidai empire that the Chinese called Western Liao. Taking advantage of disunity among the Turkish peoples living in Central Asia, he added to his side individuals and groups who were only too ready to throw their lot in with a new and promising leader. Adding these experienced warriors to a core of loyal supporters, and making full use of a plentiful supply of horses, Yelu Dashi was able to intimidate those who dared to oppose him. His tendency to retain local rulers in their positions also facilitated the smooth transition to a new empire. Yelu Dashi was succeeded by his wife, Xiao Tabuyan, who reigned as empress for three years. In all likelihood she acted as regent for Yelu Dashi's young sons after his death. His passing was certainly felt in Central Asia. In 1144 the Oghuz Turks, some of whom had been driven northwards, returned in strength and sacked several oasis cities. Other Oghuz had already trekked westwards and under Alp Arslan set up the Seljuk empire in Persia and Iraq.

A collection of balbals, Turkish grave markers, dating from the sixth century in Kyrgyzstan

Yelu Dashi's own reputation for success on the battlefield seems to have given his subject peoples reason to pause before asserting their independence. Apart from the Oghuz, there were plenty of restive Turks only waiting for an opportunity to resume the usual pattern of internecine conflict, but for nearly half a century their disputes stayed minor ones. Trouble came during the reign of Zhilugu, Yelu Dashi's grandson, who was enthroned as the last Qara Qidai ruler in 1178. A gradual decline was apparent before Genghiz Khan's general Jebe defeated a Qara Qidai army 30,000 strong in 1216. Two years later the Mongols completed the subjugation of all the land that had once formed the Qara Qidai empire. Its last ruler was Guchulug, a Turkish nobleman who had deposed Yelu Zhilugu in 1211. Guchulug was a persistent enemy of Genghiz Khan, gathering Mongol rivals around him and threatening Genghiz's hegemony over the Mongol tribes. The usurper escaped from the Mongols whom Jebe sent to capture him at Kashgar, only to be killed by them in 1218. At Kashgar the Mongol general proclaimed that every person could adhere to their own religion, thereby gaining the inhabitants' support. Other Central Asian cities were not persuaded by the proclamation, although they surrendered once Guchulug's severed head was conveyed from city to city.

A Qara Qidai gold cup

A reclining Buddha from Inner Mongolia. Before the arrival
of Islam, Buddhism was the religion of Central Asia

The Tibetan Empire

Almost forgotten today is the imperial era of medieval Tibet. So closely is
the country now associated with the Dalai Lama that it comes as something of a shock to learn how aggressive the Tibetans were under King
Songtsen Gampo and his successors. Though the process of expansion
got underway with his father, Songtsen Gampo initiated a whole series
of conquests before his death in 650. By no means an absolute monarch,
the Tibetan ruler assured his position through matrimonial alliances
with powerful clans and an adequate provision of booty, which the
conquest of Zhangzhung, a kingdom on the Indian border, conveniently
provided near the start of his reign. Originally regarded as an ally, the king
of Zhangzhung had married Songtsen's sister but her poor treatment
precipitated the attack. With the annexation of Zhangzhung, the Tibetan
plateau was subject to unified rule for the first time, and its resources
allowed the king to set in motion the growth of Tibet's empire during
the decades that followed. Songtsen was guided by Gar Tongsen, the
chief minister he had inherited from his father, who worked hard to
ensure unity among the Tibetan clans.

A statue of King Songtsen Gampo with
a bodhisattva peeping from the top of his hat

In 634 the second Tang emperor, Tai Zong, became aware of
Songtsen's expanding empire when the Tibetan king sought to avoid
conflict by proposing a marriage alliance, as he had done in Zhangzhung.
The Chinese court rejected the proposal outright, an affront that caused
Songtsen to declare that he would capture a Tang princess himself. True
to his word, in 638 the Tibetan king invaded China, withdrawing only
after a stalemate ensued. Chief minister Gar Tongtsen arrived in Chang'an
two years later, when it was agreed in light of Songtsen's expression
of regret over the invasion and a bethrothal gift of 5,000 ounces of
gold, plus several hundred "precious baubles", Princess Wencheng
should become the Tibetan queen. Apparently Emperor Tai Zong was
so impressed by Gar Tongtsen's diplomatic skills that he offered him
another princess as a bride. The minister politely declined the offer, and
instead was granted the honorary title of "Great Protecting General of
the Right". On arriving in Tibet, the Chinese princess was so horrified
by the use of red cosmetics that Songtsen banned the practice. China
never forgot Wencheng's reaction, calling the Tibetans thereafter "the
red-faced barbarians".

Peace lasted until the deaths of the Chinese emperor and the Tibetan
king. Apart from a border war with an Indian kingdom, Songtsen spent
his final years in the consolidation of his existing conquests. It seems
likely that Buddhism was encouraged in Tibet by Chinese as well as

Nepalese princesses, because Tai Zong's successor bestowed on Songt-sen the Buddhist title "Precious King", a reference to Amitabha. Tibetan tradition says that Wencheng brought the earliest image of the Buddha with her. After Songtsen's death, Gar Tongtsen virtually ruled Tibet for twenty years: to him more than his former patron, the Tibetans owed the creation of an alphabet, a law code, a central administration and the introduction of the Buddhist faith.

But Chinese penetration of Central Asia as far as the Tarim basin upset Gar Tongtsen, for whom this region was a Tibetan sphere of influence. With the aid of several oasis states he resisted the Chinese advance until he died an old man in 667. The passing of this arch imperialist made no difference to Tibetan policy because King Manglon Mangtsen, Songtsen's grandson, was just as keen on foreign conquest. The only powers in Central Asia that might have been able to stop the rise of Tibet were the Umayyad and Abbasid caliphates, but the Arab advance never reached its frontier. China was therefore left to deal with Tibet on its own, something the Tang dynasty found a challenge after the ten-year civil war begun by An Lushan in 755.

The withdrawal of western Chinese garrisons to deal with this rebellion had an immediate impact on Central Asia, where client regimes paid homage to the Tibetan king instead of the Son of Heaven. Already a day-long battle fought on the banks of the Talas river, due east of present-day Tashkent, had ended in a resounding Chinese defeat at the hands of Ziyab ibn Salih al-Khuzai, when Central Asian allies defected to the Arab side. This reverse in 751 was not in itself decisive, for both the Arab and the Chinese armies involved were badly overextended. In comparison with the trouble caused by An Lushan, it had little effect on China but there were immense repercussions for Central Asia.

Emboldened by this turn of events, the Tibetans went on the offensive and, in 763, they even occupied Chang'an, thoroughly looting the Chinese capital during a two-week stay. For the rest of the century northwestern China was at the mercy of Tibetan arms. A peace treaty between Tibet and China was eventually agreed after considerable nego-tiation, in part because the Tibetan king wanted the Tang emperor to treat him like a superior relative. It stipulated that a solemn oath should be taken in the blood of a bull representing the agricultural Chinese and of a stallion representing the Tibetan herdsmen. Ashamed at having to accept the Tibetan king's wishes, the elderly Chinese ambassador asked that the ceremony be downgraded, suggesting a threefold sacrifice of a

A Jin seal belonging to an official charged with temple administration. As it was for the Qidans and the Tibetans, medieval China was the model for the Jin invaders

sheep, a pig and a dog. As there were no pigs in the vicinity, the negotiators settled for a sheep, a goat and a dog. The Tibetan envoy, after the oath was taken and the text of the peace treaty exchanged, still remained uneasy about the Chinese attitude, and insisted that both parties should swear another oath in a Buddhist shrine.

A difficulty for the Chinese in fighting the Tibetans was the effectiveness of Tibetan armour. A Tang chronicler tells us

> that Tibetan soldiers as well as their mounts wear chain mail. Its workmanship is extremely fine. It envelops them completely, leaving openings only for the eyes. Thus arrows and swords cannot readily injure them.

It was more than fortunate for China that Tibet was soon wrecked by internal strife, arising from a clash between the monarchy and the recently established Buddhist monasteries. King Tri Songdetsen had given impetus to the new faith when, in 779, he constructed Tibet's first monastery at Samye and invited an Indian monk, the scholarly Shantarakshita, to ordain Tibetan converts as Buddhist monks. To support this monastery, particular villages were charged with the supply of food and other necessities.

As the number of foundations and monks mushroomed, and other villages were obliged to support them in the same manner, it became obvious that the Tibetan kingdom had taken on an unsustainable burden alongside the outlay required to maintain its empire. The economic crisis of ever-increasing royal patronage erupted during the reign of Tri Relpachen, when high-ranking monks were rewarded with ministerial appointments and the stewardship of royal estates. In 838 Lang Darma killed his brother Tri Relpachen in a palace coup backed by a faction favouring a return to pre-Buddhist Tibetan beliefs. The usurper set about closing down monasteries until two years later he was in turn killed by a Buddhist monk. The assassin is supposed to have disguised himself as a shaman to dance before Lang Darma, but beneath his black cloak was hidden a bow and arrow. Having slain the apostate ruler, the monk promptly disappeared.

Lang Darma's murder undermined the Tibetan empire. With the end of Songtsen's royal line, Tibet reverted to its traditional state of disunity, leaving the monasteries to fill the inevitable political vacuum. Only they could provide political authority and help to preserve the cultural identity of the Tibetans. The collapse of the Tibetan monarchy might have been viewed by the Tang dynasty as an opportunity to recover former territories in Central Asia, but wisely it decided to fix China's boundary at Dunhuang, the western terminus of the Great Wall.

Largely isolated from the rest of Central Asia after the liquidation of its medieval empire, Tibet's foreign relations were closest with Mongolia, although these did not develop until after the Mongols ceased to rule China. It was in the middle of the sixteenth century that the Third Dalai Lama accepted an invitation to visit Mongolia, leading the khan to declare Tibetan Buddhism the official religion of all the Mongols. Then Altan Khan bestowed the title Dalai, a Mongol word meaning "all-encompassing wisdom": it was also extended posthumously to his two predecessors and has been used by his successors to this day. When the Third Dalai Lama's reincarnation was found to be none other than the great-grandson of Altan Khan, Tibetan links to Mongolia became even stronger. As the Fourth, he was the only Dalai Lama who was not Tibetan.

The closeness of the Tibetans and the Mongols would lead to trouble for Tibet once the Manchus took charge of China. They struggled to vanquish the Mongols from the 1670s in the reign of the second Qing emperor Kang Xi to the 1750s in that of the fourth emperor Qian Long. What the Manchus could not tolerate was Mongol involvement in Tibetan politics, lest it endanger the Chinese empire's western frontier. It was vital to Qing foreign policy to prevent any alliance between the spiritual leaders of Tibet and the military leaders of Mongolia. So Beijing announced that the Tibetans were vassals of the Qing emperor, installing puppet Dalai Lamas when necessary. In practical terms the great Buddhist monasteries were left to their own devices, provided they concentrated solely on Tibetan matters, while Qing China took charge of Tibetan foreign relations. In the nineteenth century this division of responsibility was made clear to the British, who were then extending their authority throughout India. For better or worse, Tibet was henceforth tied to China.

The Mongol Empire

Of all Central Asian peoples the Mongols were the greatest warriors: they created an empire that covered Mongolia, China, Korea, Iran, Iraq, Afghanistan, Syria, the Ukraine, Hungary and the Caucasus. Their supremacy was even acknowledged in Southeast Asia by rulers in Burma, Cambodia and Java. What the Mongols managed to do was incorporate all the steppe tribes in a single state so that their combined military strength made Central Asia supreme during the thirteenth and the fourteenth centuries.

The Mongols were incredibly few in number, 700,000 people at most. Yet the election of Temuchin as Genghiz Khan in 1206 set them on a course of world domination. Although the meaning of Genghiz Khan is by no means clear, it conveyed the idea of a resolute leader, a characteristic reflected in the yasa, "the good and strict laws" he introduced to bring order to the turbulent steppelands. Once elected as Genghiz Khan, we are told that "he sent messengers to all tribes, whether or not they were allies, and announced his position and his justice, his laws and his generosity". Made transparent were the consequences of disobedience: even "the descendants of those who do not strictly adhere to the law will be punished, no matter how long it takes to track them down". It was a threat that was always fulfilled, as the last ruler of Qara Qidai was well aware. Guchulug's pursuers took two years to catch up with him, after his flight from Kashgar. On the death of Genghiz Khan in 1227, however, the Mongols were still only a Central Asian power. It was his sons' and grandsons' campaigns that turned them into the most feared adversary in Europe and Asia.

The secret of Genghiz Khan's success in bequeathing the chance of such a vast range of conquests was building up a personal following, rather than depending upon tribal loyalties. Most of the Mongol clans had proved fickle, electing him their leader and then showing a marked reluctance to follow his orders. This experience hardened his heart, making Genghiz Khan unwilling to delegate power to his own relations or other senior Mongols. As this distrust lasted his whole life, the slightest sign of disobedience was punished by death. But Genghiz Khan had an ability to attract devotion from his trusted commanders, who mastered the technique of mobile warfare. He also won the respect of his soldiers by seeing that they were well supplied with arms and horses, and that they received a fair share of the plunder. As a result, Genghiz Khan lost battles, never a war. "Mongol horses," Marco Polo reports, "are so well broken-in to quick-change movements, that upon the given signal, they turn instantly in every direction; and by these rapid manoeuvres many triumphs have been gained on the battlefield."

How different in outlook Genghiz Khan was from most contemporary rulers is evident in *The Secret History of the Mongols*, commissioned by his successor Ogodei Khan. It relates the greatest clash ever between the nomadic culture of the steppe and the civilisation of intensive agriculture. One revealing incident was a meeting Genghiz Khan had with two learned Turks. He asked them about the puzzling phenomenon of the city. To the Mongol leader, the city was something alien, a threat to the world of the nomads, whose arms then appeared utterly irresistible. But understanding was not the same as acceptance and Genghiz Khan always encouraged Mongol ferocity. "The greatest joy," he told his men, "is to conquer one's enemies, to pursue them, to seize their belongings, to see their families in tears, to ride their horses, and to possess their wives and daughters." The treatment of Bukhara in 1220 is representative of the Mongol approach to cities. It was plundered after a short siege and burned to the ground. Although the fire seems to have broken out accidentally, this was of no consequence to the Mongols. If Bukhara had put up stiffer resistance and caused the Mongols heavy losses, then after its capture the male inhabitants would have been massacred, except craftsmen, who were always enslaved. As every tribesman was a soldier, the continuous activity started by Genghiz Khan forced the Mongols to rely more and more on servile labour, even in the crucial task of horse breeding.

In addition, the Mongol horde proved capable of adopting military technology from other peoples and using non-Mongol troops to deploy the newly acquired weapons. Polish chroniclers relate how at the battle of Wahlstadt in 1241 the Mongols used a smoke-producing device to cause disarray among the combined forces of the Poles and the Teutonic Knights. Smoke had been available in China before the foundation of the Song dynasty, which was finally overwhelmed by the Mongols in 1276. A Chinese military handbook com-

Genghiz Khan, the founder of the Mongol empire

ments: "When savage smoke assaults men, there is no means to withstand it." Much depended on the direction of the wind. "When the wind is favourable," we are told, "the smoke will blind the enemy's eyes. You can then exploit it suddenly to strike. But should the wind become contrary and the smoke overspread your own army, you need to signal a withdrawal. You can also allow smoke to disguise your strength and order of battle." Apart from dense black smoke, there were other colours that indicated the presence of poison. The Qidans had been quick to adopt smoke as an offensive weapon, in 917 deploying it against Chinese strongholds south of the Great Wall. Other Central Asian peoples were not slow in following their example.

Genghiz Khan's struggle to achieve personal supremacy made him determined to hand on his hard-won position to a descendant. A suspicion of illegitimacy prevented him from favouring his eldest son and, as a compromise, Ogodei was chosen instead. Genghiz Khan's violent sons accepted Ogodei, whom they liked, even though they hated each other. Described as a generous person, the new Mongol leader lacked his father's iron will and made odd decisions in his cups. Once, on learning that a certain Mongol clan had forced its women into what he regarded as unsatisfactory marriages, Ogodei ordered all the girls over the age of seven and all wives married less than a year to be brought to him. Of the four thousand women thus assembled, some were singled out for his courtiers, who were required to consummate marriage on the spot. The rest were split between the khan's harem and his personal attendants. None of the women's relations present dared to protest.

It was in this strange court that Yelu Chucai made his name as a reformer. A descendant of the Qidan royal clan, Yelu Chucai had been an official in the Jin civil service but, after witnessing the senseless violence that accompanied the Mongol invasion of north China, he studied under a Chan Buddhist master who was "well versed in both Confucianism and Buddhism and very thorough in doctrine and expression". That this teacher was also conversant with Daoism indicates that he subscribed to the common origin of all three traditions. This idea was very popular then, and accounts for Yelu Chucai's attempt to champion the teachings of the three sages, the Buddha, Confucius and Lao Zi, at the Mongol court.

At first Yelu Chucai was reluctant to serve the Mongols, but as soon as he realised that he could do something to tame their ferocity, he put his administrative skills at the service of the Mongol court in Karakorum. In 1218 Yelu Chucai was summoned there by Genghiz Khan. The Mongol leader had already rallied many Qidans to his cause and

The gilded saddle and stirrups of Genghiz Khan

A Nestorian tile with Mongolian and Syriac scripts.
Even though Genghiz Khan preferred shamans, he was
careful not to antagonise the gods of other religions

they had proved faithful allies in his war against the Jin. According to
Chinese records, the sole source for Yelu Chucai's career, the audience
went like this:

> "The Qidans and the Jin," remarked Genghiz Khan, "have
> been enemies for generations, ever since the destruction of Liao.
> Now I have taken revenge for you". A strongly minded Con-
> fucian, Yelu Chucai replied, "My father and my grandfather
> respectively served the Jin emperors. How can I, a subject and
> a son, be so insincere to consider my sovereign and my father as
> enemies?" Impressed by such directness and the honest look of
> this fellow steppeman, Genghiz Khan gave Yelu Chucai a secre-
> tarial appointment at his court. He even gave him a nickname,
> "Long Beard".

Yelu Chucai's duties were both secretarial and astrological. As did all
Mongols, Genghiz Khan held natural phenomena in great respect, and

he would consult his secretary-astrologer whenever the need arose. It did not matter that Yelu Chucai interpreted these events according to the Chinese system of omens, as indicators of heavenly favour or displeasure. Correctly predicting the death of one of Genghiz Khan's enemies only served to enhance the reputation of Yelu Chucai.

Through Yelu Chucai's influence, Genghiz Khan was persuaded to summon a Daoist master to Karakorum, where Yelu Chucai hoped the new arrival would endorse the notion of Confucianism, Daoism and Buddhism working in harmony together. He thought that the Mongols might benefit from them because they combined esoteric and practical doctrines in a way that would not only appeal to the khan but even more provide a framework for stable government.

Like some Chinese emperors, Genghiz Khan was interested in acquiring the elixir of life. The arrival of a distinguished Daoist at his court must therefore have pleased him, because in China this man was regarded as an expert on longevity, even immortality. The invitation to come to the Mongol capital, which Yelu Chucai drafted for the khan, mentions the need for advice on matters of government as well as the means of prolonging life. To underscore the point in the letter, a favourable comparison is made between the Buddhist faith and the new understanding that Daoism will bring to the Mongols, once Genghiz Khan is initiated into its mysteries. It was a great disappointment for Yelu Chucai when the Daoist master showed little tolerance of Buddhism, although Confucius's moral philosophy was exempt from any of his criticisms. After the man returned to China, loaded with gifts from a grateful khan, Yelu Chucai was again on his own in arguing the value of a moderate approach in running the Mongol empire. Of the Daoist master he commented: "As our outlooks were so different, I chose not to disagree with him in public, lest there was a damaging dispute. That is why I disapproved of his words in my mind and only laughed at him in private."

It was never easy to gain Genghiz Khan's trust. When however he was convinced of a person's loyalty, he gave him his complete confidence. The public silence of Yelu Chucai is thus explained: the khan had been fascinated by Daoist lore to an extent that disagreement could have cost the secretary-astrologer Genghiz Khan's ear. It seems that Yelu Chucai kept quiet about Daoism for the rest of the khan's life, although he disliked the exemption from taxation that had been given to Daoist monks living in Mongol-controlled territory.

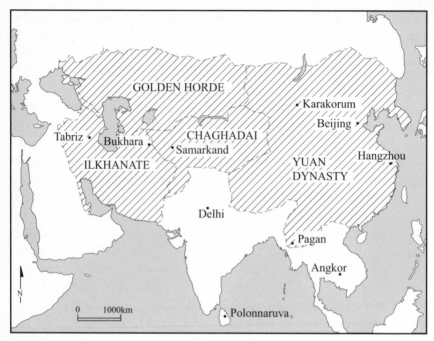

The Mongol empire

Yelu Chucai raised the issue of taxation with Ogodei Khan, when in 1234 the Jin were finally overcome in north China. By 1212 the Mongols had already conquered a large area but, with Genghiz Khan needing to fight enemies elsewhere, the Jin empire centred there grate-fully enjoyed a lull in hostilities. This ended when Ogodei led an all-out assault and killed the Jin ruler.

The new khan was not slow in appreciating the need for help in dealing with this latest territorial addition, so he accepted Yelu Chucai's advice. Had Genghiz Khan been fully aware of the extent of Qidan and Jin sinicisation, he would never have employed Yelu Chucai at all. His standard policy aimed at keeping nomad ways free from foreign entanglements. And it has to be said that the sheer size of the Chinese peasantry had always baffled the Mongols. Considered unfit as soldiers and possessing no craft skills, it was proposed to Ogodei Khan that these useless people be exter-minated and their land allowed to revert to pasture. Yelu Chucai argued strongly against this drastic proposal, explaining that if he was permitted to introduce a proper system of taxation and let the peasant farmers work in peace, he could collect enough revenue to pay for all future Mongol cam-paigns. As the promised tax flowed to Karakorum talk of genocide ceased.

In spite of ruling a huge empire, Ogodei Khan's outlook remained that of a steppe warrior. He listed his four proudest achievements as defeating his enemies in battle, creating a post system, digging wells to increase grazing land and placing garrisons among settled populations. Yet Ogodei Khan was willing to listen to Yelu Chucai's ideas until the Mongol nobles moved to oust the Qidan adviser. They most disliked his assertion of the khan's entitlement to tribute because the greater control introduced left no scope from their own exactions. Just as repugnant to them was Yelu Chucai's recruitment of former Jin administers, scholar-officials whose release he had secured from slavery. Once Yelu Chucai lost Ogodei Khan's confidence, there was nothing he could do to prevent the decision in 1239 to allow tax farming by Moslem businessmen. Yet on the death of Yelu Chucai five years later, Karakorum went into mourning and honoured his wish to be buried in the Western Hills near Beijing.

Although Yelu Chucai was convinced that the Mongols possessed the heavenly mandate to rule, he knew that this could only be maintained through an effective administration. That was why his closest friends said he died of a broken heart. Yelu Chucai's insight into Mongol and Chinese attitudes was unique, but before the accession of Kubilai Khan it was largely a wasted asset at the Mongol court. For all the acknowledgement of Yelu Chucai's long and distinguished period of service rendered to two khans, Karakorum was still no more than a steppe encampment.

After Ogodei Khan's early death through excessive drinking, his second wife Toregene acted as regent. According to Mongol custom, when the head of a family died, his widow took charge of his estate until the eldest son came of age. In the face of intense opposition Toregene managed to have her son Guyug elected as the third Mongol leader, but he died shortly afterwards in 1247. His successor, Mongke Khan, another of Genghiz Khan's grandsons, immediately ordered his two brothers, Hulegu and Kubilai, to extend and consolidate Mongol power in West Asia and East Asia respectively. Like previous khans, Mongke called up non-Mongol peoples who offered military expertise otherwise unavailable to the Mongols. He also told his brothers to refrain from wanton destruction: they were to give unconquered peoples the chance to surrender before they attacked.

For his conquest of China, Kubilai had an army 500,000 strong. Of the two brothers, Kubilai was the more ambitious and he fully exploited the conflict that shattered the unity of the Mongol empire on Mongke's death in 1259. The succession crisis exposed the personal animosities and territorial rivalries of the Mongol nobility. At the end of it Kubilai may have become "the Great Khan" that Marco Polo knew as the emperor of China, but his authority was restricted to the eastern part of Central Asia and East Asia. With three lesser khans now autonomous rulers, the Mongol empire fragmented into separate states. Never again would the Mongols pool their military forces for a joint campaign.

A key contest in the Mongol conquest of China was the five-year siege of Xiangyang on the middle reaches of the Yangzi, whose massive fortifications made the city the commanding stronghold of the river basin. To overcome the defenders' stubborn resistance the Mongolian army needed to perfect its nautical

Mongol silver passport. The front inscription requires assistance to its bearer "on pain of death"

and artillery skills. Kubilai Khan was obliged to assemble a multi-ethnic force of Mongol, Turkish, Persian, Korean, Jin and northern Chinese soldiers and sailors. For the first three years the Song dynasty was able to supply and reinforce the beleaguered garrison from its capital at Hangzhou, but a blockade then isolated Xiangyang and a major bombardment commenced. Two Moslem engineers built catapults of such size and strength that "the machinery went off with a terrific noise, which seemed to shake the earth and the sky, and everything that was hit by the enormous stones instantly collapsed". The surrender of the devastated city in 1273 left south China so dangerously exposed that the boy-emperor Gong Di was taken prisoner on the fall of Hangzhou. A few Song diehards fought on among the offshore islands, but Kubilai Khan now ruled the lion's share of the Mongol world dominion, because he was the first Central Asian to subjugate the whole of China.

From the start Kubilai Khan appreciated how he had to rely on the resources of China and on the acquiescence of his Chinese subjects. He admitted as much in a proclamation composed for him in 1260 by the Confucian scholar Wang O. Like Yelu Chucai, this adviser had been an official under the Jin emperors, for the last of whom he persuaded Kubilai Khan to grant a proper burial. In the event the ex-emperor's remains could not be found and Wang O had to content himself with a eulogy that described him as a ruler who "punished officials leniently . . . honoured Confucian studies . . . and encouraged agriculture". Heeding these words, Kubilai Khan strove to reassure China that he would behave like a traditional ruler, declaring Beijing as his southern capital.

But Kubilai Khan was very reluctant to hand over his authority to subordinates and he was quite uninterested in possessing a bureaucracy recruited by examination. To help him run his administration he preferred a mixture of foreign peoples, European adventurers such as Marco Polo. For Kubilai Khan never totally trusted his Chinese subjects, who outnumbered the Mongols living in China by 300 to 1. Given this disparity, the Mongols had to retain control of the leading positions in government if they were to survive and avoid being overwhelmed by the Chinese.

Of this state of affairs Marco Polo had only an inkling. Even though he tells us that they often talked together, how well Marco Polo knew Kubilai Khan remains a matter of conjecture. He calls the Mongol emperor "the greatest lord that ever was born", saying that Kubilai Khan was "neither too small nor too large" and boasted a "well-made nose". He was white faced, though after a drink his cheeks went red, something his Chinese advisers would have been pleased to note since a ruddy complexion

Kubilai Khan, "the greatest lord that ever was born",
according to Marco Polo

was believed to show a grateful disposition. Despite it being the custom during a banquet for "all the guests to go down on their knees and show great humility" whenever Kubilai Khan emptied his cup, the heavy drinking associated with the Mongols was rare while he sat on the dragon throne.

A Mongol banknote ostensibly worth several thousand copper coins

What really impressed Marco Polo most at Beijing was the magnificence of Kubilai Khan's palace, which was "the grandest building that has ever been . . . The main hall is so vast and so wide that a meal might be served for 6,000 people". Another thing that amazed Marco Polo was the khan's currency printing house, where "his mint is so organised that you might well conclude that he has mastered the art of alchemy". Ignored were the inflationary pressures stimulated by its printing of too many notes. This problem the Mongols consistently failed to tackle, the collapse of the paper currency in the 1330s becoming a critical factor in the fall of the Yuan, the name given to the Mongol dynasty in China.

Even before Kubilai Khan died in 1294, the economic situation was hopeless because Mongol expenditure far outstripped taxation. One non-Chinese minister after another claimed to know how to close the yawning deficit: then each of them was challenged, accused of misdeeds and finally executed. Lonely and out of touch, Kubilai Khan watched his imperial dream fade. Expeditions dispatched to Japan, Vietnam and Java overstretched military resources, while higher taxes spread unrest among his Chinese subjects.

In the early fourteenth century the strain was evident in the differences among the Mongol nobles, which in twenty-five years raised nine candidates to the dragon throne. The conflict opened the way to a partial recovery of influence by Chinese officials, but starting examinations again for would-be officials in 1315 came too late to rally lasting support for the Yuan dynasty, against whom popular rebellions steadily increased in number and size. Bloody succession struggles only tended to weaken central government further, leaving the last Mongol emperor, Togontemur Khan, with little power beyond the walls of Beijing itself. This shrinkage of authority was due in part to his indifference to everything except the imperial harem. "He was only interested in pleasure," we are told, "because he decreed that no girl over sixteen should marry before his recruitment agents had looked at her." Finding in 1368 that a rebel Chinese army was advancing on Beijing, Togontemur fled to the steppe. For some years afterwards, the Mongols maintained their claim to China but it was merely a face-saving device to cover the downfall of Mongol rule.

Tamerlane, the Sword of Islam

The surge of Mongol power shook Moslem Asia badly. How was it that all the Arabs' gains were so easily lost? As there was no answer to this sudden event, Moslem commentators looked to post-Mongol politics

Tamerlane receiving severed heads

Ismael Samani's tomb at Bukhara, constructed in the 890s. It is the oldest building in Uzbekistan

for an explanation of the castastrophe. They found it in the Turkish leaders who came to power in the aftermath of the Mongol decline. The north African scholar, Ibn Khaldun, was sure that Allah rescued the faithful by sending

> from the Turkish nation and from among its great and numerous tribes, strong rulers to defend them and utterly loyal helpers, who were brought from the House of War to the House of Islam under the rule of slavery . . . They entered Islam with the firm resolve of true believers and yet with their nomadic virtues undefiled by the ways of civilisation.

Most prominent of these new men was Tamerlane (an English corruption of Timur Lenk, "Timur the Lame"). During his rise to power he had suffered an arrow wound in the leg and, though he limped throughout his life, this injury failed to curb his explosive energy.

Born in 1336 at Kesh, south of the city of Samarkand, Tamerlane started out as a freebooter, attracted a following, and achieved power by 1370. From his capital of Samarkand, he led his army into Afghanistan,

Iran, Iraq, Syria, Asia Minor, India and almost China. Tamerlane's military success was in effect a repeat of the retinue system favoured by Genghiz Khan. At a time when tribal loyalties were under pressure from the abandonment of nomadic life, Tamerlane recruited personal followers rather than troops. These ex-nomads were joined by men from the sedentary population who served as foot soldiers and besiegers.

Through the export of violence from Central Asia, Tamerlane ensured the revival of the Silk Road as the major route for international trade, the profits from which allowed him to embellish its cities. In his beloved Samarkand he built mosques, academies, libraries and parks for the scholars, scientists, poets, philosophers and artists he gathered from the countries he conquered. The Gok Sarai, "the Blue Palace", was the seat of Tamerlane's power, a heavily fortified residence at the centre of the city: it housed his court, treasury, armoury and prison.

Although he deliberately acquired a reputation for ruthlessness to overawe subjects and opponents alike, Tamerlane was conscious of the need to balance cruelty with generosity. In such a violent age, his behaviour was not as exceptional as his method of advertising a victory. At Baghdad in 1401, a sack left 90,000 dead, their heads being cemented into 120 towers. That these people were Moslems did not worry "the Sword of Islam", for the city had refused to accept terms and obliged him

The remains of the observatory at Samarkand, where Tamerlane
settled learned men from the countries he conquered

The Gur Amir, Tamerlane's mausoleum at Samarkand

to conduct a six-week siege at the height of summer. Tamerlane saw no contradiction between bloodshed and Islam. The transition from slaughter on a battlefield one day to quiet reflection in a mosque the next posed no moral problems for him. While his army was finishing off the destruction of Baghdad, he went to the nearby tomb of a famous cleric "to implore the aid of this saint". What Tamerlane demanded was obedience to his orders: the inhabitants of Baghdad paid with their lives for defying them. In comparison with his Moslem enemies, Christians, Jews and Hindus escaped lightly. Only occasionally, as though to make up for the massacres of fellow Moslems, would Tamerlane unleash his fury against them too.

Medieval European kings dreaded the possibility of Tamerlane advancing westwards. They had no need to worry because the Central Asian conqueror was uninterested in any renewal of the Crusades, unlike the Ottoman Turks. Quite unnecessary was the praise heaped on him by Charles VI of France, who thanked this "most victorious and serene Prince" for the enlightened treatment of Christian merchants travelling in his empire, because Tamerlane was most anxious that international commerce should flourish once again. Seeing which way the wind was blowing, the Genoese colony at Pera, just across the Golden Horn at Constantinople, had already professed its allegiance and raised Tamerlane's flag.

270

But a concern with the profits derived from trade did not stop Tamerlane from planning an assault on China, the supplier of so many of the products carried by caravans along the Silk Road. From merchants who travelled this route, Tamerlane learned of the civil conflict that accompanied Emperor Yong Le's seizure of power in 1402. It seemed the perfect moment to invade and three years later he set out in the depths of winter for China. Neither intense cold nor fierce storms would deter him until his own health broke down under the rigours of the march. Tamerlane's body was taken to Samarkand, where it was laid to rest in a magnificent mausoleum, soon all that was left of his empire.

The Manchu Conquests

The last of the great Central Asian conquerors were the Manchus, who also have the distinction of ending the menace of nomad attack. Related to the Jin, who replaced the Qidans as the rulers of north China in the twelfth century, the Manchus were semi-nomads who lived in scattered villages beyond the Great Wall. They farmed, herded livestock and hunted. For the Ming dynasty, the presence of the Manchus along the northern frontier seemed at first fortuitous, because they acted as a buffer between the Chinese empire and the troublesome Mongols.

Inner part of the Forbidden City, Beijing. The Qing left this
Ming palace unchanged

271

Emperor Kang Xi, the first Qing ruler
to master the Chinese language

Because they had lived there for centuries, the Manchus were familiar
with Chinese customs and, after their takeover of China, they assimilated
to the extent that they lost their own language.

As did the Mongols, the Manchus owed their rise to power to a
single man: Nurhachi, who increased his personal following from a few
hundred men to an army 40,000 strong. An opportunity to demonstrate his new strength came in 1619 when Nurhachi defeated a large
Chinese force sent to check the growth of his influence. As a result of
this major Chinese reverse, the Koreans went over to the Manchu side.
Success on the battlefield had much to do with the banner organisation
that Nurhachi had instituted. This military system, while incorporating
tribal groups, superseded old divisions and gave the Manchu army an

unusual unity of purpose. As admission to one of the eight banners did not depend on ethnicity, the system's lack of exclusiveness helps explain the ease with which new allies were added to Nurhachi's forces.

Even though Chinese people already subject to Manchu rule were not enrolled in the banners, their labour was vital in increasing agricultural output. A campaign was launched to entice more Chinese farmers to settle beyond the Great Wall with the slogan: "In China the Ming emperor treats you badly. In the far north the Mongols enslave you. Come to Liaodong and receive land as well as a warm welcome!" The roots of the Manchu dual system of government, which separately administered the Manchus and the Chinese, originated here in the Liaodong peninsula. Its purpose, both before and after the conquest of China, was the maintenance of Manchu supremacy over the much larger Chinese population.

After Nurhachi's death in 1626, the Manchus tightened their grip on the steppelands, but they would have remained just another Central Asian people had they not exploited a Chinese civil war that followed the overthrow of the Ming dynasty in 1644. Few people then could have expected that the Manchus would rule China for so long. None of them could have realised that their dynasty, the Qing, was to be the final

Forbidden City roofs

273

Emperor Qian Long's seventieth and eightieth birthday seals

imperial house. Its last emperor Xuan Tong, better known as Henry Pu Yi, abdicated in 1911 in favour of the Republic of China.

While the Chinese civil war raged in the southern provinces, the Manchus quietly occupied Beijing and installed their ruler as Emperor Shun Zi. From the outset, a distinction was made between the Manchu followers of the new Qing emperor and his Chinese subjects, who were visually identified by the queue, which they were forced to wear so as to demonstrate their acceptance of the dynasty. Every Chinese man was required to shave his forehead and braid his hair into what Europeans soon called the pigtail.

An early sign of Manchu accommodation of Chinese tradition, however, was the adoption of Ming Beijing as the capital. They kept the layout of the imperial palace intact, although halls were refurbished or repaired at intervals. Such was the esteem of the Manchus for Chinese ways that in the end they made no changes at all, their only innovation being the Summer Palace built by the fourth Qing emperor Qian Long in the eighteenth century. Within a walled area of 346 hectares lakes were dug, pavilions and temples erected, and pathways constructed, some of them roofed as a protection from the elements. Inspired by his tours of south China, where the vast majority of the empire's population lived and accepted the legitimacy of Manchu rule, Qian Long tried to recreate its lakes and hills at the Summer Palace.

Whereas the first Qing emperor had struggled to learn Chinese, his son mastered the language, without which Kang Xi would never have been seen as a model emperor. What Kang Xi appreciated was the necessity of governing China through a ruling class that combined

Manchu-controlled military power with Chinese administrative know-how. His successors adhered to the same policy and, in 1793, Lord Macartney recognised that Qian Long's reluctance to allow any increase in international trade was connected with the maintenance of Manchu supremacy. The emperor feared the effect that outside influence might have on his Chinese subjects. What the British ambassador did not appreciate, however, was that such a restrictive attitude towards commerce with foreigners tallied with a tradition going back to Ming times. Keeping seaborne barbarians in a semi-official limbo in Guangzhou, a southern port remote from Beijing, seemed a sensible compromise, even if there was bound to be a certain amount of congestion there. As Father Amiot, a Jesuit long resident in the capital, told Macartney after the failure of his mission:

> It would have met with fewer difficulties at its outset if it had arrived before the Imperial Government had been alarmed by the news of great troubles in Europe, the inhabitants of which are indiscriminately considered by them as of a turbulent character.

A dragon holding "the pearl of wisdom" in its claw

Emperor Qian Long being carried to an audience tent to
receive Lord Macartney's unsuccessful embassy in 1793

This was of course the French Revolution. Wars arising from this upheaval
took violence in Europe all the way to Chinese shores when the Royal
Navy occupied Macao in 1802, lest the French attack this Portuguese
holding. When Chinese officials protested, the British admiral threatened Guangzhou with a bombardment, but held his fire so as to leave
commerce undisturbed.

Now it seems amazing that Qian Long failed to appreciate the
danger of a seaborne attack. Yet in the 1760s his armies had completely
subdued the Mongols and finally freed China at last from the threat
of nomad invasion. And Tibet had already been brought under the
sway of the Chinese empire, thereby securing its western frontier. Not
until the Qing dynasty was troubled by unrest in China itself, resulting
from an unexpected defeat by the British in the First Opium War of
1840–42, would its authority be questioned in Tibet, where Indian and
Nepalese raids became commonplace. Yet Britain was still prepared to
recognise Chinese suzerainty over Tibet in 1914. The establishment
of the Republic of China and a declaration of Tibetan independence by
the Dalai Lama had necessitated this final move in the Great Game.
Tsarist Russia accepted this diplomatic ploy in exchange for a sphere of
influence in Mongolia. For the land-oriented Manchus, like the Mughals
in medieval India, the real challenge was to come from the sea, which for
most of the modern era was dominated by Western navies.

Chapter 9

Medieval Southeast Asia

Do not adopt the dress of the Dutch, the Chinese, the Siamese, or the Acehnese . . . We should dress like Javanese. As wise men say, whenever people follow the dress of others, misery inevitably falls upon them.

A seventeenth-century Javanese court chronicle

Independent Vietnam

The history of Vietnam divides into two almost equal parts: a millennium of Chinese rule and, except for the brief era of French colonialism, another of national independence. During the Tang dynasty it was known as Annam, "the peaceful south", although the area under Chinese control was restricted to northern Vietnam. To its south there stood the coastal kingdom of Champa, an Indianised state whose language was entirely distinct from Vietnamese. Considering how Chinese officials in Chang'an looked upon Annam as a backwater, it is hardly surprising that they largely ignored border clashes with the Chams.

The Red river valley always remained the focus of Chinese interest. There the Vietnamese absorbed the culture of China, and used Chinese characters down until modern times. Despite the development of a Chinese-style script for the Vietnamese language, which continued alongside Chinese, recruitment to the civil service followed the Chinese model, so that candidates were expected to have mastered the Confucian classics. Today the Temple of Literature in Hanoi testifies to this enduring influence, since carved on special slabs are the names of all the Vietnamese scholars who came first in the government-sponsored examinations between 1442 and 1779. The slabs are set on the backs of eighty-two giant stone turtles.

More worrying than Champa was Nanzhou in the present-day Yunnan province, where close to the source of the Red river, at Dali, a Chinese army of 60,000 men was annihilated in 751. After this victory the kings of Nanzhou extended their power into the upper reaches of the Irrawaddy river in Burma and invaded Laos, Cambodia and northern Vietnam. In the late 850s unrest in Annam seemed to offer Nanzhou the possibility of permanent conquest, and its forces descended the Red river valley, easily brushing aside the Chinese garrison. A Chinese chronicler regrets that "in Annam were treacherous people who often rebelled", preventing the collection of taxes and complicating the task of dealing with foreign incursions. The situation became critical in 862, when Nanzhou launched a full-scale invasion aimed at expelling the Chinese forever. Only a determined counter-attack dislodged the invaders, who then shifted their attention to other parts of China. Not until Kubilai Khan invaded Nanzhou in 1253, and then added Yunnan to the Mongol empire, was this troublesome neighbour of Vietnam removed. Afterwards there was nothing to stop the southward migration of the Thai people from Nanzhou, their original homeland. By the early 1300s, they dominated the upper and middle reaches of the Mekong and the Chaophraya plain.

For the Vietnamese the conflict with Nanzhou was a very painful prelude to independence. The fragmentation of China at the end of the Tang dynasty lasted long enough for Ngo Quyen to declare himself an independent ruler. From 939 to 944 he ruled as king, but after his death there was anarchy until Dinh Bo Linh restored unity in 968. As a boy,

Van Mieu, the Temple of Literature in Hanoi. It housed Vietnam's first university from 1076 onwards

Dinh Bo Linh's conduct impressed his village enough for a palisade to be erected to keep him safe. When two yellow dragons were observed hovering over him, the villagers knew that here was someone who would "benefit his generation and bring peace to the people". Other tales underline his contempt for the Vietnamese ruling class and a preference for merchants who were capable of funding his bid for power. Though he patronised Buddhism by endowing monasteries and building temples, Din Bo Linh was very interested in Daoism because its ideas were close to traditional Vietnamese beliefs. He seems to have been trying to put a distance between his dynasty and Confucian-inclined Vietnamese scholars who regarded him as an upstart. Through Buddhism and Daoism Din Bo Linh hoped to attract the loyalty of his ordinary subjects, like the villagers among whom he grew up.

While Din Bo Linh was uniting the Vietnamese and strengthening his kingdom, the Song dynasty reunited China. To avoid conflict he sent envoys laden with tribute to the Chinese capital at Kaifeng, where they were well received. A Song edict announced that the proper relationship between Vietnam and China was that of an obedient son and a benevolent father. Diplomatic recognition of Dai Co Viet, "Great Vietnam" as Din Bo Linh's kingdom was called, inaugurated stable Sino-Vietnamese relations that lasted until the start of the Ming dynasty, when Chinese forces reoccupied the country during Zheng He's ocean voyages. In 1408 they arrived at the request of the son of its murdered king, whose own death in the confused fighting might have brought about annexation again to the Chinese empire. Such was the strength of Vietnamese opposition to this, however, that in 1427 the Ming emperor acknowledged the value of the previous relationship with Viet-

Indian-inspired sculpture from Vietnam, where the Chams adopted Hinduism

nam. The rapid Chinese withdrawal was driven by the military genius of Le Loi, who founded the Le dynasty that lasted from 1428 until 1789.

Resistance to outside interference remains characteristic of the Vietnamese outlook even now. Not only was this independent spirit forged during the struggle against China, but even more through hard-fought wars with the Khmers and the Chams. Another enemy the Vietnamese thwarted was the Mongols, who invaded in 1257, 1285 and 1287. They seized Hanoi on each occasion, but guerrilla tactics adopted by the Vietnamese under the determined generalship of Tran Quoc Tuan eventually forced them to quit the country. Emperor Tran Nhan Tuan, the general's cousin, was thus able to resume the throne in triumph.

Champa's position between the Khmer and Sino-Viet empires, both with stronger administrations and larger populations, left it in a weak strategic position that could only be sustained by constant warfare, because plunder rather than trade was critical to the kingdom's economy. As a result, Cham rulers were identified with Shiva and also Indra, the war god of the Aryan invaders of India. At present-day Nha Trang, the Po Nagar towers were once a place of royal worship. They were built in

817 by Harivarman I and dedicated to Yang Ino Po Nagar, Shiva's consort and the protector of the kingdom. Rituals at the tower complex were intended to renew royal authority by demonstrating the king's spiritual relationship with his ancestors as well as the Indian pantheon. The influence of Hinduism is even more apparent in the ruins of Vijaya, inland

Medieval Southeast Asia

from modern Danang. Possibly the Cham capital, this city was twice destroyed by Vietnamese seaborne raids during the twelfth century.

The eclipse of Cham power occurred through a massive Vietnamese invasion in 1470–71. This great push southwards was a decisive stage in Vietnamese expansion that would not stop until the Mekong delta was reached. The Cham king and fifty members of his family were captured, along with 30,000 other Chams. The men were told to adopt Vietnamese names, take Vietnamese wives, and to begin "correcting themselves". There seems to have been a genuine fear that Cham matriarchal traditions could subvert Confucianism, which had replaced similar ones in Vietnam. Final victory over Champa added valuable agricultural land as well as a strain of rice that was quick growing and could flourish even under five metres of water. This "floating rice" was adopted as far north as China, where its amazing productivity did much to transform the countryside.

Vietnamese progress was slowed by two great official families, the Trinh and the Nguyen, who split the country in two. While the Trinh were entrenched in the north around Hanoi, the Nguyen had carved out for themselves a power base farther south at Hue. A line of feeble Vietnamese emperors would have given the Trinh unlimited scope for action had not the Manchu conquest of China brought a powerful new dynasty to the northern frontier. The Nguyen were less concerned about the displeasure of the Manchus, and they welcomed many Chinese refugees as settlers at Saigon, a port the Nguyen acquired in the 1680s. The unassimilated Cham population had declined to barely 50,000, many of whom sought to preserve their self-esteem through ties with Moslem communities living in Malaya and the Indonesian archipelago.

The Khmer Empire

The foundation myth of Cambodia concerns the generosity of a dragon-lord. According to this tale, probably borrowed from southern India, a brahmin named Kaundinya appeared one day off the shore of Cambodia. When the local dragon-princess paddled out to greet the stranger, he fired from a magic bow an arrow into her boat so that she agreed to marry him. Before the wedding Kaundinya gave the dragon-princess clothes to wear and in exchange her father, a mighty dragon-lord, enlarged her dowry by drinking up the water that covered the land. He also built them a fine capital, and changed the name of the country to Kambuja.

A Khmer interpretation of Hari-hara, the deity combining the powers of Shiva and Vishnu, who together overcame the world demon Guha

Thus an Indian priest received the blessing of the existing overlord, whose gift was the water-control schemes that sustained the Cambodian kingdom. Yet another feature of the tale is the expertise of Kaundinya in sacred matters, for Cambodia unreservedly accepted the Hindu idea of kingship. As in Champa, the monarch was a living god, an actual embodiment of Shiva or Vishnu, even Hari-hara, the composite deity whose sculptured form is much in evidence at Angkor. Not so unexpected then was the development of a highly centralised state that was centred upon the raja deva, or "god-king", the focus of his subjects' religious aspirations as well as their hopes for a good life in this world.

First laid out during the reign of Yasovarman I in the 890s within a three-kilometre square, Angkor became the capital of a Khmer empire that dominated most of mainland Southeast Asia for centuries. The Khmer language belongs to the Mon–Khmer family, branches of which are found from Vietnam to the frontiers of India. Until the end of the Angkor era, Sanskrit was used for official purposes, but it did not fully supplant Khmer, which also appeared in inscriptions. After its abandonment as the capital in the 1440s, Buddhist monks continued to worship there until the arrival of the French: hence the name Angkor Wat, "the city that became a Buddhist temple". The choice of the site itself was influenced by Yasovarman's desire to place his own temple-tomb on top of a certain hill. Thirteen other rulers copied his example with the result that Angkor was transformed into a city of the divine dead, something quite alien to the Chinese approach to capital cities.

China never designed a capital around the sanctity of a king or an emperor, and never gave precedence in its layout to mausoleums for

Angkor Wat, Suryavarman II's great contribution to the Khmer capital

reigning or deceased rulers. Except for the ancestral temple, the realms of the sacred and the secular were at all times kept firmly apart. At the centre of a Chinese capital there was invariably a tower, whose function was the maintenance of order and not the worship of a divine ruler like the centrally placed temple-tombs of Khmer kings. Although some Chinese emperors were drawn more than others to the spirit world, the this-worldly tenor of Confucian philosophy set the prevailing tone for dealings with the supernatural. While the Cambodians incarnated Indian deities in their living rulers, the Chinese populated the spiritual realm with bureaucrats. This very level-headed approach, which the Vietnamese borrowed from China, explains their disdain for both Cham and Cambodian traditions.

In spite of a disputed accession, King Yasovarman established the Khmer empire as a major power. He founded Angkor, drew warring principalities firmly together and started an effective administration. Although peasants working on aristocratic and temple land were liable for taxation in kind, labour on public works and military service, Angkor was built by the enslaved, either enemy prisoners of war or captives taken in raids. Not an outright slave society, medieval Cambodia depended to

a large extent on servile labour. But its use never conformed to arrangements elsewhere, for "slaves" married members of the royal family and
owned slaves themselves. Nor, as far as we can tell, was the Indian caste
system ever introduced, unlike Indonesia.

Even while the sons of Yasovarman continued to rule at Sri Yasod-
harapura, the name by which Angkor was then known, another claimant
to the throne set up a rival court elsewhere. This was Jayavarman II. His
claim to the throne was not as illegimate as is often suggested, although
it was indirect enough for him to be labelled a usurper. Jayavarman was
briefly succeeded by his son, who in turn lost the throne to an uncle,
Rajendravarman II in 944. The new king returned the court to Angkor,
where he repaired older buildings and built new ones, including his own
temple-tomb on an island in the middle of a reservoir lake. An inscription praises his decoration of houses "with shining gold, and palaces
glittering with precious stones". Rajendravarman secured his position
through greater control over the provinces as well as successful wars. He
is described as having "a body as hard as diamond" and "a sword always
red with the blood of his foes".

Rajendravarman was succeeded by his young son, most of whose
short reign comprised a regency exercised by aristocratic officials. On
his early death in 1001, the Khmer empire broke in half and its unity
was only restored a decade later by Suryavarman I, a determined ruler
whose success may have depended on an alliance with the priestly

Monkey combat depicted at Angkor

285

An example of Indian-inspired decoration to be found on Khmer buildings.
This stone-carved face is at Angkor Thom

families who now dominated Angkor. He reduced the power of the provincial aristocracy, demanding absolute loyalty to the throne; extended
the area under cultivation by granting tracts of wasteland to new
religious foundations; advanced the western frontier to Lopburi on the
Chaophraya plain and, not least, expanded the city of Angkor. There
he constructed the largest reservoir lake, which still retains a large
body of water. Yet construction activity was not confined to the capital
because peace allowed repairs and new buildings to be commissioned
throughout the restored empire.

Reverses at the hands of the Chams in 1074 and 1080 brought
division once again to Cambodia. The political situation was not stabi-
lised until Suryavarman II ascended the throne. He was even recognised
as an important vassal by the Song dynasty, then ruling from Hangzhou,
near the Yangzi delta. The southern location of the capital naturally
drew Chinese attention to Southeast Asia and a permanent navy of
twenty squadrons protected its commercial interests in southern waters.
Suryavarman II's devotion to Vishnu led him to build the largest Khmer

monument of all, the temple-tomb and observatory now known as Angkor Wat. The miraculous deeds performed during Vishnu's incarnations are carved in relief on the temple's walls, most notably the churning of the ocean: then incarnated as the tortoise Kurma, this saviour deity helped in the production of soma, the food of the gods.

Thirty years of chaos after Suryavarman II's death, about 1150, almost destroyed the Khmer empire. The Chams sailed up the Mekong, crossed the great lake Tongle Sap, and overwhelmed Angkor. Only resolute action by Jayavarman VII, the last of the great Khmer warrior-kings, brought a respite. His bloody revenge against Champa in the 1180s and his reconstruction of Angkor, however, seem to have imposed a crushing burden on his subjects, already under pressure from the migrating Thai. More than any other king, Jayavarman tried to integrate Buddhist concepts with Cambodian ideas of kingship. As a result, he was considered to be a living Buddha, whose compassion for his people explained the reason for his occupation of the throne. It was a view of monarchy that the Thai would find most attractive.

Another example of Khmer architectural decoration.
This is a view of Banteay Srei at Angkor

A gigantic head on a roadside in Cambodia

After a Mongol raid in 1283, his successor Jayavarman VIII hurriedly sent tribute to Kubilai Khan. By the time the first Mongol embassy reached Angkor in 1296, the Khmer capital was in danger of turning into an extravagant film set. A Chinese member of the embassy noted with wonder a royal procession:

> Troops march at the head, in front of banners, flags and musicians. Several hundred palace women, wearing flowered cloth and flowers in their hair, follow holding lighted candles, even in broad daylight . . . Ministers and princes ride on elephants topped by red umbrellas. They are followed by the wives and concubines of the king in chairs and carriages, or on horseback or elephants. Their umbrellas are flecked with gold. Behind them is the ruler himself, standing proudly on an elephant, sword in hand. The tusks of this creature are covered with burnished gold.

All this was in marked contrast to Beijing where, following Chinese practice, the rare movements of the conquering Mongol emperor outside the palace entailed a general clearance of the streets. Ordinary people were never allowed to look upon the Son of Heaven.

Behind the splendid display at Angkor there were already signs of exhaustion: the last stone monument ever to be built in the capital had already been completed. Well might Khmer kings be regarded as gods incarnate, but the days of their empire were numbered: pressure from the Thai kingdom of Ayudhya made Angkor so vulnerable that, after a siege in 1431, the capital shifted downriver to modern Phnom Penh, where one king considered Christian baptism as a means of securing military aid from Spain.

The Kingdoms of Burma

Colossal standing Buddha in gilded wood at the Ananda temple in Pagan

The complicated settlement pattern of Burma, present-day Myanmar, has always tended to produce discord. Modern Burmans descend from a people who arrived in the north of the country during the ninth century. Their Sino-Tibetan language is quite different from Mon, the tongue belonging to the ancient inhabitants of the lowlands and a close relation of Khmer.

The history of Burma until modern times comprised a struggle between the kingdoms of the interior and the kingdoms of the Irrawaddy delta. Despite the abundant rainfall that makes the delta so fertile, the dry interior enjoyed distinct political advantages. First, the need for irrigation and land clearance drew farmers together as a force. A second advantage was the availability of Thai-speaking Shan auxiliaries in extended campaigns. But these northern highlanders were a double-edged weapon, as Anawrahta, the energetic warrior-king of Pagan, found in the eleventh century. This Burman state was called Arimaddanapura, or "the City that Crushes Enemies".

King Anawrahta only seems to have prevented a general coalition against Pagan through a timely marriage to the daughter

The Ananda temple at Pagan, dedicated to the
Buddha's cousin and favourite follower, Ananda.

of a leading Shan chieftain. The further expansion of Pagan's territory
southwards allowed South Asian cultural influences to penetrate the
heartland of Burma. The great scholar-monk Buddhaghosa, whose name
means "the voice of the Buddha", received a joyous reception when he
made his way to Arawrahta's court. He may well have brought with him
one of the Buddha's teeth, now enshrined in the Shwezigon temple at
Rangoon. What he certainly left behind on his return to Sri Lanka were
the standard texts of Hinayana Buddhism.

Before the rise of Pagan, another state had existed on the middle
course of the Irrawaddy. The extensive ruins of its capital Sri Ksetra,

literally "Honoured Field", are close to the modern city of Prome. According to Chinese records, its people were the Pyu but they called themselves the Tircul and spoke a Sino-Tibetan language like that of the later Burmans. Large-scale irrigation schemes allowed Sri Ksetra to flourish from the second to the ninth centuries. A Chinese embassy sent there noted fortifications that took "one day's march to go completely round. There was a deep moat and walls of glazed brick pierced by a dozen gates fitted with carved and gilded wooden doors". When Sri Ksetyra fell to a Nanzhao army in 832, a large number of its inhabitants were deported.

After the decline of the Tirculs, the delta ports were incorporated into the Mon kingdom of Hamsavati, whose capital was Pegu, founded about 825 much nearer to the sea. Hamsavati also had to endure Nanzhao raids, and later cede areas of the lower Irrawaddy valley to the incoming Burmans. Between 849, the traditional date of Pagan's foundation, and the reign of Anawrahta, which began in 1044, the historical record is scant. As did other new arrivals such as the Thai, the Burmans may have served in the forces of Nanzhao as vassals. There is no doubt that some accommodation was necessary until the late tenth century, when Nanzhao ceased to be a major power. Anawrahta's successors extended the influence of Pagan as far south as the Malay peninsula, the northern part of which was to pass in turn under Thai rule.

In and around Pagan, Burman enthusiasm for the Buddhist faith raised a forest of brick-built pagodas, temples and monasteries: today 2,000 bear witness to the city's medieval fame as a centre of Buddhist learning. But Buddhism brought no peace to Burma after Anawrahta's death in 1077, since his son was killed in a rebellion and fierce fighting was necessary to restore order under Kyanzittha. At Pagan this new king completed several temples started by his predecessor without mentioning his name in dedicatory inscriptions, suggesting a usurpation by a younger son of Anawrahta. To Kyanzittha alone, however, must be given credit for Pagan's finest building, the Ananda temple. Brilliant white towers decorated with gold rise above a series of reliefs celebrating the ministry of the Buddha, while at the centre of the temple there are four statues of him in gilded wood, each ten metres long. Kyanzittha even paid for repairs to Buddhist monuments in India, where the faith was being progressively ignored, a decline that must account for Pagan's close ties with Buddhist Sri Lanka.

Peace was shattered by the Mongols, who had crushed Nanzhao. Ignoring this warning, King Narathihapate foolishly executed Mongol

envoys and then attacked a client-state
of Kubilai Khan. The inevitable riposte
in 1287 saw the Burman army routed
and the abandonment of Pagan. Dis-
liking the tropical heat, the Mongols
only incorporated northern Burma
into their dominions and left the rest
of the country in the hands of petty
rulers. Shortlived though Mongol rule
was, the division it reintroduced in
Burma lasted till the sixteenth century,
because Thai chieftains were quick to
profit from the disorder, even in the
south. By breaking the power of both
Nanzhao and Pagan, the Mongols
encouraged the creation of Thai
client-states stretching across Burma
and what was to become Thailand.

The future Buddha cutting off his
hair before setting out on his
quest for enlightenment

Those Burmans who wished to
avoid Thai domination gradually concentrated at Toungoo in the remote
Sittang river valley. This tiny principality later formed the nucleus of
national revival, when the second Toungoo king Tabinshweti conquered
the whole of southern Burma and was crowned in 1541 at Pegu. The
strength of Tabinshweti's army lay in his ruthless mercenaries, companies
of hard-bitten Portuguese who fought alongside equally tough Moslems
from Java and India. Matchlocks supplied by the Portuguese soldiers of
fortune proved superior in accuracy, ballistic weight and rapidity of fire.
By 1546 Tabinshweti had extended his authority from the well-fortified
city of Toungoo to encompass all of Burma, except the Arakan, where
after the fall of Pagan a separate kingdom had emerged.

Even though early Toungoo kings were troubled by the revolts of
non-Burman peoples, which began soon after Tabinshweti's own Mon
guards assassinated him, they succeeded in keeping at bay the Thai as well
as the Portuguese. In 1613 King Anaukpetlun destroyed Syriam in the
Irrawaddy delta, the stronghold of Filipe de Brito e Nicote. A remarkable
example of private enterprise, Syriam was eventually recognised by
the Portuguese as a customs post, which gave de Brito access to military
supplies. These proved inadequate when attacked by an army of 100,000

men. Once he ran out of gunpowder and was unable to fire his cannon effectively, his local troops stole away until de Brito's Portuguese followers could no longer man the defences. As a punishment for looting Buddhist temples, de Brito was impaled on an iron stake, where he lingered for two days in full view of his men. However, Anaukpetlun decided to spare the lives of these cowed professionals, and for well over a century their descendants were responsible for Burma's artillery. What the fate of Syriam demonstrated was the limits of European power when confronted by the manpower resources of properly organised Asian states. Only in disunited Sri Lanka were the Portuguese able to rule an extensive territory, but even there they were struggling before the Dutch expelled them in 1658.

The Toungoo dynasty had disappeared before the Manchu emperor Qian Long invaded Burma. Freed from the nomad threat along the northern frontier, Qian Long decided to reassert China's authority in Southeast Asia. The four-year campaign in northern Burma ended in a stalemate, with the Burmese paying the same tribute to China as before. Much to Qian Long's anger his army was compelled to conclude hostilities by melting down its cannon, more easily to carry the metal home. The withdrawal confirmed the new Konbaung dynasty, which replaced Toungoo kings in 1752. Its most energetic successor and ruler was Bodawpaya, the fifth member of the new house. Before his death in 1817, he had greatly expanded Burma's borders and the royal family: his 53 wives gave birth to no less than 120 children.

The Island Powers: Srivijaya, Mataram and Majapahit

Describing a port in what today is the southernmost part of Thailand, a Chinese envoy testifies to the extent of India's influence there. We are informed that

> its market was a meeting-ground between east and west, frequented every day by more than 10,000 men, including merchants from India, Persia and more distant countries who come in large numbers to carry on trade and commerce in rare objects and precious merchandise. It contains 500 merchants' families, 200 Buddhists and more than 1,000 Hindus from India. The local people follow these religions and give their daughters in marriage to the Indians as most of them settle down and do not go away.

A Javanese scene from the *Mahabharata* in which the Pandavas lose their
kingdom in a rigged game of dice

Such was the influence of India on Southeast Asia that most early
medieval states adopted its religious and political ideas. Kings espoused
both Buddhism and Hinduism, monks and priests becoming advisers
on court ritual, besides acting as astrologers and scribes. The earliest
Indianised kingdoms so far discovered were located in eastern Borneo
and western Java and date from the fifth century. Not long afterwards
the Sumatra-based kingdom of Srivijaya began to dominate the western
part of the Indonesian archipelago and achieved renown as a centre for
Buddhist studies. Much of our knowledge about Srivijaya comes from
the writings of the Chinese monk Yijing, who stopped for six months on
his way to India in 671 so that he could master Sanskrit grammar. Of its
capital Palembang he says:

> There are more than 1,000 Buddhist monks whose minds are en-
> tirely turned to study and good works. And they consider every
> possible subject. If a Chinese monk wishes to travel westwards and
> consult the original scriptures, he should stay here for a year or
> two and prepare himself properly for the journey to India.

On his return from India, Yijing remained in Srivijaya for another four years, during which time he copied and translated Buddhist texts into Chinese. In 689, after a brief trip to China, where he had gone to recruit four assistants, he returned to Palembang and set up a translation school. Yijing was still resident when, in 695, Srivijaya first paid tribute to the Chinese emperor.

According to Yijing, the rival state of Malayu came under Srivijayan control shortly before 671. Its capital of Jambi lay to the north of Palembang. The Malay rulers of Srivijaya made their state pre-eminent in Southeast Asia's maritime commerce. Styled "Lord of the Mountain", each Srivijayan king claimed that his authority derived from the good-will of the ancestral spirits who dwelt on Sumatra's mountain slopes. As "Lord of the Isles", however, he was also believed to control the less kindly spirits of the sea. For this purpose the king threw a gold bar daily into the Musi estuary. Such an expensive method of propitiation was paid for by the profits derived from trade, but an inscription from Palembang,

Rati, the Balinese version of the Hindu goddess of maternity and fertility

dated to 683, refers to an expedition that returned home with enormous spoils. The distinction between trade and piracy has never been easy to define in the Indonesian archipelago, especially when rulers wished to safeguard their commercial interests through sudden raids. One of the reasons behind the modern development of Singapore was the protection of shipping from the attention of pirates: the Royal Navy needed a secure base that could be used to deter attacks on British merchantmen.

Although the kings of Srivijaya incorporated into their empire some previously independent riverine cities on the northern and western coasts of Java, they made no early effort to subjugate Mataram, the name given to the central part of this populous island. Central Java boasted kingdoms well before the rise of Srivijaya, thanks to its volcanic soil and a year-round growing season. It was indeed at the time of Srivijaya's heyday, from the 730s to the

Part of the vast Buddhist stupa of Borobudur in Java

1020s, that Java saw a construction boom as Hindu and Buddhist monuments were planted on hillsides and plains in their hundreds. Nothing quite matches though, the solitary splendour of Borobudur, situated to the north of present-day Yogyakarta. Its name probably means "many Buddhas". Architecturally, Borobudur is unlike anything else in Java, because a whole hill has been clothed in stone, and topped with a stupa while seventy-two smaller stupas are arranged in three concentric circles below. The monument's nine terraces record the lives of the Buddha before his enlightenment. Seen from a distance, the immense structure looks, as its designer obviously intended, like a single stupa.

Started by the Sailendra dynasty in 778 but not completed until 824, Borobudur's incredible number of carved reliefs and the painstaking manner in which they were executed explain the length of time required for the project. When the lower basement was uncovered in 1885, the care with which this work had been undertaken could be seen in the guidance inscribed there for sculptors: they were instructed to carve scenes that touched upon karma, the cause and effect of reincarnation. What the Sailendra kings wished to show their subjects was the true path that each individual must tread to follow the Buddha.

The Sailendras were related by marriage to other ruling families in Java as well as the Srivijaya royal house. After a palace coup, one deposed Sailendra king went to Palembang, where, in the 850s, he ascended the Srivijaya throne almost unchallenged. The successors of the Sailendras in Mataram tried to distinguish their own dynasties by favouring Hinduism over Buddhism. At their capital in Prambanan, also near Jogyakarta, there stand the remains of magnificent temples dedicated to Brahma, Vishnu and Shiva. Unlike those at Borobudur, they may have been intended to serve as mausoleums for kings, princes and the aristocracy in a similar manner to the temple-tombs built for Khmer kings in Angkor.

Mataram kings participated actively in the spice trade with the Chinese and the Arabs through their control of the Moluccas until, finally in 1006, Srivijaya overran Java. Respite arrived twenty years later in the sack of Palembang by the Cholas, southern Indian kings who had already

Vishnu riding on the sun bird Garuda, the enemy of serpents.
Eighteenth century, Bali

pillaged Burma. As Srivijaya failed to recover from this unexpected blow, its subsequent weakness allowed a Balinese prince by the name of Erlanga to marry a Mataram princess and restore Java's fortunes. But his devotion to Vishnu, whose incarnation he was believed to be, did not stop him from seizing temple lands and using this accumulated wealth to regenerate the island's stricken economy. Most of all, Erlanga is remembered by the Javanese with gratitude for finally establishing effective water-control schemes. By the placement of dams at strategic points, he prevented flooding and provided a regular supply of water for irrigation, long a Balinese speciality. This energetic monarch returned Java to prosperity: its ports grew rich again through trade, an entitlement that Erlanga was pleased to guarantee by charters engraved on metal sheets. Having no direct heir and fearing a contest between children born of rival concubines, Erlanga divided his kingdom into two separate states before he died in 1049.

Both states were eventually absorbed into Singasari, and later Majapahit, the last and greatest of the seaborne empires in Southeast Asia before the arrival of the Europeans. The achievement of Kertanagara in founding Singasari is the subject of the *Nagarakertagama*, an epic poem composed in 1365 by the Buddhist monk Prapanca to glorify its early rulers. We learn how Kertanagara erected a huge statue of himself as the Buddha. By then the synthesis of Hinduism, Buddhism and indigenous Javanese beliefs was complete. In the person of the king it was believed that their combined essences resided, an awsome power that Kertanagara was going to need in dealing with the Mongols, whose envoys he gratuitously insulted in 1289. Instead of accepting the hegemony of Kubilai Khan as a Chinese-style emperor, and sending tribute to the Mongol ruler's new capital at Beijing, Kertanagara tattooed the faces of the ambassadors, sending them back in disgrace.

Kubilai Khan disliked the growth of Singasari's influence, an attitude strengthened by complaints from smaller maritime states in Southeast Asia that feared the aggressive foreign policy of Kertanagara. Their tribute-bearing envoys would have raised this concern with the Mongol emperor. As a result, Kubilai Khan sent a fleet of 1,000 ships to chastise Java. But on its arrival at present-day Surabaya, from which the capital of Singasari was fifty kilometres upriver, the Mongols discovered that Kertanagara was already dead, a casualty of a local war. Remarkable though it seems, Kertanagara's son-in-law, Raden Vijaya, persuaded the commander of the expedition that he should punish those who killed Kertanagara and restore the situation. Thus Raden Vijaya ascended the throne of the new state of Majapahit, allowing the Mongols to carry away vast quantities of loot without becoming involved in a costly guerrilla war. As in Vietnam, they would have found how the jungle terrain gave plenty of scope to the Javanese for protracted resistance.

After this curious intervention there was nothing to stop Majapahit from dominating maritime trade. A chronicler relates how its "empire grew prosperous, people in vast numbers thronged its capital, and food was in great abundance". Most telling of all is the statement that "from the shores of the Southern Ocean envoys came from everywhere for an audience with the king, bringing tribute and presents". Nothing less than a second Srivijaya, the seaborne empire of Majapahit owed much to Gajah Mada, its first minister from 1330 to 1364, because he regularised

Portrait of a Javanese queen from a Hindu temple at Prambanan

the spice trade by means of collecting annual quotas as tribute. A war of succession undermined Majapahit in the early 1400s, when Malacca was founded. The development of the latter as the hub of trade routes in Southeast Asia was facilitated by Chinese protection under the great Ming admiral, Zheng He. His use of Malacca as a temporary naval base deterred both the Thai and the Javanese.

The Slow Spread of Islam

Although the Chams in southern Vietnam are known to have embraced Islam in the tenth century, Southeast Asia remained generally uninterested in that faith for another three hundred years. The activities of Arab traders hardly figure in the spread of Muhammad's message, because so few stayed on for any length of time. Although the apocryphal Malay *Annals of Semarang* credits Chinese Moslems with the spread of Islam, this may be no more than a memory of Zheng He's fleet calling at Javanese ports during the early 1400s. The great Ming admiral was a believer himself. Not until Moslem merchants from India took up permanent residence, and then married local girls, were mosques and schools necessary. According to Portuguese accounts, the towns and cities along the Javanese coast all professed Islam. Inland, it is unlikely that the new religion had yet made much headway, as substantial pockets of Hindu worshippers indicate today. Quite different then from the conflict stirred up by its adherents elsewhere was the largely peaceful penetration of Islam in Southeast Asia, although an early casualty of its iconoclasm, except in staunchly Hindu Bali, was the exuberance of Malay figurative art. Militant Islam only appeared in Java during the late sixteenth century, when hard-pressed Hindu rulers on the island were forced to ally themselves with the Portuguese.

A notable survival of Indian-inspired ways, however, were the walis, unorthodox Moslem saints who flourished on the island of Java during the late medieval era. These men behaved in a manner reminiscent of the wandering devotees of Shiva, who followed a regime that aimed at union with this Hindu deity. Shiva's followers went naked or wore a single garment, smeared themselves with ashes thrice a day, and gave worship by dancing, roaring like a bull or simply laughing. Finally, their intense asceticism granted mastery of the senses, so that they could live comfortably on a cremation ground. Somewhat less extreme was

Pangeran Panggung, the elder brother of a north Javanese sultan. This wali is famous for the saying:

Debts in gold may be settled by payment.
Debts in wisdom are carried to the next life.

Yet his unconventional behaviour scandalised the sultan when it became obvious that Pangeran Panggung was so concerned with the love of Allah that "his worldly possessions were lost and, in his actions, the wali disregarded Qur'anic law".

Pangeran Panggung is said to have caused "the passions of greed and anger" to emerge from his own body as two dogs: he named the black one Iman, "Faith", and the red one Tokid, "Unity". Wherever he went, they would accompany him, even when he attended Friday prayers. The dogs sat behind Pangeran Panggung, apparently listening to what the imam had to say. Other Moslems were furious at the presence of these "unclean" animals and even the sultan's brotherly love gave way to a hatred that led to the wali's sentence to death by burning. Taken to the pyre, Pangeran Panggung threw rice into the flames and ordered the two dogs to eat it. When they emerged with fur unsinged, bystanders realised that their master could not be burned either. To underline this point, the wali stood in the flames himself while composing a manual for the Javanese people, which the sultan took back to his palace. One of its tenets is that the worshipper must "taste the annihilation of annihilation" to understand Allah. This knowledge was vouchsafed only to those who had progressed beyond religious observance and appreciated how fasting and charity were mere "idols".

Moslems unable to understand Pangeran Panggung's mystical approach latched onto his dogs. Missing the full import of his teachings, these admirers of the wali "cherished dogs of all kinds, put collars of gold coins round their necks, bathed them with care, and provided food in precious bowls". Though still regarded as an out-and-out heretic by his more traditional opponents, this criticism does not stop Javanese people from visiting Pangeran Panggung's grave today. Moslem saints are revered for the help they can offer the living, and especially the wali, at whose tombs spiritual power is said to be heavily concentrated.

Neither the slowness of Islam's advance, nor the unusual ideas about worship championed by the walis, made any difference in the end. Once most Javanese converted, Indonesia was destined to become the world's most populous Moslem country. Java had always been the demographic anchor of the Indonesian archipelago because its fertile plains were ideally suited to rice cultivation. Now more than half of the Republic of Indonesia's 240 million inhabitants live there.

The Advent of European Power

The subsequent spread of Islam was stimulated by two factors: the development of Malacca into a major port and the arrival of Christianity under the aggressive Portuguese. In the first instance, the conversion of Malacca's ruler to Islam meant that the nodal position of the port, at the meeting point of several Southeast Asian trade routes, helped to spread the faith widely. The Ming emperor Yong Le had already given its sultan a war junk to defend his realm. Ma Huan, an official interpreter on the 1413 ocean voyage and, like Chinese admiral Zheng He a believer himself, noted with interest how "the king of Malacca and all his people follow the new religion, fasting, making penance and saying prayers". Such a reaction has nothing in common with the religious fanaticism of the Portuguese, whose own sense of identity had been forged through conflict with Moslems. When Alfonso de Albuquerque, the second Portuguese viceroy in Asia, took Malacca by storm in 1511, he told his men that its capture would destroy Islam locally and bankrupt Cairo and Mecca, besides obliging the Venetians to buy spices in Lisbon: a truly wonderful mixture of spiritual and commercial profit.

Arguably, the advent of the Portuguese did the exact opposite. Because they were never able to do more than disrupt the spice trade, the locals worked hard to keep it out of Christian hands. Within fifty years of building a fortress at Malacca, the grip of Portugal was already loosening through the energies of Aceh, a sultanate situated in northern Sumatra. Fourteen times the Acehnese launched attacks on Malacca, while they also shipped pepper and other spices to the Turkey-dominated Red Sea without apparent difficulty. There is indeed evidence of military cooperation between the Ottoman Turks and the Achenese against Portugal, so that the idea of a pan-Islamic counter-crusade against Christian intruders took root in Southeast Asia. The Portuguese repulsed all the Acehnese assaults on Malacca, but their failure to counter with any blow directly on Aceh was a sign of an increasing manpower crisis.

Even at the height of its power, the Estado da India, as Portugal's Asian empire was called, commanded no more than 10,000 men. From the outset, therefore, the Estado da India's focus was restricted to the

Alphonso de Albuquerque, whose aggressive policies laid the foundation of Portuguese power in Asia

spice trade, the most lucrative of all European markets. By planting fortresses at strategic locations and conducting regular sweeps of the sea, the Portuguese were able to add customs duties to the profits derived from their own trading activities.

Before the nineteenth century the European impact on Southeast Asia was at its greatest in the Philippines, where Spain constructed on the site of a Moslem stockade at Manila the first stone fortress. After an initial setback under Ferdinand Magellan, who in 1521 had reached Asia sailing in a westerly direction via Cape Horn, the Spanish authorities in the New World decided to convert the Filipinos and profit from trade. Magellan had been killed when he overestimated the advantage of European arms, and fell in an engagement against more than a thousand warriors on the island of Mactan. While only few Spaniards were actually killed in the attacking force of 50 men, the aura of invincibility was lost and a tactical withdrawal became necessary.

In return for leaving the rest of Southeast Asia to Portugal, Spain enjoyed a free hand in the Philippines. Without a unified political or religious authority among the 7,000 islands of its archipelago, where more than 100 languages were spoken by the islanders, the Spaniards found it easy to exploit local rivalries for their own advantage, once the healthy climate attracted permanent settlers at Manila. That the Philippines had received little cultural influence from India or China also gave Spain greater scope for moulding its peoples than Portugal ever had in the Indianised south. Both these European powers encountered Moslems, but Islam had made relatively little progress in the Philippines, with most converts living on the southernmost islands of Mindanao and Sulu.

It seems likely that the Portuguese capture in 1511 of Malacca gave Islam an unexpected boost, for the reason that the arrival of

Portuguese Malacca. Some 4,000 foreign merchants lived outside
the fortifications

Christian-Moslem conflict in Southeast Asia served to define local
resistance to European exploitation. The inhabitants of the Philippines
were to discover that Christianity would be regarded as a matter of loyalty
to the Spanish crown too. Different though the many Filipino societies
were from each other, they shared certain traditions including a belief
in a spirit world that proved helpful to Catholic missionaries. Women
were never the property of men, although the Spaniards were shocked by
how easy it was to divorce. As in other parts of Southeast Asia, women
played a major role in trade, and especially market-places. Various sources
record this fact. "In Cambodia," we are told "the women take charge
of trade," while among the Thai, "only the women are merchants, and
some of them trade considerably". "Moneychangers in Aceh are all
women," another visitor recorded, "as in Vietnam, where every man is a
soldier, and commercial operations are performed by women." This state
of affairs lasted until the 1810s, when Raffles noted on Java that

> it is usual for the husband to entrust his pecuniary affairs entirely
> to his wife. The women alone attend markets, and conduct all the
> business of buying and selling. It is proverbial to say the Javanese
> men are fools in money concerns.

Greater involvement of Westerners in international trade may have been the cause of a gradual withdrawal of Southeast Asian women from commerce during the nineteenth century.

The brutality of Spanish immigrants in the Philippines was to some degree mitigated by intermarriage with Filipino converts. The effect of conversion in lowering barriers between the rulers and the ruled would have been even greater had the Spanish authorities not decreed that for security reasons only priests were allowed to live in the interior. Missionary activity was increasingly seen as a sure method of preparing the indigenous peoples for acceptance of the Spanish state. Portuguese and Spanish settlers in Asia were unlike later Dutch, French and British arrivals, who tended to see themselves as only temporary residents. In consequence, 85 per cent of the Filipinos adopted Christianity and the church governed most areas outside Manila, acquiring great wealth as priests collected taxes and sold the crops grown by their parishioners. Not until 1842 were friars forbidden from whipping those who showed insufficient faith, often a euphemism for a spirit of independence. Just as repressive was the treatment of Chinese merchants who came to live in Manila. In 1603 Spanish records give the number of Chinese killed as 15,000.

Between 1580 and 1640, when Portugal was under the Spanish crown, the territories belonging to the Estado da India were neglected, in part because King Philip II had decided that the two colonial empires of Spain and Portugal should remain separately administered entities. A satisfactory outcome to the wars that he, and his successors, waged in Europe would have freed ships and men for overseas service, but the naval disasters against England in 1558 and Holland in 1639 seriously undermined Iberian seapower, and left ample scope for any European power intent on securing a major share of long-distance world trade.

Even before the final ratification in 1647–48 of the Treaty of Münster, by which Spain acknowledged Holland's independence, Dutch ships had already disrupted Portuguese commerce throughout Asian waters. Portuguese possessions were the chief target of attack because the Dutch realised that more could be gained by taking over the spice trade. Goa was blockaded for several years and, in 1641, the Portuguese were expelled from Malacca. There was jubilation at Batavia, the permanent base established by the Dutch in western Java. Except for Britain at the start of the nineteenth century, no power ever approached the reach of early Dutch trading ventures. Once merchants

A Chinese illustration of a Dutch vessel, whose crew were termed "Ocean Devils"

in Amsterdam were persuaded of the value of cooperation, a concerted effort was made to monopolise the import of spices to Europe. But setting up a fortified settlement at Batavia, present-day Jakarta, was to have unexpected consequences for Holland: the steady extension of its influence throughout the Indonesian archipelago laid the foundation of a land-based empire.

Impressed though Malay rulers were by the Dutch capture of Malacca, they soon came to appreciate how its new owners were intent on monopolising commerce and paying unrealistically low prices into the bargain. Supplies of tin were withheld and the Dutch resorted to force. But the attempt to take control of all Southeast Asia's trade came to nothing, because the Dutch were unwilling to turn back ships from England lest relations were strained to breaking point in Europe, where between 1652 and 1674 three indecisive Anglo-Dutch wars were fought. The last one ended in the admission that the English and the Dutch would simply have to tolerate each other on the high seas.

Eschewing the evangelism of the Spaniards and the Portuguese, the Dutch chose not to interfere with Southeast Asian customs or beliefs in case social unrest hindered trade. The only pressure put on the local population was to stimulate the production of spices. In the 1690s, for example, the Ambonese were obliged to raise the annual output of cloves to 500 tonnes, perhaps a 30 per cent increase over the decade. Elsewhere Batavia adjusted the supply of pepper, nutmeg and mace according to European demand. The overall pattern of exchange was for Southeast Asia to import cloth from India, silver from the Americas and Japan and copper coins, silk, ceramics and other manufactures from China. Like a powerful spider, the Dutch ensured that suppliers as well as consumers were entangled in their commercial web, with the result that profits of more than 100 per cent were common as goods passed from country to country. The Dutch were ruthless, slaughtering thousands of Indonesians who opposed them: in 1621, they exterminated almost the entire population of the Banda Islands. Those few spared death or enslavement were left to starve.

Where the Dutch exercised direct rule, as in western Java, the social hierarchy reflected the exploitive nature of Batavia's outlook. Dutch administrators and settlers occupied the topmost rungs, followed by Malay rulers and aristocrats who lent their support to the colonial government. Next came the non-Dutch commercial class of Chinese merchants, below whom were the mass of the indigenous population. The very lowest group comprised the enslaved, an institution that the Dutch were content to leave undisturbed, for the good reason that there was a great demand for slaves in Batavia, in outposts of the Indonesian archipelago and also at trading posts along the shipping route to Holland. Informing this rigid social arrangement was the Dutch attitude towards race. Such an unbridgeable gulf was fixed between the Dutch and the Indonesians that settlers who took local wives were not allowed to return to Holland, other than in exceptional cases. The ban was then extended to Dutchmen who used female slaves as concubines, but this did not stop them chasing good-looking Indonesians because few Dutch women ever came to live in Southeast Asia.

The Rise of the Thai

Political disintegration on mainland Southeast Asia after the intervention of the Mongols provided the Thai with their chance of power.

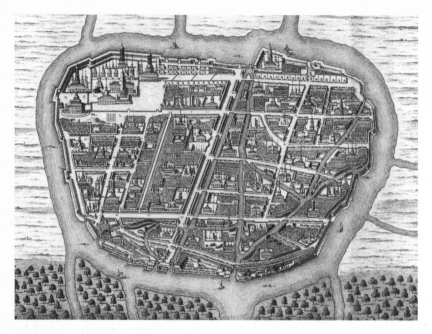

A Dutch map of Ayudhya, "the Venice of the East"

The Indianised states based on Pagan in Burma and Angkor in Cambodia were already in eclipse by the close of the thirteenth century. Although Khmer authority did not collapse with the dramatic suddenness of the Burmese kingdom in 1287, there was a lack of dynamism at Angkor that no amount of ceremony could disguise. That the later decline of Mongol strength happened to coincide with even greater Thai pressure on Angkor meant that in the fourteenth century the Khmers were left to wage a losing battle on their own.

Yet the Thai migration predated the arrival of the Mongols. For centuries the Thai peoples had inhabited the valleys leading from the Yunnan plateau. They were recruited by Nanzhao for its assaults on Vietnam and the outlying provinces of the Chinese empire. Once Yunnan had been conquered by the Mongols, however, the Thai were free to pursue their own destiny. A memory of their widespread migration is contained in the myth of Khun Borom, the divine bringer of agriculture, handicrafts, manners, learning and ritual. After a prosperous reign of twenty-five years on the plain around Dien Bien Phu, in the north of Vietnam, Khun Borom sent his seven sons to rule over the various Thai groups already spread across mainland Southeast Asia.

The story could well reflect the diffusion of power at the start of the fourteenth century, when there was a patchwork of Thai principalities stretching continuously from the Vietnamese border across the Mekong and Chaophraya rivers to the Gulf of Martaban. None of these jostling kingdoms attained sufficient power to dominate its neighbours, and it was not until the foundation of Ayudhya in 1351 by the adventurer U Thong that any sign of regional strength reappeared. U Thong, whose name means "Prince Golden Cradle", was born around 1314 into a rich Chinese merchant family. It was his marriage to a Thai princess from Lopburi that laid the foundation of Thailand's future strength: a subtle combination of Thai arms with Chinese commerce.

One account of U Thong's elevation as King Ramathibodi mentions an outbreak of smallpox, a vacant throne and the removal of the capital from Lopburi to Ayudhya. This new city, built on a downstream

The Emerald Buddha's Hall in the Grand Palace, Bangkok,
shows the influence of Khmer traditions

More Khmer influence is evident in the architecture of the
Regalia Hall at Bangkok

island, was named after the hero Rama's stronghold in the Indian epic
Ramayana: Ayudhya or Ayutthaya. The kingdom of Ayudhya soon
dominated the Chaophraya basin, while the international contacts of
its flourishing port may have stimulated further expansion down the
Malayan peninsula and along the coast of Cambodia. Proximity to what
was left of the once mighty Khmer empire undoubtedly inspired imperial ambitions in Ramathibodi and, between 1351 and 1431, there was
an almost permanent state of war between Angkor and Ayudhya. But
armed rivalry did not preclude admiration for Khmer kingship, and the
court at Ayudhya adopted its protocol wholesale, thereby inaugurating
the process by which Thailand came to absorb so much of Cambodian
tradition.

Ayudhyan society was divided into a strict hierarchy, presided over
by royal officials from leading families. As a foreign community, the
Chinese exercised political influence by assisting one court faction or
another to increase its wealth or make diplomatic contacts abroad.
Despite a great deal of assimilation, this behind-the-scenes influence

continues today, so that Thailand could be described as a Sino-Thai corporation, owing allegiance to the royal house.

The duties of royal officials were defined by King Borommatrailokanat, whose incorporation of new territories in the 1450s caused the setting up of a proper administration. Following Khmer practice, Trailok (as he is known) centralised government, distinguished between civil and military landholders, amalgamated local forces into the royal army and replaced tribal leaders with princely governors. The outcome of this reform was a stability unsurpassed anywhere in medieval Southeast Asia. The system lasted with only minor modifications right down to the nineteenth century when Western-style reforms were introduced to modernise present-day Thailand. Even then the government remained, before the constitutional revolution of 1932, which abolished absolute monarchy, largely the preserve of the nobles.

From the start, the kingdom of Ayudhya was tightly organised and controlled. Not to be underestimated, however, was the influence of Khmer speakers at the Ayudhyan court, whose vocabulary buttressed

The enormous Buddha at Wat Po in Bangkok, where the Thai king
is believed to possess the essence of this saviour

A Thai royal procession. Absolute monarchy lasted until 1932

the majesty of the throne and raised the king far above the level of his subjects. Neither Shiva nor Vishnu came to be seen as incarnate in the ruler, but rather the essence of the Buddha. Kindly benevolence and impassivity were its outward signs, a reason for current portraits of the Thai king never showing a smile or a frown, since these would indicate an attachment to worldly objects.

But worldly concerns were to trouble Ayudhya in the form of the Toungoo dynasty, named after the refuge of the Burmans after the Mongol destruction of Pagan. A Burmese invasion was only just turned back in 1593 at the battle of Nong Sarai, after which the Thai ravaged large areas of Burma itself. But the seesawing struggle ended in favour of the Burmese, when in 1767 they sacked Ayudhya. Disastrous though the Burmese attack was at the time, its long-term result was the unification of Thailand, for the territories covered by the Thai-speaking kingdoms of Ayudhya, Lan Na and Lan Sang were incorporated under the subsequent and long-lasting Chakri dynasty. The present Thai king, Bhumipol Adulyadej, who ascended the throne in 1946, is the ninth member of this dynasty to reign, his title being Rama IX.

The country's saviour was a second U Thong, whose charisma offset a Chinese ancestry. The son of a Chinese father and a Thai mother, Sin had been adopted by a noble family. At the time of the fateful

312

Burmese invasion, he was serving as governor of Tak province: hence his preferred name, Taksin. Having shifted the capital downriver to Bangkok, he established himself as a benevolent and effective ruler. He claimed that his new kingdom of Siam restored the traditions of Ayudhya, but in reality his court was cosmopolitan with the sons of Indian, Persian, Cham, Malay and Chinese families joining those belonging to old Thai ones. From his startling successes on the battlefield probably stemmed Taksin's personal difficulties towards the end of his reign. In 1779 it was clear that all was not well at court. French missionaries reported that Taksin increasingly devoted himself to religious exercises: "He passed all his time in prayer, fasting, and meditation, in order by these means to be able to fly in the air." What they regarded as Southeast Asian eccentricity was in fact the serious pursuit of immortality. Confirmation of Taksin's aim comes from his insistence on being called a Buddhist saint, even a deity: monks who refused to accord him this honour were flogged and sentenced to hard labour. Alienating the Buddhist monks, the old Thai families, the royal officials and the Chinese merchants, Taksin's fate was, in 1782, sealed when he was deposed and beaten to death inside a velvet sack. Violence could never be directly inflicted on the body of a king.

Taksin's general Chaophraya Chakri then agreed to ascend the throne. By the end of his reign as Rama I, even tributary states were content to belong to a Siam that was strong enough to protect them from the Burmese and the Vietnamese. That more dangerous enemies were on the horizon was not missed when news arrived in Bangkok of the sultan of Kedah's cession of Penang to the British. Later kings understood how modernisation represented the only means of preserving Thai independence. Even though, in 1851, Rama III bequeathed his successors a Siamese empire that was more powerful and stronger than at any previous time, he was realistic about its prospects of survival. On his deathbed the king remarked how "there will be no more wars with Vietnam and Burma. We will have them only with the West. Take care, and do not lose any opportunities to them."

The dying king believed that the British defeat of China during the First Opium War of 1840–42 had inaugurated a new international order. That as Rama IV, his brother Mongkut was able to steer Siam on an independent course remains one of the most surprising achievements of the late nineteenth century. The country's position was far from safe, with Burma and Malaya being steadily absorbed by the British and Vietnam and Cambodia coming under increasing French influence. Treaties signed with Britain in 1855, and France a year after, regularised relations with Siam, although never missing an opportunity for trade, the British also gained for its infamous Indian export, opium, the waving of import duty. The policy of playing off Britain against France was continued by Mongkut's son Chulalongkorn, or Rama V, who was probably assisted in this dangerous game by the unstated wish of both powers to avoid having a common border between their colonial holdings in Southeast Asia.

Chulalongkorn also followed his father's lead in the modernisation of Siamese society and government. Mongkut had cultivated relations with Europeans, in particular the more reasonable missionaries. Through these contacts he had acquired imported books and a grasp of the English language. His interests ranged from steam technology to the mathematics of astronomy. But it was Chulalongkorn who derived the greatest benefit from the palace governess, Anna Loenowens. Despite Mongkut's desire to hand over responsibility for the kingdom to his son when the prince came of age in 1873, both of them were stricken by malaria on a visit to peninsular Malaya to witness a solar eclipse in 1868. Not long after their return to Bangkok, Mongkut died, leaving a fifteen-year-old heir-apparent whose own health was precarious.

Once firmly established on the throne, however, Rama V began a series of reforms that revealed his concern for progress. Royal decrees sought to speed up justice, reduce corruption, control expenditure, improve the armed forces, develop communications and tackle slavery. In 1905 debt-bondage was finally abolished, one of the last vestiges of feudalism cleared away by this still absolute king. The reigns of the father and the son preserved national independence and in 1932 facilitated a bloodless transfer to a constitutional monarchy. But survival came at a price because Bangkok had to trade territory for peace with Britain and France.

Part 3

Modern Asia

Chapter 10

Modern West Asia

Here are the Arabs believing me.
Allenby and Clayton trusting me,
My bodyguard dying for me;
And I begin to wonder if all established reputations
Were founded, like mine,
On fraud.

Lawrence of Arabia

The Fall of the Ottoman Empire

The inability of the Ottomans to defend themselves determined the course of West Asian history during the early modern period. Involvement in the First World War, through a hasty alliance with Germany and Austria-Hungary that initially seemed a way of ending Ottoman weakness, only brought defeat, dismemberment of the empire, and the emergence of modern Turkey. A consequence of this abysmal failure was the rise of Mustafa Kemal—usually called Atatürk or "Father Turk"—as the guiding spirit of the new Turkish republic: he had commanded a division at Gallipoli, where the repulse of an Allied seaborne expedition in 1915–16 saved Istanbul from capture and prevented an early surrender.

That something had to be done if the Ottoman empire was to survive was borne in on Sultan Selim III by the French invasion of Egypt in 1798. Even though Napoleon fled back to France and his troops surrendered to British and Ottoman forces, the turmoil gave Muhammad Ali an opportunity to set himself up as the master of Egypt. This Ottoman officer from Albania effectively ended Istanbul's influence in this rich province, although it remained the sultan's nominal possession until 1914. In the Balkans, however, the Ottomans faced even more intractable difficulties because their Christian subjects were inflamed with nationalist ambitions that received active support from Russia. Territorial losses here were immense. Before 1860, a majority of all Ottoman subjects lived in the Balkans, while forty-five years later the European provinces held just 20 per cent of the total.

Selim tried to reconstruct the Ottoman empire on new principles. For him reform was a necessity: the separatist tendencies of the provinces had to be held in check, the armed forces needed modernisation and proper diplomatic relations were required with foreign countries. Beginning in 1793, Selim opened a permanent embassy in London and others followed in European capitals. Along with the Iranians, as the Persians were now known, the Ottomans were deeply concerned about Russian expansion. The Russians advanced in 1829 within 65 kilometres of Istanbul. The city was not taken because it might have resulted in a partition of the Ottoman empire that would be to Russia's disadvantage. But this did not stop encroachment in the mountainous Caucasus, where Russian successes pushed the frontiers of Moslem West Asia southwards. By 1870 large numbers of Moslems had left the area, their lands taken over by Christian settlers.

The reform movement that Selim sponsored failed. Its opponents were more numerous and powerful than those who supported this first attempt to jettison feudalism. Undeterred by the setback, the next sultan Mahmut II moved against the Janissaries, whom he called "nothing more than a great disorganised body into which spies have penetrated to foster disorder and to incite rebellion", and also against over-powerful families in the provinces. A rebellion of Janissaries stationed in Istanbul was put down by loyal troops and then Janissary garrisons were overcome in other cities. Afterwards Mahmut asserted his authority over hereditary leaders in the provinces, often without the use of force. Although the Ottoman

The court of the would-be reformer Selim III

empire acquired neither a new army nor an effective bureaucracy, the foundation had been laid for future improvement.

Progress proved illusive, however. The Ottomans tried to finance the expansion of their army and bureaucracy through increased taxes, but the sums raised were so inadequate that loans from Europe had to make up the difference. The burden of foreign debt was already crippling the Ottoman empire before the Balkan Wars of 1912–13 removed its remaining European possessions, except the coastal plain between Edirne and Istanbul. Provinces that in the sixteenth century had stretched to Vienna now ended a few hours' train journey from the capital. Signs of impending disintegration also appeared in the empire's West Asian provinces, where Russian pressure stimulated Armenian expectations of independence. Ottoman intercommunal relations had been comparatively peaceful until the turn of the twentieth century, when massacres of Armenians reached a climax with the killing of more than 600,000 of them. Even though orders were given for the protection of Armenians, who were entirely deported from eastern Anatolia, the trek westwards

The sultan's harem at the Topkapi Palace in Istanbul

comprised a non-stop programme of violence, especially as displaced Moslems from the lost Balkan provinces were not slow to vent their anger and frustration on the hapless deportees.

While non-Moslems were still legally inferior to Moslems, differences had been greatly eroded through the employment of Christians in government jobs and the military. Yet when the Young Turks introduced universal conscription, many Christians voted with their feet and left for the United States. A group of junior army officers and minor bureaucrats, the Young Turks had seized power in 1908 and deposed the sultan a year later. Spontaneous rather than planned, the coup changed Turkish politics forever. Why the army, the principal beneficiary of Ottoman expenditure, turned against the sultan remains unclear. These were frustrating times for Atatürk, who occupied no important post until he asked for an active command in the Gallipoli peninsula. Even then, the surrender of the Ottoman empire eclipsed any glory that he had gained in checking the Allied advance on Istanbul. Atatürk disliked Germany's exploitation of the Ottoman army for its own ambitions and soon realised that he was on the losing side in the First World War.

The eclipse of the Ottoman empire seemed to allow the victorious Allies to do whatever they liked. They were wrong: cession of remote West Asian provinces was one thing, the Greek claim on Asia Minor quite another. Once a Greek army, protected by British, French and American warships, disembarked at Izmir, the Turkish people were united in their determination to resist. The focus of resistance was Ankara, a village in the remote interior, where Atatürk rallied national opposition to the Greek invasion. Throwing back the Greek advance at Sakarya was the turning point in Atatürk's career. Casualties were about the same on each side, but the Greeks were shaken and fell back to the Aegean coast. Further defeats confirmed the hopelessness of their campaign so that in 1922 Asia Minor once again was in Turkish hands. When the fighting was over, Atatürk made peace with Greece, settling matters by a brutal but effective method of an exchange of populations. He told the people of Turkey that "the successes that our army has gained up to now cannot be regarded as having achieved the real salvation of the country". That required "new victories in science and economics". The Allies' refusal to

The Ottoman empire

Calligraphy above a doorway at the Ottoman palace in Istanbul. Such decorative script is one of the treasures of Islamic civilisation

abandon the restored sultan's government in Istanbul might have thwarted a lesser man than Atatürk, but his bold decision to abolish the sultanate, and shortly afterwards the caliphate, turned the Turkish republic into a secular state with Islam fully disestablished. As the American ambassador was informed: "Turkey is now a Western power."

Between World Wars

The loss of Mosul to British-mandated Iraq only served to confirm Atatürk's view of West Asian politics. He turned away from the Arab world, not because of hostility to the Arabs, but for the reason that they had lost their independence to Britain and France. Britain now dominated Iraq, Palestine, Jordan, Aden and the states along the Persian Gulf, while France dominated Syria and Lebanon. An exception to this European supremacy was Arabia, where the bedouin remained tribal and an Arab monarchy was acknowledged just as much as it suited them. Never really under Ottoman control, the bedouin tribesmen had revolted in 1916 and then lent support to the British offensive in Palestine and Syria. The uprising at Medina was initiated by Feisal ibn Hussein, who led an assault on the city with 30,000 men, of whom only 6,000 were armed. Not until the secondment of T. E. Lawrence—famously Lawrence of Arabia—as a permanent liaison officer was Feisal able to formulate a strategy that kept Anglo-French imperial ambitions to a degree in check. The surprise capture of Aqaba by the Arabs pre-empted an Allied naval expedition, impressed the British commander-in-chief Allenby, and allowed Lawrence to bring in much-needed weapons. With Aqaba serving as a base for operations, Arab forces inevitably came more directly in touch with the British though, from whom they were only separated by the Sinai desert.

General Allenby welcomed this development and backed Feisal as the Arab commander. Lawrence had told him how Feisal's prestige, charm and tact were the sole means of holding rival tribal leaders together. With London's approval, Allenby let Feisal's men enter Damascus, where an Arab administration was formed in September 1918. But it was a temporary triumph: France and Britain had already carved up the Ottoman provinces in West Asia between themselves. Though Lawrence claimed to be unaware of this arrangement, his credibility as an intermediary between Allenby and Feisal was over and he left for home the following month.

Arab desires were not Britain's concern. What worried London, and indeed Paris, was the political vacuum left by the collapse of the Ottoman empire after centuries of continuous rule. The search for stability explains the Balfour Declaration of 1917, which endorsed the creation of a Jewish national homeland in Palestine. This response to the growing political importance of the Zionist movement in Europe and North America was seen as a method for extending British influence. The declaration stimulated the mass migration of Jews to Palestine during the inter-war years and led directly to the creation of the state of Israel in 1948.

The creation of the Arab kingdom of Transjordan, the present-day Hashimite Kingdom of Jordan, was meant to placate Arab opinion. Its half-nomadic and half-settled population of 250,000 hardly made the new state a major player in modern West Asian politics. Even after an enlargement by the addition of part of Palestine and the influx of refugees, Jordan still had only 1.3 million people in 1949. That the Jordanians remained loyal allies to the British is quite remarkable considering the problems that Jewish emigration has caused them on the West Bank.

Not until 1988 would Jordan be prepared to abandon its claims to this part of the old mandate of Palestine.

Britain's imperial presence did not survive the Second World War. Its expulsion of the Ottomans was looked upon by some short-sighted witnesses as "the Last Crusade". Nothing could have been more unfortunate because it left the Arabs feeling that their legitimate aspirations were being cynically betrayed by Christians. The conflicting claims of Jews and Arabs erupted in open warfare in 1937 and brought about the end of the British mandate in Palestine eleven years later.

In Arabia, however, a hands-off approach suited the Arabs, who were left to decide for themselves the royal family that they preferred. Abd al-Aziz ibn Saud emerged as ruler and, in 1934, he might have taken over Yemen had Britain and Italy not intervened. Before the 1950s there was little economic change in Saudi Arabia, as the kingdom was called, for oil revenue only became substantial after the Americans, reaping the benefit of the Saudi king's profound distrust of Europeans, exploited the country's vast reserves.

An attempt to make Feisal king of Syria failed. Britain offered to evacuate its troops from Syria, handing over the province to France and the Arabs. The French accepted the evacuation but refused to acknowledge any Arab entitlement to rule. Lukewarm towards the Arab revolt, the Syrians themselves were never going to rally to Feisal's defence, choosing with reluctance to accept a French mandate instead. In Damascus, Feisal discovered that he could neither enthuse the Syrian people nor stop Arab irregulars attacking French posts near the coast. Eventually, in July 1920, he accepted the inevitable: the French occupied Damascus, bringing the short-lived Syrian Arab kingdom to an end. Because of this challenge, France did not follow the same approach to its mandate as Britain adopted in Iraq: no effort was made to devolve authority to a single Arab government and safeguard its own interests by treaty. On the contrary, France brought the Moroccan model to Syria, which comprised collaboration with local powerholders and a respect for traditional customs and institutions. Such indirect French rule was backed by an army of 15,000 French regulars and colonial troops from Africa.

Money was the cause of Britain's wish for an independent Iraq. Struggling to maintain their imperial role in the aftermath of the First World War, the British could not afford costly territorial additions. Even a noted supporter of imperialism such as *The Times* declared: "We must evacuate Mesopotamia while we can, and now is the moment." The Colonial Secretary Winston Churchill agreed. "Apart from its importance as a

A 1917 military review. Lawrence of Arabia stands at the back wearing Arab clothes

link in the aerial route to India . . . and apart from the military significance of the oil deposits," he noted, "the General Staff are not pressing for the retention of Mesopotamia . . . on strategic grounds of Imperial security." So in 1921, at a conference held in Cairo, Churchill was willing to listen to Lawrence and risk annoying the French by giving the Iraqi throne to Feisal, despite his dubbing of the Arab delegates as the "forty thieves".

Ignoring the provincial arrangements of the Ottomans, which had correctly recognised that the Kurds, Shi'a and Sunnis comprised distinct entities, the British announced the creation of a unitary state under a non-Iraqi king. Churchill and Lawrence were initially against including the Kurdish people, for whom they sought to establish Kurdistan as a buffer between Arab Iraq and Turkey. Other delegates at Cairo disagreed, possibly because they regarded the oil-rich region as an economic necessity for newly created Iraq. The sad history of the Kurds ever since bears witness to the justified fears of Churchill and Lawrence.

Yet for Churchill the Iraqi kingdom remained a good gamble. "Our difficulties and our expenses," he commented two years later, "have diminished every month that has passed. Our influence has grown while our armies have departed." But popularity eluded Feisal and he wondered just before his death in 1939 whether it was possible for Iraq to become one nation. Feisal's principal supporters were ex-Ottoman officers of Iraqi origin, who had linked their fortunes to him at Damascus. Of relatively low social standing, they looked to government service as a means of advancement. They were all Sunni from northern Iraq. Shi'a Moslems, who dwelt mainly in the south, were poorly represented in the cabinet, while the Kurds and other minority groups hardly at all. As a result, Feisal's dynasty was always fragile: between his accession to the throne in 1921 and the bloody overthrow of his grandson in 1958, fifty-seven ministries took office.

Whereas Britain seemed to have succeeded in Iraq with Feisal's kingdom becoming a sovereign state in 1932, it discovered that there was no easy solution in Palestine. The British left this mandate in disarray, hated by Jews and Arabs alike, and with their reputation tarnished in the eyes of the world. The basic problem was relations between the Palestinian Arabs and the Jewish settlers, whose numbers increased dramatically when Hitler began his anti-Semitic programme in Germany. A White Paper in 1939 aggravated an already tense situation by limiting Jewish immigration to 75,000 over a five-year period. The Arabs were not placated by the restriction because it did nothing to limit the purchase of land by Jews. More upset were the Jews, who began a campaign of violence that was only halted by the Second World War. With Britain fighting Germany, the Jews decided in the words of David Ben-Gurion that "they would fight the war as if there were no White Paper, but at the same time continue to fight the White Paper as if there were no war". The enormity of the Holocaust was bound to put the British in an impossible position. Needing an American loan to recover from the ravages of the war, Britain could not afford to antagonise Zionists in the United States; but, on the other hand, Arab goodwill was required to maintain oil supplies and the security of the sea route to India via the Suez Canal.

To a large extent Iran was unaffected by the fall of the Ottoman empire. But its need for an alliance with Britain to resist Russia indicated that the days of Safavid power were long gone. Rebellions and civil war had taken their toll before the Qajars, a Turkish dynasty, came to power at the close of the eighteenth century. While the Qajars endeavoured to prepare the country for modern times, they lacked the financial institutions that would have facilitated economic progress. There was no bank until 1888 and the credit system was rudimentary before the First World War. Possibly Shi'a clerics deliberately slowed down change, their dislike of moneylending being a more effective curb here than the opposition of their Sunni counterparts elsewhere in modern West Asia. But their influence declined after the Pahlavis usurped power in 1921. Then another Turk, Reza Khan, only became the shah after he failed to set up a republic. His coup was intended to make Iran a country whose independence could never be in doubt. Autocratic by nature, this first Pahlavi ruler modernised Iran by expanding education, improving transport, developing industry and, as far as finances allowed, strengthening the army. But Reza Khan never pursued a European-style agenda as far as Atatürk did in Turkey.

The Founding of Israel

Had the Labour government less decolonisation to handle in 1945, then it is quite possible that a fairer outcome would have resulted in Palestine. But all Clement Attlee's attention was taken up by Burma and India, the bulk of Britain's Asian empire. Leaving Palestine to Ernest Bevin was a mistake. He neither understood the problems involved nor came to grips with the muddled policy that he inherited from previous British governments. Premier Attlee expected Bevin to reach a negotiated settlement, but his foreign secretary came under intense pressure from the Americans. President Harry S. Truman was a keen Zionist for political and personal reasons. He told a gathering of Arab ambassadors: "I have to answer to hundreds of thousands who are anxious for the success of Zionism. I do not have hundreds of thousands of Arabs among my constituents."

Opposed to partition, Attlee favoured a binational state that would guarantee political and economic rights for the Jewish minority. This plan suited King Abdullah of Jordan, provided Palestine was incorporated in his kingdom. That it was unacceptable to Zionists became obvious with increased acts of terrorism. In July 1946 Jerusalem's King David Hotel was blown up, according to the terrorist leader Menachem Begin, through the Jewish invention of the "the urban guerrilla". Zionists could never countenance the idea that being Jewish was just a matter of religious belief: they wanted a separate nation in their ancient land. Ninety-one British, Arab and Jewish lives were lost in the explosion. The tit-for-tat of West

Asian violence, however, would turn such guerrilla warfare into a double-edged sword, when Palestinian Arabs resorted to suicide bombing.

All-out fighting began in 1947, after a vote by the UN General Assembly to partition Palestine into Arab and Jewish sectors, with a greater Jerusalem to be under international control. The territorial ambitions of King Abdullah blinded him to the danger of acquiring the West Bank, which soon filled with refugees smarting for vengeance against the Jews. These Palestinian Arabs had been driven there by the failure of the United Nations to send an international force to implement the mandate's partition. The Jordanian king was killed at Friday prayers in Jerusalem three years later. Against the wishes of his closest advisers, Abdullah went to the city quoting the Arab proverb: "Until my day comes nobody can harm me; when my day comes nobody can guard me."

By the time of the ceasefire at the end of 1948 the state of Israel controlled 80 per cent of the former mandate. It had a population of 800,000, of whom 80 per cent were Jewish and the remainder Arabs. By 1983 the relative balance of Jews and Arabs remained the same, although immigration had boosted Jewish numbers to four million. Cultural differences with these new immigrants were problematic during the 1950s, when Moroccan Jews rioted in Haifa over their poor job prospects, but the development of a modern version of Hebrew as the national language gradually gave all Israelis a sense of belonging. Sustained by rapid development that saw the economy grow by 10 per cent each year, as well as generous American subsidies, Israel was soon the most prosperous country in modern West Asia. Yet this exceptional progress was achieved under a constant state of siege. Most worrying for the Israelis was the spread of sophisticated technology, and especially to such an implacable enemy as Iran. Closer to its borders Hezbollah and Hamas, the more aggressive successors of the Palestinian Liberation Organisation, also acquired missiles.

Syria, Lebanon and Jordan

Britain ended French rule in Syria and Lebanon. The Anglo-Free French invasion of 1941 was a spin-off campaign that originated in neighbouring Iraq. Despite Britain's presence being reduced to two airfields, anti-British feeling in Iraq remained strong because of the increased Jewish immigration into Palestine. By treaty, Iraq should have sided with Britain on the outbreak of the Second World War, but the government of Feisal's four-year-old son was too weak to comply. When the pro-British regent was ousted and the airfields attacked, Churchill ordered an immediate invasion that caught Hitler by surprise. The British leader had no intention of allowing the new Iraqi regime an opportunity to welcome Axis forces. When Vichy France offered to provide a Syrian air link through which the Germans could supply the Iraqis from Rhodes, an Anglo-Free French invasion of Syria became inevitable. Advance units of the Luftwaffe had already got as far as Syria.

With a lenient armistice agreed in Iraq, where Jewish merchants suffered the worst casualties at the hands of outraged nationalists and free-lance looters, Britain was able to deal with Syria. Although Hitler ordered seven trains of French reinforcements to Syria, Turkey's strict enforcement of neutrality prevented their arrival. Having sacrificed his paratroopers in Crete, there was nothing Hitler could do except watch Syria's reduction. That the Vichy garrison put up strong resistance came as a surprise to everyone. Entirely cut off from either French or German reinforcements, its eventual surrender was a forgone conclusion, although 3,300 British, 1,300 Free French and 6,000 Vichy casualties were necessary first.

By 1946 all foreign troops were withdrawn and the independence of Syria and Lebanon secured. But the post-war slump undermined the Syrian economy and paralysed its government. Scaling back on military expenditure after the failure of Syrian troops in Palestine, where the Jews drove them headlong from Galilee, was bound to provoke a coup; egged on by the Americans, Colonel Hosni al-Za'im, the chief of the army staff, seized power in 1949 with little bloodshed. Installed as president, Za'im increased the size of the army from 5,000 to 27,000 men. He also enfranchised women, disapproved of traditional Arab headgear and abolished feudal titles. When he tried to negotiate with Israel, another officer took Za'im's place until 1954, when he was in turn overthrown. Whatever the benefits to Washington of these military interventions, they set a poor example to the Arab world, henceforth a periodic victim of its armed forces as the arbiter of political power. In Syria this tendency led to the establishment in 1970 of Hafez al-Assad's repressive regime. An air force general, he was the son of a minor Ottoman notable who changed the family name from Wahhish, "Savage", to Assad, "Lion".

The Ba'ath Party formed Assad's power base, a secular, socialist, pan-Arab organisation that was also used by Saddam Hussein in Iraq. It had existed as a movement since the late 1930s when it was founded by French-educated Syrian teachers. Like Saddam Hussein, Assad preferred fear to affection. Ruthless yet reflective, President Assad determined the general lines of state policy, appointed and dismissed prime ministers and cabinets, controlled other major appointments, chose members of the judiciary and could veto legislation. His closest advisers were drawn from the army and the security services. Opposition to Assad came in the 1980s from radical Moslem groups worried about his ambivalence towards the Palestine Liberation Organisation, although Syria's response to the 1982 Israeli invasion of Lebanon turned it into that state's nominal guardian.

The Palestine Liberation Organisation had transferred to Lebanon. The Israelis drove it out, hoping to find an ally in Lebanon's Christian minority, but civil war ensued and a shaken Menachem Begin resigned as Israel's premier. US Marines had no chance of enforcing a ceasefire, 241 of them dying when a vehicle packed with explosives was driven into their barracks at Beirut. After the Americans left in 1984, the continuing civil war in Lebanon almost destroyed its society as militias fought each other for territory. Beirut was reduced to a ruin, its population by 1989 sinking to 150,000.

Jordan was lucky not to be pulled fully into the slipstream of the Arab–Israeli conflict. No West Asian country endured greater territorial convulsions than Jordan, yet no other state has enjoyed greater internal stability. Politics were dominated by King Hussein ibn Talal, Abdullah's grandson, whose astute handling of affairs during a period when monarchies were no longer esteemed by most Arabs was quite masterful. In 1965 he settled the succession issue by designating his brother Hassan as heir. Even though this meant bypassing his own children, whose mother was English, Hussein believed that the dynasty could only survive through an emphasis on its Hashimite heritage, which stretched all the way back to Prophet Muhammad himself. While in 1999 the gravely ill monarch was receiving treatment abroad, news arrived that Hassan's Pakistan-born wife was already redecorating the palace. An angry Hussein returned to Jordan to die but not before dismissing Hassan and designating a new successor, Abdullah II, his eldest son by his English wife. Hussein's dying wish was that the next in line would be Hamzah, his son by his Arab-American wife, Queen Noor. But Abdullah made his own son the heir apparent in 2004. Despite this royal discord, Jordan remains an island of comparative calm amid the confusion of modern West Asia.

Iraq versus Iran

The bloody end of Feisal's dynasty in Iraq opened the way for of Saddam Hussein's dictatorship. Pro-Nasser demonstrations in Baghdad after

Egypt's nationalisation of the Suez Canal provoked the royal government to suspend the constitution and imprison hundreds of opponents. Prime Minister Nuri al-Said so detested Gamal Abd al-Nasser that he even joined Britain and France in plotting to overthrow the Egyptian leader. After the abortive Anglo-French occupation of the Suez Canal zone in late 1956, however, Nuri was politically isolated inside and outside Iraq. The climax came in 1958, when troops loyal to Brigadier Abd al-Karim Qassem, armed with heavy weapons, captured the palace and machine-gunned the royal family. Disguised as a woman, Nuri nearly escaped until someone in the crowd recognised him. The fourteen-time premier was stripped, killed, castrated and then dismembered, his legless body dragged through the streets of Baghdad behind an army lorry.

The 1958 revolution was the work of a handful of officers, a circumstance that tended to make the new government a strangely personal affair. Even though a three-man sovereignty council was formed, comprising a Sunni, a Shi'a and a Kurd, it never possessed any authority because the army held the levers of power. Overthrown in 1963, Qassem's regime left Iraq in an unstable condition until five years later the Ba'ath party became dominant. Through its ranks rose Saddam Hussein al-Takriti, the son of a poor farmer. Without any connection

The extravagant historical parade at Persepolis in October 1971

with the army, he made his way as an activist: the uniform Saddam Hussein habitually wore was that of the Ba'ath militia.

Before the two Gulf Wars, Iraq's principal foe was Iran, an Islamic republic under the control of hardline clerics, whose declared aim was to "extend the sovereignty of Allah's law throughout the world". Reza Khan's sympathy for Hitler's campaign in Russia had led in 1941 to the occupation of Tehran and the first Pahlavi ruler's enforced abdication in favour of his son, Muhammad Reza Shah. Not until 1946 did Russian and British troops finally leave a country suffering from chronic shortages and hyperinflation. The economic situation emboldened the dynasty's enemies, who called for the nationalisation of the oil industry as a way out of the financial crisis. Prime Minister Muhammad Mosaddeq, an old opponent of Reza Khan, led a coalition of secular, tribal and religious dissidents. His most important clerical ally was the anti-British ayatollah Abdul Qasim Kashani, a harbinger of the 1979 revolution of Ayatollah Khomeini. That Mosaddeq's aim also included a drastic reduction of the Shah's power galvanised the Americans and the British into action, so that subsidised opponents of the prime minister burned down his party headquarters, murdered his closest allies and turned him out of office. A compromise was reached with a triumphant Muhammad Reza Shah, whereby the British oil concession was shared among foreign companies. Anglo-Iranian Oil, renamed British Petroleum, kept 40 per cent of the annual output.

A timely switch of sides by Ayatollah Kashani and other prominent Shi'a clerics prevented Mosaddeq's fall from having religious repercussions, much to Muhammad Reza Shah's satisfaction. No longer willing to tolerate any threat to his authority, he crushed opponents, purged the army, exiled doubtful allies and, last but not least, set up a secret security agency, the US-organised Savak. Dreaded though its agents were, demonstrators still took to the streets in an increasingly urbanised country. Now impervious to all criticism, the Shah chose to show off his dynasty in a series of public events, the culmination of which in 1971 was a grand gala at Persepolis, the ancient seat of the Achaemenid kings. The three-day celebration marked the 2,500th anniversary of Cyrus' foundation of the Persian empire, at an estimated cost of £150 million.

If this expensive demonstration was not enough to annoy his people at a time of drought and famine, Muhammad Riza Shah compounded his unpopularity five years later by replacing the Islamic calendar with a Pahlavi one. It dated the years from the foundation of Persian power: thus 1976, the Moslem year 1355, became 2535. The new calendar especially outraged the Shi'a clergy, whose revenge came with the return from France of the exiled ayatollah Ruhollah Khomeini. The Shah's apparent indifference to Islam united the poor, the disenchanted and the clerics in an irresistible opposition, with the result that the self-styled successor of Cyrus had to flee to Cairo, where he died according to Pahlavi reckoning in 2539.

After the collapse of Pahlavi rule, a referendum in 1979 gave over-whelming approval to an Islamic republic, although few knew exactly what this would mean for Iran. They were soon to discover that it involved clerical authority, once Khomeini was declared the vali faqih, or "supreme guide", who controlled all civil, military, judicial and religious appoint-ments. His most powerful weapon comprised the Revolutionary Guards, a militia capable of taking on any other armed group. Its strength had reached 450,000 by the close of the 1980s and included naval as well as air force units. During the brutal conflict with Iraq that Saddam Hussein began in 1980, the role of the Revolutionary Guards became critical in sustaining the regime, both internally and externally. And this became even more the case after the death of Khomeini in 1989. The apocryphal story of the plastic keys distributed to recruits headed for the front line during the Iraq–Iran War indicates the extent of Islamisation then. It was

Ayatollah Ruhollah Khomeini returning home in 1979 after his exile in France

American missiles being fired in 2003 during the Second Gulf War

not considered worthy of notice in Iran that these guarantees of entry to paradise were stamped with the words "Made in Hong Kong".

By 1988, with both the Iraqis and the Iranians exhausted, the war halted. A bankrupt Saddam Hussein then tried to get Arab oil producers to cut production and thus increase oil prices and his income. When Saudi Arabia and Kuwait refused, the Iraqi dictator decided to lay claim to Kuwaiti oil fields. By seizing this tiny state through a lightning campaign in 1990, Saddam Hussein controlled 20 per cent of the world's known oil reserves.

Playing the anti-Israeli card failed to gain Arab support, with the result that Iraq faced a coalition made up of the United States, Britain, Saudi Arabia, Syria and even Israel. Britain's hawkish premier Margaret Thatcher stiffened the resolve of President Reagan's successor, George Bush, and 1991 hundreds of US planes and missiles, many of them launched from ships in the Persian Gulf, attacked the cities of Iraq, while the Iraqis responded with Russian-built missiles that killed people in Saudi Arabia and Israel. Bundled swiftly out of Kuwait, Saddam Hussein escaped pursuit to Baghdad, since the First Gulf War had deliberately limited objectives to avoid an Arab backlash.

Whether there should have been an advance on Baghdad remains a matter of controversy. Washington preferred to leave Iraq with enough power to pose a threat to an Iran that was bitterly hostile to the United States. This policy was flawed because Saddam Hussein's continued sabre rattling led to the Second Gulf War of 2003 and the present-day turmoil in Iraq. It also failed to moderate Iran's regional aims, perhaps to be backed shortly with nuclear weapons. Changed out of all recognition though Iraq–Iran rivalry is, its underlying tension continues to represent a danger to peace.

Saudi Arabia and the Gulf States

Somewhat eccentric to mainstream Arab politics in modern times was the southwestern tip of the Arabian peninsula, where Yemen and Aden were situated. Aden's fine natural harbour had attracted the Portuguese in 1513, but they were repulsed. During the Napoleonic Wars, the Royal Navy made use of this anchorage, but not until 1838 was Aden annexed to the British empire. The fortune of this tiny colony varied with its strategic value, which rose in proportion to Britain's declining influence elsewhere. Thus in the 1950s London declared that Aden could not expect more than internal self-government "for the foreseeable future". Yet this prediction could not have been more incorrect, once Yemen experienced an Egyptian-sponsored revolution in 1962. Because migrant Yemenis outnumbered Adenis, pressure for the union of Aden and Yemen became irresistible and, five years later, the British had to shoot their way out of the ex-colony.

During the post-colonial era there was in the Persian Gulf a gradual loosening of ties with Britain, at least until the two Gulf Wars. Oil certainly eased the transition from a medieval past to the modern world. The United Arab Emirates from its foundation in 1971 relied on an abundance of oil revenues, with Abu Dhabi the main producer. Less successful was Dubai when, in the late 2000s, it tried to turn itself into a hub of finance and tourism. Grandiose building projects had to be halted or stopped altogether through a chronic lack of funds.

As in the Gulf states, the old regime survived in Saudi Arabia, thanks to oil. And because social prestige derived from tribal power, rather than landed estates, Saudi Arabian nobles were never challenged by land reform. Cultivation was in the hands of smallholders, who were largely left to their own devices. That is not to imply any neglect, because by the 1990s the people of Saudi Arabia were much healthier, better housed and much better educated than they had been in the past. But the country was transformed politically into a centralised state that used oil revenues to sustain the Saudi monarchy. It is estimated that total membership of the royal family, including collateral branches, amounts to 20,000. Younger Saudi princes always filled ministerial posts and higher ranks in the armed forces, an arrangement that kept Saudi Arabia largely insulated from change. Almost without world comment, asylum was granted in 1979 to Idi Amin, whose toying with passengers aboard a hijacked El Al airliner prompted the famous Israeli commando rescue at Entebbe airport. The ex-Ugandan president died in his Saudi Arabian bed in 2003.

It remains to be seen whether Saudi Arabia is unaffected by the political upheaval that began in Tunisia at the start of 2011. The spread to Egypt of popular protest against long-standing and entrenches regimes was a serious development for all West Asian states, however, because so many Arabs lived in that country. Egyptian president Hosni Mubarak's initial refusal to step down after thirty years of rule hardly surprised his allies, the chief of which was the United States, although Washington was quick to advise a positive engagement with the protesters. Whereas the 1.5 billion dollar programme of American foreign aid obviously helped to sustain Mubarak in office, Saudi Arabia's own oil wealth always gave it a financial independence rare in the Arab world. Its ability to continue along a separate path had never seemed in question.

Modern Turkey

Although at first his authority derived from military success and seemed to be no more than a dictatorship, Atatürk tried very hard to create a republic based on civilian legality. His speeches were never stage-managed before large crowds as were the rallies of Mussolini and Hitler, for Atatürk always sought to convince the Turkish people by reasoned argument of the benefits of thoroughgoing social reform. He accepted the need for liberal institutions such as political parties, trades unions, a free press and freedom of speech, but he understood that a fully modern republic would not appear in Turkey overnight. Atatürk instinctively sided with the European democracies against German aggression. As the English writer George Orwell wryly commented: "In the years 1935–39, when almost any ally against fascism seemed acceptable, left-wingers found themselves praising Mustafa Kemal."

After Atatürk's death in late 1939 though, Churchill was to discover that the Republic of Turkey could not be turned into an ally during the Second World War. Not even the possibility of recovering Mosul was enough to tempt the Turks, who saw no reason to become involved in yet another European power struggle. It proved a sensible decision because Turkey had as much to fear from the Russians as the Germans. What Atatürk had made his people appreciate was the importance of Asia Minor: with the loss of the Ottoman provinces elsewhere, this was now the Turkish homeland and the new republic should concentrate upon its development. Foreign distractions were never going to be helpful, and especially those in the Arab world after 1945. Indeed, the widening gap between Turkey and other Moslem states of West Asia was bound to become even more pronounced as modernisation gathered pace.

Its logical conclusion was a request from Turkey to join the European Union. It presents a double problem for existing members: the apparent revival of Islam in Turkish society and the role of the Turkish army. Six times between 1967 and 1997, the latter obliged premiers to resign because their policies were deemed to jeopardise the secular order. But in 2010 Recep Tayyip Erdogan managed to forestall military intervention when plans came to light in Istanbul. Despite a supposedly "jihadist" past, for which he once served a prison sentence, this prime minister had wide support for his policies, including accession to the European Union. His Islamic outlook was not seen as a threat to the republic, suggesting that on this occasion the generals badly misjudged the situation. Though still regarded as a pillar of the secular order, pollsters found after the exposure of the planned coup that Turkish trust in the armed forces had sunk to a historic low of 60 per cent. This slump in popularity was confirmed later during 2010 by a referendum that agreed to curb military influence. "We have passed a historic threshold," Mr Erdogan said, "on the way to advanced democracy and the supremacy of law." As well as improving the rights of women and workers, making it harder to shut down political parties and limiting the jurisdiction of military courts, the constitutional changes were intended to permit the trial of those involved in coups.

Yet the government's popularity may not last. Increased tax on alcohol has made drink into a luxury item, to the dismay of many Turks.

"Father Turk", Mustafa Kemal, in his garden in 1923 with his wife and a friend

Consumption of raki, an aniseed-flavoured spirit favoured by Atatürk himself, is in decline and protest drinking events were organised throughout the country during 2011. Despite Islamic disdain for alcohol, it remains legal to drink in public in Turkey but not to cause disruption as a result of drunkenness. Although ministers denied that there was any ideological motive behind the higher tax, a restriction on advertising, and the curtailment of drinking at public occasions such as concerts, critics were not convinced, arguing that the real purpose of the anti-alcohol measures was placating the religious vote, which an Islamic-leaning government wants to capture. Demonstrations in Istanbul against a television drama that showed an Ottoman sultan drinking alcohol did suggest that religious conservatism was gaining ground. Possibly some of the European-style freedoms that Atatürk bequeathed to the Turkish nation will be eroded in future, but there is no question of his impact on its outlook. Whether or not Turkey joins the European Union, its emergence as a potential member is a sign of how far the country has come since the overthrow of the Ottoman empire. It is a tribute to the determined leadership of "Father Turk".

Chapter 11

Modern South Asia

King George V said: "Well, anyhow, Mr. Gandhi, remember that I can't have any attacks upon my Indian Empire." And Gandhi, who was a wonderfully good diplomat—apart from that he had wonderfully good manners—turned it away by saying: "Well, your Majesty, I mustn't enter into a political argument with you when I have received your Majesty's hospitality."

Gandhi's 1931 visit to Buckingham Palace

The British Raj

Overcoming the Marathas meant that the English East India Company was supreme in India, but this triumph did not usher in an era of peace: there were annexations right down to the Mutiny in 1857, when the larger part of the subcontinent was under British control. Even more, trading problems led to other annexations in

339

nearby Burma. A leading Burmese general by the name of Thado Maha Bandula put the conflict like this:

> The English are the inhabitants of a small and remote island. What business have they to come in ships from so great a distance to dethrone kings, and take possession of countries they have no right to?

It was the task of the Burmese to halt this encroachment. And he thought they could do so, because the English East India Company had "never yet fought with so strong and brave a people as the Burmans, skilled in the use of sword and spear". Despite wishing to avoid costly wars, Burmese pressure on the port of Chittagong left Calcutta with no choice but fight, after the small garrison placed there was destroyed by Bandula in 1824.

Although Rangoon was easily taken, the British found themselves masters of a deserted town. Except for a cellar of brandy, on which the

Britain's seizure of Rangoon added to the grievances of Hindu sepoys, who hated sea voyages

British regulars swiftly got drunk, there was nothing to sustain the expeditionary force. Farther south, a naval squadron took possession of the coastal strip of Tennasserim, where the inhabitants put up little resistance. Bandula's attempt to storm Rangoon failed, but the British were in no condition to advance, poor diet and tropical disease having taken their toll. The situation only improved when bullocks arrived from India and the local inhabitants began to reappear and offer assistance.

Now an inland advance was possible. At Danubya, not far from the city of Prome, Bandula was killed by a shell or rocket, and his army dispersed. Possibly having a gilt umbrella carried above his head turned the general into an easy target. The defeat obliged the Burmese king to accept terms, although not before in "an unbounded rage, he had ordered the wretched minister who explained the peace agreement to have his mouth cut from ear to ear". After the payment of £1 million, Rangoon was evacuated but not Tennasserim and the Arakan. The terms were quite mild: the war had cost £5 million and the lives of 15,000 British and Indian soldiers.

But complaints in 1852 from British merchants at Rangoon persuaded Calcutta that the Burmese needed to recognise British authority. Naval forces therefore seized the ports of Rangoon, Bassein

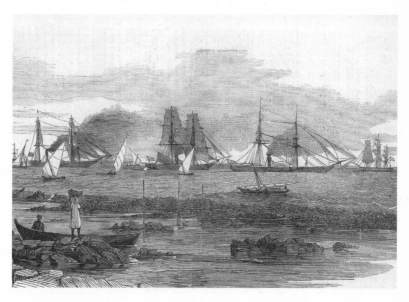

A steam squadron leaving Bombay for an assault on Burma in 1852

and Martaban. The upriver city of Pegu was also taken, despite spirited resistance. The king of Burma did not formally acknowledge the loss of a large stretch of coastline but, after a dignified silence, he informed the British that they could stay without Burmese interference.

In the subcontinent the progress of British arms was just as successful. In 1843 Sind was conquered, then Gwalior defeated a year later and, after two wars with the Sikhs, the whole of the Punjab was annexed in 1849. Nagpur and Oudh were taken over during the next decade. But in Afghanistan there was only disaster. Involvement with Central Asia resulted from Britain's concern about growing Russian influence. There seemed more than a possibility that the Russians might occupy Afghanistan and then seek to disrupt the British position in India. Here was the beginning of what later came to be called the Great Game.

In 1837 a young Scotsman, Alexander Burnes, had been sent to Kabul to settle a dispute between the Afghans and the Sikhs, both of whom claimed Peshawar. Burnes' heart was not really in the enterprise, as he liked the Afghan leader Dosh Muhammad and felt uneasy about persuading him to give up the claim. Negotiations were complicated by a Russian offer to help Dosh Muhammad, the very thing Calcutta dreaded. All that Dosh Muhammad wished to do was apply pressure on the British by appearing to enlist Russian support; but it was too much for the English East Indian Company and an army was dispatched to depose Dosh Muhammad and place Shah Shuja on the throne. It reached Kabul in the summer of 1839.

When a part of the expeditionary force did not return to India, the Afghans became resentful of Shah Shuja and his foreign supporters. Burnes' servants warned him that there was a plot to expel the British, but he was not a man to avoid danger. He remained in his house and next morning the Afghans killed him. Lack of resolution on the part of the British commander emboldened the Afghans, whose ranks were swollen by men from villages around Kabul. There was nothing to do but retreat to India: a single European, Dr W. Brydon, made it in 1842. He was an assistant surgeon in the English East India Company's employ. During the Indian Mutiny he was to be severely wounded at Lucknow, but he recovered and died a natural death in Scotland in 1873. Besides Brydon, a few sepoys eventually arrived back in British India. Even though a second British expedition was sent to free prisoners and restore prestige, the impossibility of occupying

The assassination of Alexander Burns in Kabul

such a remote and warlike country was finally appreciated. An orderly evacuation allowed Dosh Muhammad to regain his throne and rule for another twenty years.

In India there was perhaps a greater degree of understanding. English translations of ancient Indian texts appeared, some of which were used by reformers in the sati controversy. Sati, the self-immolation expected of Hindu widows on their husbands' pyres, was abolished in 1829 by the reforming governor-general Lord William Bentinck. The issue split Hindu opinion because it obliged a generation who had grown up with the rise of British power to face squarely the traditions that had shaped their society for the millennia. How was India to prepare itself for the modern world?

Another cause of traditionalist unease was undoubtedly evangelical Christianity. After his own conversion, the English East India Company director Charles Grant started to wonder whether good government or fair trading would ever be enough to bring improvement to the lives of Indians. By 1792 he was sure that the reformation of Indian society entailed nothing less than the steady introduction of Western learning accompanied by Christianity. Mission schools offered a means of achieving both objectives, while translation of the Bible into Bengali permitted missionary work to proceed amongst those who were denied a formal education. William Carey, the founder of the Baptist Missionary Society, published a Bengali version of the New Testament in 1801. A year earlier, he had been invited to teach languages in Calcutta at the new Fort William College, where English East India Company recruits were prepared for their future duties. Carey saw in the adventurousness of the trader evidence that heathen lands were not inaccessible and a reproof to Christians who preferred to ignore the wider world.

The Indian Mutiny

From Bentinck's time onwards, ideas of reform gained ground among the British in India. Central to this was the notion of the "rule of law", especially as a guarantee to property rights. But this cornerstone of British society transferred poorly to India, where joint families, village brotherhoods and community holdings frustrated any far-reaching social transformation or the spread of capitalist agriculture. Hindu society appeared stationary. Nowhere was this more apparent than in the rigidity of the caste system, whose social discrimination was at its most extreme in the treatment of the "Untouchables". Somewhat ironic was the circumstance that the British employed the largest number of these outcastes, who cleaned streets and barracks, washed clothes, slaughtered animals and made shoes. No bonus was big enough to induce other Indians to undertake such "impure" labour.

Failure to cultivate the friendship of Indians in all probability constituted the English East India Company's greatest mistake. Even an anglophile like Syed Ahmed Khan could remark:

> The Hindustanees fell into the habit of thinking that all laws were passed with a view to degrade and ruin them. The Moslems were in every respect more dissatisfied than the Hindus, and hence in most districts they were comparatively more rebellious, though the latter were not wanting in this respect.

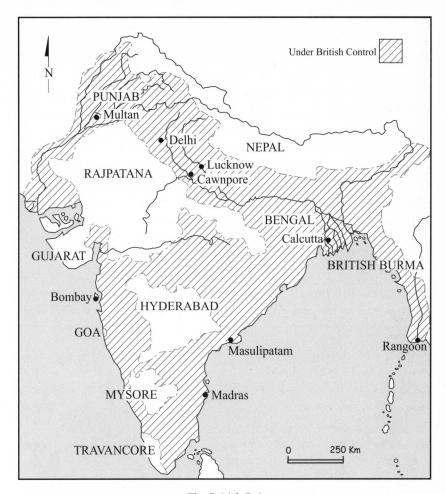

The British Raj

For most Britons service in India had come to mean little more than a career, albeit in a place that offered few attractions. One major of a sepoy regiment so disliked his military duties that he said, "You might as well think to train pigs."

The scene was thus set for an uprising among the sepoys. What brought matters to a head was the introduction of the Enfield rifle. Though muzzle-loaders like the smooth-bore muskets they replaced, Enfields used ammunition that came in the form of paper cartridges. The cartridge was opened by the soldiers using their teeth, since one hand was required to hold the weapon upright while the other held the cartridge. Because the cartridges were greased using animal fat, the composition of the grease was an issue that concerned both Hindus and Moslems. As sepoy anxiety spread across northern India, it was clear that one of the chief props of British power was about to give way. Though only troops in the Bengal army rose in revolt, and then not in every regiment, the extent of the disruption was nonetheless staggering.

Northeast of Delhi, the largely Moslem garrison at Meerut started to mutiny in May 1857, when sepoys released comrades imprisoned for refusing to handle the new cartridges. They attacked their British officers, and anyone who seemed to oppose them, before marching on Delhi and putting themselves under the command of Bahadur Shah Zafar II, the 82-year-old Mughal emperor. Obliged to speak directly to the mutinous sepoys, he told them he had no troops, no armoury and no treasury to support them. They replied, "Only give us your blessing. We will provide everything else." Fearing for the safety of his court as well as his city, Zafar reluctantly let the mutineers rally under

Disarming sepoys at Barrackpore, where one of them had
wounded two officers

his standard, the green flag of Islam. The Mughal emperor was never a war leader, and his own lack of ambition combined with an other-worldliness that made him an odd figurehead. So powerless was he that he could not stop the horses of rebel cavalrymen from trampling over the palace gardens.

Paradoxically, it was the recently conquered Sikhs who prevented the mutiny from gaining a firm grip in the northeast. They had no great reason to support the British but even less to throw their lot in with the sepoys who had helped defeat them. The Sikhs had in addition a settled hatred of the Mughal dynasty whose rulers had persecuted their own leaders. Another incentive to side with the English East India Company was the prospect of loot, when rebellious cities like Delhi were retaken. As Indian princes remained aloof from the mutiny, the sepoys occupying Delhi soon discovered that they were in an uncertain position.

News of the Meerut uprising had reached Calcutta by telegraph, before the mutineers cut the wire. After the fall of Delhi every effort was made for its recapture. British troops were summoned from other parts of India and reinforced by those destined to attack China. Another mutiny at Lucknow, between Delhi and Calcutta, was barely stopped by loyal sepoys. Elsewhere, mutinies sometimes spared British officers and their families, but this was not usual when civilian rioters joined in. At Allahabad, to the southeast of Delhi, many Hindus and Christians were killed in the city by a mob of Moslems, while British officers and civilians who took refuge in the fort there were at first in grave danger. Four hundred Sikhs under British command saved the situation, although the consumption of looted alcohol somewhat undermined their effectiveness. Timely relief by the Madras Fusiliers prevented a massacre but their colonel ordered one of his own.

At Delhi, the hapless Mughal emperor was just as appalled by the aggression of the rebellious sepoys. But he could not prevent them from killing the few Britons who had sought refuge in his palace, although Zafar knew that their slaughter condemned his own dynasty to extinction.

The British counter-attack threw up a number of unlikely heroes, one of whom was Sir Henry Havelock. This 62-year-old colonel had spent almost his entire service in India, where he had mastered several of its languages. That he had married the daughter of a Baptist missionary, and became a pious Baptist himself, may have slowed his promotion: he spent his spare time at prayer meetings and he conducted Bible classes

The Red Fort in Delhi, the last stronghold of the Mughals

for his own troops. Such was Havelock's appeal to the Victorians that streets, roads and squares were named after him when he died from dysentery in Lucknow at the end of 1857.

With the temporary rank of brigadier-general, Havelock set off from Allahabad to relieve nearby Cawnpore and support Lucknow. It was his first independent command. At Lucknow the mutineers had been driven off by loyal sepoys, but the city was not safe from attack. At Cawnpore, however, there were fewer British troops to ensure sepoy loyalty and its commanding officer, Sir Hugh Wheeler, prepared for a siege by unostentatiously placing a shallow trench and a low mud wall around two disused barracks. There he moved 59 British artillerymen with their six guns, plus 75 convalescents from the British regiment at Lucknow. Wheeler also laid in sufficient supplies to feed 1,000 people for a month. As this makeshift refuge afforded little protection against a concerted sepoy assault, Wheeler was obliged to accept an offer of safe passage in return for the surrender of his guns. Merely a trick to get the British into the open, they were ambushed when about to leave by boat. About a hundred surviving women and children were imprisoned in Cawnpore.

It was in Allahabad that Havelock heard of this atrocity, but the monsoon delayed his start for Cawnpore, so that it was not until mid-summer that he approached the city. On the way, his small force of 1,000 British soldiers, 130 Sikhs and six artillery pieces defeated the mutineers and their allies on four separate occasions. On entering the city, Havelock was disappointed to find he had arrived too late. The women and children held prisoner had been hacked to death, and their remains thrown into a well. Havelock's men were so enraged by the cold-blooded killing that they went on the rampage themselves. Even though Havelock halted the violence, news reporters sent off lurid accounts of indiscriminate slaughter.

Having no time to argue the facts of the case, Havelock pressed towards Lucknow, where a similar situation to Cawnpore existed. The presence of a British battalion helped some of the sepoys to resist the call to mutiny, but it could not hold the city on its own. As in Cawnpore, earthen defences had been made ready and concentrated within them were British soldiers along with nearly 700 Indian troops: loyal sepoys, even sepoy pensioners who volunteered their services, and a small detachment of Sikhs. In all, there were 1,600 soldiers and armed civilians. As many as 2,000 others, British, Anglo-Indian and Indian, were inside the defensive perimeter as well. A protracted siege began in the name of Oudh, whose capital had been Lucknow: the young son of the

From this audience chamber in the Red Fort, the Mughal emperor Bahadur Shah Zafar II could exercise no control over the mutinous sepoys

Delhi before the Indian Mutiny. Its fall marked the end of Mughal rule

recently deposed ruler was acknowledged by the rebellious sepoys as his replacement.

Havelock never made it to Lucknow because casualties from heatstroke were as high as those from combat, but his gallant effort was applauded in a Britain unsure about the outcome of the Mutiny. By the autumn, the worst was actually over. The spate of mutinies had reduced to a trickle, and the centre of the rising was still lodged in the northwestern provinces. Had Havelock pressed on to Lucknow and suffered an inevitable defeat, then British rule in India would have faltered. What he did not know was that the main concentration of rebels at Delhi were now much less confident of their survival. Siege guns were about to breach the walls and let three columns into the city. The attackers suffered more than 1,000 killed or wounded by the evening of the assault, but the next morning revealed that the despondent sepoys had fled.

Among those who ran away was the Mughal emperor himself. When his place of hiding became known to the British, Zafar agreed to surrender in return for a promise that his life would be spared. He was quietly removed by bullock cart, a humiliating end to a once great dynasty. His death in exile at Rangoon in 1862 rang down the curtain on Moslem India.

The End of Company Rule

The four-and-a-half-month uprising was over. It seemed that the English East India Company had survived intact until the British government decided to place its Indian possessions under the Crown. Instead of its directors' rule, there were to be in future two sources of authority: the Secretary of State for India, who answered to Parliament, and the Viceroy, who oversaw everyday administration and lawmaking in Calcutta. This radical change was in effect an admission that Britain had only just got through the Mutiny. Turning point though the military crisis was in colonial affairs, the gap between the rulers and the ruled had been widening for a long time, as more and more of the subcontinent came under British control. This fundamental change in social relations had contributed to the outbreak of the insurrection, no matter that the specific grievance was greased cartridges.

A case in point was the deteriorating status of the Anglo-Indian community, which came to occupy a no-man's-land between the Indians and the British. As early as 1786, Anglo-Indian children of deceased British officers were prevented from travelling to Britain to complete their education. To no avail, it was protested that there was no law to prevent a serving British officer with Anglo-Indian children from sending them there. Why discriminate against orphans? In 1795, Anglo-Indians were no longer permitted to serve as English East Indian Company soldiers. Thrown out of soldiering, the only profession many of them knew, there was nothing but to transfer their services to Indian princes. "It was a sad spectacle," remarked one Anglo-Indian, "the father in the Company: his son a mercenary in the pay of a late enemy Chief." Keeping the Anglo-Indian community at a distance from lucrative employment was one reason for these restrictions, another might well have been an anxiety about the emergence of a local interest group with a voice in Indian affairs. At this stage there was no suggestion of racial antagonism. Servants of the English East India Company took Indian wives or mistresses. Richard Wellesley's wife, who in 1798 had chosen not to come to India during his governor-generalship, agreed that he might keep an Indian mistress. He had written to say that the climate so aroused his senses that he could not live without regular sex. His well-born Sikh mistress not only satisfied this pressing need but she also bore him three sons before he returned home in 1805.

Ordinary British soldiers were never allowed to marry in India. Concerned about the impact of venereal disease on the low numbers stationed there, the military authorities tried to make available a supply of prostitutes subject to medical inspection. This did not stop individual soldiers from supporting favourite girls, but the prohibition on marriage drove a wedge between the rankers and Indian women. Some army surgeons took the view that the most effective way of keeping men out of the syphilis ward was to encourage a soldier to stick to one partner. Because the status of prostitutes, like that

A nineteenth-century British cartoon reflecting on Victoria's accession as Empress of India

of mistresses, carried no social opprobrium in India, supply always met sexual demand. Not until the arrival of larger numbers of British women from the 1850s onwards would the moral climate change. Victorian prudery then informed colonial behaviour and attitudes. By 1905 nearly every Indian woman was viewed as a carrier of venereal disease in "a horrible, loathsome and often fatal form". This was because, Lord Kitchener told the troops, "the common women as well as the regular prostitutes of India are all more or less infected with the disease". Its prevalence was no more than a symptom of a "diseased" society.

The demonisation of Indian womanhood was but a single part of a more general downgrading of India in the eyes of its British rulers. Oddly, Victorian feminists reinforced the notion through philanthropic works aimed at helping their "degraded" colonial sisters. They envisaged the secluded lives of Indian woman as domestic prostitution. Already the Mutiny had come to be regarded as a reaction to British efforts to improve India, "their over-eager pursuit of Humanity and Civilisation". For as long as the English East India Company ruled in the interests of commerce, and the Mughal emperor still sat on his feeble throne, Britain could not easily claim the moral high ground. After Zafar's deposition and the transfer of power to the Crown, it was possible to present the Indian empire as a natural consequence of the decay of both Moslem and Hindu institutions.

There were to be no more annexations: instead, all of the princely states were to be an adjunct of the British Raj. Their rulers received the assurance that their rights would be safeguarded, in large measure because colonial administrators were happiest dealing with a feudal order of inherited social hierarchy. Allegiance was henceforth due to Queen Victoria, who had been proclaimed Empress of India in 1877.

Gratifying though this was to the princes, whose extravagance soon became notorious in Europe, the tightening grip of the British could not be disguised. A complex and multilayered system of government dominated the subcontinent. Efficient and fair by imperial standards, the Indian Civil Service had a less attractive side in the self-assertive behaviour of its officers and their families. Social separation was the norm: the senior officers' reserve, the memsahibs' petty snobbery, the colour bar at clubs and the studious avoidance of Indian passengers on trains. All this was less tolerable for Indians than the earlier brashness of the English East India Company because it was almost everywhere. No one realised then that such triumphant imperialism was destined to last for only another 89 years.

Gandhi and Indian Nationalism

The British empire extended over one-fourth of the globe and over one-fourth of its population. According to Lord Curzon, the viceroy of India from 1898 until 1905, it represented the greatest instrument for good that ever existed. He did not share the view of Britain's duty to prepare India for self-government, no matter how far distant this might be in the future. Educated Indians were uninterested in either justice or sound administration, Curzon insisted: all they cared for was a share of executive power, for which he thought them "as yet profoundly unfitted".

But the British in India had to confront an increasingly vocal nationalist movement. Even before the rise of Gandhi, the Indian National Congress was no longer a harmless talking shop. Curzon's own abrasiveness encouraged this development: the Congress, founded in 1885 with British support, had become a trenchant critic of colonial rule. A year after the viceroy left for Britain, the Moslem League was

The Curzons' visit to Hyderabad in 1902. The Nizam is
sandwiched between his guests

founded, yet another sign that the post-Mutiny system of conservative
rule had come apart.

A breathing space was gained for the British in 1917 by a promise
of constitutional reform. Popularly named after the Secretary of State
for India, Edwin Montagu, and the viceroy, Lord Chelmsford, this
programme offered "responsible government" in the form of limited
representative democracy. On the surface, the concessions appeared substantial: three out of seven ministers on the viceroy's executive council
were to be Indian; but their portfolios lacked scope for decisive political
action, since they only covered education, public health, agriculture and
irrigation. Key ministries remained firmly in British hands. Constitutional
changes, at both central and provincial government levels, were seen as
a way of binding educated Indians to the Raj. Even so, the Conservative
Party in Britain remained suspicious of their value right up to the Second
World War.

Gandhi's return to India in 1915 transformed the struggle between
the forces of Indian nationalism and the entrenched power of Britain.
The son of a minister in one of the smallest of India's princely states,

Mohandas Karamchand Gandhi completed his education by obtaining a law degree in London. Unable to prosper in Bombay, he went to work for Indian merchants in South Africa, where the beginnings of apartheid sharpened his sense of social injustice. What he brought back from his experience of civil disobedience there was a method of embarrassing a colonial government, as well as an ability to get Hindu and Moslem Indians to sink their differences in the cause of freedom. Colour prejudice was anathema to Gandhi in all its forms, which he decided in India manifested itself in untouchability. Some Congressmen regarded his campaign to end this discrimination as an irrelevancy during the struggle against the British, others as an unnecessary assault on Hinduism. But Gandhi was not to be deflected from the task, publicly describing the 1934 Bihar earthquake as divine retribution for the sin of untouchability. Harijan, "the children of god", was to be used for members of the "suppressed classes" in future.

Gandhi's method of civil disobedience, passive resistance, which he called satyagraha, "truth force", was so effective in disrupting British rule that he later suggested that persecuted Jews should adopt the same approach in Germany. In reply, the Jewish philosopher Martin Buber pointed out the different kind of opponent his people faced in the Nazis, whose concentration camps were places of death, not just detention. He also reminded Gandhi of the sheer number of Indians who could participate in the protest movement, unlike the relatively small German-Jewish community. Indeed, the size of Indian protests were to become as much a problem for the Congress Party as for the British authorities in 1919. Riots broke out in Delhi, Ahmedabad and the Punjab. Although he deplored the looting and arson, as well as the attacks on Europeans, Gandhi blamed the police for provoking the disorder. But he was dismayed at the ferocity that his civil disobedience call had unleashed. The worst violence occurred at Amritsar, the site of the Golden Temple sacred to Sikh religion.

Rumours of the imminent collapse of British authority excited crowds so much in Amritsar that local officials asked for a reinforcement of its garrison. Before more troops arrived, the arrest of two outspoken critics of colonial rule ended in a confrontation that left six protesters dead or wounded. This shooting inflamed the crowd: public buildings were fired, telegraph and telephone wires cut and half a dozen Europeans killed in the street. When General Reginald

Dyer arrived to restore the peace and learned that a large crowd had ignored an order forbidding meetings, he went to Jullianwala Bagh to disperse the gathering by force. In the derelict garden, Dyer ordered his Indian and Gurkha troops to open fire on the unarmed crowd, killing 379 protestors and wounding more than 1,200. Amritsar was utterly cowed.

To signal the restoration of British power in the city, Dyer then issued humiliating orders, one of which required Indians to go on all fours when passing the places where Europeans had been assaulted. The end of the rioting was appreciated not only by merchants and shopkeepers, who stood to lose most through looting, but even more

The indomitable Gandhi as determined as ever in 1940 to end the British Raj

by the guardians of the Golden Temple. The latter gave Dyer a turban and a ceremonial dagger as a token of their thanks. Though he always remained convinced of the correctness of the military intervention at Jullianwala Bagh, reaction to the massacre was generally unfavourable. Congress roundly condemned the whole episode while, in the House of Commons, Winston Churchill memorably described Dyer's action as "a monstrous event, an event which stood in singular and sinister isolation . . . without parallel in the modern history of the British Empire". Forced into early retirement, Dyer did not lack supporters in Britain: they presented him with £26,000 and a golden sword inscribed "Defender of Empire". Gandhi himself thought that the disorder in the Punjab and elsewhere was organised, rather than a spontaneous outburst of mob violence. But no ringleaders were identified in what must be regarded as the most direct challenge to the Raj since the days of the Mutiny.

Throughout the 1920s and the 1930s, Congress kept up pressure for Indian independence. Feeling unhappy about its policy direction, Gandhi passed the leadership in 1940 to Jawaharlal Nehru. The same year, Chandra Subhas Bose, whose fiery temperament Gandhi deeply mistrusted, abandoned Congress altogether because of its belief in non-violent protest. Nehru was equally distressed by Bose's plan to exploit Britain's wartime difficulties, which, he held, was tantamount to offering a helping hand to Hitler. Once again Gandhi showed his political naivety in suggesting that the only way to deal with a Japanese invasion of India was completely non-violent non-cooperation. When an American journalist suggested that his Quit-India campaign, just launched against the British, could give victory in 1942 to the Japanese in China as well as India, he said: "I had not the remotest idea of any such catastrophe resulting from my action." The next year Gandhi also confessed that he had never read the India Act of 1935. He now discovered to his surprise that it gave India all the essentials of self-government. Although this piece of legislation was the blueprint for eventual independence, the Conservative Party still wished to thwart Congress by means of a federation dominated by princes, Moslems and minorities. That "half-naked fakir", as Churchill called Gandhi, had to be kept from exercising real power.

Yet an otherworldliness already seems to have enveloped Gandhi. His cherished vision of a traditional Indian way of life was doomed. Symbolically, its eclipse was marked by the choice of emblem for independent

India's flag, an Asokan chakra instead of a spinning wheel. Renowned though Asoka was as the first Buddhist ruler, he was never adamant in his insistence of non-violence. He said he would prefer his descendants to conquer without force, but should it prove necessary, he hoped they would conduct a conquest with the minimum of bloodshed. As one of his admirers noted with regret, at his funeral Gandhi's body was not carried on the shoulders of his closest followers, but on a gun carriage. "Gandhi," he commented, "had taken away the tigerish cloak of the Indian people but not their tigerish nature."

Independence and Partition

Of all the European powers in Asia, only Britain succeeded in achieving a dignified withdrawal from empire, in large measure because of Clement Attlee's determination to grant India early independence. Had the Labour Party not won a landslide election victory in 1945, the British would have found themselves struggling with a series of colonial wars. A "diehard" such as Churchill could never have adjusted to the post-war situation fast enough to avoid unnecessary conflicts. He had told the House of Commons in the debates on the 1935 Act that there was "no real practical unity in India apart from British rule".

Prime Minister Attlee, Churchill's successor, knew otherwise. He understood that preservation of Britain's influence in Asia meant nothing short of independence. What was crucial in a smooth process of decolonisation was for London to seem still in charge. It had to dictate events, and not be driven by them: it was a policy that depended upon gaining the agreement of moderate nationalists by yielding control at a pace that prevented it being seized by extremists. In the 1940s and the 1950s, Britain largely achieved this aim by reshaping the old empire into a new framework of more or less equal partners. The exception in Asia was India, where communal differences led to its split into two separate and antagonistic states.

Lack of accord in the run-up to independence suited Mohammed Ali Jinnah because it allowed the Moslem League to return to the historic "Pakistan" resolution passed in 1940 at Lahore. The creation of a separate homeland for Indian Moslems was again on the agenda. Somehow or other Indian independence had to be delivered, and Attlee decided that Lord Louis Mountbatten was the man to bring about a decision. When this final viceroy arrived at Delhi in March 1947, he was alarmed by the unsettled situation and the general assumption that partition was about to happen. Notwithstanding his royal connections, Mountbatten was far removed from previous British rulers of India. He had learned how to manipulate his superiors, allies and subordinates as Supreme Allied Commander, South-East Asia, during the war against Japan, becoming a shrewd operator at national and international levels. It is likely that his personal grasp of the political realities of power explains why Attlee chose him at this moment of crisis.

One of the difficulties facing Mountbatten on his arrival was the vanity of the Indian leadership. Not without conceit himself, the viceroy was taken aback by Jinnah, who positively enjoyed rejecting every proposal put to him, and to a lesser extent by Nehru, whose inability to measure his words was a source of acute embarrassment. Both these rivals were satisfied that they knew what was best for their followers. Another difficulty was Gandhi, still a powerful figure in the background. Unlike most Congress leaders, Gandhi could not reconcile himself to partition, and in particular any arrangement for it devised by the British.

Mountbatten had to deploy all his charm as well as all his guile to meet Attlee's chief instruction, which was for Britain to quit India in a spirit of goodwill. At once he took pains to flatter Gandhi, who responded with pleasure to this last-minute recognition by the highest of British officials. It had the desired effect when Gandhi agreed that partition was the sole means of gaining India's independence. Even then, Mountbatten told Attlee that this would have to come sooner than later, because

> we are sitting on the edge of a volcano and . . . an eruption might take place through any of the three main craters—Bengal, the Punjab and the North-West Frontier Province—at any moment.

Yet London was shaken when, at a press conference in Delhi, he said that independence could be as early as August, almost one year earlier than the projected date. Attlee took it in his stride, however, and ensured that the India Independence Act was put on the statute book in time for the transfer of power.

Because the first phases of devising the partition went without incident, Bengal and the Punjab both endorsing east–west splits, despite a strong feeling among the Sikhs that they merited a province of their own, Mountbatten could overlook an unsatisfactory referendum in the North-West Frontier Province, caused by a Congress boycott of the vote. But the viceroy was far too sanguine. As many as 700,000 people lost their lives in communal violence immediately after independence and ten million others migrated either to India or Pakistan. The rise of the Moslem League, the demands of the Congress Party and the aimless drift of British policy during the inter-war years were all factors ensuring that Mountbatten had little room for manoeuvre in 1947. His basic problem remained the missed opportunity to grant India dominion status. Only Attlee's boldness cut the Gordian knot in India but the reduced timescale that he endorsed may have facilitated the upsurge of communal violence.

Afterwards, the hostility between India and Pakistan resulted in wars during 1947, 1965 and 1971, the last of which split Pakistan in half and established Bangladesh. The decision of the Hindu ruler of Kashmir to opt for India on partition also did much to poison Indo-Pakistan relations and alienate most of the princely state's people, the Kashmiri Moslems.

Sri Lanka and Bangladesh

As a result of Attlee's support for Mountbatten, both Pakistan and India chose to remain within the Commonwealth. To get the Congress Party to abandon its republicanism to the extent of accepting the British monarch as the head of a "family" of nations was no mean achievement. To accommodate the Indian republic, a Commonwealth Conference thrashed out this formula in 1949. Just as India had been the motor of Britain's expanding power in Asia during the eighteenth century, so in the twentieth, its requirement for a different relationship drove the Commonwealth to update its arrangements in time for the accession of African, Caribbean, Pacific and Southeast Asian states. Attlee's vision of an association of free peoples could now become a political reality.

In 1948, Sri Lanka became independent within the Commonwealth, largely because it was next door to India. For some time, the great island had enjoyed a degree of self-government, a circumstance that minimised the impact of the Imperial Japanese Navy's raid in early 1942. Not that Ceylon, as Sri Lanka was then called, lacked troubles of its own. The introduction of electoral politics had sown discord between the Sinhalese and the Tamils, who were largely concentrated in the north of the island. Radical Tamils in Jaffna were dismayed when the Sinhalese used their majority to keep ministerial posts entirely for themselves. A demand for the reservation of posts for Tamil and Moslem minorities was dismissed out of hand by both the Sinhalese and the British colonial government. Especially disliked by the Sinhalese was the placement on the electoral roll of Tamils whose villages were situated in southern India. A five-year-residence requirement seemed no guarantee of loyalty to Sri Lanka. Quite forgotten in the furore was that many Hindu Tamil families had been resident for centuries.

The failure to recognise legitimate Tamil aspirations continues to fuel a conflict that continues today, despite the apparent defeat of the Tamil Tigers in 2009. Because the first communal disorder only occurred in 1956, the Labour government could congratulate itself on avoiding in Sri Lanka a painful India-style partition. It did not help that the Sinhalese became aggressively Buddhist, through combining religion with nationalism. Perhaps the country will return to a secular model but, for the moment, non-Buddhists are regarded as second-class citizens. Christians have been picked out for special treatment, with their churches destroyed in several areas. It has even been alleged that missionaries are part of an American plot to undermine Sri Lankan culture.

The third Indo-Pakistan war of 1971 assisted the birth of the third state in modern South Asia, Bangladesh. Again initiated by Pakistan, this conflict came as no surprise to India. In late 1970 Sheikh Mujibur Rahman, the leader of the Bengali Moslem Party, won an overwhelming victory in the East Pakistan elections. General Yahya Khan, the Pakistani dictator, refused to accept the result and declared martial law, thereby allowing a crackdown on Mujibur Rahman's supporters. Millions fled across the Indian border.

Needing to settle the refugee problem, the Indian government backed the Bangladeshi resistance movement, the Mukti Bahini. Fought on two fronts, the war of 1971 was altogether different in its outcome from the previous two conflicts, because the Pakistani army discovered that it could not defend East Pakistan from an Indian invasion. When, at the close of the year, the Pakistani garrison surrendered in Dacca, the Indians had 90,000 prisoners in the bag. India's ability to truncate the Moslem state depended on two things: Bangladeshi support and an effective defence along the western front. The loss of Chamb, a city southwest of Srinagar, was a small price to pay for cutting Pakistan down to size. The acquisition of nuclear weapons hardly changes the situation, because Bangladesh has managed to survive as an independent state. Yet India has not been kind to Bangladesh, because the construction of a barrage across the river Ganges not only disrupts its irrigation schemes but worsens flooding during the monsoon. Water control and deforestation remain unresolved issues between India and Bangladesh.

Chapter 12

Modern East Asia

> If we seek common ground and remove the misfortune and suffering imposed on us by colonialism, then it will be easy for us to understand and respect each other.
>
> *Zhou Enlai at the 1955 Bandung Conference of Asian states*

China's Humiliation

Lord Macartney's refusal to kowtow was given out by the Qing court as the reason for the rebuff of his mission in 1793. This ritual comprised three separate kneelings, each one followed by a full prostration with the forehead knocking the ground three times. There had been intense negotiations before it was accepted that the British envoy would be excused, in part because of the difficulty of kneeling in the tight trousers he wore.

Though "kowtow" entered the English language as a symbol of everything wrong with China, and notably its clinging to outdated customs, the truth of the matter was a marked reluctance on the part of the Manchus to open the Chinese empire to seaborne trade, since they feared the adverse effect European influence might have on their Chinese subjects. Macartney's lack of success could also be explained in the darker side of the English East India Company's trading activities. So that it could acquire sufficient silver to sustain an unfavourable balance of payments involved in the China trade, caused by massive purchases of tea, it had deliberately stimulated the production of opium in India. The English East India Company was careful to leave opium trafficking to private merchants, but this did not fool Beijing and in 1839 a special commissioner was sent to southern China with orders to stamp out the whole business. Not least because abolition of the company monopoly six years earlier had led to a free-for-all, that saw opium imports run completely out of control.

Commissioner Lin Zexu first broke up the network of Chinese importers and distributors; next he destroyed the opium stocks of Western merchants without compensation; and finally he obliged them to promise to end the odious traffic in the drug. News that Lin Zexu had also excluded the British from Guangzhou was considered reason enough to send an expeditionary force of 20 ships with 4,000 troops on board. Quite overlooked was the specific cause of the exclusion: a drunken brawl in which sailors killed a Chinese man. When none of these men were handed over for justice, Lin Zexu compelled British residents to live on their ships off Hong Kong, where they awaited the expeditionary force, which was about to humble the Chinese empire because the British were overwhelmingly superior in arms.

Hostilities against the Chinese empire were formally declared at London in 1840. Profit swept every objection aside in what became known as the First Opium War. Foreign Secretary Palmerston had cleverly insisted that it was national pride, rather than commerce, that was the issue: the freedom of British citizens abroad had to be protected at all costs. The Qing dynasty was about to discover the price that it would have to pay for this privilege. British possessions in India provided ready troops and supplies, and their shallow-draft warships could easily bombard upriver cities and towns. The steamer *Nemesis* was capable of blasting a hole in any fortress wall. The largest iron vessel ever launched, *Nemesis* allowed the British to capture the forts protecting the approach to Guangzhou, easily sink Chinese war junks and then threaten the city itself.

But the decisive phase of the First Opium War occurred when the British ships sailed northwards, capturing Ningbo and Shanghai without difficulty. Because the fall of Nanjing, an ex-imperial capital, would destroy the prestige of the Qing dynasty, a peace treaty between Britain and China was in 1842 hurriedly signed on *HMS Cornwallis*, anchored off the city.

The Treaty of Nanjing awarded Britain a very large indemnity to cover the cost of the war and the lost opium stocks; opened five ports to international trade; ceded the island of Hong Kong as a sovereign base; and, last but not least, established the principle of extraterritoriality. The total immunity the latter gave British residents from Chinese law became deeply resented, especially when they carved out for themselves privileged enclaves in the so-called Treaty Ports. The opium trade went almost unmentioned because the British negotiators disingenuously took the view that this was a matter for the Chinese authorities to sort out.

Renewed hostilities between Britain and China predictably began at Guangzhou, but on this occasion it had no connection with opium. Britain had settled on a policy of non-intervention but, with Palmerston's return to power, the Hong Kong merchants perceived an opportunity to further their interests through treaty revision. They clamoured therefore in 1856 for a stern response to the *Arrow* Incident. By registration in Hong Kong this schooner was entitled to fly the British flag and claim British protection. A skirmish with Chinese pirates led to the intervention of Guangzhou's port authorities, who boarded the *Arrow* and took into custody both the crew and the pirates. The Irish captain was not there when the police arrived. Yet this Chinese action over a Chinese-built boat, owned by a Chinese citizen, manned by a Chinese crew, sailing in Chinese waters was treated as "an insult of a very grave nature" in Hong Kong. That on sailing into Guangzhou, the *Arrow* would have lowered its flags in accordance with British nautical practice and could be mistaken as a Chinese vessel was ignored. That *Arrow*'s registration had actually expired was a technicality insufficient to stop armed action.

Riding a wave of nationalism for his gunboat diplomacy in 1857, a 72-year-old Palmerston appointed as special plenipotentiary James Bruce, the eighth earl of Elgin. Prime Minister Palmerston's instructions were brief: he was to demand, by direct negotiation with the imperial government in Beijing, the establishment of a permanent British representative there; the opening of new ports to international trade; and a Chinese promise to comply with the provisions of the Treaty of Nanjing.

At Elgin's disposal was an Anglo-French force of 5,700 men, France having decided that the execution of a Catholic missionary in south China justified taking part in the Second Opium War. It took almost a year for Elgin to reach Guangzhou because some of the soldiers

The Qing empire

had to be diverted to suppress the Indian Mutiny. Making no impression at all on the Qing court by the capture of Guangzhou, Elgin directed the expedition northwards and reached Tianjin, some forty kilometres from the imperial capital.

When it was discovered that Beijing had no intention of implementing the terms of the newly signed Treaty of Tianjin, Elgin was told to bring the Qing court to its senses. Convinced that only force would accomplish this aim, he readied siege guns to breach Beijing's ramparts, until a negotiator was lowered in a basket so that the city gates did not have to be opened. In return for keeping most of his men out of the capital, Elgin got his way and through the Conventions of Beijing obtained a lease on Kowloon, the peninsula opposite Hong Kong. But this did not stop French and British soldiers from looting the Summer Palace, the great walled pleasure ground that Emperor Qian Long had laid out northwest of Beijing. One senior British officer remarked that its sack was like "having the run of Buckingham Palace and being allowed to take away anything and everything you wanted. Things were plundered and pulled to pieces, floors were literally covered with fur robes, jade ornaments, porcelain and beautiful wood carvings".

Elgin's indifference to this wanton destruction in 1860 was roundly condemned, except by Palmerston who commented: "It was absolutely necessary to stamp by such a record our indignation at the treachery and brutality of these Tartars, for Chinese they are not." One of the looters, Charles Gordon, stayed on with his artillery corps to help the Qing dynasty put down the Taiping rebellion, which for nearly 15 years convulsed the populous southern provinces of the Chinese empire. A tragedy for this modernising movement, despite its professed Christian belief, was the coldness of Europeans living in south China, most of all those with commercial interests at stake or missionaries anxious about doctrinal differences. Painfully, the Taipings learned that Europeans were neither coreligionists nor allies against the Manchus.

Having just wrung more concessions from Beijing, Britain could see there was nothing to be gained by supporting the Christian rebels. London was content to leave the humbled Qing court as it was: an

Lord Elgin signing the Treaty of Tianjin in 1858. Qing reluctance to implement its terms resulted in the assault on Beijing two years later

anachronism in an increasingly modern Asia. Manchus such as Empress Ci Xi might cling to power, blocking any attempt at reform, but she could not prolong Qing rule indefinitely. As soon as Japan demonstrated the value of imported Western technology against the Chinese army in Korea, it was obvious that China would have to change as well. Ci Xi's imprisonment in 1898 of the ninth Qing emperor Guang Xi thwarted his Hundred Days of Reform: what she could not do was banish the ideas that informed his proposals from the public agenda.

Buoyed with the success of this intervention, Ci Xi made her second big mistake when in 1900 she backed the Boxers' attempt to expel foreigners from China by force. It was the height of folly, since their attack on the Legation Quarter would inevitably bring to its relief a punitive expedition of troops drawn from all countries with diplomats at Beijing. Members of a secret society called the Righteous Harmonious Fist had recently enlarged their sacred boxing to include assaults on Christian missions and foreign importations such as telegraph poles. Though there were only 409 armed men to resist the attack, defensible legation compounds held out until the international relief force arrived. Disguised as a Chinese peasant woman, Ci Xi had already taken her captive emperor to the northwestern city of Xi'an. "Who could ever have thought," the chastened empress is reported to have said, "that it would come to this?"

China's humiliation. Lord Elgin's triumphant entry into Beijing in 1860

The looting of an abandoned Beijing underscored the bankruptcy of Qing rule. Had it not been for the declaration of an open-door policy by the United States, whereby China was to remain a market open to all, there is every reason to believe that the spheres of influence belonging to the European powers would become sovereign possessions. The sudden death of Guang Xi in 1908, which immediately followed that of Ci Xi, left the Chinese empire ruled by a child, Pu Yi, the final Qing emperor Xuan Tong. His reign lasted until 1911.

Whereas Japan's response to the West was modernisation, that of China was revolution. Republicans such as Sun Yatsen were delighted by the new machinery of government, quite overlooking the massive jump that the Chinese people would have to make to turn the Republic of China into a democratic reality. Between the republicans and most of the population there was only one point of agreement, the correctness of overthrowing the Manchus. Within a decade of its foundation, the Republic was the plaything of warlords, regional commanders who converted their provinces into virtually autonomous areas. The vulnerability of China throughout the period of modernisation in Asia profoundly influenced the outlook of the Chinese people. They were acutely aware of the abyss into which their country sank as the imperial system declined, and republican institutions that followed its disintegration proved no match for either warlord rivalry or Japanese imperialism. Not until after the foundation of the People's Republic in 1949 would the siege of China, that began with the First Opium War, be finally lifted.

Japanese Imperialism

The task of opening up Japan to international trade fell to the United States Navy. Commodore Matthew Perry forced the shogun to accept in 1853 a letter from his president and then weighed anchor, promising to return in a year for an answer. No sooner had the smoke from Perry's steamers cleared than argument broke out over the best course of action that Japan should take.

Shogun Tokugawa Iemochi was at a loss. In theory the emperor's commander-in-chief, he was the last in a line of military dictators. It had long been the policy of such warlords to isolate the emperor from current events, and encourage the idea that he was some kind of living god involved in an endless round of ceremonies. This policy backfired shortly after Perry's return for an answer because a group of reformers were able to exploit the supposed divinity of the emperor to push through radical changes. At the time of the abolition of the shogunate and the imperial restoration, the coup seemed little more than a shift in power from one section of the aristocracy to another, but the events of 1868, which Perry's intervention in Japanese affairs had provoked, were to inaugurate a thorough transformation of the country's economy and society. The motive power for change came from the samurai, warriors who like the emperor himself had no more than a ceremonial role.

In 1872, the custom of celebrating Emperor Meiji's birth was instituted by government order as a religious festival. With Buddhism pushed aside, the way was open for emperor worship as an integral part of Japanese nationalism. Behind this traditional screen, the Meiji reformers strove to develop the strategic industries on which modern military power depended. The strain on the imperial exchequer proved too great, however, and in the financial retrenchment during the 1880s, most of the government holdings were sold cheaply to supporters in the business community, even to officials. This expedient had the accidental effect of concentrating much of Japan's nascent industrial sector in the hands of a few people with enough money to buy factories and mines. Once the initial difficulties of industrialisation were overcome, and the national economy put back on a steady course, their energetic new owners were able to dominate production.

By the 1920s, they had created huge combines such as Mitsui and Mitsubishi, each of which encompassed a great variety of enterprises, including banking, extractive industries, manufacturing companies, transportation and trading firms. It was indeed Mitsubishi, Japan's second-largest combine, that helped to create a powerful navy in its shipyards at Yokohama, Kobe and Nagasaki: they were able to supplement the hectic pace of warship construction being undertaken at imperial yards. Mitsubishi also made the Zero fighter, whose phenomenal range of 1,200 kilometres gave the aeroplane mastery of the Asian skies before the advent of more powerfully engined US fighters from 1943 onwards.

The Meiji transformation was unique. For Japan's emergence as an imperial power was so totally different from the European experience. The emperor, his court and leading reformers might wear Western-style clothes, but the constitution they announced by imperial decree in 1889 was an "immutable fundamental law". Influenced by Germany, rather than Britain and France, the new system of government was in effect an

A Japanese view of Perry's arrival at Yokohama in 1853

oligarchy of shared power between civilian politicians and military leaders, which during the 1930s tilted in favour of the latter. Revolution in China and unrest in the colonies of the Western powers seemed to create an ideal moment for an increasingly militarised Japan to strike out on its own. The result was the Pacific dimension of the Second World War, a catastrophe for imperialism throughout Asia.

The road to this conflict began in Korea with the First Sino-Japanese War of 1894–95. There Japanese intervention came about through the Tonghak movement, a parallel of the Taiping uprising in China. Its founder, Ch'oe Che'u, was another Confucian scholar denied an official career. Having burned his books, Ch'oe Che'u wandered the Korean peninsula in search of truth. Mystical experiences convinced him that he had been chosen to reshape Korean society, as the appointed agent of the supreme deity on earth. In all probability, shamanism moulded Ch'oe Che'u's basic view of god and man as inseparably linked. Slogans such as "all men are sages and princes" frightened an entrenched aristocratic order, and in 1864 the visionary was beheaded for spreading false doctrines.

Japan's equal dislike of the Tonghak movement arose from its nationalist bent, which sought to resist foreign encroachment just when Tokyo wished to assert its suzerainty over Korea. In a state of panic, the Korean government appealed to China, the traditional protector of the Korean monarchy. Defeats on land and sea obliged the Chinese to

Modernised Japan. Troops on their way to Korea in 1894

fall back on the Liaodong peninsula, where Port Arthur was a prime Japanese target. The atrocities committed in that city were regarded by Japan's admirers in the West as nothing more than an aberration, a naïve response to the cruelty for which the Imperial Japanese Army was to become notorious later on.

Korean hatred of the Japanese turned the Tonghaks into loyalists, their underground opposition prefiguring the resistance shown by the Korean people during the 35 years that their country was a Japanese colony. Some politicians were prepared to embrace Japan as a way of modernising Korea, but the blatant exploitation of the country's resources had discredited them well before Korea was annexed in 1910. It was the comprehensive defeat of Russia five years before that gave Japan a clear run in both Korea and Manchuria. Reassured by the Anglo-Japanese Alliance of 1902, which itself was an admission of the Imperial Japanese Navy's arrival in Asian waters, Tokyo did not hesitate to fight Russia, whose occupation of Manchuria and the Liaodong peninsula had inflamed Japanese public opinion.

Admiral Togo Heihachiro, a cadet at Portsmouth and Cambridge in the 1870s, bottled up Russian warships in Port Arthur and then in 1905 destroyed a Russian fleet in the Straits of Tsushima that had sailed all the way from Europe. This armada could not cope with Togo Heihachiro's fast-moving destroyers and cruisers in a two-day battle that sent most of its battleships to the bottom. As Port Arthur had already fallen after a siege that cost the Japanese 57,000 casualties out of an attacking force of 90,000 men, the Russians were obliged to sue for peace. Togo Heihachiro would only accept the compliment of a comparison with Nelson: he knew that he was no Yi Sun-sin, who single-handed had thwarted Toyotomi Hideyoshi's invasion of Korea in the sixteenth century. The Korean admiral designed his revolutionary warships himself, unlike Togo Heihachiro, whose fleet comprised British-built vessels.

But the patriotic fervour that flowed from Togo Heihachiro's humiliation of the Russians stimulated warship production to the extent that 200 major ships were launched before Pearl Harbor. The defeats inflicted on China and Russia forced the West to recognise Japan as a new power in Asia. Tokyo's attempts to exclude Manchuria from the scope of the open-door policy towards China damaged relations with Britain and the United States, but not yet to the extent that they were moved to take any action. However, events were soon to provide Japan with ample scope for further imperial advance: first, the overthrow of the Qing dynasty inaugurated the chaos of warlord politics, and, second, the First World War gave Tokyo the chance of joining the Allies and capturing the German concession on the Shandong peninsula, Qingdao.

When Britain, France and Italy endorsed Japan's claim to German rights in Shandong province at the peace conference in Versailles, popular indignation erupted in Beijing, where the Fourth May Movement, spearheaded by 3,000 university students, spread from Tiananmen Square to the houses of pro-Japanese ministers, which were burned to the ground. The impact of this spontaneous demonstration upon China was out of all proportion to its size: in towns and cities, meetings were held and a boycott of Japanese goods started.

Yet Sun Yatsen realised that public protests were inadequate for the Republic's defence. He had gone to Guangzhou and set up an alternative administration, where members of the Chinese Communist Party were allowed to join the Guomindang as "individuals" and plans were laid to crush the warlords and reunite China as a socialist state. To increase military efficiency Chiang Kai-shek was sent to a sympathetic Soviet

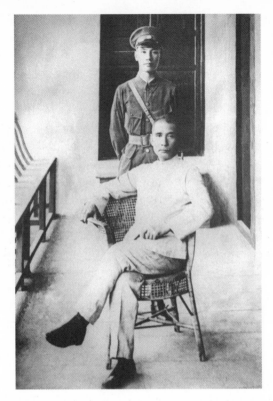

Sun Yatsen in 1923. Standing is his successor as leader
of the Guomindang, Chiang Kai-shek

Union for training and on his return became the first commandant of
Huanpu Military Academy. This appointment gave this ambitious soldier
a chance to build up a personal following within the Guomindang, so
that after the death of Sun Yatsen in 1925 he assumed the leadership
of the Northern Expedition against the warlords. At Huanpu, downriver from Guangzhou, relations between the Communists and the
Guomindang were generally amicable, because the diplomatic skills of
Zhou Enlai contributed to a unity of purpose.

By the summer of 1926 the Northern Expedition had reached the
great cities of Wuhan, Nanjing and Shanghai, but the victorious march
brought differences between the Communists and the Guomindang
into the open, as landlords and businessmen backing Chiang Kai-shek
were terrified over the social conflict being stirred up by Mao Zedong
in the countryside and Zhou Enlai in the towns. So early in 1927

Guomindang troops skirmish in Shanghai with Japanese
forces before the outbreak of the Second Sino-Japanese War

Guomindang troops were ordered to cooperate with underworld
toughs in killing strikers at Shanghai. By a quirk of fate Zhou Enlai
escaped the slaughter, which stalled the Chinese revolution for two
decades. Although Guomindang forces entered Beijing in 1928 and
restored a single Chinese government, Chiang Kai-shek only achieved
this by coming to terms with fellow warlords and, as important, giving
no offence to the Japanese.

In the blatant appeasement of Tokyo, the Generalissimo, as Chiang
Kai-shek was now called, received the active support of Japanese-educated
Wang Jinwei, China's future Pétain. Wang Jinwei was convinced that the
expulsion of the Western colonial powers from Asia depended upon an
alliance between Japan and China. Not even the dreadful treatment of
civilians at Nanjing in 1937 could persuade him otherwise and three
years later he headed a puppet government in the same city. A conservative estimate puts the number of Chinese people killed there during
the Imperial Japanese Army's reign of terror at 260,000, and there can
be little doubt that the figure would have been much higher without
the efforts made by members of the European community to establish a
safety zone. The full extent of Japanese brutality is still not squarely faced

today. When in 1988 *The Last Emperor* was screened in Japan, the film's distributor arranged for scenes of rape and murder at Nanjing to be cut, lest they annoy Japanese audiences.

But conflict between the Chinese Communist Party and the Guomindang was temporarily ended in 1936 by the Xi'an Incident. Having driven the Chinese Communist Party by the Long March to a remote stronghold at Yan'an, in Shaanxi province, Chiang Kai-shek flew into nearby Xi'an to oversee its destruction. The expeditionary commander, Zhang Xueling, and his Manchurian soldiers were much less enthusiastic: they could not understand why the Guomindang was so willing to appease Japan when their own native provinces remained occupied by the Imperial Japanese Army. At gunpoint Chiang Kai-shek was made to agree a truce and pledge himself to resist Japan.

Within a year, the outbreak of the Second Sino-Japanese War meant that the followers of Mao Zedong and Chiang Kai-shek were both engaged. But the Imperial Japanese Army soon captured many large towns and cities, the centres of Guomindang support. Chiang Kai-shek retreated inland to Chongqing in Sichuan province, where he was cut off from the outside world, except for a supply route from Russia and another from the British colony of Burma. Other than railway lines, Japanese control was restricted to urban areas and stretches of the coastline. This constituted a serious tactical error because, by the time the Imperial Japanese Army was ready to move into the countryside, Communist Party guerrillas had organised the peasants against it.

As Emperor Hirohito bitterly complained, his generals had broken their promise that war in China would not divert scarce resources from the vital air and naval buildup. So overburdened was the economy with military expenditure that by 1940 Japan could no longer pay its way. The only solution appeared to be the seizure of assets belonging to the British and the Dutch in Southeast Asia. After Japan's surrender, Hirohito said that the focus of discussion was always oil. Now it seems incredible that Tokyo should have risked conflict with the United States as well as Britain, but the immediate strategic consequences of the unannounced attack on Pearl Harbor blinded the Imperial Japanese Army to the basic weakness of Japan's position, because the easy sweep southwards gave a false impression of its strength. Admiral Yamamoto Isoroku, the author of Pearl Harbour, was under no illusion about the fate of his country in an extended war: "To fight the United States," he said, "is like fighting the world."

USS Arizona going down in flames at Pearl Harbor,
7 December 1941

In the United States and Britain the racial stereotype of the Japanese male as a slow-witted and short-sighted dwarf gave place to an exaggerated fear of his superhuman stamina and courage. The fall of Singapore in early 1942 only seemed to confirm this new view, but in the Philippines, Malaya and Burma the state of Anglo-American defences were in a poor condition. Yet the defeat at Singapore was described by Winston Churchill as "the worst and largest capitulation in British history".

With the British retreat into India, Japan was able to establish a new order in much of Asia. Its Greater East Asia Co-Prosperity Sphere promised freedom from Western exploitation within a framework of Japan-led development. The reality proved quite different as Tokyo requisitioned materials for the war effort, conscripted labour for such murderous projects as the Burma railway and flooded occupied territories with worthless currency. Despite the deteriorating economic situation, Tokyo still gambled on the possibility that the forces of Asian nationalism might be enlisted against the returning Allies. In Indonesia, and to a lesser extent in the Philippines and Burma, the gamble paid off but the dividend was too small to avert defeat. On 2 September, aboard *USS*

Missouri in Tokyo Bay, a Japanese delegation signed the instrument of surrender, thereby liquidating the Japanese empire.

The People's Republic of China

The aftermath of the Second World War, with which the Second Sino-Japanese War had merged, was as profound for China as it was for Japan. Neither country could escape the far-reaching transformation that so dramatically altered the political landscape in the 1940s.

The sudden ending of hostilities caught the Guomindang short, while providing ample scope for the Chinese Communist Party to extend its influence. President Truman offered Chiang Kai-shek financial and military assistance and he ordered one million Japanese troops in Manchuria and north China to remain under arms until they could be replaced by Chiang Kai-shek's or US forces. Because of his warlord outlook, the Guomindang leader thought that the latest American military equipment would be enough to secure his position. Once Washington had rejected feelers from Mao Zedong for a top-level conference, civil war in China could not be avoided.

The rush to take over cities in Manchuria was Chiang Kai-shek's greatest error because, with Mao Zedong's guerrillas in effective control of the countryside, he simply inherited the difficulties of the Imperial Japanese Army. Had he chosen to secure south China first, and at the same time tried to reassure the peasants by introducing a measure of land reform, then the Guomindang might have been able to push northwards without peril. Guomindang forces were instead seen to ally themselves with the defeated Japanese and those Chinese units that had actively assisted the invaders.

In the meantime, the People's Liberation Army, as Mao Zedong's forces were now called, moved freely through the rural areas, setting up bases for future operations in mountainous areas as far south as the Yangzi river valley. While Chiang Kai-shek tried to counter this dangerous infiltration, Mao Zedong launched an all-out offensive. There was very little the Generalissimo could do to stop the advance of the People's Liberation Army: by 1949 units had reached the Yangzi, where shell fire drove *HMS Amethyst* aground. Despite the frigate's dramatic escape downriver, the Royal Navy's discomfiture marked the end of gunboat diplomacy. The shelling restored the great river to Chinese

On 1 October 1949 Mao Zedong proclaims the People's Republic in Beijing

ownership: it was no longer an international waterway, a designation forced upon China in the nineteenth century.

The sequel to the *Amethyst* Incident was strained relations between Britain and the People's Republic, which Mao Zedong proclaimed in Beijing on 1 October 1949. Truman now knew that Chiang Kai-shek was a lost cause. Of the 2.5 billion dollars that Washington had given in aid, the president said: "I'll bet you that a billion dollars of it is in New York banks today . . . It's all for those grafters and crooks; rest of the people in China don't matter." The flight of a Guomindang remnant to Taiwan left Truman unmoved, although his political opponents blamed him for "losing" China, as if it were his to lose.

Not until the outbreak of the Korean War returned US troops to mainland Asia would Washington offer any assistance to the Guomindang. But with the United States so worried about the Soviet Union, there was never any chance of better relations with the People's Republic: it would take major clashes between Chinese and Russian troops in 1969 to dent American belief in a unified communist bloc.

Under the Chinese Communist Party material progress was impressive, although observers were surprised by the disagreement within its leadership over the Great Leap Forward in 1959. Because of his interest in the countryside, Mao Zedong was the first Chinese leader to appreciate the revolutionary dynamic in the agrarian revolts that had punctuated imperial history. Before anyone else, he understood that in China, unlike Europe, political control was strongest in the urban areas: hence his strategy against the Guomindang was "encircling the cities with the countryside". Now Mao Zedong decided it was the moment for the peasants to lift industrial output by means of smelters in their backyards. The initial increase in production was excellent, in spite of the poor quality of much of the village steel. But more worrying was a drop in the cereal harvest, caused by bad weather as well as the dispersion of labour into too many projects. Instead of taking note of the warning signs and rethinking strategy accordingly, Mao Zedong pressed on with the Great Leap Forward until famine forced a halt. Perhaps as many as ten million people died in 1960 and, though this figure is low in comparison with any of the bitter years of the 1920s and 1930s, it was the first occasion since the founding of the People's Republic that there were so many deaths caused by malnutrition.

As a result of this failure, Mao Zedong's influence was severely curtailed until the Great Proletarian Cultural Revolution that raged between 1966 and 1969. It represented his final attempt to stimulate a continuing revolution. Sensing the discontent of the young, Mao Zedong used those who joined the Red Guards to assault "capitalist-roaders" within the Chinese Communist Party itself. They were directed by his third wife Jiang Qing, a Shanghai actress whom Mao Zedong married in Yan'an. It was as much a tragedy for him as it was for China that the Great Proletarian Cultural Revolution appealed so strongly to Jiang Qing's thwarted theatrical talents.

The summer of 1967 was the high-water mark of cultural agitation, when people with Western-style clothes or possessions were harassed in a xenophobia reminiscent of the Boxers: Zhou Enlai had to protect Sun Yatsen's widow because her hairstyle was considered offensive. Comparative calm returned to China only after the invention of the People's Liberation Army in 1969.

The judgement of Deng Xiaoping was that the period from 1966 to 1976 had been a "Ten-year Catastrophe". His strictures were given dramatic form at the trial of Jiang Qing in 1980, when along with others she was convicted of hounding 34,274 people to their deaths. The total number of casualties remains unknown, although the nature of the cultural upheaval never remotely reached the extremes of Soviet terror. Yet it has to be accepted that the experience was very unpleasant indeed for many Chinese, peasants and urban workers alike. Deng Xiaoping's political strength derived from his realisation of how much the People's Republic yearned for stability after a series of uninterrupted mass movements. So Deng Xiaoping introduced reforms that blurred the Maoist dichotomy between the city and the countryside, allowing greater autonomy on the land and in state-owned factories. But in contrast to the introduction of market forces in Russia though, these changes were infinitely more successful because price increases were never allowed to approach the chronic inflation suffered under Chiang Kai-shek's regime.

This did not stop protest taking a bloody turn in Tiananmen Square in the summer of 1989. The tragedy was watched by millions outside China, because television crews were still in Beijing after the visit of Mikhail Gorbachev, then the Soviet Union's president. His arrival gave protesting students a unique opportunity to embarrass the Chinese authorities, already on the defensive through reports of riots in Tibet. Foreign viewers were initially surprised by the restraint of both the Political Bureau and the student leaders, whose complaints were focused upon official corruption. When it became known that rallies in support of the Tiananmen Square demonstration were being staged elsewhere in China, Deng Xiaoping called in the People's Liberation Army and cleared the students away. The brutal crackdown on the "counter-revolutionaries" astounded the world, although President George Bush blocked extreme measures against the People's Republic. The president felt a great deal of sympathy for Deng Xiaoping, whose modernising programme was doing so much to bring China back into the international community.

Good relations with Britain stemmed from Deng Xiaoping's own recognition of how much the People's Republic gained from the colony of Hong Kong. It was China's biggest trading partner and provided 70 per cent of its foreign investment. And Deng Xiaoping was anxious to prevent a flight of capital from Hong Kong on its return to China in 1997, something that Margaret Thatcher, the British prime minister, could do nothing to stop. Putting a brave face on the inevitable she declared as nothing less than a stroke of genius the formula "one coun-try, two systems", quite overlooking that this had always been Deng Xiaoping's intention for the money-making colony.

After Deng Xiaoping's death, the People's Republic weathered the 1990s financial crisis in Asia without difficulty, unlike slow-footed Japan. The absence of regulatory monitoring had already led to a bad debt problem for many Japanese banks, whose excessive lending repre-sented 70 per cent of their business. The economic downturn only made the situation worse. Banks in the People's Republic were less affected, because private enterprise still functioned as a supplement to the public economy. By 2000 it was admitted that private enterprise was not just a useful support, but rather an organic part of "socialism with Chinese characteristics". As a result, the People's Republic was put on the path to its present-day domination of world trade.

The Korean War

In the thirty-five years that followed the Japanese annexation in 1910, Korean nationalists did what they could to free their country from an oppressive colonial administration. But until 1943 there was no sign of any Western concern for the fate of Korea, then suffering badly as its resources were drained to sustain Japan's war effort. Whatever the reason for this delay, the United States and Britain had inadvertently created the conditions for the partition of the country.

Situated between Russia, China and Japan, the strategic posi-tion of the Korean peninsula went unnoticed in both Washington and London. Forgotten were the old rivalries between Russia and Japan for dominance, once the Chinese empire was in its final decline. As late as the Potsdam Conference in mid-1945, the Americans were still worried about the projected casualties of an invasion of Japan, so the defeat of Japanese units on the Asian mainland was left to the Soviet Union.

The dropping of the atomic bombs on Hiroshima and Nagasaki ended Japanese resistance at the very moment Russian forces overran northern Korea. Fearing that the whole peninsula might fall to them, US troops were rushed from Okinawa and the American commander, Douglas MacArthur, decided that it made sense to work through the existing Japanese authorities. The Koreans naturally found intoler-able the continuance in office of a colonial government from which they were supposed to be liberated. It was, a US intelligence officer concluded, "one of the most expensive mistakes ever made". In North Korea, on the other hand, Japanese soldiers were at once disarmed and colonial officials arrested, the day-to-day administration passing to a provisional government formed by Kim Il-sung. Koreans living in the American part of the peninsula looked with envy on this development, especially when MacArthur replaced the Japanese with their long-serving collaborators.

Although Washington got the United Nations to recognise its favoured regime, the Republic of Korea, as the lawful government, there already existed in the north the Soviet-backed People's Republic of Korea. As far as the United States was concerned, Korea lay beyond its defence perimeter in Asia, as indeed did the Guomindang bastion on the island of Taiwan. Noting this lack of interest, the North Koreans launched a surprise attack in 1950. During the ensuing struggle the South Korean army lost 350,000 men killed or missing, and 250,000 wounded; another 100,000 civilians were forcibly moved to North Korea. Thirty-three thousand Americans lost their lives and 106,000 were wounded. Against this, North Korea is estimated to have suffered 500,000 casualties, and China a staggering 900,000. By the end of 1953, few in the West believed any more that the Korean War had been necessary.

The involvement of the People's Republic in the conflict was a result of President Truman's decision to advance all the way to the borders of China and the Soviet Union. Containment had been replaced by rollback. Mao Zedong preferred to rely on China's traditional border policy of "letting the barbarians fight each other", and stay out of what he considered to be a Korean civil war, until MacArthur threatened more than the conquest of North Korea. Had this pugnacious commander-in-chief not been so contemptuous of the idea of a buffer zone along the Chinese border, there is no reason to suppose that Beijing would have opted for war. But there was the nagging possibility that Washington might be tempted to back Chiang Kai-shek in a bid to recover the Chinese mainland, perhaps through an invasion from Korea.

Once the border seemed threatened, the People's Liberation Army hit American-led forces with such devastating impact that they took to their heels in headlong flight. Everywhere carefully laid ambushes awaited retreating columns, because the Chinese had infiltrated the mountainous interior. This unexpected intervention changed the whole course of the war, ensuring that the peninsula would stay divided as it was at the end of the Second World War.

With China fully committed, MacArthur suggested a blockade of its coastline, bombing its factories, a diversionary attack by the Guomindang from Taiwan and, last but not least, an overland advance into north China. When these proposals were turned down flat in Washington, and the Truman administration chose a peaceful solution to the Korean conflict, MacArthur blew his top. Used to having his way, the general dared to criticise the peace move openly. With his sacking in early 1951, the main obstacle to a negotiated settlement was removed and two years later an armistice was eventually signed.

The Rise of the Pacific Rim

The chief beneficiary of the Korean War was Japan. Billions of dollars poured into the country, which served as the main base for forces fighting on the Korean peninsula. Military procurement accounted for nearly 40 per cent of Japan's foreign currency earnings, and generated demand in a wide range of industries, which later switched production to exports. As the Japanese premier Yoshida Shigeru said, the war was nothing less than "a gift from the gods", because it laid the foundation of Japan's present-day economic strength.

Relieved that Emperor Hirohito had survived the Allied occupation of Japan, which lasted from 1945 until 1951, Yoshida Shigeru was pleased to trade the throne's loss of divinity for a democratic system of government that allowed Japan to return to the world stage as a major power, albeit an economic one. Alliance with the United States offered protection against Russia and China while opening up the American market to Japanese goods. That Japan, the catalyst for so much change in modern Asia, acted as the frontrunner of the Pacific Rim is not surprising. Because it was the first Asian country to develop an industrial economy, its ability to influence events outside the People's Republic of China lasted for as long as the Chinese continued their revolutionary travail.

Once Deng Xiaoping came to power, the pre-eminence of Japan was effectively challenged. By the first decade of the twenty-first century, China looked less like a country in transition from socialism and more like an industrialising country in transition from its agrarian past. Concerned though the Chinese Communist Party has remained about political control, there is much more individual freedom and openness than in Mao Zedong's day.

Another "Asian Tiger", the Republic of China based on the island of Taiwan, also coped well with the 1990s financial crisis. Behind this success stood sound economic policies, since the Taiwanese had liberalised finance, upgraded industry and relaxed import controls. Its technology-intensive manufacturers were thus able to enhance their already large share of the world's computer markets. Making a virtue out of their own restricted domestic market, these energetic entrepreneurs had resisted the temptation to develop Taiwanese brand names. They were content to act as the unmentioned makers of components, even complete products, from bicycles to computers. Another strategy for overcoming the smallness of the Republic, and one that points towards eventual reunion with the People's Republic, was the export of businesses to the Chinese mainland, where more than 40,000 are presently in operation. One shoe company was thus able to increase its workforce from 10,000 to 120,000, turning itself into the world's biggest shoemaker.

Chapter 13

Modern Central Asia

The gatling's jammed and the colonel dead
And the regiment blind with dust and smoke.
The river of death has brimmed his banks,
And England's far, and Honour a name,
But the voice of a schoolboy rallies the ranks,
'Play up! Play up! And play the game.'

Sir Henry Newbolt

The Russian Advance

Had the Ottomans not persisted in fighting interminable, and ultimately ruinous, wars with Austria in the Balkans and Venice in the Mediterranean, then the Russians would have struggled to advance into Central Asia. Having annexed the Crimea in 1783, they were able to conquer most of Central Asia between 1865 and 1884. Until directly under attack, its Turkish-speaking peoples remained absorbed in their own rivalries and quarrels: there was no power to rally them against imperial Russia. Only Istanbul could have taken the lead here.

Unlike the rush to Siberia in the 1580s, after Moscow's reduction of all rivals on the European side of the Urals, expansion in Central Asia was comparatively methodical and slow. That is until the final stage of conquest when, like the rest of the European powers, Russia scrambled for colonies. A weapon that Russia deployed against the mobile peoples of the steppelands were the Don Cossacks. They were supplied with arms and encouraged to raid towards the southeast, where they also looted settlements belonging to the Ottomans and their allies. But the Cossacks' independent spirit, and an unruliness that often caused them to participate in popular revolts, made the Russians cautious. In the mid-seventeenth century, fortifications were therefore added to the southern frontier, shortly before the arrival of the Kalmyks. These newcomers were of Mongol stock.

Having travelled all the way across Central Asia, the Kalmyks settled in the mid-seventeenth century on what today is the southern Russian steppe. Rather than meet them in battle, the Russians allowed the Kalmyks to cooperate with the Don Cossacks in raids on the Crimea. At the start of the eighteenth century, the Kalmyks were recognised as a major power by several competing states: Tsarist Russia, Ottoman Turkey and Qing China. In the case of the latter, Manchu arms were soon to reach the oases of Turkestan, south of the Tianshan mountain range. Emperor Qian Long's conquest of that area ended the nomad threat to China, because incorporation within the Chinese empire meant that the local khans were no longer solely in charge of their peoples. Their warlike followers were split up in the banner divisions of the Qing army and stationed across the whole of Xinjiang.

On the arrival of the Kalmyks, Russia's grip on the steppelands was still weak and so these nomads were treated as semi-autonomous allies. The extent of their independence was evident in the contact that they maintained with China, to which tribute missions were dispatched regularly. The sudden decision to leave the Volga river valley in 1770 was a result of growing Russian pressure: the spread of agricultural settlements on grazing land; the increased number of fortifications; interference with the workings of their own system of government; and excessive demands for cavalrymen to serve in wars against the Ottomans. When in 1769 some 10,000 Kalmyks returned home early from one campaign, defying Russian orders, it was obvious that a turning point had been reached. What the Russians did not really understand was the Kalmyk need to tend herds and keep raiding Kazakh tribesmen at bay.

One leading Kalmyk put the situation in these stark terms. So determined was Russia to limit the rights of the Kalmyks that unless they soon migrated elsewhere, they would be condemned to live in areas unsuited to the nomad way of life. "Either we bend our necks under the yoke of slavery," he told the Kalmyk nobles, "or we leave the Russian empire now and avoid destruction." Convinced by this argument, Ubashi Khan planned an exodus at the start of 1771, taking advantage of the fact that a great many Russian troops were then away fighting

A Kazakh horseman, one of the "steppe beasts" according to the Russians

against the Ottomans. About 170,000 Kalmyks set off. Perhaps as many as 50,000 of the nomads stayed behind, unwilling to face the gruelling trek eastwards. Later, Ubashi Khan claimed that the failure of the Volga to freeze right over had prevented their crossing with the rest. The epic migration was a near disaster because winter frosts, hunger, disease and Kazakh attacks reduced Kalmyk numbers by half.

Chinese historians tended to overlook the terrible suffering involved when they described the event as an heroic escape from Russian oppression. Emperor Qian Long was the benevolent father who welcomed the Kalmyks home. What went unsaid concerned the smallness of the Kalmyk nation: no longer big enough to compete on its own with other nomad peoples, Ubashi Khan had to accept Manchu conditions for settlement in China. So instead of being permanently incorporated into the Russian empire, the Kalmyks joined the Qing military system.

After the departure of the Kalmyks, Russian colonisation was accelerated by grants of land to gentry who were prepared to bring their peasants and settle as farmers. But this extension brought Russia into contact with the Kazakhs, a Turkish people driven westwards by more powerful nomad groups. In the 1720s, the desperate Kazakhs overran the Central Asian khanates. The inhabitants of Samarkand, the pride of Tamerlane, fled, while Bukhara was besieged, its gardens and fields trampled by the Kazakh herds. Other Kazakhs moved farther west in search of a new homeland, which brought them well within the orbit of Russian interests.

Russia's appetite for Asian trade, its search for natural resources, and its political ambitions in Central Asia led to close contact with the Kazakhs. Tsar Peter the Great appreciated how even though "the Kazakhs were unreliable nomads", they stood at the gateway to Asia. He urged his military commanders to spare no effort or cost in making them Russian subjects.

According to the Russians, the Kazakhs were then divided into three hordes: the Lesser, the Middle and the Greater. The Lesser and the Middle hordes were estimated to comprise 80,000 households, or more than 300,000 people. Though an overall figure is lacking for the Greater Horde, it was capable of fielding 50,000 horsemen. Proximity to Russia's border led to the acceptance of overlordship by Abulkhayir, the khan of the Lesser Horde. In return for the payment of 4,000 fox skins annually, Abulkhayir Khan was guaranteed Russian protection. When in 1731, however, an ambassador named Muhammed Tevkelev arrived to execute an oath of allegiance to the tsar, he discovered the khan's court in disarray. Kazakh nobles would simply not agree to becoming imperial subjects: the khan had not bothered to undertake the customary consultation with them, but acted entirely on his own initiative. A peace treaty was one thing, they insisted, submission to Russia another. So Tevkelev did not mince his words:

> The Russian empire is in high repute among many states in the world, and it is not befitting such an illustrious monarch to have a peace treaty with you, steppe beasts, because the Russian empire has no fear of the Kazakhs and not the least need of them, while the Kazakhs are in great danger from Russian subjects.

Abulkhayir Khan, together with a few supporters, pledged an oath of allegiance on the Qur'an, but most of the nobles refused point blank.

The motives of Abulkhayir Khan are obscure. He seems to have genuinely welcomed protection from his nomadic enemies as well as valuable presents from the Russians. The khan even told Tevkelev, before he left, that he had no objection to having a Russian fort built

Two views of Kashgar, a Moslem city that was pivotal in the Great Game

close to his border, so that he could lure his anti-Russian opponents there with promises of presents and have them arrested, then deported. When Tevkelev reported the deep divisions within the Lesser Horde, it was decided to build Fort Orenburg on the Ural river as a means of pacifying the Kazakhs and expanding trade links with Central Asia.

Tevkelev's diplomatic mission had highlighted the dilemma that faced Russia on its steppe border. It was possible to overawe the nomads sufficiently to insist upon their status as subject peoples but, by doing so, the Russian empire acquired an onerous duty: the responsibility for protecting them in a world where inter-tribal conflict was a way of life.

Hardly unexpected therefore was the consequence of Russia's advance, for almost at once it became embroiled in Central Asian politics. The pledge of protection was evoked by Abulkhayir Khan when the Mongolian Oirats demanded tribute and hostages. The Oirats possessed a large army equipped with artillery capable of threatening Russia's fortified defences, so the governor of Orenburg told them to desist. But the habit of internecine warfare was too deeply rooted for such an intervention to work for long: not only did the different steppe peoples constantly fight each other, but supposedly pro-Russian Kazakhs even raided Russia.

More effective than threats of intervention was the encouragement of trade with newly founded Russian towns. Between 1743 and 1747 the Kazakhs traded more than 14,000 horses and 28,000 sheep. But Abulkhayir Khan's death at the hands of the khan of the Middle Horde in 1748 revealed how fundamentally unstable conditions remained. Russia had yet to learn that conventional military operations were ineffective against the nomads, whose numbers and mobility ruled out direct control. The only solution was to exploit tribal divisions and allow feuds to take their inevitable toll. D. V. Volkor, the Orenburg governor in 1763, pointed out how the Kazakhs, and their neighbours, were like children. Only in time they would grow up as responsible adults under Russia's benevolent guidance.

After the nomads chose to settle down, Volkor confidently predicted, would this happen because "the almighty civilisation at the hands of the emperor was such that it could transform nature, and through the wisdom of the grand sovereigns and the obedience of subjects . . . the winters are turned into summers, and the summers into winters". What Nuraly, the new khan of the Lesser Horde, made of this harangue is not recorded. But he must have been acutely aware of an increased Russian military and economic presence on the steppe. All the signs of

A towering minaret at Turfan, one of the Central Asian cities
incorporated into the Chinese empire

impending change were there, although unlike the Kalmyks, none of the
Kazakhs ever felt that they had to move away.

The apparent suppression of the Kazakhs seemed to justify Volkor's
outlook, but large areas of Central Asia were still outside Russian control. Regarded as the most important was Bukhara, where the Turkicised
Mangits founded a final emirate in 1785. They succeeded in reducing
the power of Uzbek tribal chieftains, whose followers formed the bulk
of the population, and ruled through a Persian-speaking bureaucracy of
ex-slaves. But the regime's despotic nature made it incapable of grasping
the changes that were happening in Central Asia, so its leader missed

entirely the Russian advance that reached Bukhara in 1863. As no effort was made at reform under imperial Russia, an almost medieval society survived there until the 1920s.

Elsewhere, the last independent rulers before the Russian conquest were Uzbek Turks. As their dynasties at both Khiva and Khoquand had been founded through violence, they were never really secure. This did not stop Khoquand, however, from competing with Bukhara for primacy in Central Asia. Situated astride the old Silk Road, Khoquand was well placed with borders adjoining Russia and China. Neither of these powers wished to lose Khoquand's friendship, so its khans skilfully played one off against the other. British India was also a factor in this balancing act, which was subsumed in the Great Game. The Russians won this contest in most of Central Asia: they began their final conquest by taking Tashkent in 1865 and completed it with the acquisition of Merv in 1884. The oasis city near the Afghan border had been one of the earliest Arab settlements in the region.

Merv's passing under Russian rule caused panic in Britain, a state of mind that someone mischievously called an attack of Mervousness. In 1895 the British and the Russians finally came to an agreement about the southern frontier of Central Asia. The area to the north was designated by the Russians as the Governorate-General of Turkistan with its capital at Tashkent, but it included the two protectorates of Bukhara and Khiva as well. Kazakhstan became part of the Governorate-General of the Steppe.

The Great Game

Although the final defeat and exile of Napoleon in 1815 eliminated any French threat to British India, there was still danger from the Russian advance into Central Asia, a largely unexplored part of the continent. To gain a better picture of this area, the English East India Company and later the Crown were prepared to let young officers undertake journeys into its remotest corners. Commonly known as "shooting leave", the pursuit of game was a convenient cover for espionage. Separately, surveyors were secretly mapping the borderlands of India, but there was plenty of scope for intrepid individuals to participate in the Great Game. Courage was at a premium in this covert competition with Russia because those who took part knew that they were expendable.

As Francis Younghusband, head of a trade mission sent to Tibet in 1903 reflected about the whole business:

> We and the Russians are rivals but I am sure that the individual Russian and British officer like each other a great deal better than they do the individuals of the nations with which they are not in rivalry . . . We are both playing a big game.

The son of an Indian Army general, Younghusband was fascinated by life on the frontier, which he saw as a British preserve. Whereas the viceroy, Lord Curzon, wanted a commercial treaty and an agent in Lhasa so as to hinder Russia's designs on Tibet, Younghusband longed for nothing less than a British protectorate and the liberation of the Tibetans, "slaves in the power . . . of ignorant and selfish monks". Both Curzon and Younghusband preferred to gloss over the bloodshed that accompanied the mission, the slaughter of a poorly armed group of Tibetans on the way to Lhasa. Whether Russia intended to meddle in Tibetan affairs is a moot point, even though Curzon's fears were shared in London. The subsequent Anglo-Russian Convention suggests that intrigue by the Dalai Lama was a factor in the British calculations, because one of its provisions stipulated that neither Russia nor Britain should seek concessions in Tibet or send representatives to Lhasa or negotiate with Tibet except through the Chinese government.

On its ratification in 1907, Curzon criticised the Convention's details. The "bargain," he said, was "doubtful in respect of Afghanistan, bad in respect of Tibet, and worse in respect of Persia". While Curzon was mistaken about Afghanistan, which Russia willingly conceded was within Britain's sphere of influence, his points about Tibet and Persia were not unreasonable. The former never seems to have seriously tempted the Russians, while the division of the latter into spheres of influence between Russia and Britain greatly upset the Iranians. But from Britain's viewpoint, Iranian anger was less critical than the security of its Indian empire, which the Convention essentially guaranteed. It also ended the Great Game, although a similar rivalry between the Russians and the Americans persists among the Central Asian republics today. The violent overthrow of the Kyrgyzstan government in early 2010 was swiftly accepted by Russia, whose continued support for the impoverished country may depend on the closure of the vital US airbase at Bishkek. It supplies troops and equipment to Nato operations in Afghanistan.

High minarets such as this one at Bukhara have always fascinated
visitors, including Genghiz Khan

Before the Tibetan mission, Younghusband had been allowed
"shooting leave" on many occasions. His first took him towards Mongolia
and China, where he met up in 1885 with Mark Bell in Beijing. This
soldier was gathering intelligence and, discovering Younghusband's
enthusiasm for adventure, he recommended that he should travel back
to India via Turfan and Kashgar, negotiating the edge of the Taklimakan
desert. After the British minister in Beijing secured for him a further
absence from his regimental duties, Younghusband set off with two
Chinese companions. Only one of them stayed the course, even though
the crossing of the Himalayas was made more difficult by another of
Bell's recommendations: "the unexplored but direct road by the Mustagh
Pass to Baltistan and Kashmir".

This section of the border between Chinese Tibet and British
India, a treacherous snow-covered pass, had never been negotiated by a
European before. Afterwards Younghusband told his father that "when
we reached the bottom and looked back, it seemed utterly impossible
that any man could have come down such a place". The route that he
had followed made Younghusband an immediate reputation in India as
an enterprising explorer and a fearless secret agent. He was not allowed

to rejoin his regiment for long before other special assignments came his way. Impressed though he could not fail to be by his local guides through deserts and mountains, their self-reliance and pluck was not enough to erase his own sense of British superiority, the besetting sin of the late nineteenth-century Indian empire. Younghusband could even say of his loyal companion on the way back from Beijing that "he was a Chinaman, and therefore not a perfect animal", while the Gurkhas who ensured his safety in Tibet were "brave, cheery little men, but they have the wits of a hog". Buddhism alone seems to have had an effect on Younghusband, despite his complete disdain for its Tibetan form.

Lord Curzon can be said to have informally joined the Great Game before his appointment in 1899 as viceroy of India. He had long aspired to this appointment and his extensive travels across Asia were a conscious preparation for its duties. In the 1880s he travelled through Russia to Baku, where he took a boat across the Caspian. Then he boarded a train to Bukhara on the recently opened Transcaspian Railway. At Samarkand, then the railway's terminus, he transferred to a horse-drawn cart for the journey onwards to Tashkent, where the Russian governor invited him to stay. The whole of Central Asia fascinated Curzon, who found its inhabitants "a far less extortionate and rascally lot than their fellows in the marts of Cairo and Stamboul". At this time, the future viceroy did not regard Russian suzerainty as a problem for British India. His espousal of a forward policy was a later development that during his period of office meant that more than 50 per cent of the Indian budget went regularly to the military. What seems to have changed Curzon's mind about Russia was its extension of the railway system throughout Central Asia. It was an idea that also appealed to Halford J. Mackinder, the eminent British geographer. In 1904 Mackinder wrote:

> A generation ago steam and the Suez Canal appeared to have increased the mobility of sea power, relative to land. Railways acted as feeders to ocean-going commerce. But trans-continental railways are now transmuting the conditions of land-power, and nowhere can they have such effects as in the closed heart-land of Euro-Asia, in vast areas in which neither timber nor accessible stone was available for road-making. Railways work wonders in the steppe, because they directly displace horse and camel mobility, the road stage of development has been omitted.

Here were the means of continental power. "Russia," Mackinder boldly asserted, "replaces the Mongol Empire." It has not quite worked out like that. Yet the Russians still control a considerable expanse of continental Asia, unlike the British, who chose to transform their seaborne empire into a commonwealth of free nations.

Afghanistan, the Land of Bones

Nowhere in Asia was British foreign policy less successful than in Afghanistan. The first foray in 1838–42 ranks as one of the worst reverses ever suffered by British arms. Intervention resulted of course from the Russian advance. The British wanted to make sure that Afghanistan was ruled by Shah Shuya who was favourably inclined towards them. Planning for the campaign was lax, almost as if an invasion of Afghanistan were no more than extended "shooting leave". Along with 15,200 soldiers in the expedition went 38,000 servants, together with brass bands, bagpipes, polo ponies, packs of foxhounds, and 30,000 camels burdened with supplies. The officers of one regiment needed two camels to carry their cigars. Even so, the rugged terrain of Afghanistan ensured that the expeditionary force ran out of provisions and had to purchase on the march flocks of sheep at exorbitant prices. Opposition eventually found its target in the 4,500-strong garrison left behind in Kabul to support Shah Shuya. This beleaguered force tried to fight its way to India but, in the event, only one man got through. The British nominee was dethroned and Afghanistan returned to its usual condition, a country dominated by the feudal bands belonging to tribal warlords.

A second British force of 6,000 men then set off to secure the release of prisoners held by the Afghans. On the way to Kabul it had to fight a series of battles. Also encountered were the grisly remains of British skeletons and desiccated corpses "thrown in heaps of eighty or a hundred" and in places completely blocking the road. In retaliation, Afghan villages were burned, their vineyards and orchards destroyed, while outside Kabul itself the tomb of Mahmud ibn Sebruktigin was desecrated. The first Moslem invader of India from Central Asia, this Ghaznavid sultan had destroyed the famous Hindu temple in 1026 at Somnath: its sandalwood doors supposedly adorned his tomb, so they were carried back to India in triumph. In actual fact the looted doors were of a later date. Though they saved face by means of this second invasion, the British had gained nothing at all in Afghanistan.

Another equally unnecessary invasion of the country began in 1878, simply because a Russian envoy had been received in Kabul.

British troops on the move in the Second Afghan War

Cholera added to military ineptitude until Sir Frederick Roberts, later commander-in-chief of the Indian Army, restored the situation. With 10,000 troops, and a smaller number of camp followers, Roberts achieved an orderly evacuation from Kabul in 1880, but warned Britain that Afghanistan should be left alone. He added prophetically:

> It may not be very flattering to our amour propre, but I feel sure that I am right when I say that the less the Afghans see of us the less they will dislike us. Should Russia in future years attempt to conquer Afghanistan, or invade India through it, we should have a better chance of attaching the Afghans to our interests if we avoid all interference in the meantime.

A century later, the Russians did dispatch an occupation force of 100,000 men, with a conspicuous lack of success. Advanced weaponry proved just as incapable of weakening the tribal warlords' grip on the rural areas and outlying towns. Today American-led Nato forces in Afghanistan are not doing very much better, especially as the Taliban have learned how to deploy home-made explosive devices alongside roads.

That Russian tanks and missiles were no more effective than rifles and mules should have given the West pause for thought. But there was little reflection after the terrorist attacks on New York and Washington on 11 September 2001 thrust Afghanistan into the limelight. No one bothered to ask why it has been so difficult to dominate that country militarily.

Several reasons can be adduced for the sturdy independence of the Afghans. First, the country's history of invasion initiated a tradition of self-reliance and mutual antagonism, because each part of the country sought to protect itself from external and internal foes. Second, there is

British troops crossing the perilous Bolan Pass, gateway to
and from the Indian subcontinent

the inhospitable Afghan landscape, which makes holding on to valuable tribal domain a matter of life and death. A third reason is the mixture of peoples living there, whose differences are not eased by the fact that most of the population speak languages that are Persian based. Smaller ethnic groups also include Mongols and Arabs. Robust independence, the badge of the hillsman, is to be seen everywhere.

Only two invaders have ever subdued the peoples of Afghanistan. These were the Macedonians and the Mongols, but their approaches could not have been more different. Alexander the Great sought to conciliate the tribal leaders once he had demonstrated the strength of his own army in 329 BC. He married Rauxnaka, Roxane in Greek, the daughter of a prominent warlord in the area close to present-day Kabul. She had caught the king's eye because Roxane was "the loveliest woman the Macedonians had seen in Asia, with the one exception of Darius' wife". Whether Alexander was genuinely in love with her is open to question, but the political advantages of such a match were immense, for all parties concerned. Leaving Roxane's father to hold Afghanistan on his behalf, and adding locally raised forces to his multi-ethnic army, Alexander could safely invade northwestern India.

Utterly opposed to any kind of goodwill was the Mongol use of terror to quell their enemies. Just how pitiless Genghiz Khan could be was clear at Bamiyan in central Afghanistan, where in 1221 one of his grandsons was killed. The Mongol khan ordered the extermination of all living things in the great valley: people, animals, birds. Little is known about Genghiz Khan's personal life other than he took a new wife home after each campaign. Unlike Alexander, his taste in women seems to have had more to do with the pleasure he found in bed than political calculation. And the Mongols would have considered the idea of dynastic marriage a sign of weakness anyway.

Siberia and Mongolia

The fur trade informed Russia's interest in Siberia. This "soft gold" comprised pelts of squirrels, otters, martens, beavers, ermine, mink, foxes and sables. In the early eighteenth century furs amounted to one-third of the value of Russian exports to the rest of Europe. So depleted were these animals in the Urals and the western part of Siberia, however, that traders were obliged to move ever eastward in search of unexploited regions. Already the Cossacks had reached the Pacific Ocean and crossed the straits separating Asia and America, which meant that well before Russia acquired a major port on either the Baltic or the Black Sea, it possessed permanent harbours in Asian waters. Alaska was not sold to the United States until 1867.

By this date the Russians had come to view the politics of Siberia as an extension of the Great Game, or the Tournament of Shadows as they called international rivalry with Britain. The Kurile island chain was handed over to Japan for outright possession of the large island of Sakhalin in 1875. After the defeat of the Russian army and navy in 1905, Japan recovered southern Sakhalin, so that Stalin made the Soviet Union's entry into the war against the Japanese in 1945 conditional on the recovery of the Kuriles and Sakhalin. He also gained a free hand over Mongolia at the Allied Conference at Yalta earlier that year.

Eastern Siberia rose in significance for Russia in direct proportion to the decline of Manchu power. Not wishing to miss out in the distribution of spoils during the Second Opium War, which culminated in the Anglo-French capture of Beijing in 1860, the Russians forced the Qing government to cede an area the size of Texas north of the Amur river. Hard pressed by the British and the French, there was no desire in the Chinese capital for another war in the northeast and appeasement of Russia seemed a prudent expedient. But this loss, and that of the Soviet-sponsored Republic of Mongolia, has not been forgotten by the Chinese, as George Bush discovered at a meeting with Deng Xiaoping in 1989. Then the American president learned at first hand how much the Chinese leadership distrusted the Russians, when Deng Xiaoping said:

> Mr President, you are my friend. I hope you will look at a map to see what happened after the Soviet Union severed Outer Mongolia from China. What kind of strategic position did we find ourselves in? Those over fifty in China remember that the shape of China was like a maple leaf. Now, if you look at the map, you see a whole chunk of the north cut away . . . The strategic position I have mentioned is very unfavourable for China.

The future of Mongolia and the territory lost to China in Manchuria now constitute the greatest unresolved issue of the period of Western colonialism in Asia.

The border clashes in 1969 between Russian and Chinese forces reminded the world of this dispute, aggravated by the build-up of Soviet forces along China's northern border. Hundreds of soldiers were killed and wounded on both sides before a truce was agreed. In the throes of the Great Proletarian Cultural Revolution, the Chinese Communist Party may well have misjudged Russian manoeuvres as a criticism of this far-reaching event, but the snuffing out of the "Prague Spring" during the previous year added to the uncertainty felt in Beijing. Just as Soviet Russia had invaded Czechoslovakia, so military pressure might be exerted on China to toe Moscow's ideological line. Although few could have seriously expected a full-scale attack, the border clashes exposed the very different socialist outlooks of the Chinese and the Russians. In the event, they also revealed a comparative weakness in the People's Liberation Army's firepower. Investment in heavy weapons immediately ensued.

Mongolia was late in coming under Russian control. Added to the Chinese empire by the Manchus, the Mongolian homeland only escaped from Beijing's rule in 1911. Chinese troops reoccupied the country in 1919, only to be driven out two years later by Russian and Mongol forces. The population of Mongolia was then slightly more than half a million, a low figure incorrectly attributed to Buddhist monasticism. The birth rate seems always to have been low among Central Asian nomads.

The price of protection from China in 1921 was a political and social revolution directed by the Soviet Union. In the late 1930s a "Mongol Stalin", Choibalsan by name, went so far as to stage show

Vladivostok, Russia's port on the Sea of Japan, was an early acquisition

402

trials of his own. Their target was Buddhism, and their high point was the closure of the great monastery of Erdene Zu at Karakorum, the old Mongol capital. To underline this cultural change in 1940, a new alphabet based on the Cyrillic script replaced the traditional Mongol one: notice was being given that a close association with the Russians represented Mongolia's future.

Until the 1960s the Republic of Mongolia only had diplomatic relations with the Soviet Union and its satellites, plus China. Nothing seemed to stir in Mongolian affairs until Mikhail Gorbachev's reforms made change respectable. Some Mongolian leaders were already aware of the outmoded nature of the Soviet model, and a multiparty system favouring free enterprise and a market economy was introduced in 1992. The country's isolation had first been eased by Britain, which established diplomatic relations in 1963. Other European countries followed this lead, even the United States finally acknowledging that the Republic of Mongolia was not a Russian stooge.

The Central Asian Republics

Under the tsars, the Moslems of Central Asia were treated as second-class citizens, a complete reversal of the attitude taken by Moslem states to those who rejected the teachings of the Prophet. The great advantage that an inferior status bestowed upon Moslems was exemption from military service, although manpower shortages at the height of the First World War caused their conscription as manual labourers behind the front line, mainly for digging trenches. So disliked was this work that there were rebellions, most notably among the Turkish Kyrgyz tribesmen. Their violent repression in 1916–17 caused large numbers to flee into the neighbouring Chinese province of Xinjiang.

The Bolshevik revolution not only ended the persecution but seemed to offer self-determination to all the subject peoples of the former Russian empire. But the Great Game was about to reappear in a new form in 1919 when Stalin declared how

> Turkestan, because of its geographical position, is a bridge connecting socialist Russia with the oppressed countries of the East, and in view of this the strengthening of the Soviet regime in Turkestan might have the greatest revolutionary significance for the entire Orient.

Such global ambition looked suspiciously like tsarist imperialism dressed up in Marxism. Hardly surprising then in Central Asia was an immediate polarisation between its Moslem and Russian inhabitants. At Tashkent the Russian minority took control to the exclusion of others, while in Khoquand a predominantly Moslem regime formed. Because the latter included members whose lukewarm, even antagonistic, attitude towards Bolshevism was known, the Tashkent government suffered no rebuke from Moscow when it stormed Khoquand in 1918. Similar efforts by Moslems to gain control over their own affairs failed elsewhere. Only in 1924 did Moscow concede a degree of autonomy in Kazakhstan, which was confirmed by a founding convention held at Orenburg. Four other Soviet socialist Republics were set up afterwards: Uzbekistan, Kyrgyzstan, Turkmenistan and Tajikistan.

What this arrangement neatly prevented was the formation of a huge Turkish Soviet Republic. Because Moscow feared such a potentially powerful state coming into existence in Central Asia, the old imperial policy of divide and rule was dusted down and put back into use. Each

The Ark fortress at Bukhara, where in 1918 a 20-strong
delegation of Russian Bolsheviks was executed

Central Asian republics

republic ostensibly contained a distinct people, ignoring the circumstance that, with the exception of the Tajiks, all their dialects belonged to a common Turkish tongue, which could easily sustain one large Central Asian polity. A reason for Moscow's blocking any such development was the large number of Russian residents. Settlement had been ongoing throughout the imperial era, especially in Kazakhstan, the earliest region to ally itself with Russia. For tsarist rule had been largely sustained through large-scale migration and the growth of towns.

Although Moscow liked to pose as the champion of oppressed colonial peoples and, after their attainment of independence, the stern opponent of neo-colonialism, its own ruthless exploitation of the Central Asian republics reached unprecedented proportions. The whole area became one gigantic cotton farm, where the lack of investment in agricultural machinery meant that the cotton crop was harvested by cheap labour, including that of children. Uzbekistan, Turkmenistan and Tajikistan were the main producers of cotton.

Forced settlement of nomads and the collectivisation of their herds provoked resistance and repression. During the 1930s the Kazakhs lost as much as two thirds of their people. The underpopulated steppe was then settled by Russians who helped to prepare the way for the ill-conceived "virgin lands" campaign of the Nikita Khrushchev era. The attempt to cultivate areas only suited to pastoralism inevitably led to erosion and deforestation. The wholesale loss of topsoil went unheeded, as did the disaster inflicted upon the Aral Sea. Draining its waters for the benefit of cotton production stands as the supreme symbol of all that was wrong with Russian-driven agriculture in Central Asia. But Moscow's blatant disregard for the environment did not stop there. Kazakhstan endured 468 nuclear tests over four decades.

With Mikhail Gorbachev's accession to power, Moscow came to recognise how much the Soviet Union had stagnated through a reliance on central planning. His brave attempt to improve the economic system through perestroika, "restructuring", opened the floodgates in such a manner that the Soviet Union itself broke up. In Central Asia the new openness predictably brought to light corruption on a massive scale, since well-placed local officials were found to have regularly falsified export figures of cotton to line their own pockets. But this dishonesty pales into insignificance when compared with the below-the-market prices dictated by Moscow for the cotton and other commodities extracted from all the Central Asian republics.

Unable to put a brake on popular demands for self-determination in Central Asia, or indeed other parts of the Soviet Union, Moscow could only watch the disintegration of its socialist empire. In 1991 Kyrgyzstan, Uzbekistan, Tajikistan, Turkmenistan, and Kazakhstan all became independent republics. Their experiences since then have been varied. Authoritarian regimes established themselves in Uzbekistan and Turkmenistan, while more democratic arrangements prevailed in Kazakhstan and Kyrgyzstan. A really difficult adjustment happened in Tajikistan, where civil war was seen as a struggle against Islamic fundamentalists. Even though this may not have been a true picture of the conflict, which returned ex-communists to power, Tajikistan's long border with Afghanistan could have allowed the Taliban to lend support. An additional encouragement to cross-border cooperation would have been the Persian-based language spoken by the Tajiks and the Afghans. Of the Central Asian republics, Tajikistan is the outsider, a non-Turkish-speaking state whose cultural links are with Iran and Afghanistan.

There are signs, however, that old tribal rivalries have reappeared. At Osh in Kyrgyzstan, the city was torn apart in 2010 by fights between Kyrgyz gangs and Uzbek residents, who comprised 40 per cent of its 250,000 inhabitants. Losing control of the situation in Osh as well as other towns, the Kyrgyz authorities appealed to Russia for military assistance, but Moscow hesitated to intervene.

Chapter 14

Modern Southeast Asia

If we want democracy, it should not be Western democracy, but a democracy that gives life, that is, political-economic democracy that guarantees social welfare!

Sukarno at a 1951 rally

The Dutch East Indies

East of India the British acquired territory in their struggle against France. When it was learned that the French had obtained permission to refit vessels at Aceh in northern Sumatra, the Royal Navy insisted that a similar anchorage be found, because strong monsoon winds prevented its ships from finding a sheltered harbour on the east coast of India during the winter months. A base was secured near the Straits of Malacca at the island of Penang by Francis Light, a naval officer who had assisted the sultan of Kedah in 1785, when he was attacked by Indonesian pirates.

A grateful sultan offered Penang as a base, believing that the Royal Navy would deter Kedah's enemies. Before Light died in 1794, the new colony was several thousand strong, many of its residents Chinese merchants seeking to escape Dutch domination of Southeast Asian trade. Although the new settlement weakened the trading position of Dutch Malacca, it was a less satisfactory anchorage than the Royal Navy had hoped. Not until Thomas Stamford Raffles founded Singapore in 1819 would a first-rate harbour become available. That year, he persuaded the sultan of Johore to grant permission for English East India Company occupation of the island.

When Holland fell under the sway of Napoleon, the Dutch ruler William V had fled to England and taken up residence at Kew. In what are known as the "Kew Letters", he instructed Dutch colonial officers to surrender their holdings to Britain, so that they would not fall into French hands. Armed with this authority, the English East India Company moved to take over the Dutch East Indies, but at first Batavia refused to comply. Once under English East India Company control, there was discussion in Calcutta about whether this sizable territory should be retained. Richard Wellesley's large acquisitions of territory in India were then bearing fruit, and along with the new revenue derived from the occupied Dutch territory, Calcutta was able to remit £10 million annually to London over and above the provision of funds for company investment in Asian trade.

To administer the Dutch East Indies, Raffles was appointed to the governorship of Java in 1811. Exploiting the confusion that followed the British takeover, Hamengkubuwana tried to recover his throne at Yogyakarta in central Java. But his misunderstanding of the recent confrontation between the British and the Dutch combined with an uncooperative attitude towards Raffles' administration to destroy his court. In 1812, British troops and Indian sepoys, supported by soldiers provided by Hamengkubuwana's rivals, captured Yogyakarta after an artillery barrage. The city was looted and the sultan deposed once again. The impact of this conquest was enormous, because it was the first occasion on which a hereditary leader had been sent into exile. It explains the overwhelming response in 1825 to Pangeran Dipanagra's call for an uprising against re-established Dutch rule. Of royal Yogyakartan descent himself, Pangeran Dipanagra defied Batavia for almost five years, some 200,000 Javanese and 8,000 Dutchmen losing their lives in the uprising.

Apart from the military intervention at Yogyakarta, Raffles is remembered in the annals of colonial history as a great reformer, except by the Dutch. In rejecting what he termed the "perverted liberalism" of

An early view of Singapore. In 1915 an Indian regiment mutinied
there when its Moslem rankers learned that Turkey had sided
with the Central Powers

Raffles in the 1830s, governor-general Johannes van den Bosch imposed
the cultuurstelsel, or "culture system", in which Javanese farmers had to
devote one-fifth of their labour or 66 days each year to the cultivation of
export crops for the Dutch authorities. Profit was again the order of the
day, as an impoverished Holland attempted to recover from Napoleon.
To its amazement, the Dutch East Indies provided 19 per cent of all government revenue in the 1840s, a figure that grew to 31 per cent over the
next two decades, an entirely different situation to the Philippines, which
the United States took from Spain in 1898. There American investment,
according to President William McKinley, was intended to "educate the
Filipinos, and uplift and civilise them".

No such notion ever entered the heads of Dutch colonial officials,
despite a great deal of soul searching in Holland itself. They were only too
aware of the need for British support in the maintenance of their Southeast Asian empire. Because London preferred the Dutch to the French
as neighbours, the 1871 Anglo-Dutch Treaty of Sumatra gave the green
light for a Dutch attack on Aceh, one of the last pockets of Indonesian
independence. Yet the uncompromising approach of Dutch colonialism
drew widespread criticism, as Western newspapers asked how it was that
a tiny country like Holland could go on plundering the whole Indonesian archipelago. President Franklin D. Roosevelt openly complained

about the living conditions of colonial peoples generally, and the inhabitants of the Dutch East Indies in particular, despite his own forbears. Yet Washington remained anxious about Japan, which it feared might exploit Indonesian nationalism in what was a strategically important area. This gradual shift in American thinking delighted Batavia, which announced that the word "Indonesia" could no longer be used. Relations between the Dutch and the Indonesians then hit rock bottom as police surveillance was stepped up: the popular village sport of pigeon racing was outlawed to prevent bad news becoming known. Even though the fall of Holland to Germany in 1940 could not be kept a secret, the feebleness of the Dutch resistance to the Japanese two years later astonished the local population.

The British Possessions

With the return of peace in Europe in 1815, the British government allowed the Dutch to reoccupy the East Indies on condition that they ceded Malacca and recognised the British claim to Singapore. Without a rival, Britain could afford to dictate the shape of colonial Asia, for France had ruined itself and much of Europe too, leaving the United Kingdom as the dominant world power.

Under the Anglo-Dutch Treaty of 1824, Borneo was left to the Dutch but they never bothered with that great island's northern coast. The unexpected development of North Borneo, the present-day Malaysian state of Sabah, was therefore the result of British private enterprise. Almost a throw-back to the English East India Company, the granting of a royal charter to the British North Borneo Company in 1881 was intended to keep other powers at bay, without the bother of annexation. Germany and Belgium had both shown an interest in trading ventures there. London was quite happy in the Philippines for the Spaniards to tidy up the last corner of independent Southeast Asia, the Sulu sultanate, but no other Europeans had permission to intrude.

From the start of Spain's involvement with the Philippines, the Moslem inhabitants of Mindanao and Palawan had launched raids on its coastal settlements to the north. Similar to the troublesome Acehnese in Sumatra, the Moros were not finally brought under direct colonial rule until the late nineteenth century. London refused a request for assistance against the Spanish offensive: the Sulu sultan was advised to pray instead, not entirely misplaced advice as a Dominican friar in Manila had already

The simplicity of James Brooke's house in Kuching was at
one with his relaxed rule

preached a Christian crusade against Islam. This was small consolation
for the Moros, as the sultan's subjects were called, because they were
forcibly annexed a decade before the arrival of the Americans, who never
grasped the reason for their own unpopularity, either before or after
Philippines gained independence in 1946.

An earlier example of British private initiative in Borneo was the
creation of Sarawak by James Brooke. Born in India, the son of an English
East India Company official, Brooke tired of commerce and purchased a
schooner, arriving at Singapore with a crew of 20 in 1839. His inspiration was Raffles' governorship of Java, which he believed had signalled
a new way forward through positive collaboration between Europeans
and Asians. He said that

the experiment of developing a country through the residence of a
few Europeans, and by the assistance of its native rulers has never

411

A Land Dayak longhouse in Sarawak. The "Head House" above only boasted four shrunken heads in the 1960s

been fairly tried; and it appears to me, in some respects, more desirable than the actual possession by a foreign nation . . . Above all it insures the independence of the native princes, and may advance the inhabitants further in the scale of civilisation, by means of this very independence, than can be done when a government is a foreign one, and their natural freedom sacrificed.

The arm's-length policy of the English East India Company gave plenty of scope for Brooke's radical experiment. He went to what was to become his capital, Kuching, and helped put down a rebellion against the sultanate of Brunei by Land Dayaks and Malays. Raja Muda Hassim, the heir apparent to the sultanate, welcomed this assistance and in 1843 Brooke became governor. From the start there was a notably relaxed atmosphere in Kuching, which had much to do with the new governor's genuine liking for the people, whom he considered to be the worthy "possessors of Borneo".

Support from British warships in the suppression of Sea Dayak pirates allowed Brooke to consolidate his own position and overawe Brunei, which in 1844 ceded the island of Labuan. Steam navigation required plentiful supplies of coal, something deposits in Sarawak and Labuan could go someway to meet. London was never really comfortable with Sarawak as a separate kingdom but because its coastline commanded one of the two sea routes to China, the Royal Navy insisted upon its protection. The French in Cambodia and Vietnam controlled the other sea route.

British intervention in Malaya only occurred in the 1870s, when disturbances among tin miners seemed to provide other European powers with an excuse to intervene. The appointment of "residents"— the title used in British India—to advise Malay rulers on all matters, save religion and custom, brought peace without full annexation. James Brooke would have approved of that, but not the free run that was allowed to big business.

Typical was the attitude of Sir Frank Swettenham, who rose through the ranks of the colonial civil service to become governor of the Straits Settlements of Penang, Malacca and Singapore. He was committed to modernisation through improved communications and shipping facilities, but these American- and British-financed projects were for the benefit more of international capitalism than of the local people. Other than the nobility, Swettenham argued that English should not be taught to Malays, even though it was becoming essential for any employment outside villages. In 1890, he wrote in an official report on Perak that it was inadvisable "to attempt to give children of an agricultural population an indifferent knowledge of a language that to all but a few would only unfit them for the duties of life and make them discontented with anything like manual labour". Towards the Chinese, whose industriousness was a relief after the laziness of the Malays, Swettenham recommended a friendly but distant relationship that underscored who was the master. After all, most of the Chinese immigrants were either shopkeepers or manual labourers. As for the Indians, who came to work largely on rubber estates, their physical separation from the rest of the population clearly defined their social position.

According to Colonial Office in 1934, Hong Kong was "the most self-satisfied of all colonies, except Malaya". Rural disturbances and strikes in the mines were always interpreted in Kuala Lumpur as local grievances, unlike the growing opposition in Burma to British rule. With the Imperial Japanese Army stalled in China, and Tokyo edging towards an assault on Western colonial holdings in Southeast Asia, the strategic position of Burma assumed vital importance in military planning. Japanese agents recruited nationalists like Aung San with a promise of independence within the Greater East Asia Co-Prosperity Sphere. After the first Japanese air raids on Rangoon at the end of 1942, Aung San's followers covered most of southern Burma, and notwithstanding initial British mistakes in dealing with the Japanese

Royal Navy vessels overawe Brunei in 1846. Within forty years, North Borneo, Sarawak and the remnant of Brunei were all British protectorates

A British attack on Borneo pirates. Singapore was established as a
Royal Navy base to facilitate such actions

invasion, the Imperial Japanese Army had the advantage of superior
intelligence. But the honeymoon period between the Imperial Japanese
Army and Aung San's Burmese Independence Army was short-lived.
The announcement of a Japanese military administration for Burma
meant that Japan had broken its word. Switching to the Allied side was
unavoidable, Aung San told the commander of the Fourteenth Army,
William Slim: "If the British sucked our blood," he said, "the Japanese
ground our bones."

French Indochina and Thailand

By aligning with Japan in 1942, Thailand could have ceased to be the
only Southeast Asian country to avoid European colonial rule. The declaration of war on Britain and the United States was made by Luang
Phibunsonkhram, a dictator who had been involved in the 1932 coup
that ended an absolute monarchy. An admirer of Hitler, this forceful

Part of the Royal Palace at Phnom Penh. Its riverside location allowed
French gunboats to overawe Cambodian kings

general had already changed the name of the country from Siam to Thailand, a move intended to make it attractive to Thai speakers throughout mainland Southeast Asia. He also wanted to put residents of Chinese descent in their place. One reason for Luang Phibunsonkram's willingness to side with the Japanese was the support they had provided during the Franco-Thai War of 1940–41, which resulted in the recovery of territory lost to French Indochina. When the United States cancelled the sale of fighter planes and bombers, Japan stepped in and offered planes, guns and torpedoes. A reward for voluntarily joining the Greater East Asia Co-Prosperity Sphere, the general calculated, would be the Thai territories incorporated into British holdings in Burma and Malaya.

France had pushed its way into mainland Southeast Asia because it represented the last remaining colonial prize. "Indochine", the name by which the French knew the countries they occupied there, well described the two distinct traditions they endeavoured to amalgamate in a single empire. At its two extremes were Vietnam and Cambodia: the former, despite its long resistance to Chinese domination, was a country profoundly influenced by Confucianism; the latter, though a shadow of its former glory, was the lineal descendant of an Indian-inspired king-dom. French authority was first established in the Mekong delta shortly after the Anglo-French capture of Beijing, but not until 1874 did the Vietnamese emperor Tu Duc cede the southernmost part of his country. Sickly and pessimistic by nature, this ruler was almost resigned to French domination of Vietnam. Exploration of the Mekong was used by France as an excuse to claim rights over adjacent Cambodia and, later in 1887, over landlocked Laos.

The Cambodian practice of taking Thai and Vietnamese princesses as royal consorts in Phnom Penh inevitably produced two court factions: one pro-Thai, another pro-Vietnamese. It was the former that blocked a treaty with France in 1856, correctly guessing that the French would help Cambodia to recover the Thai-occupied provinces of Battambang and Siem Reap. In 1863, France got its treaty, which stipulated that the Cambodian king had to agree to "all the administrative, judicial and commercial reforms that the French government shall judge, in future, useful to make their protectorate successful". Doubtless a gunboat anchored within sight of the royal palace had an effect.

The Thai were also about to discover the same disadvantage of a riverside capital. The killing of a French officer by Thai troops in Laos

In 1893 French gunboats forced their way upriver to Bangkok

417

brought matters to a head. In 1893 gunboats threatened Bangkok until it was agreed that Laos should become a French protectorate. France's takeover of Vietnam had already happened a decade earlier, when Chinese forces sent to aid Vietnamese resistance were soundly defeated. In Hue, Vietnamese emperors tried to retain some prestige for their Chinese-style government, but Confucian learning no longer seemed a necessity in a Western-dominated world. Ho Chi Minh abandoned such study and began learning French, "better to know the colonial enemy".

Only in French Indochina did the level of anti-colonial unrest reach Indian proportions. Efforts to ferment a full-scale rebellion failed, but by the 1930s naked force alone was keeping the Vietnamese people down. Once Tokyo supported the Thai recovery of lost territories and occupied Vietnam in preparation for entry to the Second World War, the days of French authority were over. The only power to which officials in French Indochina could have looked for help was Britain but, after the fall of France, the Royal Navy had bombarded French warships in north African ports to stop them falling into Hitler's hands. All diplomatic

In 1884 French action in north Vietnam ended China's suzerainty

Southeast Asia in 1941

relations had been severed and an attack on Gibraltar was even launched from Vichy airfields in Algeria.

The Greater East Asia Co-Prosperity Sphere

Imperial Southeast Asia was entirely overturned by the Japanese in 1941–42. Western confidence and prestige plummeted with defeats as widespread as Hong Kong, the Philippines, Malaya, Singapore, Burma and Indonesia. As Tsuji Masonobu, staff officer responsible for operations during Yamashita Tomoyuki's lightning campaign in Malaya, commented well after the Japanese surrender:

> In military operations we conquered splendidly, but in the war we were severely defeated. But, as if by magic, India, Pakistan, Ceylon,

Burma, the Dutch East Indies, and the Philippine islands one after the other gained their independence overnight. The reduction of Singapore was the hinge of fate for the peoples of Asia.

Britain never recovered from the fall of Singapore, where 85,000 troops surrendered to a Japanese expeditionary force a third of that size. "Mr Quickly-Quickly", as Yamashita Tomoyuki was known to his men, had outmanoeuvred and bluffed the British garrison. To disguise the lack of shells, he ordered a colossal bombardment of the island before the leading troops landed, which deeply impressed the defenders, who were still unaware that they actually faced fewer Japanese soldiers. "I was very frightened," Yamashita Tomoyuki admitted later, "that the British would discover our numerical weakness and lack of supplies, and force me into disastrous street fighting."

The poor state of the defences in Malaya and Singapore was repeated elsewhere, including the great American naval base at Pearl Harbor, which succumbed to a surprise attack by the Imperial Japanese Navy. But American industry soon made good the damage done to the US Pacific Fleet, whereas the Japanese were unable to replace the aircraft carriers they lost shortly afterwards at the battle of Midway.

British soldiers surrendering at Singapore on 15 February 1942

This shift in the balance of power, however, was not immediately apparent. Conquered Southeast Asian peoples had no choice but accept Japan's new order, the so-called Greater East Asia Co-Prosperity Sphere. The savage behaviour of the Imperial Japanese Army seems to have been looked upon by many senior officers as a useful method of cowing occupied territories. Most feared was arrest by the Kempeitai, the Japanese military police, whose arbitrary response to daily events was totally unsettling. Failure to bow properly could warrant detention or death. Yamashita Tomoyuki's own contempt for the Chinese explains the brutality in Singapore, where thousands of men between the ages of 15 and 50 were either thrown overboard to drown at sea or executed in improvised prison camps.

Although the Japanese tried to placate most local leaders, and especially in Indonesia where they feared as much as the Dutch the ability of Moslem clerics to rouse the people, the grim reality of the Greater East Asia Co-Prosperity Sphere could not be long disguised. There was no prosperity when Japan began to strip each area of its resources for the war effort. While famine struck Java in 1944, some 300,000 starving Singaporeans had to be resettled as farmers in Malaya.

Because the United States had promised independence to the Philippines, the Japanese were more cautious in their occupation, except when it came to surrendered Filipino soldiers. One Japanese officer bluntly told them: "Like it or not, you are Filipinos and belong to the Oriental race. No matter how hard you try, you cannot become white people." That death marches consumed the lives of American as well as Filipino prisoners-of-war hardly endeared the Imperial Japanese Army to the Filipino public; yet there were still nationalists who espoused Japan's declared intention of ending Western colonialism. As happened in supposedly independent Burma, they discovered that their freedom of action was strictly limited. The Filipino administration in Manila had less authority under the Japanese than previously under the Americans.

One liberation movement sponsored by Tokyo had an unexpected impact on Burma. Its aim was the freeing of India from British control and its instrument was Subhas Chandra Bose, who rejected Gandhi's attachment to non-violence and was impatient to have an Indian army fighting alongside the Japanese. Using funds extracted from the Indian business community in Malaya, Bose attracted 18,000 Tamil workers from the rubber estates and recruited Indian soldiers captured on the fall of Singapore. Few Indian officers responded to his call, although they had had to tolerate discrimination before the Japanese victory. A colour

A second atomic bomb exploding above Nagasaki, 9 August 1945

bar prevented their membership of Singapore's clubs, unlike British officers from their own regiments.

The attempt by Bose's Indian National Army to suborn Indian troops in the British Fourteenth Army met little success. Once Bose's recruits were found incapable of taking part in actual engagements in Burma, they were abandoned by the Japanese. The defeat of the Imperial Japanese Army there was unprecedented, with 100,000 men killed by the recapture of Rangoon in early 1945. The desperate effort to invade the Indian borderlands was almost the last major operation launched by Japan. From mid-1944 onwards the Americans began an island-hopping campaign towards Japan that reached the islands of Iwo Jima and Okinawa via the Philippines. Waves of suicide pilots could do nothing to stop this advance. The divine wind, the kamikaze, that had thwarted the Mongol invasion of Japan in the thirteenth century was reincarnated to little purpose in the bomb-planes that buzzed around US warships.

Yet this fanatical gesture, plus the heavy casualties inflicted on the Americans on Iwo Jima and Okinawa, caused Washington to reconsider strategy. Instead of a seaborne invasion of the Japanese islands, President Truman decided to drop atomic bombs on the cities of Hiroshima and Nagasaki. Even then, Tokyo hesitated to surrender until Emperor Hirohito said how "ending the war is the only way to restore world peace and to relieve the nation from the terrible distress with which it is burdened". Between them, the president and the emperor had ended the Pacific dimension of the Second World War, liquidating the Greater East Asia Co-Prosperity Sphere at a stroke.

Post-War Decolonisation

Even if Singapore's surrender was insufficient to bring down the curtain on Western colonialism, the sweeping election victory of the Labour Party in Britain certainly was. The 1945 landslide ensured that the British were spared the agony of colonial wars, unlike the Dutch in Indonesia and the French in Indochina. Prime Minister Clement Attlee's decision to grant India early independence ensured that decolonisation soon followed in Southeast Asia.

British intentions were transparent in the speed with which Burma gained its independence. Not even the assassination of Aung San, by a political rival, caused Attlee to hesitate, so that in late 1947 Burma became free, and left the Commonwealth. Its withdrawal was not unexpected, Attlee noted, because murder had removed the one man who could have maintained Burmese membership. Misjudging the post-war situation in spectacular fashion, Churchill savaged Labour's Burma policy. He condemned the agreement in these terms:

> I did not expect to see U Aung San, whose hands were dyed with British blood and loyal Burmese blood, marching up the steps of Buckingham Palace as the plenipotentiary of the Burmese government.

Yet blood was the very stuff of Burmese politics: assassins machine-gunned Aung San and his entire cabinet three months before the date of Burma's independence. The perpetrators of the massacre were quickly brought to justice, and a period of national mourning lasted several months. The martyrdom of Aung San had one beneficial effect, albeit only a temporary one, because it left no room for the bickering that typified Burmese political debate. In its grief, the country was not prepared to tolerate any argument on the eve of its freedom. The goodwill did not last, however, because in 1949 the Karens rose in revolt. The mass desertion of Karen soldiers from Burma's army gave this uprising great strength for, along with other hillsmen, they had formed the backbone of the resistance movement during the Japanese occupation. Even today there is determined resistance in the pursuit of a separate Karen state.

Back in power, a more realistic Churchill refused an American appeal to assist the French in Indochina. Believing that they were beyond help, the British premier rejected Washington's domino theory of a communist takeover of Southeast Asia. He had already appointed Sir Gerald Templer to govern Malaya and win "the hearts and minds" of its peoples to beat the communists there. Summing up the situation, Templer said "the shooting side of the business is only 25 per cent of the trouble". With a remit to prepare for independence, the unorthodox general not only contained the communist insurgency but in the election of Tunku Abdul Rahman also produced a premier-in-waiting. This ex-playboy was the brother of the Malay sultan of Kedah, a leader the British feared would aim at an old-fashioned dictatorship. Their fears proved groundless because the Tunku, or "Prince", understood the need for communal harmony and in the Alliance Party he incorporated the Malayan Chinese Association and the Malayan Indian Association along with UMNO, the United Malay National Organisation, which was formed in 1948 as a protest against British moves to create a common citizenship for all inhabitants within a unitary state comprising the Malay sultanates and the Straits Settlements, excluding Singapore.

Washington was deeply impressed by the emergence of a pro-Western political party in Malaya coincident with the terminal decline of French Indochina. Not perhaps so well appreciated by the Americans was a British design to protect its commercial interests under the protective umbrella of independence. Just as in the late nineteenth century, the creation of the dominions freed Britain from the task of running large swathes of its empire, so after the defeat of Japan effective arrangements for self-government in Southeast Asia allowed business as usual in ex-colonies wherever a reliable national government was in power. The Tunku's Alliance Party proved an excellent partner in stemming the excesses of Malay nationalism.

If Malaya gave Britain initial cause for concern, the kingdom of the Brookes in Sarawak represented an imperial anomaly of antique proportions. There was no sympathy in London for its survival as a sovereign state, with the result that the last "white rajah", Vyner Brooke, ceded his kingdom to Britain in 1946. Significantly for post-colonial differences between the state of Sarawak and the federal government of present-day Malaysia, most Sarawakians opposed cession. One British governor was actually assassinated in 1949 and it took all the skills of his successor, Sir Anthony Abell, to restore Sarawak to its usual condition of friendliness. A latter-day James Brooke, Abell's obvious enjoyment of its 40 distinct peoples led to his repeated terms as governor. Not long after his departure, Sarawak held its first general election, a timely opportunity to transform itself into a self-governing state before the formation of Malaysia.

Having formally transferred power to Tunku Abdul Rahman in 1957, the British had to decide what to do about the Borneo territories including oil-rich Brunei. There was additionally the need to prevent Singapore becoming an independent communist state, given its strategically important location at the junction of key international sea routes. Even in Sarawak, the attraction of the People's Republic of China to Chinese youths had caused a worrying exodus to both China and Indonesia. Those who went to the latter were to fight alongside Indonesian

Singapore's Lee Kuan Yew with his Malaysian counterpart Tunku Abdul Rahman

soldiers during Confrontation, which Sukarno declared in opposition to Malaysia in 1963.

Once Indonesia called off this border war in 1966, Britain knew that Malaysia had solved the problems it faced as the last major Western colonial power in Asia. A federation linking all remaining possessions, except Hong Kong, with already independent Malaya seemed a perfect postcolonial solution. At the very last moment, Brunei stood aside, but North Borneo, Sarawak and Singapore joined. For Lee Kuan Yew, Singapore's first prime minister, Malaysia meant a welcome end to British rule but not its military presence, because he seems to have been uncertain then over the long-term survival of a predominantly Chinese community situated in the midst of the Malay world. He knew that the British provided much of Singapore's foreign earnings, a circumstance that drove him to stimulate the local economy during the 1970s as Britain withdrew its forces. After Singapore had quit Malaysia in 1965, this was a matter of urgency, although Lee Kuan Yew reminded Singaporeans how "from 1819 right up to the 1930s there was a prosperous Singapore without either a British naval or air base". The island's survival depended on three things: a stable society that would encourage investment; the capacity of the population to adapt and the level of promised British aid. "It would be foolish to believe," he warned, "that others can do for us what we as a people and organised as a representative government can do for ourselves."

Correct though his assault on discriminatory legislation was, Lee Kuan Yew's own political ambition contributed to withdrawal from the Malaysian federation. Yet even Mahathir Mohamad, Malaysia's controversial premier from 1981 to 2003, came to appreciate towards the end of his long period in office that the entrenched rights afforded Malays would have to be lessened, with greater scope given to Chinese and Indian citizens. Mahathir was prepared to admit openly that the Malays had frittered away their privileges.

An odd mixture of realist and autocrat, the Malaysian premier was always prepared to speak his mind. Responding in 1986 to criticism over the "barbaric" execution in Kuala Lumpur of two convicted Australian drug smugglers, Mahathir reminded Canberra that many Australians are descended from convicts". Two years later, when more than one hundred Australian MPs protested about his detention without trial of political opponents, he bluntly replied: "When Australia was at the same stage of Malaysia's development, you solved your aborigines problem by simply shooting them."

Today, the continued vulnerability of Singapore is demonstrated by its close alliance with Brunei, another post-colonial mini-state. The British defeat of a rebellion led by Azahari, a local politician opposed by its sultan, was not enough to persuade Brunei to join Malaysia. Brunei chose to rely instead for its defence on the hire of a battalion of Gurkhas, so that its 380,000 inhabitants uncannily resemble those living in certain Arab sheikdoms. Substitute desert for jungle and the diminutive sultanate could be a second Kuwait.

The Republic of Indonesia

To some educated Indonesians, the Meiji programme of modernisation had seemed to point the way for fruitful cooperation with Japan. What they came to appreciate, however, was that the Greater East Asia Co-Prosperity Sphere was no better than the Dutch East Indies. Only one aspect of

President Sukarno rallies Indonesians against the return of
the Dutch colonial authorities

427

Taman Ayun temple at Mengwi, a Hindu place of worship in Bali

Japanese rule was an improvement: the ending of the racial prejudice that had bedevilled colonial relations for centuries. But this hardly compensated for Japan's ruthless exploitation of Indonesia's resources.

The future Indonesian president, Sukarno, was under no illusions about Japanese intentions as long as the war lasted, but he took advantage of public platforms to disparage the Dutch and stimulate nationalist aspirations. As he reminded the Javanese in 1943, "the fate of our people is in our own hands and not those of others". Once they recognised that the Allies could not be held at bay, the Japanese asked Sukarno and Mohammad Hatta, another prominent nationalist, to devise a formula for cooperation and draft a constitution for an independent republic. The new state was to incorporate under a strong presidency not only the territories of the Dutch East Indies but those belonging to Britain in Malaya and Borneo as well. The Indonesian leaders did not want independence as a gift from Tokyo, so Sukarno proclaimed the Republic of Indonesia on 17 August 1945.

Because the Netherlands had no troops available, and British forces were already spread thin in Southeast Asia, London expected the Dutch to negotiate with the nationalists in Java as had happened successfully in British Burma. But it had not reckoned with Hubertus van Mook, the governor-general of the Dutch East Indies. He resented the lightness of the British touch, wrongly believing that Dutch authority could be restored with the application of force. And he correctly guessed that Labour government had little enthusiasm for restoring Dutch colonial rule, when decolonisation was very much part of its own agenda.

Ignoring London's desire for a political settlement, the Dutch strung out talks with the nationalists until it was obvious they would have to recover Indonesia themselves. After the British withdrawal, the Dutch tried to subdue the whole of Java and secure economically important areas in Sumatra, by diverting funds provided by the United States for post-war reconstruction in Europe. When this "police action" failed, van Mook was obliged to reopen talks with "a terrorist so-called government". Once the Soviet Union showed an interest, however, the United States ditched Holland with the result that an independent Indonesia became inevitable.

While the Republic of Indonesia was diplomatically referred to as the Netherlands–Indonesian Union, nobody expected any mutual relationship to last. One omission from the final agreement was Western New Guinea—or West Irian, as Sukarno called it—where a continued

A typical Javanese village with its paddy fields

Dutch presence was a source of post-colonial antagonism. Not that this represented the limits of Indonesian ambitions, because in the 1960s Sukarno promoted territorial claims against Malaysia, and in 1976 Indonesian forces took over the Portuguese colony of East Timor. Its liberation by an Australian-led international peacekeeping force in 1999 marked the last Asian decolonisation.

A struggle for unity has typified Indonesian independence, which many islands in the sprawling archipelago viewed as no more than Javanese domination. It did not help that economic development was concentrated on Java, where the overwhelming majority of Indonesians lived. Jakarta, the new name given to Batavia, witnessed unprecedented growth, its population doubling twice between 1945 and 1961. Despite having a democratic system of government, politicians discovered how difficult the Indonesian army was to handle. The situation only worsened as President Sukarno exploited factional and regional divisions to assume executive authority. In 1959, he replaced parliamentary with "Guided Democracy", wrapping himself in the trappings of power. Despite serious rebellions, Sukarno held on to power with the support of the Indonesian Communist Party and the armed forces, an uneasy alliance that triple-digit inflation ended with a bloody military coup in 1965, when perhaps as many as 500,000 people died.

A relatively unknown general by the name of Suharto then assumed control, ending Confrontation with Malaysia and pushing Sukarno into retirement. The Indonesian army portrayed itself as the country's saviour until in 1998 Suharto's vaunted "New Order" collapsed before popular protest amid cries of "corruption", "cronyism" and "nepotism". Before his overthrow, the general had invaded East Timor, an annexation that came back to haunt Indonesia. Even now, there is dismay that none of the military leaders responsible for the dreadful treatment of the East Timorese have been brought to justice. It is estimated that one-third of East Timor's inhabitants died during the 24 years of Indonesian rule.

The Tragedy of Vietnam

The United States was slow to abandon Suharto in comparison with military leaders in South Vietnam because this earlier withdrawal of support had stemmed from defeat in the field. Totally different from that of the British was the French approach to its colonies in 1945: Clement

430

"Uncle Ho". The leader of Vietnamese resistance to the
French and the Americans, Ho Chi Minh

Attlee's idea of a Commonwealth, "a free association of free peoples"
was anathema to Paris, where a reassertion of imperial power seemed an
almost psychological necessity after the German occupation.

The French inability to restore colonial rule in Indochina should
have warned the Americans about opposing Vietnamese nationalism.
But with the British getting the better of the communist insurgency in
Malaya, Washington came to the conclusion that Ho Chi Minh should,
and indeed, could be beaten. It was a misjudgement that would lead
to the tragic Vietnam War and the United States' first defeat abroad.
In a last gamble to bring the Viet Minh, "the Vietnamese League", to
a decisive battle, the French allowed the garrison at Dien Bien Phu, a
fortified base northwest of Hanoi, to be cut off. It was a mistake because

they underestimated Vo Ngyuen Giap, the most skilled field commander of the late twentieth century. He forced the garrison to surrender just before an international conference in Geneva recognised the independence of North Vietnam. With the French gone a year later in 1955, the United States was left as the sole protector of South Vietnam.

In 1956 South Vietnam's president, Ngo Dinh Diem, refused to hold the elections agreed at Geneva because he feared Ho Chi Minh would win. Opposition to his American-sponsored government steadily mounted, with even the Buddhists joining in the protest movement. Self-immolations of monks on Saigon's streets cost Ngo Dinh Diem Washington's favour when a reporter heard the president's sister-in-law draw a parallel between monks, who neither moved a muscle nor uttered a sound when they burned to death with petroleum, and barbecues, a word her daughter had picked up from American military advisers. American public opinion reacted so badly to this remark that President John F. Kennedy was forced to press Ngo Dinh Diem to introduce reforms.

Frustrated South Vietnamese generals interpreted Kennedy's anger as their moment to assume power, which they did with the blessing of the US ambassador. Photographs of Ngo Dinh Diem's blood-splattered body dismayed Americans, but not as much as that of Kennedy's assassination in Texas, shortly afterwards. At this moment, the United States still had a limited role compared with the deployment of 525,000 troops at the height of the Vietnam War. Because Lyndon Johnson, Kennedy's successor, was determined in 1964 to stop "Southeast Asia going the way of China", this massive escalation could not be avoided once the North Vietnamese understood that there could be no peaceful reunification of Vietnam. While the South Vietnamese military hierarchy played musical chairs for the political leadership, the United States poured in soldiers and supplies. Two strong men eventually came to the fore: Nguyen Cao Yy, an admirer of Hitler, as vice-president and Nguyen Van Thieu as president. At last, Washington seemed to have South Vietnamese leaders who promised to provide political stability, a prerequisite for the safety of its troops.

Realising at long, however, last that the conflict was beyond US strength, the next president Richard Nixon tried to win the peace by a massive bombing campaign, the tonnage dropped on North Vietnam between 1969 and 1971 being greater than that expended in all theatres throughout the Second World War. So destructive was the onslaught that Ho Chi Minh, just before his death, advised the Hanoi administration to let the Americans leave without hindrance,

Despite this display of technology in 1967, the United States was
heading for defeat in Vietnam

once much vaunted Nixon's "Vietnamisation" programme had run its
course. There was little point in carrying on fighting when it was obvious
that South Vietnam could never survive on its own.

Yet before Nixon withdrew the troops, he backed in 1970 a South
Vietnamese invasion of Cambodia, a country hitherto spared the horrors of
ground fighting, with the aim of cutting the Ho Chi Minh trail, the main
supply route for the Viet Minh. Considering how King Norodom Sihanouk
had said nothing when American bombs had already rained down on eastern
Cambodia, the welcome given to Lon Nol's ousting of him in Washington
seems extraordinary. Guessing that his anti-communist credentials would
impress the Americans, the Cambodian general seized power when the king
was abroad and then allowed the south Vietnamese to invade Cambodia, an
action that later handed power to the Khmer Rouge.

By early 1973, Lon Nol's authority was restricted to refugee-filled
towns, fed by airlifted American rice. When the planes came no more,
the Khmer Rouge sent nearly everyone to the countryside. The decision
in 1975 to empty the towns seems to have been a long-standing Khmer
Rouge intention, possibly because its rank and file, recruited from the
poorest sections of the peasantry, saw it as a just end to the parasitic
rule of an urban hierarchy. An impoverished peasantry was no longer

prepared to sustain by its toil a privileged modern capital like some latter-day Angkor. The Khmer Rouge leader Pol Pot justified the evacuation in terms of the Paris Commune: this had failed, he said, because the proletariat had not exercised dictatorship over the bourgeoisie. Whatever the exact cause of this drastic measure, resettlement decimated the Cambodian people, with as many as three million deaths. It was brought to a close in 1978 by a Vietnamese invasion of Laos and Cambodia, whose purpose was the expulsion of the Khmer Rouge. Relieved though they were to be rid of these revolutionaries, Cambodians feared that their country would become a Vietnamese colony. With the fading of the Cold War, the Vietnamese army withdrew in 1989 but many settlers stayed behind. Possibly the Sino-Vietnamese border clashes a decade earlier were attempts by Beijing to rein in Hanoi's territorial ambitions. The exact origin of the brief conflict is hard to fathom, although it is not impossible that Deng Xiaoping gave the People's Liberation Army its head because of his continued need of its support in the run-up to the trial of Mao Zedong's widow, the leader of the Gang of Four.

By then, the Vietnam War was well and truly over. With the Americans gone and South Vietnamese president Nguyen Van Thieu behaving like a dictator, Hanoi let the ingenious Giap mount a three-month campaign that reunited Vietnam in early 1975. Nguyen Van Thieu had already made his escape by a US transport plane, taking his family with him as well as sixteen tonnes of gold and silver from the vaults of the national bank.

Filipino Democracy

The first Southeast Asian colony to attain sovereignty in 1946, the Philippines was not essentially changed by independence. Allowed a large measure of self-government, the political pattern had already set because large landowners were the chief collaborators with the Americans. They pulled the strings behind the two main parties, the Nacionalista and the always Liberals.

Unlike Indonesia, the other great island state, the Philippines had developed no indigenous anchor equivalent to medieval Java. Its archipelago remained without a stabilising point until the Spaniards made Manila their capital. Colonial rule left an indelible Christian impression that provided the basis for national identity, but as the United States discovered on supplanting Spain in 1898, there were strong separatist

Mass opposition to President Marcos led to his exile in 1986

tendencies at work beneath Filipino resistance to an America administration. Besides the belligerent Moros in the south, whose conversion
to Islam preceded the arrival of the Spaniards by more than a century,
rivalry between Catholics was marked by entrenched regional antagonisms, whose tussles for power facilitated Ferdinand Marcos' rise.

From the start of his political career Marcos made no secret of his
ambition. "If you are electing me just to get my services as a congressman for the pittance of 7,500 pesos a year, don't vote for me at all",
he shouted at rallies during his first campaign in 1949. "This is only
the first step. Elect me a congressman now, and I pledge you a president
in twenty years". He was duly elected, at the age of thirty-two the
youngest member of the House of Representatives; then in 1959 he
became a senator with a landslide majority; and finally, well within
the timescale that he had set for himself, Marcos was elected president
in 1965 and re-elected in 1969.

It may be the case that this swift climb to the highest office affected
his judgment, because Marcos admitted that he was tired of the chore
of elections and spoke of replacing democracy with "constitutional
authoritarianism". He used the presidential privilege of declaring martial
law in 1972 to overcome the prohibition on a president serving more
than two terms. Initially, his dictatorship was not unpopular because the

"New Society" that he advocated seemed to promise land reform, an end to official corruption and large-scale foreign investment. But even such an astute handler of the American political system as Marcos could not disguise the weakness of his regime indefinitely. His assassination of Benigno Aquino in 1983 at Manila airport after exile in the United States exposed a degree of desperation that shocked the world.

It was now obvious to Ronald Reagan, the second-term American president, that Marcos had lost his grip on the Philippines. He could no longer deal with either armed rebels or the rising demand for a fair presidential election. Despite vote rigging in the snap election he called in 1986, there could be no question that Corazon Aquino, the widow of Benigno, had won. When Marcos moved towards his own inauguration, the people of Manila took to the streets and physically surrounded the presidential palace in non-violent protest. Fearing civil war, the Filipino army abandoned Marcos, who fled the country in a US plane. The new president Corazon Aquino inherited massive foreign debts, a mutinous army and a growing rebel movement, but for the great land-owners it was business as usual. Yet Marcos' downfall was overwhelmingly due to the courage and determination of vast numbers of the Filipino people, many of whom took great risks to bring democracy back to their country.

The leadership of the Catholic church was quick to recognise the popular mood and lend its support to the new government. Church services almost became occasions for rousing political sermons. But during her troubled presidency, Corazon Aquino came to depend on Fidel Ramos, the defence minister and army chief. In 1992 he was the first soldier to be elected president, but with a mere 23 per cent of the votes cast. When six years later Joseph Estrada duly replaced him, it looked as though the Philippines was following the US example in choosing a former film star. But he was more vulnerable than President Reagan once it emerged that Estrada had taken bribes. That the 1990s economic crisis was then putting immense pressure on the peso left him with no choice but to resign. Troubled though Filipino democracy was by the Marcos and Estrada débâcles, its problems bear no real comparison with the tumult in Thailand, where King Rama IX witnessed no less than five military coups during his reign.

The Rise of Present-Day Asia

We all seek a better future for our people. But, given the different circumstances of natural and human resources, agricultural or industrial backgrounds, and industrial and technological competence, we have to chart different courses for that goal.

Lee Kuan Yew in 1971 at the first Commonwealth Conference to be held in Asia.

Recognition that China, India and Indonesia possess key world economies is an indicator of how much has changed in Asia. The troubles of the nineteenth and early twentieth centuries are now things of the past, along with the temporary triumph of imperial Japan. Because it was the first Asian state to modernise its economy, the Meiji reformers were able to pursue ambitions on a par with those of the Western colonial powers. The Imperial Japanese Navy was the most obvious feature of this new status, which Britain first recognised in the Anglo-Japanese Alliance of 1902. Yet the patent inability of the Imperial Japanese Army to subdue China set the scene for the Pacific dimension of the Second World War—Japan's rash assault on the colonies of the United States and Britain. Initial victories as widespread as Hong Kong, Malaya, Singapore, the Philippines, Indonesia and Burma shattered the myth of Western superiority. Everywhere Japan's opponents were taken by surprise, but this apparently irresistible advance was not destined to last.

A chastened Emperor Hirohito admitted after Japan's total defeat that:

> Our people believed in the imperial country and were contemptuous of Britain and the United States. Our military men placed too much weight on spirit and forgot about science.

Ingenious though this explanation of failure was in shifting the blame from his subjects to their poor equipment, defeat came as much from Japan's own cultural traditions as anything else. A marked indifference to the sufferings of subject Asian peoples gave the lie to the Greater East Asia Co-Prosperity Sphere, whose benefits were reserved solely for the Japanese. Possibly as many as 2.5 million Javanese died of starvation during 1944 when stockpiles of rice were being created on the island for a long war. Atomic bombs dropped on Hiroshima and Nagasaki—perhaps the scientific edge of the Allies that Hirohito had in mind—certainly brought the Second World War to an abrupt end, yet the devastation they caused was not enough to restore Western prestige.

Alone among the European leaders, British premier Clement Attlee saw how Asia had changed. Just as Japan's overrunning of the West's colonial possessions had rung down the curtain on imperialism there, so Attlee's decision to grant India early independence meant that decolonisation was inevitable, despite the refusal of Holland and France to face political reality.

Liquidation of the British empire was to have an impact right across the Asian continent. In West Asia, the British withdrawal was complicated by the foundation of Israel, an event that still unsettles the region today. Intense pressure from Washington on a London already overburdened by decolonisation must take most of the blame. Only Turkey escaped this conflict through Atatürk's disestablishment of Islam. Inherited religious differences elsewhere resulted in friction both within and between countries as diverse as Syria, Iraq and Iran. Opposition to Israel comprises one of the few policies that these states share.

In South Asia the independence of India and Pakistan in 1947 was not achieved, however, without communal violence, a horror that Gandhi had devoted his life to contain. The subsequent emergence of Bangladesh as a sovereign state was essentially a continuation of the subcontinent's unresolved cultural antagonisms. The days of religious equipoise that had typified Akbar's reign were long past, even though the economic activity that sustained the Mughal empire still informed India's economy. Its recent surge, ill distributed though the new wealth is, explains the European interest in Indian commerce from the arrival of the Portuguese in 1498 onwards.

It was in Southeast Asia that British handling of decolonisation gained its greatest successes with Myanmar, Malaysia and Singapore, in stark contrast to the failures of the Dutch in the East Indies and the French in Indochina. But here the Cold War complicated the situation to the extent that the United States almost assumed a neo-colonial role that culminated in the tragedy of the Vietnam War. Already conflict had occurred in East Asia, where the Korean War effectively isolated the People's Republic of China and provided Japan with an unexpected economic boost. Like "A gift from the gods", according to its premier Yoshida Shigeru, was US military procurement during the early 1950s. The billions of dollars that poured into Japan gave it a second opportunity to dominate the region, albeit this time strictly in terms of commerce.

Once China ended its revolutionary travail under Deng Xiaoping, moving from state control towards a free market, Japan's position as a leading Asian economy was under threat. China's phenomenal development since then seems incredible. Its massive balance of payments surplus gives Beijing financial leverage, even over the United States, but this growth has come at a high price. Inflation, uneven development, corruption and crime could all upset China over the next decades. Not entirely forgotten are the comments made by senior communists about the effect that Deng Xiaoping's espousal of modernisation was having on the young: they were criticised for being indifferent to social issues and overly preoccupied with personal interests.

China is nonetheless a dominant player in both Asian and world affairs. Another rising star is the Republic of Indonesia, for long overlooked because the Dutch East Indies was always regarded as a colonial backwater. One reason for this was an archipelago of some 14,000 odd islands that forms this predominantly Moslem country. It is inhabited by more than 300 distinct peoples, not including those living in Irian Jaya. And the

439

fact that they speak more than 250 regional languages caused President Sukarno to insist immediately after independence on the use in primary schools of Bahasa Indonesia, the national language. Based on the Malay spoken in central Sumatra, it contains additional elements from other languages, above all Javanese. Sukarno had been aware of language differences from his earliest years because his father was a Javanese teacher in the employ of the Dutch, who married a local girl when he was working on the island of Bali.

Arguably the Indonesian republic is a product of colonialism because no previous indigenous state ever exercised control over such a far-flung area. But modern idea though it is, an independent Indonesia was always the aim of nationalists opposing Dutch rule throughout the early twentieth century. Their attainment of this goal has turned the archipelago into a formidable power, whose natural resources of oil and gas are sufficient to support the emergence as a major economy. A fundamental weakness remains its geographical configuration: people living on islands at a distance from Jakarta tend to feel remote and politically sidelined.

China, India, Indonesia and possibly Turkey, with the fastest growing economy of all, will set the pace in a newly resurgent Asia, the most significant historical event of our time. Their very different outlooks need to be understood if there is to be any appreciation of the direction that events are likely to take. The world simply has no choice but come to terms with their preferences and expectations, because in the era of globalism no continent can stand on its own. We are all involved in the future together.

Glossary

apartheid   a word describing the racial discrimination that typified Dutch colonialism.

ajivikas   followers in ancient India of a philosophy of predestination. It held that asceticism could in no way speed up the attainment of enlightenment.

ayatollah   the title used by senior clerics in Iran: it means "the sign of God".

bhakti   "way of devotion", the special attachment of a devotee to a Hindu deity. Such fervent worship first appeared in south India during the seventh century.

bodhisattva   a Buddhist whose compassion for the sufferings of others causes him or her to postpone the attainment of full Buddhahood. Avalokitesvara, "the celestial bodhisattva", is the prime example of assisting those who wish to follow the Buddha's path.

brahmins   sometimes **brahmans**, members of the Hindu priestly caste.

bushido   "the way of the warrior" in medieval Japan. The status of a fighting man, or samurai, was rigidly defined and difficult to acquire.

chan   a Chinese form of Buddhism that bore no Indian imprint at all. Its practical approach to enlightenment also made it popular in Korea and Japan, where it was called son and zen respectively.

cultuurstelsel   "culture system" introduced by the Dutch in Indonesia. It required farmers to cultivate crops for export.

dalai lamas   have exercised secular and religious authority in Tibet since the late medieval period. The title dalai, meaning "all-encompassing in wisdom", was bestowed on the Third Dalai Lama by the Mongol leader Altan Khan in 1577.

dasyus   the name given to the dark-skinned peoples whom the intruding Aryans overthrew in the Indus valley.

ensi   the Sumerian title of a city prince. In most cases the office was hereditary, although there seems to have been an assembly of elders whose opinion the ensi had to take into account when reaching important decisions.

feng shui "wind and water", the present-day version of geomancy.

han'gul the indigenous alphabet of Korea. It was introduced in 1446 because "the sounds of the Korean language differ from those of China and are not easily conveyed in Chinese characters".

harijan "children of God", was the name that Mahatma Gandhi insisted upon calling the "suppressed classes", the so-called "Untouchables" who were excluded from Hindu society. Hari is another name of the saviour god Vishnu.

ilkhan "lesser khan", the title adopted by Hulegu so as to show respect for his brother Mongke Khan, the leader of the Mongols. It was meant to indicate a subordinate role.

imam the officiating cleric in a mosque.

kamikaze "the divine wind", or typhoon, that destroyed the Mongol fleet in 1281. During World War Two the name was adopted by the pilots who flew bomb-planes against Allied warships.

karma the idea that one's present position in society is determined by the net effect of all one's previous actions in past lives. It is the reason for Hinduism being as much a social system as a religion because one's caste depends entirely on the operation of karma.

khalifat Allah "the deputy of Allah", the caliph.

khan the leader of a nomadic people.

ksatriyas warriors, the caste from which Hindu rulers arose. The Buddha was born into it, although his father may have been a prominent nobleman, rather than a king.

lugal the Sumerian title of a king. Gilgamesh was a legendary lugal.

nirvana "enlightened extinction", freedom from life illusion, the state of mind first attained by the Buddha.

perestroika "restructuring", a description of the changes taking place in the Soviet Union under Mikhail Gorbachev.

raja deva "god-king". How far Southeast Asian rulers were actually believed to be divine is now difficult to establish, but the idea of divine kingship certainly took root in Cambodia and Indonesia.

rishis "wise men" who frightened even the Hindu gods.

samurai Japanese warriors who served a feudal lord. Their status had to be confirmed by the shogun, since exemplary action on the battlefield was not in itself enough to acquire it.

sati "widow burning", the self-immolation of Hindu widows. It was abolished by the British in 1829.

satyagraha "truth force", the guiding principle of Gandhi who believed there was divinity in every human breast.

shogun "generalissimo", in theory the Japanese emperor's commander-in-chief but usually the most powerful warlord.

stupa a monument containing relics of the Buddha. The raising of a mound, or stupa, in which to enshrine teeth, bones or ashes was an old Maghadhan custom put to a new use in early Buddhism.

sudras servants, the lowest Hindu caste.

sultan a Moslem ruler. Seljuk rulers called themselves sultans rather than khans after their conversion to Islam.

sunyata "emptiness", the fundamental nature of the world according to the Buddha. It formed the basis of Nagarjuna's philosophical analysis of illusion in second-century India.

tian ming "the mandate of Heaven", the cornerstone of Chinese political theory from Confucius onwards.

tokharika a woman of Tocharian descent.

tsars Russian emperors.

vaisyas farmers, the second-lowest Hindu caste.

vali faqih "supreme guide", the title that Ayatollah Ruhollah Khomeni assumed on his return to Iran in 1979.

varna the Hindu class system dividing society into four castes, in order of precedence brahmins, ksatriyas, vaisyas and sudras.

wali heterodox Javanese saints, the bane of traditional Moslems.

wang the ancient Chinese character for king, whose four strokes bear witness to the ruler's chief role as mediator between the heavenly realm and the world.

yasa the Mongol law code that Genghiz Khan introduced in 1206 so that order would be established in nomadic society.

yin–yang the two interacting forces that the Chinese believe to coexist in the world.

Further Reading

Chapter 1: Ancient West Asia

Bottéro, J., *Religion in Ancient Mesopotamia*, translated by T. L. Fagan, Chicago, 2001.

Boyce, M., *Zoroastrianism. In Antiquity and Constant Vigour*, Costa Mesa, California, 1992.

Briant, P., *From Cyrus to Alexander, A History of the Persian Empire*, translated by P. T. Daniels, Winona Lake, Indiana, 2002.

Burkert, W., *Babylon, Memphis, Persepolis. Eastern Contexts of Greek Culture*, Cambridge, Massachusetts, 2004.

Cotterell, A. (ed.), *The Penguin Encyclopaedia of Ancient Civilizations*, London, 1988.

Dalley, S., *Myths from Mesopotamia. Creation, The Flood, Gilgamesh and Others*, Oxford, 1989.

Hammond, N. G. L., *Alexander the Great. King, Commander and Statesman*, London, 1981.

Kramer, S. N., *History Begins at Sumer*, London, 1958.

Oates, J. *Babylon*, London, 1979.

Ringgren, H., *Israelite Religion*, translated by D. Green, London, 1966.

Sherwin-White, S. and Kuhrt, A., *From Samarkhand to Sardis. A New Approach to the Seleucid Empire*, London, 1993.

Soden, W. von, *The Ancient Orient. An Introduction to the Study of the Ancient Near East*, translated by D. G. Schley, Grand Rapids, Michigan, 1994.

Chapter 2: Ancient South Asia

Allchin, B. and R., *The Rise of Civilization in India and Pakistan*, Cambridge, 1982.

Brockington, J. L., *The Sacred Thread. Hinduism in its Continuity and Diversity*, Edinburgh, 1981.

Bronkhorst, J., *Greater Magadha. Studies in the Culture of Early India*, Leiden, 2007.

Buitenen, J. A. B. van, *The Mahabharata*, Chicago, 1973 onwards.

DeCaroli, R., *Haunting the Buddha. Indian Popular Religions and the Formation of Buddhism*, Oxford, 2004.

Ling, T., *The Buddha*, London, 1973.

O'Flaherty, W. D., *Rig Veda*, Harmondsworth, 1981.

Thapar, R., *Early India. From the Origins to AD 1300*, London, 2002.

Westerhoff, J., *Nagarjuna's Madhyamaka. A Philosophical Introduction*, Oxford, 2009.

Wheeler, Sir Mortimer, *The Indus Civilisation*, Cambridge, 1953.

Williams, P., *Buddhist Thought. A Complete Introduction to the Indian Tradition*, London, 2000.

Zimmer, H., *Philosophies of India*, edited by J. Campbell, Princeton, 1951.

Chapter 3: Ancient East Asia

Bielenstein, H., *The Bureaucracy of Han Times*, Cambridge, 1980.

Bynner, W., *The Way of Life According to Lao Tzu*, New York, 1944.

Chang, Kwang-Chih, *Shang Civilization*, New Haven, 1980.

Cotterell, A., *The First Emperor of China*, London, 1981.

Ho, Ping-ti, *The Cradle of the East. An Inquiry into the Indigenous Origins of Techniques and Ideas of Neolithic and Early Historic China, 5000–1000 BC*, Hong Kong, 1975.

Ivanoe, P. J., *Confucian Moral Self Cultivation*, Indianapolis, 2000.

Lewis, M. E., *The Early Chinese Empires. Qin and Han*, Cambridge, Massachusetts, 2007.

Rubin, V. A., *Individual and State in Ancient China. Essays on Four Chinese Philosophers*, translated by S. I. Levine, New York, 1976.

Smith, D. H., *Confucius*, London, 1973.

Watson, B., *The Tso Chuan. Selections from China's Oldest Narrative History*, New York, 1989.

——, *The Analects of Confucius*, New York, 2007.

Yu, Ying-shih, *Trade and Expansion in Han China. A Study in the Structure of Sino-Barbarian Economic Relations*, Berkeley, 1967.

Chapter 4: Ancient Central Asia

Barfield, T. J., *The Perilous Frontier. Nomadic Empires and China, 221 BC to AD 1757*, Oxford, 1989.

Beckwith, C. I., *Empires of the Silk Road. A History of Central Eurasia from the Bronze Age to the Present*, Princeton, 2009.

Cosmo Di, N., *Ancient China and Its Enemies. The Rise of Nomadic Power in East Asian History*, Cambridge, 2002.

Cotterell, A., *Chariot. The Astounding Rise and Fall of the World's First War Machine*, London, 2004.

Frye, R. N., *The Heritage of Central Asia. From Antiquity to the Turkish Expansion*, Princeton, 1966.

Hildinger, E., *Warriors of the Steppe. A Military History of Central Asia, 500 BC to 1700 AD*, Cambridge, Massachusetts, 1997.

Kelly, C., *Attila the Hun. Barbarian Terror and the Fall of the Roman Empire*, London, 2008.

Lewis, M. E., *China Between Empires. The Northern and the Southern Dynasties*, Cambridge, Massachusetts, 1990.

Mallory, J. P. and Nair, V. H., *The Tarim Mummies. Ancient China and the Mystery of the Earliest Peoples from the West*, London, 2000.

Sinor, D. (ed.), *The Cambridge History of Early Inner Asia*, Cambridge, 1990.

Tarn, W., *The Greeks in Bactria and India*, Cambridge, 1951.

Chapter 5: Medieval West Asia

Abulafia, D., *Frederick II. A Medieval Emperor*, London, 1988.

Axworthy, M., *Empire of the Mind. A History of Iran*, London, 2007.

Bennison, A. K., *The Great Caliphs. The Golden Age of the Abbasid Empire*, London, 2009.

Cook, M., *Muhammad*, Oxford, 1996.

Ferrier, R. W., *A Journey to Persia. Jean Chardin's Portrait of a Seventeenth Century Empire*, London, 1996.

Findley, C. V., *The Turks in World History*, Oxford, 2005.

Hillenbrand, C., *Turkish Myth and Muslim Symbol. The Battle of Manzikert*, Edinburgh, 2007.

Imber, C., *The Ottoman Empire*, Basingstoke, 2002.

Kaegi, W. E., *Byzantium and the Early Islamic Conquests*, Cambridge, 1992.

Kennedy, H., *The Prophet and the Age of the Caliphates*, Harlow, 1986.

——, *The Court of the Caliphs. The Rise and Fall of Islam's Greatest Dynasty*, London, 2004.

Khatibi, A. and Sijelmassi, M., *The Splendour of Islamic Calligraphy*, London, 1996.

Mohring, H., *Saladin. The Sultan and His Times, 1138–1193*, translated by D. S. Bachrach, Baltimore, 2008.

Runciman, S., *The Fall of Constantinople, 1453*, Cambridge, 1965.

Tyerman, C., *Fighting for Christendom. Holy War and the Crusades*, Oxford, 2004.

Chapter 6: Medieval South Asia

Basham, A. L. (ed.), *A Cultural History of India*, Oxford, 1975.

Chandhuri, K. N., *Trade and Civilization in the Indian Ocean. An Economic History from the Rise of Islam to 1750*, Cambridge, 1985.

Cooper, R. G. S., *The Anglo-Maratha Campaign and the Contest for India. The Struggle for Control of the South Asia Military Economy*, Cambridge, 2003.

Cotterell, A., *Western Power in Asia. Its Slow Rise and Swift Fall, 1415–1999*, Singapore, 2010.

Khan, I. A., *Gunpowder and Firearms. Warfare in Medieval India*, New Delhi, 2004.

Lawson, P., *The East India Company. A History*, London, 1993.

Malik, J., *Islam in South Asia. A Short History*, Leiden, 2008.

Moon, Sir Penderel, *The British Conquest and Dominion of India*, London, 1990.

Mukhia, H., *The Mughals of India*, Oxford, 2004.

Nicoll, F., *Shah Jahan. The Rise and Fall of the Mughal Emperor*, London, 2009.

Pearson, M. N., *The New Cambridge History of India, Volume 1.1, The Portuguese in India*, Cambridge, 1987.

Peebles, P., *The History of Sri Lanka*, Westport, 2006.

Richards, J. F., *The New Cambridge History of India, Volume 1.5, The Mughal Empire*, Cambridge, 1993.

Shelat, J. M., *Akbar*, Bombay, 1965.

Stein, B., *A History of India*, Oxford, 1998.

_____, *The New Cambridge History of India, Volume 1.2, Vijayanagara*, Cambridge, 1989.

Chapter 7: Medieval East Asia

Berry, M. E., *Hideyoshi*, Cambridge, Massachusetts, 1989.

Ch'en, K. K. S., *The Chinese Transformation of Buddhism*, Princeton, 1973.

Cotterell, A., *The Imperial Capitals of China. An Inside View of the Celestial Empire*, London, 2007.

Dreyer, E. L., *Zheng He. China and the Oceans in the Early Ming Dynasty, 1405–1433*, New York, 2007.

Fitzgerald, C. P., *The Empress Wu*, Melbourne, 1955.

Kitagawa, J. M., *Religion in Japanese Society*, New York, 1966.

Kuhn, D., *The Age of Confucian Rule. The Song Transformation of China*, Cambridge, Massachusetts, 2009.

Lee, Ki-baik, *A New History of Korea*, Cambridge, Massachusetts, 1984.

Lewis, M. E., *China's Cosmopolitan Empire. The Tang Dynasty*, Cambridge, Massachusetts, 2009.

Mote, F. W., *Imperial China 900–1800*, Cambridge, Massachusetts, 1999.

Needham, J., *The Grand Titration. Science and Society in East and West*, London, 1969.

Sampson, Sir George, *A History of Japan 1334–1615*, London, 1978.

Souryi, P. F., *The World Turned Upside Down. Medieval Japanese Society*, New York, 2001.

Wechsler, H. J., *Mirror to the Son of Heaven. Wei Cheng at the Court of T'ang T'ai-tsung*, New Haven, 1974.

Chapter 8: Medieval Central Asia

Allsen, T. T., *Culture and Conquest in Mongol Eurasia*, Cambridge, 2001.

Beckwith, C. I., *The Tibetan Empire in Central Asia. A History of the Struggle for Great Power Among Tibetans, Turks, Arabs and Chinese during the Early Middle Ages*, Princeton, 1987.

Biran, M., *The Empire of the Qara Khitai in Eurasian History. Between China and the Islamic World*, Cambridge, 2005.

Brown, T., *The Troubled Empire. China in the Yuan and Ming Dynasties*, Cambridge, Massachusetts, 2010.

Cosmo Di, N., *Warfare in Inner Asia (500–1800)*, Leiden, 2002.

Crossley, P. K., *The Manchus*, Oxford, 1997.

Kapstein, M. T., *The Tibetans*, Oxford, 2006.

Marozzi, T., *Tamerlane. Sword of Islam, Conqueror of the World*, London, 2004.

Ratchnevsky, P., *Genghiz Khan. His Life and Legacy*, Oxford, 1991.

Rossabi, M., *Kubilai Khan. His Life and Times*, Berkeley, 1988.

Shaumian, T., *Tibet. The Great Game and Tsarist Russia*, New Delhi, 2000.

Waley, A., *The Secret History of the Mongols*, London, 1963.

Chapter 9: Medieval Southeast Asia

Coe, M. D., *Angkor and Khmer Civilization*, London, 2003.

Coedès, G., *The Making of South East Asia*, translated by H. M. Wright, Berkeley, 1966.

Higham, C., *The Civilization of Angkor*, London, 2001.

Lockard, C. A., *Southeast Asia in World History*, Oxford, 2009.

Reid, A., *Southeast Asia in the Age of Commerce 1450–1680, Volume 1, The Land Below the Winds*, New Haven, 1988.

——, *Southeast Asia in the Age of Commerce 1450–1680, Volume 2, Expansion and Crisis*, New Haven, 1993.

Rinkes, D. A., *Nine Saints of Java*, translated by H. M. Frozer, Kuala Lumpur, 1996.

Strachan, P., *Pagan. Art and Architecture of Old Burma*, Oxford, 1989.

Taylor, K. W., *The Birth of Vietnam*, Berkeley, 1983.

Wyatt, D. K., *Thailand. A Short History*, New Haven, 1982.

Chapter 10: Modern West Asia

Dawisha, A., *Iraq. A Political History from Independence to Occupation*, Princeton, 2009.

Gans, C., *A Just Zionism. On the Morality of the Jewish State*, Oxford, 2008.

Gilbert, M., *Israel. A History*, London, 1998.

Hanioglu, M. S., *Preparation for Revolution. The Young Turks, 1902–1908*, Oxford, 2001.

Hulsman, J. C., *To Begin The World Again. Lawrence of Arabia from Damascus to Baghdad*, New York, 2009.

Keddie, J. C., *Modern Iran. Roots and Results of Revolution*, New Haven, 2006.

Lawson, F. H. (ed.), *Demystifying Syria*, London, 2002.

Mango, A., *Atatürk*, London, 1999.

Menoret, P., *The Saudi Enigma. A History*, translated by P. Camiller, London, 2003.

Meyer, K. E. and Brysac, S. B., *Kingmakers. The Invention of the Modern Middle East*, New York, 2008.

Robbins, P., *A History of Jordan*, Cambridge, 2004.

Shlaim, A., *The Politics of Partition. King Abdullah, the Zionists, and Palestine 1921–1951*, Oxford, 1988.

Chapter 11: Modern South Asia

Adams, J., *Gandhi. Naked Ambition,* London, 2010.

Barua, P. P., *The State at War in South Asia,* Lincoln, Nebraska, 2005.

Bayly, C. R., *The Raj: India and the British 1600–1947,* London, 1990.

Bose, S., *A Hundred Horizons. The Indian Ocean in the Age of Global Empire,* Cambridge, Massachusetts, 2006.

Dalrymple, W., *The Last Mughal. The Fall of a Dynasty, Delhi, 1857,* London, 2006.

Gandhi, M. K., *An Autobiography: The Story of My Experiences with Truth,* Boston, 1957.

Gilmour, D., *Curzon,* London, 1994.

Hardy, P., *The Muslims of British India,* Cambridge, 1972.

Harris, K., *Attlee,* London, 1982.

Richards, D. S., *Cawnpore and Lucknow. A Tale of Two Sieges—Indian Mutiny,* Barnsley, 2007.

Saul, D., *The Indian Mutiny,* London, 2006.

Singh, J., *Jinnah: India, Partition, Independence,* Karachi, 2010.

Voight, J. H., *India in the Second World War,* New Delhi, 1987.

Zaheer, H., *The Separation of East Pakistan: The Rise and Realization of Bengali Muslim Nationalism,* New York, 1994.

Chapter 12: Modern East Asia

Bergère, M.-C., *Sun Yat-sen,* translated by J. Lloyd, Stanford, 1998.

Bodde, D., *Peking Diary. A Year of Revolution,* London, 1951.

Boyle, J. H., *China and Japan at War 1937–1945. The Politics of Collaboration,* Stanford, 1972.

Chae-Jin Lee, *Zhou Enlai. The Early Years,* Stanford, 1994.

Ch'en, J., *Mao and the Chinese Revolution,* Oxford, 1965.

Gelber, H. G., *Opium, Soldiers and Evangelicals. England's 1840–1842 War with China, and its Aftermath,* Basingstoke, 2004.

Hastings, M., *The Korean War,* London, 1987.

Jones, F. C., *Japan's New Order in Asia: Its Rise and Fall,* Oxford, 1954.

Keene, D., *Emperor of Japan. Meiji and His World, 1852–1912,* New York, 2002.

MacFarquhar, R. and Schoenhals, M., *Mao's Last Revolution,* Cambridge, Massachusetts, 2006.

Màdaro, A., *The Boxer Rebellion,* translated by E. Tomlin, Treviso, 2001.

Murfelt, M. H., *Britain, China and the Amethyst Crisis of 1949*, Annapolis, 1991.

Pu Yi, *The Last Manchu. The Autobiography of Henry Pu Yi, Last Emperor of China*, translated by P. Kramer, London, 1967.

Waley, A., *The Opium War Through Chinese Eyes*, London, 1958.

Chapter 13: Modern Central Asia

Hopkirk, P., *Trespassers on the Roof of the World: The Race for Lhasa*, London, 1983.

——, *The Great Game: On Secret Service in High Asia*, London, 1990.

Khodarkovsky, M., *Russia's Steppe Frontier. The Making of a Colonial Empire, 1500–1800*, Bloomington, 2002.

Lattimore, O., *Studies in Frontier History: Collected Essays 1928–1958*, London, 1962.

Mehra, P., *The Younghusband Expedition*, London, 1968.

Meyer, K. and Brysac, S., *Tournament of Shadows. The Great Game and the Race for Empire in Asia*, Boston, 1999.

Perdue, P. C., *China Marches West. The Qing Conquest of Central Eurasia*, Cambridge, 2005.

Rowe, W. T., *China's Last Empire. The Great Qing*, Cambridge, Massachusetts, 2009.

Soucek, S., *A History of Inner Asia*, Cambridge, 2000.

Stephan, J. J., *The Russian Far East. A History*, Stanford, 1994.

Vogelsang, W., *The Afghans*, Oxford, 2008.

Chapter 14: Modern Southeast Asia

Aldrich, R., *Greater France. A History of French Overseas Expansion*, Basingstoke, 1996.

Allen, L., *Singapore 1941–1942*, London, 1977.

Ang Cheng Guan, *The Vietnam War from the Other Side. The Vietnamese Communists' Perspective*, London, 2002.

Bayly, C. R. and Harper T., *Forgotten Wars. The End of Britain's Asian Empire*, London, 2007.

Bizot, F., *The Gate*, translated by E. Cameron, London, 2003.

Black, I., *A Gambling Style of Government: The Establishment of Chartered Company Rule in Sabah, 1878–1915*, Kuala Lumpur, 1971.

Further Reading

Bonner, R., *Waltzing with a Dictator. The Marcoses and the Making of American Policy*, London, 1987.

Brands, H. W., *Bound to Empire. The United States and the Philippines*, Oxford, 1991.

Brocheux, P., *Ho Chi Minh. A Biography*, translated by C. Duiker, Cambridge, 2007.

Butcher, J. G., *The British in Malaya 1880–1941. The Social History of a European Community in Colonial South-East Asia*, New York, 1992.

Chandler, D. P., *Brother Number One. A Political Biography of Pol Pot*, Boulder, Colorado, 1999.

Collis, M., *Raffles*, London, 1966.

Frederick, W. H., *Visions and Heat. The Making of the Indonesian Revolution*, Athens, Ohio, 1989.

Gottesman, E., *Cambodia After the Khmer Rouge. Inside the Politics of Nation Building*, New Haven, 2002.

Issacs, A. R., *Without Honour. Defeat in Cambodia and Vietnam*, Baltimore, 1983.

Marr, D. G., *Vietnam, 1945. The Quest for Power*, Berkeley, 1995.

Milner, A., *The Malays*, Oxford, 2008.

Myint-U, Thant, *The Making of Modern Burma*, Cambridge, 2001.

Reece, B., *The White Rajahs of Sarawak. A Borneo Dynasty*, Singapore, 2004.

Regnier, P., *Singapore. City-State in South-East Asia*, translated by C. Hurst, London, 1987.

Ricklefs, M. C., *A History of Modern Indonesia*, Basingstoke, 1981.

Simpson, H. R., *Dien Bien Phu. The Epic Battle America Forgot*, Washington, 1974.

Tarling, N., *Imperialism in Southeast Asia. A Fleeting, Passing Phase*, London, 2007.

Vickers, A., *A History of Modern Indonesia*, Cambridge, 2005.

Wain, B., *Malaysian Maverick. Mahathir Mohamad in Turbulent Times*, Basingstoke, 2010.

Index

Index

Index

Index

Index

Jews, xiii, xvii, 19, 20, 21, 22, 26, 27, 28, 30, 37, 104, 143, 147, 148, 149, 150, 153, 167, 248, 323, 324, 326, 327, 328, 329, 336; see also Israel and Palestine

Jiang Qing (Mao Zedong's wife), 380, 381, 434

Jin dynasty (China), 105, 125

Jin state (China), 223, 248, 260, 262, 271

Jinnah, Mohammed Ali (Moslem leader), 358, 359; and the creation of Pakistan (1947), 358

Johnson, Lyndon B., (US president), 432

Jordan, xviii, 322, 323, 324, 327, 328–330

Kalmyks (nomads), 387, 388, 392

Kang Xi (Qing emperor of China), 255, 272, 274

Kanishka (Kushana king), 66, 67, 68, 127

Karens (Burma), 423, 424

Kassites (Babylonian dynasty), 13

Kautilya (Indian minister), 58

Kazakhs (nomads), 387, 388, 389, 391, 392, 405

Kazakhstan, 114, 393, 405, 406

Kennedy, John F. (US president), 432

Kertanagara (Javanese king), 298

Khalaji, Ala al-Din (Ghurid sultan), 183, 184, 190

Khmer empire (Cambodia), 280, 282–289, 297, 307; see also Angkor

Khmer Rouge (Cambodia), 433, 434

Khomeni, Ayatollah Ruhollah (Iranian leader), 332, 333

Khrushchev, Nikita (Soviet leader), 405

Khun Borom (Thai hero), 308

Khusrau II (Sasanian king), 38, 39, 40

al-Khuzai, Ziyab ibn Salih (Arab general), 253

Kimmerians (nomads), 120, 121

Kim Il-sung (North Korean leader), 383

Kim Pu-sik (Korean minister), 227

Koguryo (Korean state), 101

Korea, xiv, xvi, xvii, 100, 101, 128, 129, 132, 133, 214, 215, 225–230, 231, 235, 236, 238, 244, 256, 272, 371–373, 382, 384; and the growth of slavery, 227; and hereditary privilege, 225, 226, 371

Korean War (1950–53), 379, 382–384, 439

Koryo dynasty (Korea), 226, 227, 228

Kotte (Sri Lankan dynasty), 192

Krishna (incarnation of Vishnu), 51, 52, 57, 65, 69, 197

Kubilai Khan (Mongol leader), 167, 235, 239, 263–266, 278, 288, 292, 298; becomes emperor of China, 264, 265

Kukkuli (Mitannian horse trainer), 16, 17; see also chariots

Kurdistan, 325

Kushanas (Central Asian dynasty), xiv, 66, 67, 68, 69, 127, 128; see also Da Yuezhi

Kuwait, 334, 335, 427

Kwangjong (Korean king), 227

Kyanzittha (Burmese king), 291

Kyrgyz see Turks

Kyrgyzstan, 394, 406

Lang Darma (Tibetan usurper), 255

Lao Zi (Chinese philosopher), 89, 90, 259; see also Daoism

Laos, 63, 278, 417, 418, 434

Later Han see Han dynasty

Lawrence, T. E. (of Arabia), 323, 325

Le dynasty (Vietnam), 280

Lebanon, xviii, 322, 328–330

Lee Kuan Yew (Singaporean premier), 426, 437

Legalism (Chinese philosophy), 87, 97, Leo I (pope), 138

Li Ling (Chinese commander), 123, 124

Li Shimin see Tai Zong

Li Si (Chinese minister), 90, 92, 94, 95; and the Burning of the Books (213 BC), 92

Index

Index

Index

Index